THE STOLEN BONES OF
ST. JOHN OF MATHA

IBERIAN ENCOUNTER
AND EXCHANGE
475–1755 | Vol. 10

SERIES EDITORS
Erin Kathleen Rowe
Michael A. Ryan

The Pennsylvania State
University Press

ADVISORY BOARD
Paul H. Freedman
Richard Kagan
Marie Kelleher
Ricardo Padrón
Teofilo F. Ruiz
Marta V. Vicente

The Iberian Peninsula has historically been an area of the world that fostered encounters and exchanges among peoples from different societies. For centuries, Iberia acted as a nexus for the circulation of ideas, people, objects, and technology around the premodern western Mediterranean, Atlantic, and eventually the Pacific. Iberian Encounter and Exchange, 475–1755 combines a broad thematic scope with the territorial limits of the Iberian Peninsula and its global contacts. In doing so, works in this series juxtapose previously disparate areas of study and challenge scholars to rethink the role of encounter and exchange in the formation of the modern world.

OTHER TITLES IN THIS SERIES
Thomas W. Barton, Contested Treasure: Jews and Authority in the Crown of Aragon

Mercedes García-Arenal and Gerard Wiegers, eds., Polemical Encounters: Christians, Jews, and Muslims in Iberia and Beyond

Nicholas R. Jones, Staging Habla de Negros: Radical Performances of the African Diaspora in Early Modern Spain

Freddy Cristóbal Domínguez, Radicals in Exile: English Catholic Books During the Reign of Philip II

Lu Ann Homza, Village Infernos and Witches' Advocates: Witch-Hunting in Navarre, 1608–1614

Adam Franklin-Lyons, Shortage and Famine in the Late Medieval Crown of Aragon

Sarah Ifft Decker, The Fruit of Her Hands: Jewish and Christian Women's Work in Medieval Catalan Cities

THE STOLEN BONES OF ST. JOHN OF MATHA

FORGERY, THEFT, AND SAINTHOOD
IN THE SEVENTEENTH CENTURY

A. KATIE HARRIS

THE PENNSYLVANIA STATE UNIVERSITY PRESS
UNIVERSITY PARK, PENNSYLVANIA

Library of Congress Cataloging-in-Publication Data

Names: Harris, A. Katie, 1969– author.
Title: The stolen bones of St. John of Matha : forgery, theft, and sainthood in the seventeenth century / A. Katie Harris.
Other titles: Iberian encounter and exchange, 475–1755 ; v. 10.
Description: University Park, Pennsylvania : The Pennsylvania State University Press, [2023] | Series: Iberian encounter and exchange, 475–1755 ; vol. 10 | Includes bibliographical references and index.
Summary: "Investigates an incident of holy relic theft in Rome, the lengthy legal case that followed it, and the larger questions that surrounded saints' remains in seventeenth-century Catholic Europe"—Provided by publisher.
Identifiers: LCCN 2023017660 | ISBN 9780271095356 (hardback) | ISBN 9780271095363 (paper)
Subjects: LCSH: Theft of relics—Italy—Rome—History—17th century. | John, de Matha, Saint, 1160–1213—Relics. | John, de Matha, Saint, 1160–1213—Cult. | Trinitarians—History—17th century.
Classification: LCC BX2333 .H37 2023 | DDC 235/.2—dc23/eng/20230614
LC record available at https://lccn.loc.gov/2023017660

Copyright © 2023 A. Katie Harris
All rights reserved
Printed in the United States of America
Published by The Pennsylvania State University Press,
University Park, PA 16802–1003

The Pennsylvania State University Press is a member of the Association of University Presses.

It is the policy of The Pennsylvania State University Press to use acid-free paper. Publications on uncoated stock satisfy the minimum requirements of American National Standard for Information Sciences—Permanence of Paper for Printed Library Material, ANSI z39.48–1992.

Contents

LIST OF ILLUSTRATIONS   vii
ACKNOWLEDGMENTS   ix

   Prologue: The Crime   1

1 Relics and Relic Culture in Early Modern Europe   5

2 "Well, If They Are So Ancient, What Saints Do They Have?":
   St. John of Matha in Trinitarian Tradition   23

3 Forgery and Sainthood in the Seventeenth Century   57

4 Uncertain Saint: The Case Before the Congregation of Sacred Rites   107

5 "A Very Difficult Business": Proving the Bones of
   St. John of Matha in 1715 and 1721   143

   Epilogue   167

   NOTES   173
   BIBLIOGRAPHY   197
   INDEX   221

Illustrations

1. Mosaic at San Tommaso in Formis   42
2. Printed prayers and antiphons from the English breviary, 1649   83
3. Printed prayers and antiphons from the English breviary, 1649   84
4. Medieval breviary pages, date unknown   99
5. Medieval breviary pages, date unknown   99
6. Medieval breviary pages, date unknown   100

Acknowledgments

This book has taken too long in becoming. It has gone through so many false starts and so many different forms that I hardly know where to start. I owe so many long-standing debts of gratitude to so many people. I am very grateful to the granting agencies that supported the projects that eventually became this book: the American Academy in Rome, the Renaissance Society of America, the American Philosophical Society, and the Academic Senate of the University of California, Davis. Thanks are also due to the staff of the many institutions in Spain and Italy where I conducted the archival research on which this book rests. Special thanks to Fr. Pedro Aliaga Asensio, O.SS.T., who so graciously welcomed me into the Trinitarian house in Rome at San Carlino alle Quattro Fontane and granted me access to the exceptional materials housed in the archive there. This book took a lot longer than either he or I expected, and I thank him for his patience. Many thanks, too, to Fr. Javier Carnerero, O.SS.T., who facilitated my last-minute return to San Carlino. Monsignor Giancarlo Zichi and his friendly staff at the diocesan archive in Sassari were very kind and helpful. Corinna Ricasoli and her colleagues at Archivitaly helped me get access to critical materials in Rome at a time when the COVID-19 pandemic made international travel utterly impossible. The interlibrary loan specialists at the University of California, Davis, library were enormously helpful in getting me materials, while the staff at the Robbins Collection Library of the University of California Berkeley School of Law went above and beyond by granting me special temporary borrowing privileges that made my work much easier. I am particularly grateful to the many libraries and archives around the world that have digitized their early modern materials and made them available to the public.

Portions of chapter 4 appeared in my article "Stolen Saint: Relic Theft and Relic Identification in Seventeenth-Century Rome," in *The Quest for Certainty in Early Modern Europe: From Inquisition to Inquiry, 1550–1700*, edited by Barbara Fuchs and Mercedes García-Arenal (Toronto: University of Toronto Press, 2020), 159–97, and are reprinted here with permission of the publisher.

In the years that have passed since I first started the project that eventually morphed into this book, I have passed through more personal and professional highs and lows than I ever would have imagined when I started out. Some of my thanks are due to colleagues who helped me with questions and problems that developed in the course of research and writing; others are due to friends who lent me a hand in other ways: James Amelang, Emily Albu, Adam Beaver, David Biale, Jessica Boone, Brad Bouley, Liam Brockey, Joan Cadden, Ian Campbell, Michael Cuthbert, Vanessa de Cruz Medina, Simon Ditchfield, the members of the Association for Spanish and Portuguese Historical Studies email list, Jill Fantauzza, Barbara Fuchs, Mercedes García-Arenal, Ellen Hartigan-O'Connor, Lu Ann Homza, Michelle Leigh, Lisa Materson, Ean Murphy, Katrina Olds, Lorena Oropeza, Erin Rowe, John Rundin, John Slater, John Smolenski, Daniel Stoltzenberg, Kathy Stuart, Valentina Tikoff, Natalie Troxel, Stefania Tutino, and many others. Many thanks, too, to the audience members and commentators at seminars, workshops, and conferences held by the Johns Hopkins University, the University of Exeter, the University of Arkansas Fayetteville, the Pontificia Universidad Católica de Chile, UC San Diego, UC Los Angeles, UC Davis, UC Merced, the Huntington Library, the University of York, the Sixteenth Century Studies Conference, the Association for Spanish and Portuguese Historical Studies, the Mediterranean Seminar, the Renaissance Society of America, SHADYC (CNRS-EHESS, Marseille), TELEMME-MMSH (Université de Provence), and CARE (EHESS, Paris). Many thanks, too, to the two anonymous readers who read the manuscript, whose comments and critiques have made this book much better. I also thank Ellie Goodman and the amazing staff at Penn State University Press, who have done so much to bring this project to fruition. Needless to say, all responsibility for any errors lies wholly with me.

My deepest thanks goes to my family, who have helped me, supported me, and lifted me up, especially when things seemed very bleak indeed. My son, who has lived with this book his whole life, taught me that it is people, not scholarship, that love you back. My sisters and their families critiqued chapters, helped me puzzle out translations, and patiently listened to me ramble on about topics that must surely have been very tedious indeed. My parents—all four of them—have helped me in more ways than I can count. They worked their networks and drove for hours to get me otherwise-inaccessible books. They emailed me articles and helped me think through key ideas and read through the manuscript with careful eyes and sharp red pencils. They rode to my rescue in times of trouble and caught me when I fell. Above all, my mother, Nancy Flowers, has been unwavering in her support for me and all my endeavors. Her love for me has been my rock. This book is for her.

PROLOGUE: THE CRIME

On March 18, 1655, the eve of the feast of St. Joseph, at eleven o'clock at night, two Spanish friars, lay brothers of the traditional, or Calced, branch of the Order of the Most Holy Trinity and of the Captives, left their Roman monastery and hurried out into the night.[1] Slipping quietly through the darkened streets, they made their way from their monastery, located in the Via Sistina near the Piazza Barberini, to the church of San Tommaso in Formis, almost three kilometers away on the Caelian Hill.[2] The small church and its adjoining cloister had once numbered among the twenty privileged abbeys possessed by the Benedictines in Rome, but in 1209, the site was handed over by Pope Innocent III to St. John of Matha (ca. 1160–1213), the founder of the Trinitarian Order. The Trinitarians rebuilt the site (preserving in the process the first-century arch, or *fornix*, that gave the church its name) and constructed a hospital to serve the poor, the sick, and pilgrims to the Eternal City. By 1389, however, the friars had lost control of the buildings and the rents associated with them, owing in part to the order's support for the antipope Clement VII (r. 1378–94) in the Western Schism. Since then, except for a brief period in 1572–73 and an even briefer one in 1605, the church was one of many properties possessed by the canons of the chapter of St. Peter at the Vatican, who in 1639 leased the church and its associated buildings to the ever-expanding urban villa of Girolamo Mattei, Marquis of Giove.[3] Largely abandoned in a semirural sector of Rome, its hospital half in ruins and reduced to service as a granary, San Tommaso in Formis was a vulnerable target.[4]

Armed only with an iron pry bar, a flint and steel for striking a light, and a candle, Gonzalo de Medina and José Vidal scaled the garden walls that flanked the church but found the doors locked tight.[5] They nearly abandoned their quest out of fear of making noise and being caught, but the discovery of a wooden ladder strengthened their resolve, and together they climbed it to reach the windows that provided light to the building's interior. They ripped away the linen curtain that substituted for window glass and clambered into the church, bringing the ladder with them. Once inside, they struck a light. The flickering candle would have revealed that the walls of the little church were decorated with frescos commemorating their order and its primary ministry, the redemption of Christian captives in Muslim lands.[6] Together, Vidal and Medina made their way toward a marble sarcophagus raised on pillars against one wall of the church and marked by an inscription that identified the tomb as that of St. John of Matha himself.[7] Taking up the pry bar, Medina approached the tomb, but the sudden sound of three howls, like those of a dog, stopped him in his tracks. The two terrified friars extinguished most of their candles and sought out the source of the chilling sounds, but none could be found. "Brother," said the panicked Vidal, "it must be that God does not wish us to take this holy body." "Let us pray first," replied Medina. The two offered prayers and vows and then set to work.

Using the iron bar, Vidal opened the tomb, creating a hole large enough to admit his head and an arm. Inside, he discovered not one but three bodies. The bones of the saintly founder of the Trinitarians were in the middle, set apart from the others, and on his skull was a handwritten prayer to the saint drawn from the order's English breviary. On either side, pushed to the corners of the tomb and marked with identifying inscriptions, were the remains of John of England and Miguel Laínez of Spain, two of the order's earliest generals.[8] The two thieves noted that while the two generals' bones were yellowed, those of St. John of Matha were unusually white and quite long. The friars venerated the remains and reverently kissed Matha's skull and then proceeded to remove his bones, placing them in a hastily improvised sack fashioned from Medina's woolen undershirt. They carefully replaced the pieces of the tomb so that it appeared intact and exited the church by the same window they had entered, taking care to return the ladder to its original location. Medina and Vidal again traversed the city under cover of night. This time, their route included a victory lap, as it took them past the church of San Carlo alle Quattro Fontane and the house of their rivals in religion, the Spanish brothers of the Discalced, or reformed, branch of the Trinitarian Order. Though it was the wee hours of the morning and a time when no bell should be ringing, they heard a bell sound within the Discalced monastery, an event that the pious thieves interpreted as a miracle in honor of the saint whose remains they bore. Medina and Vidal returned, undetected, to their monastery and hid their prize in a chest in Medina's cell. They then retired for the night, each taking a key to the chest.

For eighteen days, the friars kept their secret, but eventually news of the theft reached the ears of their superior, Pedro Arias Portocarrero, the Calced Trinitarians' *procurador general*, or solicitor general at the papal court, who took possession of the remains. He ordered the two thieves to return to the church in order to retrieve the other two bodies and to leave in the tomb a note, written out and signed by himself, that explained and documented the removal of all three. He also prepared an identical copy of the note to accompany Matha's bones.[9] On the night of April 6, Medina and Vidal braved a dangerous thunderstorm to return to the church of San Tommaso in Formis. Despite the near disaster of Medina's fall from the church window and the loss of a shoe, they accomplished the task, but in the process, they broke the lid of the tomb, a misfortune that ensured that the crime would eventually be discovered.[10] Given the general neglect in which the church of San Tommaso in Formis languished, it was some days before the theft became known. By April 11, the archpriest of the Vatican chapter, Cardinal Francesco Barberini (1597–1679), had opened an inquiry into the affair, and by mid-August, Medina, Vidal, and Arias had been tried and convicted in the court of the cardinal vicar. On August 30, a warning was posted on church doors throughout the city of Rome and its district. The *monitorio* ordered the thieves to present themselves before the court within eighteen days and threatened penalties ranging from loss of status to prison, exile, and galley service for noncompliance.[11] The culprits, however, were long gone. Fearing punishment, Medina and Vidal had left Rome for Naples shortly after completing the second theft. Arias fled with the remains to the safety of the hospital attached to San Giacomo degli Spagnoli, the Spanish national church, prominently located on the Piazza Navona.[12] Having first entrusted the bodies of the two generals to the Spanish ambassador in Rome, Don Diego Tagliavia de Aragón y Mendoza (1596–1663), Duke of Terranova, Arias disguised himself as an Augustinian friar and sneaked out of the city to join his confrères in Naples. Together, the three boarded a galley and spirited the stolen bones away to the safety of Spain.[13]

I

RELICS AND RELIC CULTURE
IN EARLY MODERN EUROPE

By the thieves' own account, their motives were pious. According to Gonzalo de Medina, the two friars had stolen the bones because they "were in a church that was not [Trinitarian], and did not receive the appropriate veneration, because the church [of San Tommaso in Formis] was half ruined [and] in an unpopulated area within the city of Rome."[1] Their crime was the product of a tradition of reverence for the bodies of the saints that was as ancient as the saints themselves. From the second century onward, members of the early Christian community gathered the remains of pious people martyred for the faith at the hands of hostile authorities and venerated them in remembrance of their sacrifice and of the promise of the coming Resurrection. By the fourth century, believers had overcome traditional taboos against touching the dead and began to parcel out the remains of martyrs, dividing them up and spreading them and their cults throughout the expanding Christian world.[2] With the end of persecution in the fourth century, the profile of the saint shifted, and martyrs were joined by confessors, "not those who had died for their faith but those who had lived for it, in a heroic and resolute way."[3] As the cult of the saints blossomed over the succeeding millennium, so too did the veneration of their bodies, around which there developed a rich array of beliefs and practices. Bodily remains, corporeal relics, were accompanied by contact relics, bits of clothing or other objects that had been in intimate contact with the body of the saint, dust or oil from the tomb, or even water in which the saint's holy bones had been washed. The most sacred and most sought-after relics were those of Christ and his mother, but throughout medieval Europe, Christians enthusiastically venerated the bodies of saints both famous and obscure.

As these bits and pieces of the holy dead began to circulate, so too did fears about fraud and about distinguishing saintly remains from those of everyday Christians. Already in the early fifth century, St. Augustine worried about imposters masquerading as monks who peddled "the limbs of martyrs, if indeed [they are] of martyrs," to the faithful.[4] Seven centuries later, the historian Guibert of Nogent complained of the dangers posed to the laity by the veneration of dubious saints' bones and decried those who profited from their credulity, while the stock comic figure of the corrupt cleric and his questionable relics found in late medieval writers like Chaucer, Boccaccio, and Masuccio Salernitano suggests that the problem persisted.[5] Thus, the questions raised by the friars' criminal act in 1655 were not new. While Medina and Vidal (and their superior, Pedro Arias Portocarrero) may have sought to ensure that their founder received proper veneration, their pious misdeed instead cast the very identity of the bones into doubt. Were the bones stolen from San Tommaso in Formis really those of St. John of Matha? And was the body now in Spain one and the same as that which had lain in the tomb? What of the bones of other saints—how certain could one be of the identity and authenticity of their remains? How was one to know and to recognize the bodies of the "very special dead"?[6] Until Matha's relics could be certified as truly belonging to the saintly founder of the Trinitarian Order, they could not be presented to the faithful as objects for devotion—a hindrance that could seriously affect the order's public standing and impede its ability to gather funds to support its central mission, the ransoming of Christian captives from slavery in Islamic North Africa. The Trinitarian Order would now have to prove the identity of Matha's stolen bones to the eagle-eyed members of the Congregation of Sacred Rites, the papal institution charged with overseeing the veneration of the saints and of their bodies. It would take three attempts and nearly seventy years for the order to win its case.

The uncertainties raised by Matha's bones, and by all saints' relics, took on a particular urgency in the context of the sixteenth and seventeenth centuries, as Protestant critiques shook the cult of the saints to its very foundations. Whereas Catholic humanists had sought to rein in superstitious practices and reform popular devotion, Protestant reformers were set on pulling down the entire edifice of traditional devotion to the saints and their remains. For Martin Luther, relics "ought long ago to have been condemned, even though there were some good in them," since they were "without God's word neither commanded nor advised. It is a completely unnecessary and useless thing."[7] Jean Calvin went further, thundering against the veneration of relics as "the mother of idolatry." It was an "execrable sacrilege," he declared, to give worship to "dead and insensible creatures" rather than to "the one living God."[8] In towns and cities across Protestant Europe, reforming crowds swept the altars clean, pulling down images and burning and destroying the once-holy bones, sometimes ritually "disenchanting" them with parades and public expositions that parodied traditional acts of veneration.[9]

The response of the Catholic Church to the threat of Protestantism came in many forms, chief among them the ecumenical gathering known as the Council of Trent (1545–63).[10] The council aimed to counter Protestant critiques by clarifying and affirming Church doctrine and by reforming beliefs and practices through the reinforcement of the borders between the sacred and profane. In 1563, the assembled prelates took up the question of the cult of the saints and of their relics. They affirmed the validity and importance of the saints and relics but also tasked bishops with regulating the cult:

> All superstition must be removed from invocation of the saints, veneration of relics and use of sacred images; all aiming at base profit must be eliminated; all sensual appeal must be avoided, so that images are not painted or adorned with seductive charm; and people are not to abuse the celebration of the saints and visits to their relic for the purpose of drunken feasting, as if feast days in honour of the saints were to be celebrated with sensual luxury. And lastly, bishops should give very great care and attention to ensure that in this matter nothing occurs that is disorderly or arranged in an exaggerated or riotous manner, nothing profane and nothing unseemly, since holiness befits the house of God.[11]

In the years and decades that followed, the council's decrees were taken up and implemented by provincial councils and reforming bishops. In so doing, ecclesiastical officials found themselves forced to contend with the questions and doubts that could surround relics, especially those that were newly discovered or those, like the bones stolen from the little church in Rome, that were poorly documented or acquired by questionable means.[12]

The veneration of relics was but one part of the cult of the saints, one of Western Christianity's most important forms of cultural expression. Like the faithful themselves, the saints were human, but they were understood to be a special class of people, extraordinary in their virtues and piety. They were also seen as ideal examples of Christian living, role models for imitation. Though they were remembered for their exemplary lives, death marked not their ends but their beginnings, as they transcended its boundaries and linked Heaven and Earth both in their physical presence and in their continuing power as members of the heavenly assembly before the throne of God, with whom they interceded on behalf of the living. Whether they were martyrs for Christ or whether they were women and men who had lived lives of exceptional holiness, saints were invoked by Christians of all social levels and petitioned in times of need. They responded by working miracles, healing the sick, and saving the imperiled. Their stories were told and retold in hagiography; their images could be found in churches and chapels, homes and streets. People named their children after saints and left goods and property to them in their wills. They sought saints out in nearby shrines or traveled to distant pilgrimage centers, where they commemorated the saints' interventions with votive paintings and wax images of body parts miraculously healed. People called on the saints for their aid before going into battle and childbirth or when seeking a cure or a lost sheep. The saints, in sum, were firmly interwoven with all aspects of medieval Christian social, religious, and political life.[13]

Relics and relic culture were not some morbid, marginal oddity of Catholic religious life; rather, they occupied an important position within the sprawling complex of beliefs and practices that surrounded the saints. Carefully stored in ornate reliquaries and housed in altars and shrines, relics were regularly sought out by petitioners seeking a cure and pilgrims fulfilling a vow. Cathedral churches and rich abbeys accumulated treasuries of holy bodies, and kings and emperors magnified their greatness with collections of priceless and powerful saintly remains. Other people, if they were wealthy and pious enough, wore tiny relics contained in pendants around their necks. People swore oaths on the bodies of the saints and carried them into battle; they transported the relics in processions of celebration and rogation. A gift of a relic could seal an important alliance or family tie, while a dispute over competing claims to a holy body could provoke much bad blood and wind up in court.[14] Relics might also be acquired by means of *furta sacra*, holy theft, while others, lost or hidden, were discovered in relic *inventios*, inventions. Despite legal prohibitions on the sale or purchase of holy bodies, relics were also a commodity exchanged within an exclusive and often clandestine market.[15]

All of these practices rested on the relationship between the saints and their bodily remains. Unlike images, relics did not represent the saint's likeness or recall her to memory—they *were* the saint and made her presence palpable in the here and now. Operating on a logic of *pars pro toto*, any fragment made present the whole of the saintly body and thus the saint herself. In the words of the fourth-century bishop Victricius of Rouen, the whole of the saint resides in even the smallest shred, since "what is divine cannot be diminished, because it is wholly present in the whole. And wherever it is anything, it is whole."[16] In relics, the visible fragment made manifest the invisible whole. For this reason, its identity was of paramount importance, since what was venerated was not just anybody's body, but that of the saint, because of the person that she had been and still was. "We do not venerate a lifeless body [of the dead saint]," said St. Thomas Aquinas, "for what it is in itself, but by reason of the soul which was once united to it and which now enjoys God; by reason also of God whose servants they were."[17]

The concepts and customs surrounding the cult of the saints and their physical remains did not spring up fully formed but grew and changed over time, and for this reason, scholars of medieval and early modern Catholicism have long pointed to the saints as interpretive tools with which to understand broader dynamics within culture and society. Cults came into being and disappeared, were promoted or suppressed, in ways that reflected and responded to the changing concerns of each age. The wonder-working missionary saints of the early Middle Ages, for example, saints like St. Columba and St. Patrick, offer a window into the dynamics of Christianity's expansion beyond the Mediterranean, while the emergence of lay female saints St. Marie d'Oignes and St. Francesca Romana can tell us much about the values and expectations of Europe's increasingly city-centered society after 1200.[18] The cult of relics, too, reveals much about the societies in which it took root. For example, the custom of swearing oaths on relics, a common practice in the ninth, tenth, or eleventh centuries, gradually gave way by the later Middle Ages to swearing on the Gospels, as an increasingly universal religious culture influenced more local and regional traditions.[19] As Julia M. H. Smith has pointed out, "Relics were a small subset of much larger issues. On the one hand, they epitomized the weighty cultural meaning vested in saints and sanctity in early modern Catholicism as well as the deep anxieties surrounding them. On the other, they refracted long-term evolutions and tensions in western thought, as new forms of knowledge, changing modes of proof, and different methods of reasoning marked the transition from Scholasticism to Enlightenment."[20]

In just this way, the uncertainties surrounding the identity of St. John of Matha's stolen bones were representative of a broader collection of concerns and changes that surrounded holy bodies. In an age of persistent interconfessional conflict and reforming impulses both within and outside the Catholic Church, relics were a focal point for anxieties about fraud and forgery, the boundaries between the sacred and the profane, and the relationship of human beings to the divine. As the physical remains of holy women and men, relics were inherently ambivalent: they were both things and people, both mundane and exceptional. Like another object of contemporary controversy, the consecrated Eucharistic Host, relics brought the material and the spiritual into a meaning-laden tension, and, like the Host, they concealed their holiness under their ordinary appearance. Removed from their ornate reliquaries and separated from their identifying documents or inscriptions, to the naked eye, there was little that distinguished a holy person's remains from those of a common sinner. A few saintly bodies made themselves known through miracles, revealing the truth of their sanctity through their ability to move without human intervention, their healing exudate and unearthly light, their sweet smells and resistance to decay and, by extension, proving the Church's claim to be God's true institution.[21] Miracles were not, however, unproblematic evidence of a bone's identity, and most relics stubbornly refused to demonstrate their holiness. Just as one could not be sure of the identity of the remains said to belong to the Trinitarians' founder, it could be difficult to be fully certain of the identity or authenticity of any of the relics held up to the faithful as those of saints.

These concerns overlapped with broader changes at work within the cult of the saints during the early modern centuries. While the saints and their remains remained as important in sixteenth- and seventeenth-century Catholic devotional life as they had been before Luther, new institutions like the Congregation of Sacred Rites and revived ones like the Inquisition reworked the standards for the creation of new saints and the veneration of existing ones. Their aim—to defend the Church's ancient traditions while trimming back the exuberant excesses of popular superstition—drew on trends at work in other areas of early modern intellectual and religious life. New developments in philological and historical scholarship, for example, challenged traditional understandings of holy people and their bodies. In a push to craft a more solid, credible, and certain foundation for sacred history and for the Church's claims to unchanging historical continuity, writers of hagiography, ecclesiastical history, and related genres adopted the new techniques, sources, and perspectives pioneered by Renaissance humanists. The destabilizing effects of these innovations on sacred history and on the veneration of the saints could be felt throughout the Catholic world, as Church leaders trimmed the liturgical calendar, suppressed doubtful cults, and reworked concepts of sanctity to fit the needs of a new, revitalized Catholic Christianity. Similarly, methods and modes of thought developed among the practitioners of an increasingly empirical new science effected changes in the saint-making process, as doctors, surgeons, and even mathematicians were brought into canonization cases to assess critically alleged miracles and the bodies of candidates for sainthood.

Proving Identity Within a Culture of Relic Knowledge

The Stolen Bones of St. John of Matha examines the theft of the relics of St. John of Matha and its lengthy legal aftermath as a means of investigating the cultural meanings and anxieties invested in the relics of the saints and the changing modes of thought with which early modern Catholics approached them. Matha's stolen remains and the almost seventy-years-long campaign to secure their identity offer a unique opportunity to open up and explore the questions that surrounded relic identity and authenticity in seventeenth-century Europe: How could one know whether an object said to be a relic of a saint truly belonged to that saint, and how certain did one need to be about that knowledge? How could one tell the remains of the saints from those of the common dead or, worse, from those of an animal? What kinds of evidentiary instruments could prove the identity and authenticity of an alleged relic? What kinds of knowledge could be brought to bear on holy bodies? Were miracles necessary or sufficient evidence, or were other proofs needed? In the coming chapters, I explore the changing ways in which early modern Catholics sought solutions to these uncertainties. I argue that the bodies of the saints were objects of a specialized knowledge, surprisingly understudied by modern historians, that had its own conventions, proof strategies, procedures, and values. Through a close study of the events and arguments surrounding Matha's stolen bones, this book traces some of the contours of that knowledge.

In 1655, at the time of the theft, St. John of Matha (d. 1213) was not yet formally canonized. A product of the same evangelical ferment from which emerged such well-known saints as St. Francis (d. 1226) and St. Dominic (d. 1221) and of the same climate of interfaith conflict that fostered the Crusades, St. John of Matha was a professor of theology in Paris whose visionary experiences drove him to found the Order of the Most Holy Trinity and of the Captives, aka the Trinitarian Order or the Trinitarians, a new religious establishment dedicated to ransoming Christian captives from slavery in Islamic lands. In the centuries that followed, his spiritual sons and daughters of the Trinitarian Order committed their energies more to their charitable mission than to venerating their founder. By the late sixteenth century, however, the

Trinitarians were increasingly claiming Matha as a saint, and by the 1620s, this informal, uncanonized sainthood had become an embarrassment. The order's leadership set the wheels in motion to win approval of his cult and, with it, papal affirmation of his saintly status.

The case to establish the identity of Matha's stolen relics thus operated in tandem with the campaign to shore up his sainthood. The documentation marshaled to ensure Matha's place among the company of the saints was critical to proving the identity of his remains, but the origins and authenticity of that documentation were themselves the subject of controversy. *The Stolen Bones of St. John of Matha* examines how the Trinitarians mobilized the past to achieve results in the present as chroniclers of the past crafted a new history for their order, a history based in no small part on an ambitious program of invention and forgery. Even as historians of all genres, including ecclesiastical history and hagiography, adopted new methods and evidentiary expectations, for some, forgery remained a resource, the disreputable handmaid to more legitimate forms of historical writing. In an era in which the process of saint-making was increasingly rigorous, legalistic, and grounded in written records rather than in other forms of proof, the Trinitarians' reliance on forged documents and an imagined past was both typical and risky. This book uncovers the ways in which history and historical invention and forgery were created and deployed as a form of proof within the culture of knowledge around the bodies of the saints.

Early modern discussions of how questionable relics might be identified and authenticated pointed to many acceptable forms of evidence, many dating from the earliest origins of the cult of the saints in late antiquity. Commentators on relics laid out a wide array of possible indicators, ranging from divine revelations and miracles to pilgrimages and processions. In practice, however, seventeenth-century ecclesiastical authorities operated within a more restrictive regime of proof that favored what one writer of the time described as "human evidence," that is, the physical appearance of the remains, multiple forms of textual and historical documentation, reliable witness testimony, and local traditions.[22] These preferences, I argue, were representative of the tendency toward the centralizing, standardizing, and streamlining of sanctity and saint-making, a tendency that had already been slowly transforming the medieval cult of the saints since at least the twelfth century, when popes began to assert their exclusive right to judge and to declare just who may be venerated as a saint. The specialized culture of knowledge that surrounded the bodies of the saints reflected that transition in its blend of traditional and modern modes of thinking about and interpreting the evidence for sanctity.

The Stolen Bones of St. John of Matha maps out some of the key aspects of the culture of relic knowledge by exploring how the Trinitarians deployed lines of reasoning and proofs that met early modern evidentiary preferences while also situating them within older modes of knowing. The friars presented their case in multiple hearings between 1669 and 1721 before the Congregation of Sacred Rites. Through a close reading of the arguments presented before the congregation, I examine how the Trinitarians produced their proofs, which centered on the bones' material qualities, their documentary support, their place within the order's history and tradition, and the testimony of witnesses, and how the Trinitarians located their proofs within a framework of Scholastic concepts of individuation, identity, change, and persistence. I also consider how, when existing evidence was found to be inadequate, the friars produced new proofs by doubling down on forgery and their order's invented history and by enacting carefully scripted acts of inspection and viewing that blended highly traditional methods of relic recognition with a pragmatic and empirical approach to the holy that reflected new trends at work in the broader intellectual culture of early modern Europe.

Because the Trinitarians' arguments for the identity of Matha's stolen bones depended on human testimony and human memory, it opened them to doubts about the credibility and certainty of their evidence. They sought to address those doubts by emphasizing another characteristic of relic knowledge, a lesser form of certainty known as "moral certainty." A common feature on the scientific and philosophical landscape of the seventeenth century, moral certainty was regularly invoked in casuistry, moral and natural philosophy, law, and elsewhere. It offered an acceptance of doubt and an acknowledgment of the limits—but not the impossibility—of human knowledge. I examine how the Trinitarians applied moral certainty to the case of their founder's remains, revealing in the process how the category accommodated the uncertainty and inherent ambiguity of relics.

Thinking with Saints

In recent decades, interpretations of the religious transformations of the early modern period have undergone a thoroughgoing sea change. Scholars have stepped away from older narratives grounded in a supposed gulf between a Protestant sphere that was "disenchanted" and modern and a Catholic sphere that embraced the magical and, by extension, a nonmodernity often dismissed as "medieval." Similarly, models that presumed an opposition between religion, especially Catholicism, and changes in science and medicine have largely been discarded. Studies on sanctity and sainthood and on closely related concepts like the miraculous and the demonic have repeatedly revealed the ways in which "religious authorities alternately collaborated with philosophers in studying the natural world, viewed natural philosophy as a separate sphere of knowledge, or, indeed, even opposed certain investigations into nature."[23] While Protestants largely discounted miracles, early modern Catholics promoted them as irrefutable signs of the Church's supremacy and monopoly on truth. As recent scholarship has shown, miracles and other manifestations of the sacred were not accepted acritically; they required interrogation, testing, verification, and authentication, processes that overlapped with and participated in contemporary developments in natural science and medicine. For example, Fernando Vidal's work on miracles explores the ways in which saint-making and experimental natural philosophy shared an understanding of the role of testimony in making knowledge, while Bradford Bouley's recent study on autopsies performed on the bodies of candidates for sainthood in the sixteenth, seventeenth, and eighteenth centuries reveals how ecclesiastical officials brought recent developments in anatomy to bear on a means for knowing and recognizing holiness and how the Church looked to the expertise of university-trained physicians in interpreting the saintly body.[24]

Studies like these demonstrate how sanctity and sainthood were not merely products of the culture and society in which they were rooted; they were sites on which people could work out concepts and concerns, new ideas and nagging uncertainties. The saints, as Simon Ditchfield has suggested, were "good to think with," for sixteenth- and seventeenth-century Catholics and for twenty-first-century historians alike.[25] Holy people and concepts of holiness were one arena in which people contended with the pervasive crisis of certainty at work within early modern European culture. This was an age in which long-established certainties were brought into question. Unexpected continents, for instance, reworked the map, and the strange inhabitants of those continents occasioned doubts about how to interpret alien cultures. Likewise, encounters with the fauna and flora of distant lands and the new empirical methods being developed by scientists strained traditional natural philosophy to the breaking point. Religious upheaval transformed Truth into competing confessional truths, and Christians found themselves grappling with uncertainty about the relationship between truth and the appearance of truth and the discernment of the true from the false, reality from appearance, being from seeming.[26]

While contemporaries explored these issues in arenas that ranged from witchcraft trials and exorcisms of the demon possessed to concerns about counterfeit converts and handwringing about Machiavellian dissimulation, the saints and their bodies offered a particularly rich terrain on which to work out the uncertainties inherent in knowing and recognizing the sacred.[27] In taking up the question of the early modern culture of relic knowledge, this book speaks to a growing literature on saint-related subjects, such as pretended sanctity; the many new cults that blossomed, waned, or were suppressed; and ideas about miracles and the miraculous.[28] It also engages a growing body of work on early modern historical forgery, on hagiography and other forms of sacred history, and on the friction between historical and doctrinal truth.[29] Relics have been largely incidental to these researches, however, and those few that have included the bodily remains of the saints within the scope of their analysis have focused mainly on the *beati moderni*, the recent holy dead under consideration for canonization. Most of the existing literature on relics deals with the medieval cult, rather than its early modern continuator, and to date, only a handful of scholars have plumbed the ways in which early modern Catholics investigated and authenticated the thousands upon thousands of ancient or medieval holy bodies scattered in churches and chapels across the Catholic world or uncovered in *inventios*.[30] This book builds on this small body of scholarship, using the case of St. John of Matha's stolen bones to examine the largely unstudied regulatory and evidentiary regime that surrounded the early modern cult of relics. As key parts of the devotional landscape, relics and relic culture served as a critical proving ground on which early modern Catholics contended with the uncertainty that surrounded the discernment of the sacred and worked out their ideas about evidence, authenticity, and doubt.

Part of what made relics both fruitful and challenging to think with is their very material nature. The bodies of the saints were both wholly unique and utterly generic objects, and early modern Catholics struggled to contend with the fact that a relic was both sacred and mundane, that it was simultaneously a very special, very unique person and a very common object. The materiality of the relic was critical to its meaning and to its place in the lived religion of Catholics of all social levels. In this book's exploration of the culture of relic knowledge, it participates in scholarship's recent "material turn," a turn to material culture and materiality as a way of opening up new questions, especially within the study of religion.[31] In examining the arguments and practices with which the Trinitarian Order sought to establish the identity of Matha's remains, this book uncovers some of the ways in which the ecclesiastical authorities who crafted the culture of relic knowledge confronted relics' very materiality and the tools and assumptions they brought to that encounter. I do not attempt, however, to address all of the practices and performances through which Catholics engaged with relics, nor do I claim to have encompassed the entirety of relic knowledge. Unofficial or lay modes of encountering the divine in the material remains of the saints, such as the production of little buns containing the ashes of martyrs, or liturgical practices, such as grand public relic displays on feast days, do not appear here much, for the simple reason that they did not figure in the evidence and arguments brought to bear on the case of St. John of Matha's stolen bones.[32] My hope is that these omissions will prove productive terrain for other researchers into the materiality of relics.

St. John of Matha and the Trinitarian Order in Contemporary Scholarship

For centuries, the Order of the Most Holy Trinity and of the Captives was a regular feature on the religious landscape throughout France and Spain (and elsewhere). Trinitarian monasteries were fixtures in many cities and towns, and Trinitarian friars regularly circulated among the population, collecting funds to pay for the ransoming of Christian captives. Given the order's ubiquity, it is a bit surprising that it has not been the focus of much sustained scholarship. While the Trinitarians' medieval past has been the object of important research by Giulio Cipollone and James Brodman, among others, the early modern period is comparatively unknown.[33] There are a handful of older works, most notably those of Paul Deslandres and Antonino de la Asunción, that remain indispensable, and the more recent scholarship of Juan Pujana and Bonifacio Porres Alonso has shed new light on the order's reform and of its redemptorist pursuits.[34] A new wave of work on the Mediterranean slave trade has also brought the Trinitarians much deserved attention. Most recently, Daniel Hershenzon has explored the crucial role of the Trinitarian friars (among others) in the system of enslavement and redemption that bound together the early modern Mediterranean. His study, together with other recent works, makes clear the order's centrality in the political economy of ransom.[35] Beyond these, however, one finds a curious paucity of studies that focus in on the order and its inner workings, institutional culture, and ethos or on its connections with the society around it during the early modern centuries. And if secondary scholarship on the Trinitarian

Order is skimpy, sustained work on its cult of its founding father, St. John of Matha, is nearly nonexistent. The only real exception to this rule is the work of María Cruz de Carlos Varona, whose excellent 2005 doctoral dissertation on images and the veneration of Trinitarian saints in the Calced (traditional) Trinitarian monastery in Madrid has become a landmark in the order's historiography. To date, only De Carlos Varona and Lisa Beaven have written about the theft that stands at the center of this book. The legal struggle that followed has never been studied.[36]

This state of affairs is due in no small part to the order's fate in the upheavals of the late eighteenth and early nineteenth centuries. Unlike the Jesuits, the Trinitarians did not have a strong tradition of centralized administration. Rather, each monastery or convent seems to have undertaken the maintenance of its own papers, a responsibility that some houses seem to have fulfilled better than others. When the order was suppressed in France in 1790 and underwent exclaustration in Spain in 1835 or, in the case of England, was wholly dissolved in 1534, much documentation was destroyed or disappeared. Other records were probably lost when the traditional wing of the order went extinct in 1894 and its last remaining monastery was handed over to the Dominicans. As a result of these vicissitudes, state archives absorbed some of the order's records, but the events of the eighteenth and nineteenth centuries, coupled with the wars, invasions, floods, fires, and other usual calamities of history, mean that it can be surprisingly difficult to write about the order's past.

While many sources have disappeared, however, some have survived, and *The Stolen Bones of St. John of Matha* is closely based on a wealth of manuscript and printed material written primarily in Latin, Spanish, Italian, and French. Few of these materials have ever been examined by modern researchers. The lion's share of the sources related to the case of Matha's stolen bones are housed in the archive at San Carlino alle Quattro Fontane, the Trinitarian monastery in Rome. I found other materials in different repositories around the Eternal City, including the Vatican Library, the Vatican Archives, the Archive for the Congregation for the Doctrine of the Faith (i.e., the Roman Inquisition), and the Biblioteca Angelica, as well as in Madrid at the National Library of Spain and the Royal Academy of History. Due to the harsh realities of time and money and especially to the chaos created by the outbreak of the COVID-19 pandemic, some materials were entirely inaccessible, while others I could consult only in their digitized form. Thus, readers will also find cited manuscript material from libraries and archives that lie farther afield, like the State Public Library in Palma de Mallorca or the rare books collection of the University of Granada. Digitizing initiatives like the ones that made these resources available are a godsend to researchers; my hope is that by making public how essential they have been to this project, I can help foster better awareness of the great need for their continued funding and support.

The Structure of This Book

Together, the manuscript and print sources gathered from libraries and archives in Rome, Madrid, and beyond form the foundation for the chapters that follow. Chapter 2 returns to the crime first introduced in the prologue and situates it within the broader context of the history and institutional culture of the Trinitarian Order. The chapter charts the development of the Trinitarian Order from its origins in southern France in the late twelfth century and its spread throughout France, the Iberian Peninsula, and other parts of Europe, and its splintering in the sixteenth century into competing wings of Calced (traditional), Discalced ("unshod," reformed, or observant), and Reformed (a separate observant group). Smaller and less well known than other religious groups founded in the same period, the Trinitarians were nevertheless key players in their main area of activity, the Mediterranean slave trade. Unlike many other orders, however, by the late 1620s, the Trinitarians had not yet undertaken the formal canonization of their founder, St. John of Matha, and his legendary companion, St. Felix of Valois. Drawing on a wide array of medieval and early modern sources, I trace the development of Matha's cult and demonstrate that, until the late 1500s, Matha does not seem to have been particularly important to his spiritual sons and daughters. By the turn of the century, however, in an era of increasing emphasis on standardization and centralized control over the cult of the saints, Matha's uncanonized status had become a pressing issue. In effect, Matha was a problem for the order long before the 1655 robbery, and after the theft, the two issues, the recognition of his long-standing veneration—and, by extension, his sainthood—and the authentication of the relics' identity, would be closely intertwined. Chapter 2 concludes by examining the Trinitarian Order's first efforts toward the authorization of Matha's cult: a reworked and modernized saintly *vita* published in 1630 and a failed petition in that same year for extension to the whole of the order of the "English breviary," a supposedly medieval liturgical commemoration of the two founders.

Chapter 3 picks up the question of the case for Matha's immemorial veneration and the narrative thread of the 1655 theft and moves with the thieves and their booty across the Mediterranean from Italy to Spain. The historical narratives and documentation crafted in support of Matha's cult would become load-bearing supports for the case to prove the identity of his stolen relics. This chapter focuses in on the writing of histories and the concomitant forging of sources as a central part of the order's campaign to win recognition of Matha's immemorial cult. I examine the work of two historian-forgers who both "invented" missing historical evidence. The first, a Trinitarian friar named Juan Figueras Carpi, laid the groundwork by crafting a fully developed life of St. John of Matha and a detailed recounting of his order's more than four hundred years of existence, both grounded in imaginary authors, invented traditions, and forged documents—including the very same English breviary that had been the focus of the failed 1630 petition discussed in chapter 2. The second, a historian-for-hire named Antonio Lupián Zapata, built on Figueras's work to create new documents that would help shore up the shaky foundations of the Trinitarian Order's new history and its case for Matha's canonization. I contextualize the work of the two forgers within contemporary developments in historical theory and method and argue that for early modern historians, especially those writing in the service of religious truths, historical criticism, forgery, and a generous approach of "pious affection" were all compatible.

In 1666, armed with the evidence created by Figueras and Lupián, the Trinitarian Order won the formal recognition of Matha's ancient cult and could finally address the problem of the identity of their founder's stolen bones. Chapter 4 follows the case back to Rome, where in 1669 the Discalced Trinitarians petitioned the Congregation of Sacred Rites for a ruling that would confirm the relics' identity as the remains of St. John of Matha. While theoretical discussions of relic knowledge commonly pointed to a wide array of possible proofs, in practice, investigating Church authorities preferred physical evidence and documents as tools for evaluating both relic identity and the closely related issue of relic authenticity. In the first third of the chapter I examine a collection of legal briefs developed for the case to uncover how the Trinitarian legal team met that evidentiary requirement and linked the question of the identity of Matha's relics—that is, their sameness through time—to their unchanging material qualities, especially their size and color, and to the documentary support provided by an extract from the same forged English breviary discussed in chapters 2 and 3. The second third of chapter 4 connects the Trinitarians' evidentiary approach to another aspect of relic knowledge, moral certainty. Through a close analysis of one legal brief, I trace the history of this category and its use in a wide range of intellectual arenas and argue that as an interpretive mode, moral certainty took into account the inherent ambivalence of relics. In the final portion of the chapter, I analyze why these strategies failed. While the cardinals and their advisers appear to have accepted moral certainty as the correct kind of certainty for relics, they rejected the evidence adduced in support of the case as untrustworthy and incomplete. I connect the congregation's objections in the case of Matha's relics to broader trends as Rome sought to bring the cult of the saints under tighter control and discipline.

Chapter 5 follows the case of Matha's stolen bones from 1669 to 1715 and 1721, when it again came before the Congregation of Sacred Rites. I contextualize the renewed effort within, on the one hand, sharpening internal disputes between different wings of the Trinitarian Order and, on the other, the military conflict that played out in the Iberian and Italian Peninsulas in connection with the War of Spanish Succession (1701–14) and the concomitant upheaval in the international political order. In the wake of the failed petition of 1669, the Trinitarians sought to create new, more acceptable evidence in 1671 by putting the relics through a formal act of inspection. This act, a "recognition," brought to bear on the bones other aspects of relic culture by using the senses, especially sight and touch, as ways of knowing. My analysis contextualizes the event in relation to other acts of relic inspection, quasi-scientific testing, and medical inspection and connects it to the role of witnessing in early modern natural science. These practices demonstrate how the cult of the saints and relic knowledge did not stand alone and isolated from the cultural and intellectual movements at work in other areas of inquiry.

The new evidence created in 1671, together with a renewed emphasis on the Trinitarians' invented past and on the forged documents on which it relied, formed the foundation of the order's second failed attempt in 1715 and a third, successful effort in 1721. My discussion devotes special attention to the role of Prospero Lambertini, who, during his long career within the Congregation of Sacred Rites and later as Pope Benedict XIV, helped consolidate ideas about proof and evidence within saint-making and within relic culture as well. Lambertini's personal intervention into the framing of the arguments proved critical to the Trinitarian Order's final victory. Using an eyewitness account probably written by the Trinitarians' main representative in Rome, I examine how under Lambertini's guidance, the Trinitarians reframed the evidence to meet the changing standards of early Enlightenment historical criticism as it was being developed by scholars like Jean Mabillon and Ludovico Antonio

Muratori. In the end, it was as much canny political maneuvering as it was arguments and evidence that finally pushed the congregation to confirm the identity of Matha's stolen remains. An epilogue concludes by following the fortunes of Matha's bones through the eighteenth and nineteenth centuries and into the upheavals of the Spanish Civil War (1936–39), when new questions may have arisen about the identity of the remains.

2

"WELL, IF THEY ARE SO ANCIENT, WHAT SAINTS DO THEY HAVE?"

St. John of Matha in Trinitarian Tradition

Medina and Vidal's decision to steal the body of St. John of Matha during the early months of 1655 was strategically timed. The death of Pope Innocent X on January 7 had left Rome and the whole Catholic world in a suspended state, a liminal period known as a *sede vacante*. During such moments when the throne of St. Peter sat empty, the streets of the Eternal City became stages for protest and pasquinades, riots and jurisdictional jockeying, the settling of scores and collective violence against law officers and Jews. Papal government largely ceased functioning for the duration of the interregnum, and the *sbirri* (constables) of the governor of Rome, the city's most powerful agent of papal judicial authority, and the members of the civic artisan militias were hard-pressed to contain the explosive violence.[1] This period of license and lawlessness offered a window of opportunity to the two thieves, and its imminent closing with the election of Alexander VII on April 7 must have lent an air of urgency to their return visit to the little church the night before.

The crime was a serious one. The theft of holy relics had a long and distinguished history—medieval hagiography is littered with accounts of purloined bodies, some obscure, some belonging to Catholic Christianity's most famous and powerful saints. While in the ninth through the twelfth centuries monastic and urban communities often resorted to *furta sacra* (sacred theft) in order to supply themselves with holy bodies, by the mid-seventeenth century such actions were neither common nor condoned.[2] By the early thirteenth century, canon law had come to define relic theft as a crime of sacrilege.³ Early modern legal specialists disputed the details, but most agreed that even when committed out of devotion to the saints, relic theft was "mortal sacrilege, because it took away a holy object against the will of the owner."⁴ The conviction of Medina and Vidal in the court of the cardinal vicar carried correspondingly heavy penalties. Had they not escaped to Spanish-controlled Naples, the two would have been sent off to row for ten years in the galleys that plied the Mediterranean. Since the court could not prove that Arias had himself taken part in the crime but only that he had ordered the lay brothers to do it, the punishment meted out to him was much lighter, a mere three years of imprisonment, loss of voting privileges within his order, together with a number of other, lesser penalties. It is unlikely that any of them actually served out these punishments.⁵

Arias, like his confrères, took refuge in a center of Spanish power. In an age of nascent national identities, national churches were important sites of collective affiliation and identification for expats resident in the Eternal City. The Spanish national church, San Giacomo degli Spagnoli, was just one of several sites around the city associated with Spanish prominence and presence, an expression of the "informal imperialism" exercised by the Spanish Crown over Rome.⁶ While the church and its adjoining hospital do not seem to have enjoyed the same diplomatic immunity extended to the district surrounding the ambassador's palace on the Piazza di Spagna, Arias's decision to flee to safety in San Giacomo suggests that there, too, Spanish fugitives from Roman justice could find temporary shelter.⁷ Though the number of Spaniards resident in Rome had much declined since its peak in the late sixteenth and early seventeenth centuries, they remained an important group among the legions of foreigners who made the city their home. Spaniards in Rome hailed from all parts of the Iberian Peninsula and from all social levels. At the top of the expatriate community was the Spanish ambassador and the Spanish cardinals, who together played critical roles in advancing the Crown's interests and shoring up support among the many players at the papal court. At the bottom, thousands of working-class Spaniards in Rome found employment and patronage from their wealthier compatriots. Not surprisingly, many of those in the middle were members of the clergy. While some served in the papal administration or were attached to the households of cardinals, others had come to Rome in the hopes of winning a benefice. Still others, like Medina and Vidal, were present in the city as residents in religious establishments or, like Arias, had come to Rome to represent the interests of their religious orders or home monasteries.⁸

The Trinitarian Order was just one among many religious congregations present in Rome. Like all monastic orders, it had its own accumulated communal history, its own institutional culture, and its own particular, Trinitarian way of doing things. This chapter situates the theft of Matha's relics within the context of the Trinitarian Order and its veneration of its founder. It traces the order's origins in northern France in the late twelfth century and its spread throughout France to the Iberian Peninsula and to England, Flanders, and the Levant and sketches the contours of the order's primary charitable mission, the ransoming of Christian captives from slavery in Islamic North Africa. Unlike the order's main rivals in this arena, the friars of the Order of the Blessed Virgin of Mercy, or Mercedarians, by the late 1620s, the Trinitarians had not yet undertaken the formal canonization of their founder. The chapter follows the development of the Trinitarian Order's legend of St. John of Matha and that of his (apocryphal?) companion, St. Felix of Valois, from the early thirteenth century and finds that until the last decades of the sixteenth century, Matha does not seem to have been particularly important to his spiritual sons and daughters.

By the turn of the century, however, Matha's saintly status and lack of veneration had become an increasingly pressing issue, thanks to a changing religious climate and internal reform movements within the order itself. The situation was further complicated in the 1620s by new papal requirements that suppressed the cults of uncanonized holy people unless their devotees could prove that they had been venerated for a minimum of a century. The chapter examines the Trinitarians' first efforts to lay the groundwork for Matha's canonization, a reworked and modernized saintly *vita* published in 1630 and a failed petition in that same year for extension to the whole of the order of a supposedly medieval liturgical commemoration of the two founders. In effect, Medina and Vidal's crime and the problem it created of the relics' identity was a sudden plot twist in the existing campaign to secure St. John of Matha's status as a saint. After the theft, the two issues, canonization and relic identity, would be closely intertwined.

Origins and Development of the Trinitarian Order

The Order of the Most Holy Trinity and of the Captives originated in France in the late twelfth century, a product of the same evangelical ferment that produced the Franciscans and the Dominicans and of the climate of interfaith conflict that fostered the Crusades. According to Trinitarian tradition, its founder, John of Matha (ca. 1160–1213), was born to a noble family in Faucon-de-Barcelonnette, in Provence. Matha studied theology in Paris, where he was ordained a priest in 1193. Trinitarian hagiographical tradition holds that as Matha celebrated his first Mass, he experienced the vision that would shape his mission. At the key moment of elevation, as he lifted the consecrated Host above his head, he saw Christ holding in each hand the chains that bound two captives, one white (a Christian) and one Black (a Muslim). Matha interpreted this mystical vision as a sign that he was to found a new religious order, one dedicated to the ransoming of Christians ensnared in the slave trading and warfare that characterized Muslim-Christian relations in the Mediterranean. Working together with the hermit Felix of Valois (d. 1212?), in 1194 Matha founded the Trinitarians' first house at Cerfroid, in the diocese of Meaux, some eighty kilometers northeast of Paris. Innocent III (1160/61–1216), in 1198, the first year of his papacy, extended his protection to the new mendicant order and authorized its monastic rule, and in 1209, he transferred possession of the church of San Tommaso in Formis to Matha and the Trinitarians.[9]

The new order spread quickly outward from the mother house at Cerfroid—by 1213, the year of Matha's death, there were more than thirty Trinitarian houses scattered through northern France, Occitania, Castile, and Aragon and one in Rome (and possibly others in other sites in Italy).[10] Over the course of the thirteenth century, the order also expanded into Portugal, Gascony, Flanders, the Levant, and the British Isles.[11] In France, the friars were also synecdochally known as the Mathurins, for their Parisian residence at the church of Saint-Mathurin, or as the Donkey Brothers (*frères des ânes*), since their original rule required them to eschew horses and mules for transport as a sign of their humility.[12] By the end of the fourteenth century, Aragonese Trinitarian houses could be found in cities like Valencia, Lorca, Barcelona, and Palma de Mallorca.[13] Many of the Trinitarian houses also had hospitals or hospices, places where the sick, the poor, and needy travelers could find care. Some of these hospitals were under the charge of Trinitarian sisters, who took the customary vows of poverty, chastity, and obedience and observed the order's rule like their male counterparts; however, the only convent of full-fledged Trinitarian nuns that predated the sixteenth century was the house at Avingaña, founded in 1250.[14]

By comparison to some of the monastic groups founded around the same time, such as the Franciscans or the Dominicans, the Trinitarian Order was fairly small. By the 1560s, there were some ninety male Trinitarian houses in

France, four in Portugal, and fifty-nine in the Spanish kingdoms, as well as four convents of Spanish Trinitarian nuns and a residence in Algeria. While in theory the whole order was governed by a minister general based in Paris, in practice the Trinitarians were deeply divided by nation and by degree of adherence to their rule.[15] Until 1654, only the four northernmost French provinces regularly participated in the order's general chapter meetings at Cerfroid, and Trinitarian provinces outside of these bounds operated largely independently of the minister general. The houses in England, Scotland, and Ireland had either ceased to exist or been disbanded in the Protestant reforms, and Iberian Trinitarians, separated into Aragonese, Castilian, Andalusian, and Portuguese provinces, for the most part functioned autonomously, following their own constitutions and governed by their own provincial leaders.[16] Contemporary political rivalries and alliances exacerbated these national divisions. During the Western Schism (1378–1418), Spanish and French Trinitarians threw their support behind the Avignon papacy, while those of England and Portugal supported the popes based in Rome. In the chaos of the schism and the Hundred Years' War, Portuguese and English friars sought their own superiors, unvetted by the minister general in France, and dissentions over leadership and offices multiplied. Not until 1429 was unity restored.[17] Over the course of the sixteenth century, however, when papal policy tended to favor Spain, Spanish Trinitarians seem to have attained "absolute autonomy." They enjoyed special privileges and even distinguished themselves from their French confrères by wearing different-colored capes over their habits.[18] Indeed, though the highest leadership of the order remained in French hands, the Spanish wing's prominence persisted at least until the 1630s, especially under the leadership of the Hispanophilic minister general Louis Petit (d. 1652).[19]

National differences between the friars were further complicated by the division of the Trinitarian Order into observant (Reformed and Discalced) and traditional (Calced) strands. Like many other monastic orders, the Trinitarians felt the spirit of revival and reform that swept through the Catholic world in the wake of the Council of Trent (1545–63). The Portuguese Trinitarians were the first to experience reform, as part of a general monastic reform ordered by the Portuguese Crown in 1545.[20] Efforts to reform the Spanish monasteries began in the mid-1560s and gathered steam in the 1580s. In France, an independent movement centered in Pontoise had resulted in the creation of a Reformed branch of the Trinitarian Order by the late 1570s. At its peak, this branch of the Trinitarian family had twenty-four houses, all within the territories of France.[21] In the Spanish kingdoms, efforts on the part of the Crown to reform the order resulted in both a reenergized traditional Calced branch and another observant group, the Discalced Trinitarians.[22] Founded by Friar Juan Bautista de la Concepción (1561–1613), a Castilian mystic known for his austerity, in 1599, the Discalced Trinitarians received their authorization as a separate branch within the order. With the patronage of Francisco Gómez de Sandoval y Rojas (1553–1625), the powerful Duke of Lerma, the Discalced Trinitarians were able to establish a prominent presence at the court in Madrid by 1605. Urban VIII granted the Discalced branch full independence from the Calced leadership in the 1630s, and by 1659, there were twenty-six Discalced houses in Castile and Aragon, divided into three provinces, as well as the interprovincial residence in Rome at San Carlo alle Quattro Fontane.[23] By the 1620s, French Discalced Trinitarians had created their own separate branch within the order. Their monastery in Rome was located across the street from that of their Discalced Spanish colleagues, at the small church of San Dionisio alle Quattro Fontane. By the middle of the seventeenth century, the divisions within the Trinitarians were so firmly established that each branch and each nation within the order maintained its own representative agents at the papal court, and each cultivated its own patrons and protectors.[24] While the key differences between reformed and traditional Trinitarians were in their degree of adherence to the order's rule—Discalced observance was significantly stricter and more austere than that of the Calced wing, for example—the different branches were careful to separate themselves from each other even visually, with different-colored habits emblazoned with different versions of a red and blue cross.

While the four branches—Calced, Spanish Discalced, French Discalced, and French Reformed—remained members of the same Trinitarian family, relations among them could be tense, even rancorous. During the latter decades of the sixteenth century, Calced Trinitarians in Spain resisted the establishment and expansion of their Discalced rivals, sometimes with violence. In 1600, for example, Juan Bautista de la Concepción himself was attacked and imprisoned by a group of Calced Trinitarians who resented the loss of their monastery at Valdepeñas.[25] Likewise in France, in the midst of a protracted struggle between Minister General Louis Petit, a Calced Trinitarian, and the fractious, breakaway Reformed and Discalced branches, relations could sometimes turn violent. On the eve of the feast of the Epiphany in 1638, Reformed friars then in control of the mother house at Cerfroid struck out against their rivals by throwing a picture of Petit into the monastery's privy and by stripping one unfortunate Calced friar naked and forcing him to skip rope for three-quarters of an hour. When the vicar general, the Calced friar Raymond de Pallas, attempted to intervene, he was rewarded with a punch to the temple.²⁶ As the existence of the Discalced branch became a fait accompli, the rivalry between the two played out in other arenas. In Spain, the courts were often a preferred site for disputes between the two branches, as Calced Trinitarians attempted to keep their Discalced confrères from collecting funds for the redemption of captives.²⁷ In one case in 1619, the Calced Trinitarians of Castile suggested that the Discalced friars' contemplative bent made them ill suited for the worldly work of "bargaining over caps and merchandise," a quality that was to their credit "but is very damaging to [the work of] redemption." They argued that the Discalced friars, unsuited to the rough-and-tumble of haggling for captives, ought to be compelled to hand over to their more experienced Calced colleagues the funds they had earmarked for redemptions.²⁸ Despite this hostility, however, Calced, Discalced, and Reformed Trinitarians continued to share a common history, traditions, ethos, and charism. Individual members and houses of the different branches and nationalities often collaborated with each other—the iron bar used by the two Spanish Calced thieves to pry open the tomb of John of Matha, for example, was loaned to them by their unwitting French Discalced colleagues at the monastery of San Dionisio alle Quattro Fontane.²⁹ Others looked to divine signs of reconciliation and cooperation, such as the miraculous discovery in Seville on July 16, 1621, the festival of the Triumph of the Cross, of a tree whose timber revealed images both of the pointed cross *pattée* of the Calced Trinitarians and of the plain cross of the Discalced branches.³⁰

For Trinitarians of all stripes, redemptions continued to be a central part of the order's mission. Throughout the early modern Mediterranean, both Muslims and Christians captured, held, and enslaved members of the rival religion and engaged in a thriving trade in human misery. The data are incomplete and the numbers much contested among scholars, but estimates suggest that three hundred thousand to four hundred thousand Moroccan and North African subjects of the Ottoman Empire were held in the Iberian Peninsula between 1450 and 1750, while another five hundred thousand Muslims were held in slavery in mainland Italian territories between about 1500 and 1800. Enslaved Muslims could also be found on the islands scattered through the Mediterranean—on the tiny island of Malta, for example, some thirty-five thousand to forty thousand Muslims were sold as slaves in the 1600s and 1700s. Similar numbers of Christians were captive in North Africa and elsewhere, enslaved and sold by the corsairs who infested the waters throughout the zone.³¹ Indeed, the size of the cross-Mediterranean slave trade between 1450 and 1700 was at least equal to that of the Atlantic trade in kidnapped and enslaved people from sub-Saharan Africa.³² Between the sixteenth and the nineteenth centuries, perhaps three million people, both Muslims and Christians, experienced enslavement within (mostly) southern Europe and North Africa.[33] These estimates do not, of course, come close to the many millions who suffered in the Atlantic slave trade, especially after its dramatic expansion during the eighteenth century, but they do testify to the pervasiveness of the practice and the persistently conflictive relations between Muslims and Christians within the Mediterranean.[34]

From the earliest origins of the Trinitarian Order, it had been dedicated to the ransoming of captive Christians—the order's very first mission was carried out in Morocco in 1199—and despite the internal divisions that plagued it, redemptions remained key to the friars' charism in the early modern period.[35] Indeed, so important was this task that the Trinitarians' original 1198 monastic rule specified that a full third of each monastery's income was to be reserved for redemptions. Though this provision was often modified or ignored as financially unworkable and troublesome for donor relations, its inclusion in the original rule is indicative of the centrality of redemptions in the order's charitable project.[36] The number of Trinitarian rescue expeditions is difficult to estimate since documentation for the order's first three centuries is sparse, but French Trinitarians conducted at least fourteen missions by the end of the fifteenth century, while Castilian friars carried out at least twelve during the 1400s. These campaigns freed captives held throughout the Islamic Mediterranean but especially in Algiers, Tunis, and Morocco (including Fez, Tetuán, and Salé) and in the kingdom of Granada, the last outpost of independent Islamic political power in the Iberian Peninsula.[37] After the capture of Granada in 1492, the Spanish monarchs began to turn their expansionist energies to the lands across the Strait of Gibraltar. The Portuguese Crown had held territory in coastal Morocco since the conquest of Ceuta in 1415, and Spain's leaders soon joined their Portuguese colleagues in expanding "their Crusaders' fantasy of conquest, colonization, and Christianization" to campaigns in sites across North Africa.[38] The imperialist efforts of Ferdinand (r. 1479–1516 and Isabella (r. 1474–1504), Charles V (r. 1516–58), and Philip II (r. 1558–98) were matched by their Ottoman counterparts, Suleiman the Magnificent (r. 1520–66), Selim II (r. 1566–74), and Murat III (r. 1574–95). Captive-taking became a side product of the frequent clashes between Spanish and Ottoman armies and navies. The available sources do not identify whether the Christians freed in Trinitarian expeditions during the sixteenth century were primarily soldiers or civilians, but they do show that the order's redemption efforts moved across the strait, as Castilian friars staged redemption expeditions in Fez, Tunis, Algiers, Tetuán, and Vélez de la Gomera.[39]

By the late 1570s, both the Ottomans and the Spanish began to turn away from their persistent struggle for control of the Mediterranean, and by 1581, the two had signed a truce that put an end to major military action.[40] In the decades that followed, North African corsairs stepped into the vacuum left by the imperial fleets, and battlefield captures gave way to an epidemic of high-seas attacks on hapless travelers and coastal raids that ranged as far west as the Canaries and as far north as Ireland and even Iceland.[41] Whereas most fifteenth- and sixteenth-century captives seem to have been primarily war trophies, the seventeenth century marks the full flowering of a complex and coherent system of capture, enslavement, and ransom. The most famous of those who were freed by the Trinitarians was the novelist Miguel de Cervantes, who spent five years in captivity in Algeria until he was redeemed by the Calced friar Juan Gil in 1580 for the hefty sum of five hundred gold *escudos*.[42] Most other captives were less exalted, often simple soldiers and sailors in service to the Crown or luckless fishermen and travelers captured on the high seas.[43] As corsair activity increased and the number of captives rose, so too did the redemptive activity of the Trinitarians and other groups and individuals involved in the rescue of enslaved Christians, increasing to expeditions approximately every three years.[44] While reliable numbers are hard to come by, it is clear that the number of redemption expeditions and redeemed captives expanded significantly during this period, due partly to the energizing, militant spirit of post-Trent Catholic culture and partly to new policies of royal supervision and funding. From about 1575, the Trinitarian Order and its rival, the Order of the Blessed Virgin of Mercy, or Mercedarian Order, were brought into ever closer alignment with the Spanish Crown's political and religious priorities through increased royal administrative oversight.[45] Using funds gathered from members of lay Trinitarian brotherhoods, from pious bequests and donations from members of the general public in Spain and the Spanish colonies abroad, from government councils, and from the families of captives, as well as income from annuities and real estate rents, between 1580 and 1767, Calced and Discalced Spanish Trinitarians redeemed more than eleven thousand enslaved prisoners held in Algiers, Fez, Tetuán, Tunis, and elsewhere.[46] Though the French Trinitarians did not experience the same degree of state involvement and oversight, they were similarly active, and the number of their redemption missions rose from a mere handful during the sixteenth century to more than twenty expeditions to North Africa between 1600 and 1700 (plus an additional one to Ottoman-ruled Hungary in 1602).[47]

The Trinitarians were thus key agents active within a thriving commerce that traversed political and religious frontiers and bound together both shores of the Mediterranean in a shared economy.[48] In addition to their work as redeemers, Trinitarian friars also ministered to the physical and spiritual needs of captive Christians through their hospitals located within the *bagni*, or prisons, of Algiers and Tunis. This dimension of the Trinitarian mission in North Africa seems to have developed during the seventeenth century, as the numbers of Christian captives began to grow precipitously. The first of the Trinitarian hospitals in Algiers was founded in 1612, and by 1672, there were six such institutions that provided medical services, clothing, and food to Christians of all confessions, including Protestants, as well as religious services, counseling, and basic education for captive Christian children. Similar hospitals were established in Tunis in the early eighteenth century.[49]

The friars of the Order of the Most Holy Trinity and of the Captives were not the only religious present in Islamic North Africa and engaged in the redemption of enslaved Christians. While members of other orders, including Jesuits, Discalced Franciscans, Capuchins, and Lazarists, could be found ministering to captive Christians and sometimes undertaking redemption missions, the Trinitarians' main competitors were the friars of the Order of the Blessed Virgin of Mercy.[50] Founded in Barcelona in the first decades of the thirteenth century, the Mercedarians emerged out of the same context of persistent interreligious conflict that produced the Trinitarians, and the order's central task, to "visit and deliver those Christians who are in captivity and in the power of Saracens or of other enemies of [Christian] law," closely mirrored that of the Order of the Most Holy Trinity and of the Captives.[51] Both orders depended heavily on donations and bequests to fund their redemptions, and from the mid-thirteenth century onward, the rivalry between the two over access to financial sources led to frequent litigation and much bad blood. Indeed, so entrenched was the culture of discord between the Trinitarians and the Mercedarians that the first formal constitutions of the Order of the Blessed Virgin of Mercy, promulgated in 1272, explicitly forbade the admission of any would-be friar who had been a Trinitarian and permanently excluded any Mercedarian who, having left to join the Trinitarians, wished to return.[52] Conflict between the two orders was particularly acute in the kingdom of Aragon, where the Mercedarians' roots were deepest and where they had a history of royal patronage, but similar legal battles raged for decades between Trinitarians and Mercedarians in France, in Castile, and in other parts of Iberia, so much so that in 1597, Pope Clement VIII forbade the founding of Mercedarian houses in Lisbon "in order to avoid the lawsuits over the redemption of captives that may arise between them and the friars of the Most Holy Trinity," a prohibition that was extended in 1636 to the whole of Portugal.[53]

While the redemption of captives constituted the order's main mission, not all Trinitarians were engaged in fund-raising, rescue, or ministry to the poor and sick. The Trinitarian community in Paris, established in 1229 at the church of Saint-Mathurin, was the order's most prestigious scholarly center, with close ties to the University of Paris. It hosted many of the university's most important gatherings, especially those of the faculty of theology.[54] In April 1521, for example, a meeting of the university's theology professors in the monastery of the Mathurins formally condemned the writings of Martin Luther—and in 1533, the church of Saint-Mathurin was the site of the rector Nicolas Cop's scandalous sermon in favor of the Protestant doctrine of justification by faith alone.[55] From 1291, the monastery of the Mathurins served as the university's storage and sales center for parchment, a critical commodity for the university community.[56] The Trinitarians' Parisian house was home to some of the order's leading scholars during the medieval centuries. Minister General Jean Halboud de Troyes (d. 1439), for example, dean of the faculty of theology of the University of Paris in 1432, figured among the theologians who condemned the future saint Joan of Arc, while Minister General Robert Gaguin (1433–1501), one of the leading lights of humanist scholarship in late medieval France, served as dean of the faculty of law and as a diplomat for King Charles VII (r. 1483–98).[57]

Reliable records from the first few centuries of the order's existence are few, but Trinitarian friars do appear in positions of prominence as chaplains or confessors to royal or noble patrons in France, especially during the thirteenth and fourteenth centuries. Minister General Nicholas (d. 1257), for example, accompanied King Louis IX on crusade to Egypt, where he was captured together with the monarch, while Minister General Thomas Loquet (d. 1357) was chaplain and almoner for Gaucher de Châtillon (d. 1329), constable of France, and Friar Henri Sachebren served Count Robert d'Artois of Beaumont-le-Roger (1287–1342) as chaplain.[58] The kings of Navarre also seem to have had an affinity for the Trinitarians. In 1239, for example, a Trinitarian friar named Simon served Theobald I (1201–1253), while thirty years later, Jean Boileau, minister general between 1272 and 1291, was chaplain first to Theobald II (1239–1270) and then to Henry I (ca. 1244–1274) of Navarre.[59] Even in England, where the order remained small and marginal, Trinitarians could also be found in positions of trust. The Trinitarian house at Knaresborough, in North Yorkshire, enjoyed the particular patronage of Richard of Cornwall (1209–1272), who chose two friars, Ralph and William de Wolvele, to represent his interests in Rome in 1246 and 1259, respectively.[60]

The order's fortunes took different trajectories in the different Iberian kingdoms. While the Trinitarians were not absent from Aragon or wholly ignored by its monarchs, royal patronage and privileges in that kingdom were directed primarily toward their rivals, the Mercedarians. In Castile, the order enjoyed greater royal favor. For example, as members of the order accompanied the troops of King Fernando III in his push down the Guadalquivir River against the small Islamic kingdoms and principalities of Al-Andalus, the monarch rewarded the friars for their service by founding Trinitarian houses in Úbeda (1234), Córdoba (1236), Jaén (1246), and Seville (1248). The order found royal favor in Portugal as well. Queen Isabel of Aragon (1271–1336) worked with her confessor, Friar Estevão Soeiro of Santarem, to sponsor the construction of the Lisbon monastery's church, for example. In the fifteenth century, we find Friar Miguel de Contreras serving as confessor to the Portuguese queen Leonor de Avis (1458–1525), while in Castile, his confrère Simón de Camargo (1415–1477) served as a royal chaplain to Juan II, Enrique IV, and Ferdinand and Isabella.

By the sixteenth century, reform movements within France and the Iberian Peninsula brought focus and renewal to the Trinitarians, both among the Reformed and Discalced branches and within the traditional Calced wing of the order. The reforming trend and the closer relations between the Trinitarians and the Spanish Crown seem to have raised the order's profile, and by the mid-seventeenth century, members of both branches regularly occupied important positions in service to the Church and the French and especially the Spanish monarchs.[61] Minister General Bernard Dominici (1517?–1597), for example, whose fiery oratory won him renown as a "hammer of heretics" during the French civil wars between Catholics and Protestants, served as personal adviser and preacher to Charles IX (r. 1560–74) and Henry III (r. 1574–89).[62] Similarly, the Calced friar and future saint Simón de Rojas (1552–1624) shaped royal hearts and minds in his capacity as friend and adviser to King Philip III; confessor to Isabel of Bourbon (1602–1644), consort to Philip IV; confessor to Ana Mauricia (1601–1666), queen of France and mother of Louis XIV; and preceptor and tutor to two of Philip III's children, Carlos (1607–1632) and the flamboyant "Cardinal-Prince" Fernando (1609–1641).[63] By contrast, his Discalced counterpart, Tomás de la Virgen (1587–1647), exercised an informal influence from his sickbed in the Madrid monastery through an extensive correspondence with the Duke of Lerma, the Count-Duke of Olivares, Isabel de Borbón, and leading members of the Spanish noble and ecclesiastical establishment.[64] Trinitarians at court could be found serving in other capacities, including as royal preachers. While few achieved the renown of the poet, royal preacher, and Calced friar Hortensio Félix Paravicino (1580–1634), whose close relationship with both the Duke of Lerma and Philip IV and his favorite Gaspar de Guzmán, Count-Duke of Olivares, won him a seat on numerous important government councils, others, like the Calced friars Juan de la Vega (ca. 1520–1579), Bernardo Suchet de Quiñones (ca. 1594–1647), Juan de Almoguera (1605–1676), and Manuel Guerra y Ribera (1638–1692), won recognition and honors at court for their eloquence in the pulpit.[65]

Other members of the order ascended to episcopal leadership. By the 1540s, several members of the order had been raised to the position of auxiliary bishop, while one, Diego de Gayangos (ca. 1460–1522), died shortly after being named bishop of Jaén.[66] Toward the end of the century, the Calced friar Jerónimo García (d. ca. 1590) was named to the see of Bosa, in Sardinia, while his confrère Diego Gómez de Lamadrid (1529–1601) served for many years as the bishop of Badajoz. Rafael Díaz de Cabrera (1565–1630) served as bishop of Mondoñedo and of Tui.[67] While the order did not expand into Spain's overseas colonies until the late nineteenth century, Trinitarian prelates could also be found in the Americas. The Calced friars Luis de Córdoba y Ronquillo (ca. 1590–1640), Fernando Ramírez (d. 1652), Fernando Núñez Sagredo (d. 1639), Juan Damián López de Haro (1581–1648), and Juan de Almoguera, for example, occupied the sees of Cartagena de Indias, Panama, León (Nicaragua), Puerto Rico, and Arequipa, respectively, while the Discalced Trinitarian Diego Morcillo Rubio de Auñon (1642–1730) served as both archbishop of Lima and viceroy of Peru.[68] Trinitarians were also well represented among the professoriate of Spain's universities and as theologians in the service of the Holy Office of the Inquisition.[69]

Forgotten Founders

The order's growing prominence was not matched, however, by its saints. By the late 1500s, the only members of the celestial court to whom the Trinitarians could lay claim was their founder, St. John of Matha, and his cofounder and companion, St. Felix of Valois. But even they were not unproblematic. As one of the thieves later acknowledged, until the removal of Matha's relics, they had lain alone in the half-ruined church of San Tommaso in Formis, beyond the control of the order that he had established.[70] More importantly, their status as the remains of an acknowledged saint had recently been imperiled. In an age in which successive popes sought to tighten up the standards and procedures for the creation of new saints and regulate the veneration of existing holy men and women, even long-established cults were subject to new scrutiny. The Council of Trent reaffirmed the veneration of the saints, and the creation in 1588 by Pope Sixtus V of the Congregation of Sacred Rites and Ceremonies, a department within the papal administration charged with the examination of candidates for formal sainthood, signaled the turn toward ever greater regulation, but it was the establishment of new rules by Pope Urban VIII that marked the beginning of the Trinitarians' difficulties. A decree promulgated on March 13, 1625, by the Congregation of the Holy Office of the Inquisition prohibited the faithful from rendering public veneration to holy people without previous papal authorization. The regulation directly affected nascent cults of men and women who, at the time of their death, had acquired a reputation for sanctity but who had not yet been formally approved for veneration. Would-be devotees could no longer engage in common acts of devotion, such as displaying pictures of deceased holy men and women with halos or nimbuses or burning candles at their tombs; instead, a papal brief in 1634 specified that proponents of candidates for sainthood would now have to prove to the authorities in Rome that their would-be saints had *not* received public veneration before their authorization.[71]

On the surface, it appeared that the new rules would not apply to a figure like John of Matha, since a paragraph within the decree specified that exceptions would be made for older cults grounded in the consensus of the Church or scriptural tradition, and the papal brief of 1634 further specified that in order to qualify for the exception, cults must be at least a century old, dating from 1525 or earlier. However, though the Trinitarians of the sixteenth and seventeenth centuries venerated their founder as a saint, there was no record of Matha's having ever received formal canonization. In Christianity's earliest centuries, saints were established by local acclamation through acts of veneration by individuals and communities. Saint-making gradually came under the control of bishops, who arrogated to themselves the power to recognize and authorize saints and their cults and to control access to miracle-working saintly remains. By the eleventh century, saint-making had also become an arena for papal power. As the influence of the papacy expanded, papal pronouncements came to vie with episcopal actions to recognize and confer the status of saint. In 1215, the Fourth Lateran Council decreed that no new relics could be venerated without papal approval, and in 1234, Gregory IX formally limited canonization of saints to the papacy.[72] Over the course of the following centuries, a slow but insistent push to centralize and to bureaucratize the process increased the papacy's control over saint-making, and after the Council of Trent, the standards for evidence of sainthood became increasingly rigorous. The decrees of 1625 and 1634 thus marked a culmination in expanding papal authority over the holy. In order to ensure the licitness of the cult rendered to Matha and the status and prestige of the order, the friars would now have to embark on the demanding bureaucratic process of formal recognition of his long-standing veneration—and thus, by extension, his sainthood.

Like the procedures for the formal beatification and canonization of the *beati moderni*—recently dead men and women with a reputation for holiness—the judicial process for obtaining papal recognition of an ancient or medieval saint's immemorial cult, and thus "equivalent" canonization, was complicated and demanding. While the exact course varied from case to case, in general, the local religious authority or ordinary—in this case, the minister general of the Trinitarians and the leaders of the independent Trinitarian provinces of Castile or Aragon—would order a two-pronged inquiry. On the one hand, the friars to whom they delegated the task would investigate the would-be saint's current reputation for sanctity and "heroic virtue" and the miracles attributed to them; on the other, they would look into the history and unbroken existence of the cult in order to establish that it qualified as a *casus exceptus*, a case that met the criteria for exemption from the new rules published in 1625 and 1634. For both investigations, witnesses would be examined on what they knew of the holy person's reputation and veneration and what they had heard about the cult from their elders. Investigators appointed by the ordinary would also examine all available documentation, including manuscript materials, printed histories, and inscriptions on stones, walls, and buildings, that testified to the antiquity of the cult and veneration of the candidate as a saint. They would also seek specialists to give evidence about the existence and age of other material vestiges of the cult, such as ex votos and other offerings left by the faithful, pictures and sculptures of the candidate, or tombs and altars erected in their memory.

When these investigations were complete, the case would be remitted to the jurisdiction of the Holy See and the Congregation of Sacred Rites. If the candidate's merits passed muster and the official commissioned by the congregation judged the proofs to be sufficient evidence of veneration since time out of mind (or at least since 1525), the case, once confirmed by the Congregation of Sacred Rites and the pope, would be qualified as a *casus exceptus*, and their cult would be recognized as licit and permitted where already established. Having reached this milestone, the candidate's cult could eventually be extended to the Church universal by adding them to the

Roman Martyrology, the Church's official calendar of saints and blesseds, and/or providing them with their own, individualized liturgical commemorations (a "proper" Mass and office). Unlike more recently dead candidates for sainthood, this expansion of veneration did not include a definitive papal statement on their sanctity; rather, it simply acknowledged and regularized their existing status as saints.[73]

By the 1730s, this complex process was codified as an "equivalent beatification" (the recognition of immemorial veneration) that eventually led to an "equivalent canonization" (the expansion of that cult to the whole of the Church). However, these terms do not seem to have been in use before this period, and their apparent clarity hides the fact that for the seventeenth century, the moment at which a holy person with an ancient cult might be considered merely beatified or fully canonized could vary a good deal depending on one's perspective. In theory, the difference between the two was one of permission versus obligation. Beatification allowed the veneration of a holy woman or man within a restricted geographic region or a particular community, often a religious order; canonization, by contrast, elevated that person's cult to the whole of the Catholic world and made it required for all. In practice, despite these well-known distinctions, contemporaries might interpret the confirmation of an immemorial cult as a canonization rather than a beatification. The friars of the Mercedarian Order, for example, hailed the 1628 confirmation of the immemorial cult of their founder, St. Pere Nolasc (Pedro Nolasco) (1189–1256), as a full canonization.[74] In the case of St. John of Matha and St. Felix of Valois, even among the saint-making specialists of the Congregation of Sacred Rites, the deliberations around an ancient saint's long-standing veneration were understood as tantamount to "allowing all of the effects of solemn canonization."[75]

The stakes for achieving fully canonized status were high. Within early modern European society, origins and ancestry shaped social rank and the rights and privileges that accompanied it. Genealogical thinking and the assumption that origins were key determinants of social and legal status, character, even religious orthodoxy or deviance applied as much to corporate entities like religious orders as they did to individuals, kinship groups, or ethnic groups. Religious communities like the Trinitarian Order regularly conceived of themselves as "families" that traced their origins from a founding mother or father figure whose nobility and saintly virtues continued to manifest themselves in his or her modern-day sons and daughters. By this logic, an uncanonized or otherwise questionable founder weakened the whole edifice and left the Trinitarians vulnerable to rivals who might call into question their rights and privileges—rivals like their main competitors, the friars of the Order of the Blessed Virgin of Mercy, who regularly contested the Trinitarians' right to solicit donations from the faithful. By comparison with their Mercedarian rivals, the friars of the Most Holy Trinity were late to the saint-making game. Like John of Matha, Pere Nolasc, the founder of the Mercedarians, lacked evidence of any formal canonization. The basic facts of his life were hazy—his hometown and the dates of his birth and death were fixed by tradition, rather than verifiable historical evidence—and because he had been buried in a common grave, there were no relics to venerate. But much like the Trinitarians, the Mercedarian friars had just weathered a painful split between those who preferred the traditional observance and an enthusiastic Discalced movement that sought to recover the order's lost past and deepen its religious vocation. For the reforming Mercedarians, the order's reorganization and spiritual reawakening were necessarily also an engagement with its earliest history, since "the spiritual apparatus of the Order, not to say the religious priorities of the age, demanded the individuality afforded by a canonized patriarch."[76] In 1622, the Discalced Mercedarians took up the project. With the assistance of some forged records that conveniently supplied the missing biographical details and of some well-placed financial inducements to Cardinal Antonio Barberini (1569–1646), Urban VIII's brother, by September 20, 1628, they had achieved the recognition and authorization of Nolasc's immemorial cult. On October 11 of the same year, Urban VIII permitted the Mercedarians to honor Nolasc with a common office and Mass.[77] The Mercedarians also succeeded in winning the beatification of Ramon Nonat (d. 1240), one of Nolasc's earliest followers, in November 1625.[78] The 1620s and 1630s saw an explosion of hagiographical writing about Nolasc, Nonat, and other Mercedarian saints, the cases for four of whom were also initiated in Rome between 1626 and 1630.[79]

The case of St. John of Matha contrasted uncomfortably with that of St. Pere Nolasc and was made considerably more difficult by the fact that until the 1500s, he does not seem to have been venerated with much enthusiasm or focus. During the first four centuries of the order's existence, Trinitarian accounts of the founder were sparse narratives that focused less on Matha's virtues or deeds than on the miraculous circumstances that surrounded the papal authorization of the Trinitarian rule and habit. One narrative strand, probably the earliest, had at its center Matha's vision of Christ and the captives. One example, a mid-thirteenth-century prose text from Normandy on the "origin and reason why this order, that is, of the Holy Trinity and of Captives was established, and by such a miracle and revelation was founded," described John of Matha (here called "Johannes Provincialis," or John of Provence) as an exceptionally devout and God-fearing professor of theology in Paris, who yearned to live a life in religion and was sometimes teased for his devotion. Seeking to placate his friends and "a reasonable cause to recite the hours and pray," he took holy orders and prayed that God would show him which religious order to join. On the day of his first Mass, as he prayed to God to reveal to him the order that he should choose, Matha experienced the vision of Christ and the two captives: "On raising his eyes to heaven, he saw the majesty of God, and [he saw that] God [was] holding in his hands two men with chains on their ankles, one of which appeared to be black and deformed, the other thin and pale." The attending worthies, who can be identified as Maurice de Sully (d. 1196), bishop of Paris; Robert, abbot of Saint-Victor; and the scholar Prevostin of Cremona (ca. 1135–1210), witnessed Matha's hesitation in completing the consecration of the Host, "and raising up their eyes, the bishop, the abbot, and Master Prevostino saw the same, and they glorified the Lord, and then they roused him and [on] recovering, [he continued] to celebrate [the Mass]." After this shared miracle, the three worked with Matha to create the rule and encouraged him to seek papal authorization for his mission. Matha went first to Cerfroid, where he recruited four hermits to the new order, and then on to Rome.[80] The authorities in Rome rejected Matha and his letters of support from Paris "and considered him and such a bishop to be stupid." The defeated Matha turned back toward Paris. Shortly thereafter, however, the pope experienced the same vision that had appeared to Matha. The pope, "grieved that he had not fulfilled [Matha's] petition," sent out emissaries to recall Matha to Rome, saying, "Let the Lord send him to me." The text noted that Innocent then fulfilled Matha's request and concluded abruptly, not with an account of the saint's death, burial, or posthumous miracles but with the comment that the Trinitarian Order was established in 1198.[81]

Evidence suggests that this text probably reflected the order's foundational story in its earliest form. A chronicle, roughly contemporaneous with the Trinitarian prose text, that recounted the establishment of the Franciscan order in England described Matha's story in terms very similar to the Trinitarian prose account: "But the brothers of the Order of the Trinity, which was divinely established during [the papacy of] Innocent III [by] the theologian Master John, [after] Jesus Christ appeared to him while he celebrated [Mass] in the presence of the bishop and clergy of Paris, came into England long before [the Franciscans]."[82] Likewise, the famous mosaic at San Tommaso in Formis depicted the vision of Christ in similar terms. Thanks to an inscription just below it, the image, a roundel inside a marble aedicule above an arched doorway that once led to the monastery's hospital, can confidently be attributed to Jacopo Cosmati and his son, Cosma, two members of a famous Roman clan of artists and architects renowned for their skill in decorative mosaic work. Their participation in the work, together with evidence from another, very similar Cosmati mosaic, suggests a likely date of 1210—just one year after Matha received San Tommaso in Formis from Innocent III and three years before the founder's death. While we cannot know for sure, it seems very possible that Matha himself had a hand in shaping the mosaic's imagery, which centers on an enthroned and haloed Christ Pantocrator, who looks directly out toward the viewer. In his right hand, he holds the right wrist of a white man, who holds in his left hand a staff capped with the Trinitarians' red and blue cross. The white captive's near nakedness and shackles mark him as a slave, but his rope or chain bonds seem to lead toward Christ's throne, perhaps in the act of unbinding. Christ holds in his left hand the left wrist of a Black man, who bears the same indicators of bondage but whose restraints show no sign of coming undone; instead, the Black captive holds the lead to his own shackles in his left hand. An inscription around the border makes clear the meaning of the image: "Sign of the Order of the Holy Trinity and of the Captives" (Signum Ordinis Sanctae Trinitatis et Captivorum). Matha himself appears nowhere in the mosaic, nor does he figure in the order's earliest official seals, which likewise featured the image of Christ with the two captives (fig. 1).[83]

By the second half of the thirteenth century, some Trinitarians had begun to embroider this bare-bones narrative with miracle stories. A white stag that was said to have appeared to Matha and his hermit companion featured on seals issued by the Trinitarian monasteries at Fontainebleau in 1276 and Cerfroid in 1303, and it is possible that a seal issued in 1253 by the minister general of the order included an image of a haloed Matha himself.[84] However, most of the surviving evidence suggests that the narratives surrounding the order's origins shifted to downplay or even obscure Matha's role, making the Holy Trinity the founder of the order through the agency of Pope Innocent III, rather than Matha. Already by 1263, the Trinitarian axiom that the order was established not by humans but by God himself was a key element of the Trinitarian imaginary, but the moment of foundation had shifted from Matha's original vision of Christ and the captives to a repetition of that vision experienced by Innocent III as he conducted Mass in the Lateran Palace in Rome, a repetition that came to substitute an angel for Christ.[85] This change, which highlighted the order's close ties to Innocent III

Fig. 1. Mosaic at San Tommaso in Formis. Photo: author.

and to papal authority more broadly and which closely resembled similar papal visions in the legends of Sts. Francis and Dominic, was reflected in a mid-thirteenth-century devotional poem copied in 1444 by Pierre Muguet, a Trinitarian friar at Châlons-sur-Marne.[86] The poem—which centered on the encounter in Rome between Matha, his as-yet-unnamed hermit companion, and the pope, here mistakenly called Honorius—left out entirely Matha's own revelation of the two captives and instead elaborated on a different moment of the order's divine authorization: the pope's vision and his establishment of the Trinitarian habit and rule. The text explained how the pontiff, having invoked the Holy Spirit to approve the Trinitarian habit and rule, "sees an angel dressed / in white and placed above / the sign of the cross in this form: / The angel has in his hands / two men, Christian / [and] Saracen are [their] names. / They signify that the pagan / and this Trinitarian Order / will make exchanges."[87] On finishing the Mass, the pope informed the two hermits that God had confirmed their order through the vision of the angel and bestowed on the two the rule and habit that they had sought. "Behold the approved order," sang the poet, "not made by saints / but by supreme

God alone." Similarly, the account recorded in the 1490s by Robert Gaguin, a celebrated humanist and minister general of the Trinitarian Order from 1473 until his death in 1501, eliminated Matha's vision entirely and instead offered a detailed retelling of the appearance of the angel to Innocent III and the pope's authorization of the Trinitarian habit and rule to Matha and his collaborator. Gaguin, who appears to have drawn on much-older accounts of lives of the founders, filled out Matha's bare-bones biography a bit and listed new hagiographic details surrounding Innocent's vision—its location in the Lateran Palace, the names of the attending cardinals. He also recorded Matha's death and burial in the church of San Tommaso in Formis in 1213 and threw in a few tidbits describing Matha's virtue—his asceticism, devotion to prayer, and dedication to preaching—but like the previous accounts, he omitted the hagiographical commonplaces like posthumous miracles or wonder-working relics that were typical of a thriving cult.[88]

Somewhat different versions of the founding of the order appeared in two poems, one in English, one in Latin, probably composed in the fifteenth century by a friar or friars attached to the Trinitarians' house at Knaresborough. While the two poems differed in their details, both from each other and from the versions described by Gaguin and by Pierre Muguet, they both located the moment of foundation in Innocent III's revelation. Neither poem named John or Felix. In the Latin text, the poet described how the two anonymous hermits, who had been living a holy life in the "desert" of Cerfroid (which is also left nameless), went to the pope in search of a rule. "At the moment when the pope / celebrated the Mass before the people / by revelation of the King of Heaven / appeared a white garment. / Marked with a cross / which, according to the testimony of a writer / to the humble and virtuous [hermits] / the pious pope gave." Having received papal approval of the rule and the habit, the two hermits then established ("innovabant") the order. The origin of the order, noted the poet, was under the patronage of the Trinity. The English poem contained a more conventional account of the founding of the order. The poet, who noted the diversity of opinions about the Trinitarians' origins and the lack of written accounts, sang of "twa heremites," who, inspired by God, wrote a "boke" or "byll"—that is, the proposed rule—and presented it to the pope, here unnamed. The pontiff prayed on the matter and consulted his advisers, and as he sang Mass, "Appered ane aungell bright of ble / And kest a clething att hys kne / And badde hym take that clething tyte / Þairin to cleth hym men perfyte. / The pape doune falland wyth hys handes / Loued our Lord þat hys seruaundes / Sway saues and comforthes ay / And grauntes all þaim þat þai for pray. / He toke this clethinge cleyn and whyte / And þarein cledde þase heremytes tyte / Badde þaime in crese and multyply / Here to lyffe a halely." The two hermits then journeyed "over streme and strand" to succor and redeem captives in the Holy Land. "Þan þus began the order fre / That ys off the Haly Trinite."[89]

Thus, there is little evidence that by the beginning of the 1500s, the Trinitarian Order venerated its founding fathers. Notably, none of the surviving medieval accounts of the order's origins title Matha or Valois as "saint," and most leave the two founders anonymous and/or subordinate their role to that of Innocent III and the Trinity itself. Sixteenth-century narratives of the order's origins and of its founders differed little from their medieval predecessors. Most published accounts of the origins of the Trinitarian order seem to have been based on Gaguin's version, which apparently circulated widely in manuscript. For example, the short historical account included in the order's first printed breviary, published in Paris in 1514, focused primarily on the miracle of Innocent III's vision and the authorization of the order and the rule.[90] A complete version of Gaguin's account was published a few years later, in a Trinitarian breviary printed in Valencia in 1519, and again with other historical notes on the order gathered by the Catalan friar Miguel Borrell in *Reformatorium Fratrum O.SS. ac individuae Trinitatis, Redemptionis captivorum, Aragoniae Provinciae* (Barcelona, 1563).[91] A related narrative tradition preserved Matha's mystical experience but subordinated it to that of the pope. Published in 1586 in Douai by Friar Jacques Bourgeois (b. 1525) as a preface to an edition of the order's rule, the account reduced Matha's vision of the angel to a single sentence but dealt in detail with the appearance of the angel to Innocent III and the pope's subsequent authorization of the Trinitarian habit and rule.[92] For the most part, however, Gaguin's account, either in full or in summary, seems to have become the standard version, repeatedly reprinted in publications intended primarily for internal use within the order, such as manuals, constitutions, and lists of indulgences.[93] These books affirmed the central role of Innocent III and ascribed the order's origins to God himself (or, more rarely, directly to the pope, "founder of this religion").[94] For example, a woodcut on the back of the title page of *Regula et constitutiones fratrum ordinis Sanctissimae Trinitatis Redemptionis Captiuorum* (Seville, 1573) displayed an image of Father, Son, and the dove of the Holy Spirit surrounded by the Trinitarian motto, "Here is the approved order, made not by saints but by supreme God alone"; an epigram at the beginning of a similar text published in 1591 in Lisbon praised "God, Triune and One, the author of this noble order."[95]

Matha was similarly absent from Trinitarian liturgy.[96] The original rule of 1198 required the friars to follow (with some minor changes) the liturgical practices of the Augustinian canons of Paris's Abbey of Saint-Victor, and while the liturgical calendar adopted in 1247 gave double honors to St. Augustine, it made no mention whatsoever of either Matha or his hermit companion.[97] The tendency to leave Matha on the liturgical margins persisted well into the sixteenth century. An illuminated manuscript missal donated to the Trinitarians' house in Paris by Minister General Nicolas Musnier (d. 1545), for example, included no mention whatsoever of the founders; instead, it stressed the order's long-standing affiliation with papal power with an image of God the Father dressed in papal regalia.[98] Neither did they appear in a 1545 Trinitarian breviary from Seville, nor were they listed among the saints to whom Trinitarians must render honors in Borrell's *Reformatorium*. Similarly, a manual to the Trinitarian liturgy published in Seville in 1593 omitted any commemoration of Matha but instead noted, "the second feast of St. Agnes, which falls on January 28, is celebrated in our order with the solemnity of a patron, because our sacred religion was founded on that day."[99] The date is significant—the feast of St. Agnes, according to Gaguin, was the day on which Innocent III experienced his miraculous vision.[100]

If the Trinitarians' tradition of a divine foundation and their emphasis on the intervention of Innocent III left John of Matha at the margins of the order's hagiographic tradition, so too did the order's traditional deep veneration for the Holy Trinity. The Trinitarians' monastic rule required all of its churches to be dedicated to the Trinity (although in practice, the friars regularly bowed to patron preferences and accepted grants of already-named churches). It was not until the 1670s and the establishment of a new monastery in Matha's hometown of Faucon-de-Barcelonnette that the Trinitarians dedicated their first church to their founder.[101] Medieval commentators highlighted the order's characteristic devotion to the Triune God. The Dominican writer Humbert of Romans (d. 1277), for example, noted that "with reason are they called the Brothers of the Trinity," since "they must be specially devoted to the Trinity and therefore imitate it."[102] That imitation was often indirect, through the tripartite division of each monastery's assets, for example, or through the friars' habits—white tunics emblazoned with a red and blue cross. The mid-thirteenth-century poem copied by Friar Muget, for example, unpacked the symbolism of the habit as emblematic of Christ's sacrifice and of Christian virtues: "The white color of your garment / signifies that you are chaste / and pure as whiteness; / The cross is, so that you may know, / witness of the passion of Christ: / red and blue signify [this]."[103] Others interpreted the Trinitarians' attire as symbolic of the Trinity itself. According to the breviary printed in 1519 in Valencia, "For three colors are on the habit of the friars themselves: white, blue, and red. White represents the Father, whose beginning is without beginning, and white is the highest color, mixed with no other color. The color blue, which conveys a kind of tarnishing and degrading, signifies Christ, whose body was broken and bruised in the torture and pain of his passion. Red, wherein is signified ardor, expresses the Holy Spirit, which is fire and inspires flames in the hearts of the true believer."[104] Similarly, the Trinitarians' emphasis on the Trinity colored the interpretation of the mosaic at San Tommaso in Formis included in *Institutio, regula, priuilegia, constitutiones, c[a]erimoniale, & formularium Ordinis Sanctissimae Trinitatis redemptionis Captiuorum*, published in Zaragoza in 1584. This text described the mosaic, "where appears now not the Angel, but the image of the Trinity itself, holding two captives, and the cross of the Order appears, and letters of gold saying 'Sign of the Order of the Holy Trinity and of Captives.'" In Innocent's vision of the angel, he recognized the sacred enigma of the Holy Trinity, which mystery the mosaic more clearly conveyed.[105]

Even in the little church of San Tommaso in Formis, where John of Matha had lived and died, the Trinitarians' strong identification with their order's miraculous origins and thus with its particular mission, the redemption of Christian captives, left their founder at the margins. While the building was thoroughly remodeled in 1663, leaving no remains of its medieval form, sixteenth-century descriptions of the church mentioned no images of the saintly founder but instead included depictions of the Trinitarians' journeys to Muslim lands.[106] Testimony taken in 1526 in connection with the order's endless lawsuit with the Vatican chapter, for example, noted that "on the front of the aforementioned church or hospital there were and at present are and are found certain ships with friars marked with the cross depicted as if navigating in the exercise of redemptions, according to their [founding] rule, and in a like manner [appears] the figure of a camel and men carrying sacks of money to denote the said redemption, which [figures], while they appear to be ancient, however are still extant and manifest, and they are the particular insignia of the Order of the Most Holy Trinity and Redemption of Captives."[107] There seems to have been a similar decorative scheme inside the church. The 1625 edition of Ottavio Panciroli's *I tesori nascosti nell'alma Città di Roma* observed that "in the chapel where is [the body of] Blessed John, the founder of this order, is depicted a great ship, on which are some of [the order's] brothers, who are going to Algiers to rescue Christians, and on the land are many mules loaded with money and other things for the same purpose."[108] These accounts omitted any mention of any images or statues of Matha or Valois.

These traditions left John of Matha in relative obscurity, so much so that for writers outside the Trinitarian Order, Matha could be invisible or even absent. For Jerónimo Román y Zamora (1536–1597), an Augustinian chronicler writing in 1575, Matha was "Juan Marense," a French gentleman.[109] Similarly, in 1581, the historian Paolo Morigia (1525–1604) (a member of the Congregazione dei Gesuati) tried in vain to discover the Trinitarians' origins: "So, this congregation had its beginnings in a brother John, but of what nation he may have been I do not know since I could not find it out, because at the time I was our order's solicitor general in Rome, [the Trinitarians] did not have monasteries in Italy."[110]

There are clues, however, that both in France and in Iberia, devotion to St. John of Matha among the Trinitarians was on the rise in the sixteenth century. Statues of Matha and Valois installed in the early sixteenth century in the main altar retable of the Trinitarian monastery in Burgos, for example, suggest veneration toward the order's founders, as does their inclusion in the frescos that were painted on the ceiling of the Trinitarian church in Cuéllar (Segovia) in the 1590s. Similarly, the existence of a devotional poem composed in 1544 by a youthful Jacques Bourgeois (who later authored one of the order's key historical accounts) may reflect both personal devotion to the saint and his companion and hagiographic traditions not preserved in the order's sparse written accounts of their lives and deeds.[111] Other hints can be found in the many publications sponsored by the order. For example, while the aforementioned 1514 Parisian breviary centered the role of Innocent III over that of Matha and Valois, it designated the two founders as "saints" (*sancti*), a title that became increasingly common in Trinitarian texts over the course of the century. The 1572 address delivered before Pope Gregory XIII by Friar François Bouchet, a Parisian theologian and vicar general of the order, described Matha as "that father St. John of Matha, theologian [and] doctor," while the aforementioned manual on the order's rule and constitutions called him both "saint" and "founder."[112] Publications meant primarily for the order's lay supporters also referred to "St. John of Matha." One example, the Pamplona 1611 edition of *La institución o fundación de indulgencias del Orden de la Santíssima Trinidad de la Redempción de Captivos*, a frequently reprinted guide to the indulgences offered to the faithful by the order, invoked "the new soldiers of Jesus Christ, St. John and St. Felix"; another, similarly titled text published in Douai that same year described Matha as "that holy doctor John."[113]

Other evidence for Matha's growing importance can be found in the Trinitarians' persistent efforts to regain possession of San Tommaso in Formis.

By the late fourteenth century, the order had lost control of the church and its associated buildings and properties to the Vatican chapter, and throughout the fifteenth century, the church remained shuttered, opened only on December 21, the feast day of its titular saint, the Apostle Thomas. While we have no mentions of Trinitarian visitors at the grave of their founder during the fourteenth and fifteenth centuries, the angry reaction of would-be Trinitarian pilgrims to the tomb in 1532 to the Vatican chapter's major structural renovations to the complex suggests that by the early sixteenth century, devotion to Matha was on the rise.[114] By the early 1570s, Minister General Bernard Dominici was pushing hard to recover the property. We can glean his arguments from the bull that briefly granted San Tommaso in Formis to the Trinitarians in October 1571: not only were friars greatly inconvenienced and their proper observance of the Trinitarian rule imperiled by the lack of a permanent home in Rome, but the church that housed the tomb of their "first major and general minister" was "not merely occupied, but profaned by lay people and secular clergy."[115] While the Trinitarians enjoyed possession of San Tommaso in Formis only briefly—by December 1572, the Vatican chapter again controlled the complex—the concerns documented by the bull and the fact that the order immediately launched into a lengthy lawsuit to recover the property suggests that the Trinitarians were motivated both by possessiveness and by a nascent veneration for their founder.[116]

While Matha did not figure in the Trinitarians' medieval liturgical tradition, there are hints of changes afoot there, too. According to Juan Bautista de la Concepción, the founder of the Trinitarians' Discalced wing, a group of Portuguese friars asked Pope Sixtus V (r. 1585–90) for permission to offer liturgical honors to St. John of Matha and St. Felix of Valois. The pontiff responded by telling the friars to bring him evidence of the founders' longlasting cult: "'Fathers, bring me information about how, since forty years ago up to now, these saints are on the altars in paintings, and with haloes, before whom the people pray'—giving them to understand that for this [proof of cult] he would give [the Portuguese friars] what they asked." It was unclear, lamented the reformer, whether the Portuguese Trinitarians ever followed up on the pope's request, with the result that "[the founders] would be on the altars for a thousand centuries, venerated and held [as saints], if it is not that, because [the Trinitarians'] devotion ended, their veneration ended."[117]

John of Matha and Felix of Valois loomed particularly large for Juan Bautista de la Concepción and his followers, who sought in them and in the order's primitive rule the models of religious life that guided Juan Bautista de la Concepción's reforming Discalced movement.[118] The two were the order's "foundations" and "first fathers," in whose footsteps the Trinitarians should walk and whose "spirit"—that is, their charism, discipline, poverty, and charity—was the same as that followed by the members of the fledgling Discalced movement: "If in the beginning of our holy Religion the spirit that was communicated to it came from Heaven, and from there came down the fire that seared our first fathers [i.e., John of Matha and Felix of Valois] and burned them with a charity so great that it caused them to act in such immense works of charity, why should we wish now a different spirit?" Instead, argued the reformer, what was needed was a return to the order's origins and thus the elevation and imitation of its founders, to whom honor and veneration were overdue. He exhorted the Discalced friars to arm themselves against vice and praised those who were gifted by God with so great "an ardor, a devotion, a desire, a craving" for their saintly founders that they would go thousands of miles to seek out their holy relics, if only they could.[119] For Juan Bautista de la Concepción, the Calced branch's inattention to the founders and to other saintly members of the Trinitarian family was an embarrassment. In his account of the establishment of the Discalced wing, the reformer recounted an awkward conversation that took place in Rome in 1598 or 1599. When he and another Discalced friar discussed the antiquity of the various religious orders with two Spanish noblewomen, his companion correctly asserted that the Trinitarians' foundation predated both the Franciscans and the Dominicans. "The other good lady must have been more devoted to St. Francis than to the Trinity. She responded, 'Well, if they are so ancient, what saints do they have?' I found myself suddenly [tongue-]tied. 'That is what we are after, madam,'" replied the reformer.[120] Reflecting later on the discussion, Juan Bautista de la Concepción came to find a deeper meaning in his response: "But these words that I suddenly said—'that is what we are after'—I have often remembered in order to fulfill them: that in this reform, one takes up the job of seeking the saints of this Religion that have been lost, and in the meanwhile [until] they appear, search to be true saints ourselves."[121]

By the sixteenth century, devotion to Matha's semilegendary cofounder, St. Felix of Valois, was also expanding. As we have seen, Matha's companion and collaborator was either absent or unnamed in the order's earliest histories. By the mid-fourteenth century, however, Felix seems to have been incorporated into the Trinitarians' iconography, since according to witness testimony collected in 1630, he appeared alongside Matha in a series of painted panels commissioned by Minister General Thomas Loquet (d. 1357) for the altar of the mother house at Cerfroid, as well as in images held by Trinitarian monasteries in Murcia and Salamanca, each dating to the foundation of the house (1272 and 1330, respectively).¹²² By the 1490s, the nameless figure had become "Felix of Valois, a hermit."¹²³ Other texts suggest that Felix was slowly acquiring a legend of his own. The Celestine friar Benoit Gonon's 1625 *Vitae et sententiae patrum occidentis*, for example, drew on the thirteenth-century accounts and Gaguin, together with other "antiquis monumentis" held at the order's monastery in Avignon, to create a more rounded image of the pious and humble hermit. In Gonon's account, Felix figured as a dear friend and helpmeet to his more prominent companion, from whom he tearfully parted when John returned to Rome and Felix remained to oversee the monastery at Cerfroid. There, Felix "governed by word and example his brothers and subjects, and spurred them to discipline and to the love of God, such that day by day the number of brothers increased."¹²⁴ His death was that of an exemplary monastic leader: feeling his end draw nigh, he called all the friars to him; exhorted them to observance of the divine commandments, of monastic discipline, and of perseverance; blessed them; "and, fortified by the most holy sacraments of the Church, quietly gave up his glorious soul to the Savior."¹²⁵ Over the course of the seventeenth and eighteenth centuries, other writers expanded on these hagiographic details and endowed the once shadowy hermit with a full *vita* that stressed his sanctity of life, his eremitical virtues, and, increasingly, his alleged links to the French royal house.¹²⁶

First Efforts in the Campaign for Canonization

Thus, by the late 1620s, when the leaders of the Trinitarian Order took up the task of winning recognition of St. John of Matha's immemorial cult, they were responding both to the increasingly urgent social and political imperative to ensure that their founder be a fully authorized saint and to the rising importance of Matha as a focus of devotion for Trinitarians of all stripes. That he had not yet received formal papal acknowledgment of his holiness did not make him less of a saint for his spiritual daughters and sons, who by the first decades of the seventeenth century seem to have assumed that he was and always had been a saint. Sainthood and canonization were not necessarily one and the same. Even after saint-making had become first an episcopal prerogative, then a papal one, there were still saints whose status as such rested primarily on the acclamation of their communities, rather than the judgment of any central authority. But it was precisely these cults that the decrees of 1625 and 1634 were meant to bring under papal control, and in order to comply with the new requirements, Trinitarian authorities would have to contend with the awkward facts that, in truth, little was known about Matha and that neither he nor his hermit companion had been the focus of much sustained, enthusiastic devotion during the preceding centuries. Any campaign to regularize his cult would have to find a way past these considerable obstacles, ideally by gathering witness testimony that would prove his long-established cult and by providing a saintly *vita* that would furnish the evidence of holy life and posthumous miracles that were expected of an established saint and that would help foster increased devotion to the saint among the order's members and among its lay friends and patrons. The perennial divisions by nation and branch within the order made any unified effort impossible, however. The project seems to have been a largely Spanish, especially Castilian, undertaking—I have found few indicators of direct involvement by the order's French central leadership—and in the pursuit of this goal, the Calced and Discalced wings followed separate strategies in Rome and in the court of public opinion.

In 1630, the Discalced Trinitarians made their first attempt to meet the challenge of Matha's life and cult by publishing a new hagiographic life of the saint and his companion, Gil González Dávila's *Compendio histórico de las vidas de los gloriosos san Iuan de Mata i S. Félix de Valois*.[127] Though the author was a Dominican friar, the text was clearly written at the behest of the Discalced Trinitarians, who sought to advance themselves and the cause of their founders in Rome.[128] Dedicated to Cardinal Francesco Barberini (1597–1679), nephew of Pope Urban VIII and one of the most influential power brokers in Rome, fully half the volume was devoted to the history of the Discalced branch.

González Dávila's *vita* elaborated on the elements established by Gaguin and others, filling out the narrative and adding new episodes to Matha's life, such as his eremitical experiments in southern France and his preaching in Paris. He also larded the tale with the evidence of sanctity that was common to most saints' lives, such as a vision of the Virgin that appeared to his pregnant mother, his exemplary death, the deathbed discovery of the metal chains and cilice that testified to his rigorous physical discipline, his veneration and burial by Innocent III, and posthumous miracles, including a healing oil that had flowed from the saint's tomb and miraculous recoveries by a paralyzed woman and four blind people. While the traditional, established sources for Trinitarian history (Gaguin, Bourgeois, and Borrell) figured prominently among González Dávila's source materials, he gave no citations for these new details—an omission that may suggest that he drew on hagiographic traditions about John of Matha then circulating in Trinitarian oral culture, perhaps especially among friars of the order's Discalced wing.[129] It is very likely that he also drew on material provided to him by the Calced Trinitarian chronicler and forger Friar Juan Figueras Carpi, whom we will meet again in chapter 3.[130]

While the Discalced Trinitarians put their efforts behind González Dávila's new book, the Calced Trinitarians took a different tack. In that same year, 1630, the Calced Trinitarians of Castile and Aragon took up the question of Matha's ancient cult as part of a larger petition to the Congregation of Sacred Rites for the permission to use throughout the whole order a liturgical commemoration of Sts. John of Matha and Felix of Valois, said to have been conceded by Pope John XXII (r. 1316–34) to Trinitarian houses in England, Scotland, and Ireland.[131] The designated representative for the case, Friar Jerónimo Vélez Matute, presented ten expert witnesses to be interrogated in Rome in the court of Cardinal Vicar Marzio Ginetti on the question of the antiquity of the veneration of the two.[132] Only three of the group of witnesses were Trinitarians; the others were ecclesiastical figures well connected in Rome, France, and Spain, such as Gonzalo Fuentes de Albornoz, a professor in the Jesuit college at the University of Alcalá de Henares, and Luke Wadding (1588–1657), an Irish Franciscan well known for his erudite historical scholarship. Together, the ten witnesses provided rather general and unspecific attestations of the antiquity of the cult and of the sanctity of John of Matha and Felix of Valois. The witnesses affirmed a general account of the history of the order, its text drawn from the biography of the saints included in Benoit Gonon's *Vitae et sententiae patrum occidentis* (1625), and confirmed the antiquity and authenticity of various memorials to Innocent III's vision and the divine founding of the Trinitarian order, including the mosaic at San Tommaso in Formis and other representations at the mother house at Cerfroid, the inscription on Matha's tomb, and the liturgical commemoration of St. Agnes's feast day. They further corroborated the saints' long-standing reputation as founders of the order and of its mission to Christian captives and listed historians (mostly modern) who testified to these well-known facts. Most witnesses supplemented these general affirmations with more personal testimony about the tangible indicators of veneration of Matha and Valois, including ancient and modern haloed images, altars dedicated to them, and Masses said in their honor at Trinitarian monasteries throughout France, Spain, Portugal, and Italy. None, however, described the images in any detail or whether they depicted any hagiographical events or characteristics (other than the apparition of the by-now-canonical angel), and none mentioned any particular miracles worked through the two saints—though all affirmed that they had heard from their elders of the saints' miraculous intercessions.

The witnesses were also questioned as to what they knew of the "English breviary," a volume containing liturgical honors devoted to John of Matha and Felix of Valois that was supposedly granted by the pope to English, Irish, and Scottish Trinitarians in the early fourteenth century. It seems probable that the Calced Trinitarians of Castile built their case for the founders' immemorial cult around this mysterious document, which we will examine in greater detail in chapter 3, as a way of simplifying the process of winning papal recognition, since the extension of the province-specific liturgy to the whole of the order would be very likely to help clear the way to papal recognition of their immemorial cult.[133] It may also be that they reasoned that this petition would lay the groundwork for a separate, more comprehensive campaign for their founding fathers' immemorial veneration and, by extension, their sanctity. The witnesses' testimony about the English breviary was fairly generic; all simply confirmed that it was common knowledge that the liturgical commemoration of the two founders had been conceded to the provinces of the British Isles by John XXII and that the text of the office and its versicles was to be found in a manuscript volume from 1340 currently located in London. The breviary and its text (which neither the witnesses nor the questioners described in any detail) appear here as simply one of many arguments for the antiquity of the Trinitarians' veneration of their founders.

The Calced Trinitarians submitted the declarations of the ten witnesses in Rome, together with others gathered from Trinitarians in Toledo, Cuellar, Segovia, Arévalo, Logroño, and Naples, to the Congregation of Sacred Rites for consideration.[134] Unfortunately, the assembled cardinals seem to have found the evidence for the English breviary and, by extension, for Matha's immemorial cult to be insufficient. On June 6, 1631, they turned down the request for extension of the Anglican office to the whole of the Trinitarian Order on the grounds that according to a November 20, 1628, decree, it was not enough to prove that an uncanonized saint had a Mass or office of their own, but one must also demonstrate that that veneration, Mass, and office had been in use since time immemorial. Since there was no evidence that the English office had been in uninterrupted use and John XXII's decree could not be found, the Trinitarians' efforts were fruitless at this time—or so goes a Calced Trinitarian's official account of the events.[135] However, a report from Francisco Antonio Diez de Cabrera, the Spanish Inquisition's agent in Rome, suggests that other issues were at play. In a letter dated August 18, 1655, Diez de Cabrera informed Inquisitor General Diego de Arce y Reinoso

(1585–1665) about the theft of Matha's body and noted aspects of the crime that might properly fall under the jurisdiction of the Spanish Holy Office:

> What may pertain to us, and which, as I have said, I was warned about by a serious and learned person, is that these fathers removed these bodies from here in a box with the title "Corpora sanctorum Joannis de Matha et sociorum" [bodies of the saints John of Matha and associates]. This being [the case], [the] first [aspect of interest to the Spanish Inquisition is] that in the tomb where they were there is no more memorial than "hic iacet frater Joannes de Matha" [here lies the body of brother John of Matha]. The second, that neither does this brother John of Matha have the title of saint, nor any sign of cult, because he was in a tomb placed in the wall without an altar, lamp, nor any other sign of cult. The third, that having tried a few years ago [i.e., 1630] to prove that this friar John of Matha and friar Felix of Valois, who were the first founders of this order, had immemorial cult, the Congregation of [Sacred] Rites ordered that [the commissioners] look again at [the place] in Rome were the body was, and that the commissioners, having gone to do the examination, and finding the body without any cult, expelled the friar who was soliciting [the case], who is a certain master [Jerónimo] Vélez, who frequents this court, telling him that he had come to fool the pope, that how could images [of Matha and Valois] have legitimate cult if the body that was in Rome did not? [and] that this was not a land of infidels, that if friar John of Matha had been a saint, since he had lived and died here, there would have been some sign or memorial of his being held as such. In sum, they did not want to listen any more to this friar, and despite this having happened, this person tells me that in the province of Andalusia, these religious, both Calced and Discalced, have introduced prayers to him and publicly celebrate the feast of this John of Matha on their own authority, and it is probably the same in that province [of Castile?]. This person fears that with the bodies they have stolen from here they may make noise, putting them on an altar exposed to the cult and veneration of the people. He has asked me that I inform you, as I am now, so that you may order what may be needed.[136]

Perhaps the loss of San Tommaso in Formis and the constant litigation between the order and the Vatican chapter over its possession made access to the tomb difficult and irregular, but together with the scant veneration documented in the Trinitarians' own hagiographical and liturgical literature, the scene reported by Diez de Cabrera and the commissioners' outraged scolding of Friar Vélez strongly suggests that the Trinitarian leadership's zeal to regularize the status of their founder outpaced his popularity among the members of the order and that things were not exactly as they had been presented to the Congregation of Sacred Rites. Vélez's own correspondence with his superior, Friar Hortensio Paravicino, provincial of Castile, indicates the Trinitarians' difficulties were grounded in a kind of culture clash. In a letter dated October 5, 1630, Vélez lamented that despite his efforts, the case was going very badly: "I have made many efforts and it has cost me much sweat and exhaustion, if I can recover [from] so much dishonor that we have [from] not having our founders given [canonization] as saints." The ringleaders of the opposition within the Congregation of Sacred Rites—Cardinals Giovanni Battista Pamphili (1574–1655; the future Pope Innocent X) and Agustín Spínola (1597–1649), who "por ser nacional," that is, because he was Spanish, Vélez had hoped would favor the Trinitarians' goals—claimed that the order had left the body of its founder wholly without veneration. The fundamental issue, he noted, was a difference in attitude: "There [in Spain] they understand [canonization] as a thing of little importance, and here [in Rome] they [consider it] so [important] that these cardinals would be astonished and they say a thousand things that are not fit to be heard."[137] The case was not helped by Vélez's constant lack of sufficient funds to offer the customary financial incentives or to seek royal backing.[138] The Calced Trinitarians seem to have tried again to win the extension of the English office in 1646, this time with letters of support from the Spanish monarch Philip IV, but to no effect.[139]

Whether the inquisitor general ordered any follow-up to the unauthorized cult to Matha in southern Spain alleged in Diez de Cabrera's 1655 letter remains uncertain, but it would not be surprising if he had—it would not be the first time that Spanish Trinitarians had been investigated by the Holy Office for their veneration of their founder. Four years earlier, in 1651, an anonymous informer alleged that the liturgical honors rendered to Matha and Valois by the friars of the Calced monastery of Madrid had violated Urban VIII's decrees prohibiting veneration of uncanonized saints. The provincial, Cristóbal de Astiaso Zapata, countered the charges by presenting evidence of the antiquity of the founders' cult—evidence that included, among other documents, the same testimony gathered from the ten witnesses in Rome in 1630. In the light of these proofs of immemorial cult, the Inquisition dropped the case, and all Trinitarian monasteries continued to render solemn public cult to Matha, even, in Madrid, with the attendance of the Suprema, the Spanish Inquisition's highest body.[140]

The 1655 theft of St. John of Matha's bones thus threw fuel on the fire of an already heated controversy surrounding the veneration of the saint. According to Medina and Vidal's own testimony, their crime was meant to ensure that the Trinitarians' founder received proper honors and to thumb their noses at their Discalced rivals, who were said to have tried to steal the body for themselves.[141] It may also have been a preemptive act to secure the body for Spain against any French claims in advance of a special international general chapter meeting that was to be held in Rome the following year.[142] As we will see, however, the two friars' most likely motive for the theft was the campaign for Matha's immemorial cult; that is, the daring break-in and relic robbery is best understood as a strategic act intended to rescue Matha's remains from an embarrassing oblivion in San Tommaso in Formis and to remove them to Spain, where they could help foster the saint's growing cult among the members of the order and, eventually, among the laity. But instead of securing Matha's veneration, Medina and Vidal had unwittingly opened a Pandora's box of problems. In order for the relics to be given public veneration, the order would now have to prove that the bones now located in Spain were the same as those that had lain for centuries in the tomb in the little church in Rome. The Trinitarians' quest for Matha's canonization through papal recognition of his immemorial cult quickly became intertwined with a second, equally difficult legal process of establishing the identity of his remains.

3

FORGERY AND SAINTHOOD
IN THE SEVENTEENTH CENTURY

Having successfully evaded capture in Rome, Friar Pedro Arias Portocarrero and the two thieves set sail from Spanish-controlled Naples with the stolen bones of St. John of Matha carefully wrapped in white taffeta and padded with cotton and stored in a beechwood box lined with turquoise and gold brocade.[1] Once safely arrived on Spanish soil, Arias made his way to Madrid, where he settled into his cell in the city's Calced Trinitarian monastery. The monastery was one of the city's more prominent religious houses. Established in 1562, shortly after Madrid had been raised to the status of capital by King Philip II, it boasted a spacious, modern church and cloister located in the very heart of the city on the Calle de Atocha, one of Madrid's most important thoroughfares.[2] There, Arias faced the dilemma of what to do with Matha's holy remains. Yes, he had escaped the Roman *sbirri* and certainly he was safer in Spain, but relic theft was a grave crime. Nor was he wholly beyond of the reach of papal justice, since the nuncio had been tasked with the arrest of the three fugitives and, indeed, had opened a case against them.[3] Perhaps planning his next moves, Arias waited for some three weeks before taking action.[4]

But the Spanish wing of the Trinitarian Order enjoyed strong ties to Spain's political and cultural elite, and eventually Arias brought the question to Francisco de Arcos (d. 1674), minister provincial for the Calced Trinitarians of Castile. Arcos, who was both a respected scholar and a royal preacher with excellent connections in the court of King Philip IV, presented the case directly to the monarch, who offered to write to Rome on the order's behalf and commanded that the relics be entrusted to the nuncio for safekeeping.[5] On November 24, 1655, Arcos, Arias, and Jerónimo Vélez Matute, the order's *visitador*, gathered, presumably in the palace of the nuncio, not far from Madrid's main square, the Plaza Mayor. There, they handed over the bones of St. John of Matha to Carlo Camillo Massimo, the papal envoy in Spain.[6] In the presence of a notary, Nuncio Massimo opened the box and found inside "a large skull with the remainder of the [other] bones of the body, [which were] extraordinarily white." Just above the skull, he noted, were a prayer and an antiphon, or sung response, in honor of the saint.[7] After taking depositions from Arias and the others who testified to the identity of the bones, Massimo's secretary pressed the nuncio's personal seal on red wax in four places on the cords that bound the box.[8] Sealed and secured, the coffer was then placed inside a second box with a green taffeta lining. Officials filed a notarized record of the handover in the nunciature's archive and preserved the relics until they could be consigned in late 1656 to Cardinal Carlo Bonelli, Massimo's successor.[9] These measures were insufficient, however, to ensure the proper identification of Matha's body, and in June 1657, Medina, Vidal, and Arias reconvened at the nuncio's tribunal in Madrid to testify about the events and the identity of the body that they had stolen. The witnesses recounted the crime, describing in detail the location, disposition, appearance, and identifying inscriptions of the three bodies in the tomb. The matter went no further, however, since Arcos's contacts in Rome told him that the theft was too recent and feelings too raw for the authorities to consider a petition to transfer Matha's bones to Madrid's Calced monastery.[10] In the meantime, the relics were safely stowed in the nuncio's oratory.[11]

In effect, the surrender of the relics in 1655 and the thieves' testimony in 1657 reasserted the universal political and spiritual authority of the Holy See over the relics and the wayward Trinitarians' initiative.[12] Both actions were also cleanup operations, retroactive efforts to remedy the awkward reality that, as one anonymous official of the Madrid nunciature put it, "when the said holy body was stolen in Rome, [neither] the friar who took it from the tomb in which it lay [nor] the one who brought it to Spain and who held onto it before handing it over to the apostolic nuncio took any care at all to prove its full identity, and they could have changed the said relics, and substituted other, profane ones."[13] Without a proper paper trail, with a notary and sworn witnesses, how could one be sure that the relics in Madrid were the same as those that had lain in the tomb in Rome, and how could would-be devotees be certain that they were venerating true holy relics, rather than the bones of the common dead? Nuncio Massimo's 1655 testimony and the 1657 depositions from Arias, Vidal, and Medina soon became important parts of a larger effort to secure the identification of the stolen bones as the remains of St. John of Matha. While Arcos and the rest of the Calced Trinitarians may have been content to set the matter aside until the anger of the powerful canons of the Vatican chapter had subsided, by the second half of the 1660s, the leaders of the Discalced branch seem to have seen the theft as an opportunity to assert the prominence and pull of their own wing of the Trinitarian family. As one Calced critic commented sourly, "impelled by their usual genius for sticking their noses into everything," the Discalced Trinitarians in 1667 began to gather information for a formal petition for identification of the relics to be considered by the Congregation of Sacred Rites.[14] Established in 1588 by Pope Sixtus V, the Congregatio Sacrorum Rituum is best known as the body that oversaw the formal processes of beatification and canonization of saints, but its purview also extended to larger issues of liturgy, ceremony, and cult. Relics, too, came under the congregation's authority—since the thirteenth century, authentication of the remains of candidates for beatification and canonization had been the exclusive province of the pope, while bishops held jurisdiction over newly discovered relics of known, approved saints.[15] The Council of Trent, an ecumenical council assembled to clarify Church doctrine, root out internal problems, and rebut Protestant critiques, affirmed this division of labor in its twenty-fifth session but specified that particularly doubtful or questionable cases must be remanded to a provincial council and that the pope must also be consulted.[16] The identity of the relics of St. John of Matha came under papal purview not because they had been stolen from the pope's own episcopal see and were now in the hands of the papal envoy but because of the grave doubts that surrounded them. For these reasons, it was to the Congregation of Sacred Rites that the Discalced Trinitarians directed their case for the identification of the stolen bones.

But first there was another, even more pressing issue for the Trinitarian Order to address: the ongoing question of the immemorial cult and, by extension, the saintly status of John of Matha and Felix of Valois. This issue also came under the purview of the Congregation of Sacred Rites, and so closely was the identity issue tied to the success of the immemorial cult case that it was not until the latter was resolved that the order could really address the former. In part, this was due to the kinds of proofs the two issues required, as both relied heavily on historical evidence. As we saw in chapter 2, Urban VIII's decrees in 1625 and 1634 prohibiting public veneration of unauthorized holy people spawned the development of a process for recognition of a saint's immemorial cult and, eventually, the extension of that cult to the whole of the Catholic world—that is, the saint's canonization. Such cases depended on a wide array of proofs, including witness testimony, material vestiges, and especially documentary evidence, such as chronicles, annals, and other histories; papal bulls, episcopal and royal decrees; wills, donations, and other legal instruments; and any other written sources that could prove to the cardinals of the congregation the antiquity of a cult. This preference for documentary evidence was not limited to immemorial cult cases but could also be found in the congregation's approach to beatification and canonization more generally. Over the course of the seventeenth century, the process of saint-making was increasingly of an "intensely legalistic rather than theological cast" and colored by "a thirst for written evidence and a rigour in its examination without precedent in the history of canonization."[17] For recently dead holy women and men, gathering written records was usually relatively straightforward, since witnesses were still living and the letters, biographies and autobiographies, and other texts that documented a candidate's heroic virtues, holy reputation, and miracles could be easily acquired. But for those who had died centuries before, advocates and devotees could face major hurdles in successfully seeing their candidate down the path to sainthood. In 1645, for example, doubts about the authenticity of a key piece of documentary evidence—a thirteenth-century miracle register—halted the case of Pope Gregory X (r. 1272–76) for almost eighty years.[18]

As we have seen, Trinitarian tradition and liturgy had long left St. John of Matha at the margins, and only in the last decades of the sixteenth century did Trinitarians both Calced and Discalced start taking an active interest in him and in his cofounder. This left the order at a considerable disadvantage, since it meant that there were very few indicators, written or otherwise, of uninterrupted veneration of Matha in the centuries since his death in 1213. The new, more hagiographically embellished *vita* published in González Dávila's 1630 *Compendio histórico* was a good start, but it did not go far enough, and the failure of the 1630 petition for extension of the English breviary to the whole of the order suggested that more and better evidence would be needed to prove that Matha and his cofounder had long been the focus of devotion within the order. In order to make the case for Matha's immemorial cult, the Trinitarians needed something they did not yet have: documentary proof of cult dating from the thirteenth, fourteenth, or fifteenth centuries.

The 1625 decrees and the evidentiary demands they created intersected with another problem: the paucity of sources for and studies of the history of the order more generally. Historically, the Trinitarians had been an avowedly active, rather than contemplative or scholarly, order: "Our rule deals with exterior things, like the redemption of captives and the care of the poor," noted Juan Bautista de la Concepción, founder of the Discalced branch.[19] While it seems probable that most Trinitarian houses would have had some kind of repository for important papers and books, the depredations of time, such as fires, floods, wars, sieges, and the Protestant-Catholic struggles of the sixteenth century, meant that many key documents had disappeared. The original Trinitarian rule of 1198 made no mention of libraries or archives, nor did its various revisions over the centuries, and later Trinitarian historians bewailed their forefathers' lack of concern for the order's documentary foundations. It is small wonder, then, that by 1594, a reforming general congregation of Castilian Trinitarian monasteries ordered that every establishment must have its own library, in a designated space or room, with a Bible, concordances, and the works of St. Thomas Aquinas, the doctors of the Church, and the saints.[20] Even so, we know little about the holdings of any Trinitarian libraries prior to the eighteenth century. What few inventories remain suggest that most were fairly modest collections.[21] The order's establishment in Paris boasted an important library founded by its most celebrated scholar, the humanist friar Robert Gaguin, and the monasteries in other major cities like Madrid and Barcelona were well endowed, but their early modern manuscript and print holdings have long been dispersed and can only be partially reconstructed through stray references made by seventeenth- and eighteenth-century bibliographers and other scholars.[22]

It is difficult to believe that the Trinitarian Order would have wholly ignored its own past, but it seems that by around 1500, beyond a brief text by Gaguin that recounted the names and accomplishments of the order's generals from John of Matha through 1472, there survived not a single full account of the Trinitarian Order's more than three hundred years of history.[23] Whatever annals or chronicles that may have been composed in the preceding three centuries were either missing or destroyed, and the handful of library catalogues that survive do not suggest any special concern for the history of the order.[24] Nor is there any reliable evidence of any medieval chronicles or document collections that recorded the histories of individual monasteries—that is, none have survived into the present, and as we will see, our main early modern witnesses for the existence of these now-vanished sources are of very questionable credibility. By comparison, many of the other mendicant orders founded in the same period could boast numerous historical texts. The earliest Carmelite history dates from at least 1281, for example, and over the course of the fourteenth, fifteenth, and sixteenth centuries, Carmelite historians continued to produce an extensive corpus of historical scholarship. Similarly, Franciscan friars began producing chronicles of their order by the late 1250s.[25] For many orders, internal reform movements and revivals between the late fourteenth and early sixteenth centuries were the impetus to historical scholarship.[26] Likewise, the reforming ethos of the Council of Trent found expression in a wave of historical works that proclaimed the antiquity and rigor of the monastic orders they chronicled.[27] By 1588, even the Mercedarians, the Trinitarians' traditional foes, had begun appointing chroniclers to begin the work of recording that order's poorly documented past.[28]

Given this dynamic, it is not surprising that by the end of the sixteenth century, just as reform movements within the Trinitarian Order were gathering steam, some members had begun to inquire into their order's past. Repeated reprintings of Robert Gaguin's brief account of the founding of the Trinitarian order that, as we saw in chapter 2, was regularly included in manuals, constitutions, lists of privileges and indulgences, and other books meant mainly for internal use suggest a developing historical conscience. So too do longer manuscript histories, like Antonio Raposo's (d. 1547) *De revelatione et institutione Sacri Ordinis Sanctissimae Trinitatis*, Marcos de Moura's two-volume *Historia dos instuidores e instituicão da Ordem da Santissima Trinidade e das excellencias e grandeza della* (ca. 1595), or Bartolomé de Gaona's *Tabla sinóptica sobre la fundación de la Orden de la Santíssima Trinidad* (1595).[29] These texts are now lost, and we cannot know precisely what they contained, but it seems likely that they did not quite meet the order's needs, especially in the light of the 1625 decrees. What the Trinitarians required, it seems, was both hard documentary evidence for Matha's long-standing veneration and a thorough recounting of the whole of the order's past, one that connected the lives and deeds of its founding figures to its growth and activities throughout the succeeding centuries. The situation called for someone who could meet both imperatives, someone who excelled as an archival sleuth and as a crafter of narrative but who also had the skills, imagination, and audacity to do whatever might be needed in order to meet the demand for written proof. It called for a scholar who was both a talented historian and a daring forger.

The combination was not as unusual as it may sound. Historical forgery and historical scholarship require many of the same skills, such as a firm command not just of events but of the language, style, scripts, assumptions, and whole mental worlds of past eras. The same Renaissance humanists who pioneered new techniques of textual criticism, more exacting standards for historical documentation, and a growing attentiveness to historical context sometimes turned their scholarly skills to fabricating ancient and medieval texts. For example, the celebrated scholar Desiderius Erasmus (1466–1536) forged a treatise by the third-century writer St. Cyprian of Carthage, and Carlo Sigonio (d. 1584), a renowned specialist in the histories of early Rome and medieval Italy, won lasting scorn from his colleagues for his fabrication of Cicero's lost *Consolatio*.[30] In an age in which scholarly methods were shifting, the line between critical historical and literary scholarship and forgery was blurry, and projects in historical erudition could also be projects in historical invention. Scholars like Pirro Ligorio (ca. 1512–1583) fabricated hundreds of classical inscriptions as a way of re-creating the ancient world to present it in full, not in the fragmentary way in which its remains had survived.[31] Others, like Giovanni Nanni, aka Annius of Viterbo (ca. 1432–1502), or Curzio Inghirami (1614–1655) turned to forgery out of local or national patriotism.[32] Others seem to have created false documents and histories out of baser motivations, like Alfonso Ceccarelli (1532–1583), a historian-*cum*-forger for hire who specialized in fabricated genealogies, wills, and other legal instruments.[33]

Specialists in sacred history, a broad category that included a wide range of genres, from martyrologies and hagiography to religious history of all types, including the history of individual religious orders, were not immune to the trends at work in secular historical scholarship. In the fifteenth and early sixteenth centuries, writers began to apply the new historical methods to Church history and hagiography. Equipped with the new philological and historical methods, as well as an increasingly skeptical attitude, sacred historians began to look beyond miracle stories and other traditional sources to textual, epigraphic, and other testimony for the lives of the saints.[34] This trend grew more pervasive after Trent, as scholars submitted the history of Christianity and of the Church to new scrutiny. Cardinal Cesare Baronio (1538–1607), author of the *Annales ecclesiastici* (1588–1607), brought careful source criticism and new textual and material evidence to his chronicle of the earliest centuries of the Church and to his revision of the Roman Breviary and the revised Roman Martyrology (1586).[35] In the early seventeenth century, Jesuit hagiographers known as the Bollandists undertook a similar project. Starting in 1643, Heribert Rosweyde (1569–1629), Jean Bolland (1596–1665), and their followers published the *Acta sanctorum*, a monumental project that sought to reevaluate the earliest documentary sources for the lives of the saints and eliminate their more apocryphal elements.[36] In so doing, they sought to create a more credible and certain foundation for sacred history and for the Church's claims to unchanging historical continuity.

For some sacred historians, however, the new historical methods and evidentiary expectations threatened to undermine dearly held devotions.

These scholars embraced the new norms but found ways to support underdocumented saints with wishful interpretations of inscriptions and other difficult sources. Dionisio Bonfant (d. 1637), a theologian and jurist from Cagliari who created hundreds of new saints for his hometown with imaginative—and erroneous—readings of inscriptions from Christianity's earliest centuries, was an extreme example, but similar tactics were deployed by local historians throughout Europe.[37] Others turned to forgery, not as a crime but as a pious act that aimed to transform unsubstantiated but cherished legends into historical facts by firmly grounding them in textual and material proofs. The most notorious of these devout forgers was Jerónimo Román de la Higuera (d. 1611), a Jesuit from Toledo, Spain. In order to counter the challenges posed by Cardinal Baronio's works, which, following a careful reexamination of the hagiographic sources, gave short shrift or even omitted many saints and legends that were locally popular but lacked the proper documentation, Higuera fabricated a series of texts that later came to be known as the *falsos cronicones*, or false chronicles, of Dexter, Maximus, Luitprand, and Julián Pérez. These forgeries, ostensibly medieval chronicles, confirmed many beloved traditions, such as the evangelization of Spain by the apostle St. James the Greater, as well as providing a profusion of saints, martyrs, and other holy figures for the earliest centuries of Iberian Christianity. Although sharp-eyed critics soon questioned their authenticity, Higuera's forged chronicles quickly became foundational documents for devout and patriotic local historians across Spain.[38]

If sacred history frequently served as a site on which treasured traditions were defended, it was also terrain on which rival entities and institutions competed for power and prominence. The cities of Toledo and Santiago de Compostela, for example, fought out their competing claims to be the seat of the primate of Spain—that is, the highest-ranking archbishop within the Spanish kingdoms—both through lawsuits and through treatises on the lives of their patron saints and on the ecclesiastical histories of their communities.[39] Similarly, religious orders deployed annals, chronicles, and hagiographies in order to assert their "excellencies"—their "antiquity, sanctity, and the quantity and quality of services rendered to the monarchy, the society, the Church itself."[40] In a competitive religious landscape, where monastic and mendicant orders jockeyed with one another and with the secular clergy for members, donations, patronage, and prestige, chronicles, annals, and histories were important means of promotion and propaganda. These texts also help foster internal institutional memory and group identity, promoting a sense of belonging. Some of those who wrote on behalf of a religious order enriched their narrative by claiming key figures from the past. Carmelite historians, for example, engaged in an extended debate with detractors from other religious orders over whether the Carmelites could claim to have been founded by the biblical prophet Elijah, long before Christ. Others went further, appropriating spiritual luminaries from other religious orders to elevate their own. In one case, a controversy that dated from the early seventeenth century (if not earlier) and continued for decades pitted the Franciscans against the Augustinians, who claimed that St. Francis had originally been a hermit living under the rule of St. Augustine.[41] Writers of these monastic histories often made their cases through imaginative readings of existing documents or inscriptions; others turned to Higuera's false chronicles and other invented sources. Still others resorted to forgery themselves.

In effect, the Trinitarians confronted many of the same issues that faced other communities and institutions encumbered by a poorly documented past even as they vied for social prominence and the privileges that it afforded. To compete with other religious orders, especially the Mercedarians, the Trinitarian Order needed to mobilize the past in order to meet the requirements of the present—to ensure its prominence by proving its antiquity, its long service to the Crown, the Church, and the whole Christian community, and its tradition of exemplary piety and deep devotion. More importantly, in order to solve the problems posed by Urban VIII's decrees, the Trinitarian Order needed a writer who could find—or create—the necessary evidence for Matha's immemorial cult and compose a compelling narrative of the order's past while obeying the ever more stringent scholarly norms demanded of would-be historians. Only with these proofs in place and with the question of Matha's status as a saint resolved could it take up the problem of the identity of his stolen bones. This chapter examines the strategies by which, over the course of several decades, the order met the evidentiary demands posed by the 1625 decree. Over the course of the 1630s, 1640s, 1650s, and 1660s, the Trinitarians established the foundations for proving the antiquity of Matha's veneration. While the case drew on a wide range of proofs, it rested primarily on the creative scholarship of Friar Juan Figueras Carpi, a historian/forger of some real talent. During the 1630s and 1640s, from his ingenious pen emerged a fully developed life of St. John of Matha and his companion and a detailed recounting of the order's more than four hundred years of existence, both grounded in forged documents, imaginary authors, and invented traditions. One in particular—the same English breviary that, as we saw in chapter 2, had already been the focus of a failed petition before the Congregation of Sacred Rites in 1630—became the cornerstone for the order's developing case for the founder's immemorial cult. An outpouring of hagiographical and historical texts during the 1640s and 1650s disseminated the new documents and the narratives that they supported, but it appears that they were not sufficient to win the Trinitarian Order's case in Rome. Beginning in 1661, a second forger, a chronicler named Antonio Lupián Zapata, created new documents and shored up the shaky foundations of others manufactured by Figueras. In 1665, armed with these new proofs, the order successfully made its case before the Congregation of Sacred Rites. By the end of the decade, the question of Matha's and Valois's immemorial cult, and thus their status as full-fledged, recognized saints, had been fully resolved. Only then could the Trinitarians turn their attention to the 1655 theft and the identity of Matha's stolen bones.

Juan Figueras Carpi

The challenges posed to the Trinitarians' founding fathers by the 1625 and 1634 decrees regulating the veneration of uncanonized holy people were considerable. Fortunately, a solution was already at hand, and the first steps had already been taken. In 1628, a provincial chapter of the Calced Trinitarians in Salamanca nominated Friar Juan Figueras Carpi to serve as general chronicler. According to one mid-eighteenth-century commentator, he hailed from Albalat de Pardines (now called Albalat de la Ribera), a town some thirty-six kilometers south of Valencia. He seems to have entered the Trinitarian Order in Castile, though where and when is unknown. Where he pursued his education is likewise unknown, but by 1634, he already held a master's degree in theology and had served the order as a preacher. Friar Figueras seems to have been a true archive hound—within six years of his appointment as general chronicler, he had collected material from Trinitarian houses throughout Spain, Portugal, France, and Italy. In late 1633, he settled down in the order's Calced monastery in Genoa, and by September of the following year, he had completed the first volume of his history of the order, *Annales sacri Ordinis Ssmae. Trinitatis de Redemptione Captivorum*. While Figueras's *Annales* never reached print, they seem to have circulated in manuscript, and they also formed the foundation for his later published work, the *Chronicum Ordinis Sanctissimae Trinitatis de redemptione* (Verona, 1645). Figueras is said to have died in Málaga in the 1660s or 1670s.[42]

Beyond these few facts, we know little about Figueras or his life. What else can be uncovered suggests that the friar had a penchant for imaginative storytelling. By 1634, Figueras was styling himself "Provincial and Vicar

General for England, Scotland, and Ireland." He claimed to have received this title (wholly honorific, given the Trinitarian Order's total suppression in the British Isles in the course of the Protestant Reformation) in 1631 in transfer from its original possessor, Friar Juan Hynde de San Martín (d. 1643). According to an anonymous pamphlet (ca. 1644) most probably written by Figueras himself, Figueras had journeyed to England to preach and to minster to its beleaguered population of Recusants, or secret Catholics. On August 15, 1630, shortly after saying Mass in a private home in Hounslow, a village about ten miles outside London, he was captured by English authorities and clapped in jail for eleven months. There, he encountered his English confrère Juan Hynde de San Martín, who transferred the honorific position to him shortly before Figueras escaped from the prison and, presumably, from England.[43] These events cannot be confirmed, nor is there any real proof that Figueras ever visited England. There is also some evidence to suggest that the order's leadership in Cerfroid may have attempted to punish him for his unsanctioned appropriation of the honorific title, but he seems to have persisted in its use since it appears everywhere throughout his published and unpublished work.[44]

The story points toward Figueras's inventive posture toward the past, both his own and that of his religious order. Upon his appointment as general chronicler, Figueras took up the task of writing the Trinitarians' history with enthusiasm, energy, and imagination, qualities he poured into his *Annales* and, later, the *Chronicum*. Together, the two texts offered a compelling new vision of the Trinitarians' obscure history, one replete with details about the order's origins, expansion, and activities; its many illustrious members; and, of course, its saintly founder. Previous accounts, like those compiled by Gaguin and Bourgeois, had portrayed Matha as a pious professor with eremitical tastes and mystical tendencies but revealed little about the man himself. Figueras's pen transformed Matha into a multidimensional figure: a learned scholar, a dedicated preacher, a zealous inquisitor, a trusted diplomat, a brave missionary, an exemplary ascetic, a charismatic miracle worker. The obscure medieval saint emerged from the shadows as a man fully grounded in his historical context and a model for modern emulation.

Figueras first floated many of these new particulars in the *Annales*. This multivolume work traced Trinitarian and European history from 1153, the supposed year of Matha's birth, to 1333. The *Annales* thus combined a hagiographic life of the founder with a history of the Order of the Most Holy Trinity and of the Captives, including its foundation, its establishment of houses throughout Europe, its leaders and prominent members, and its many expeditions into Islamic lands to redeem captive Christians. Moving year by year, Figueras paired the events of Matha's life and the history of the order with contemporary events in European military, political, and religious history. This expanded framework laid the groundwork for many of the new hagiographic and historical facts revealed in the text. Discussion of the origins and errors of the heretical group known as the Cathars, for example, offered a context for Matha's public disputations and erudite writings against both the Cathars and the Waldensians, writings that Figueras claimed to have seen in Florence, in the library of the Grand Duke, and in Rome, in the collection of Cardinal Federico Barberini.[45] Similarly, an extended consideration of the ancient and medieval history of San Tommaso in Formis, the little church that was the Trinitarians' first possession in Rome, framed Innocent III's grant of the property to the order, Matha's exemplary oversight of the Trinitarians' first general chapter meeting there, and his establishment of the order's dedication to hospitality and to the redemption of captives.[46]

These new details rested on an impressive body of evidence. Figueras showed himself a skilled and resourceful scholar whose indefatigable research uncovered a wealth of sources, both manuscript and print, with which he enriched his account of Matha's life and deeds and the history of the order. For example, Figueras drew on histories of the medieval Church by Abraham Bzowski (Bzovius; 1567–1637) and Severin Binius (1573–1641), as well as the papal epistolary registers held in the Vatican archives, to authenticate Matha's previously unknown diplomatic service in 1200 to Innocent III as his chaplain and legate to Dalmatia.[47] Similarly, manuscript sources newly discovered in the archive of the order's monastery at Avingaña—the first Trinitarian house in Iberia—documented Matha's hortatory words to the monastery's first leader.[48] Well-known, key events in Matha's life, such as his vision of Christ / an angel and the two captives, likewise benefited from Figueras's deep research. While Figueras stressed Innocent III's miraculous vision in 1198 as the key moment in the foundation of the Trinitarian Order, he gave significant weight to Matha's previous revelation, which he dated as having occurred some five years earlier. His retelling drew on thirteen different sources, ranging from recent publications like Gil González Dávila's 1630 life of Sts. John of Matha and Felix of Valois to a hagiographical manuscript on parchment held by the Trinitarian monastery in Burgos.[49] Other episodes in Figueras's account reflected novel hagiographic details found in newly discovered documents or in existing legends about the saint that circulated in oral form among the friars. Figueras's recounting of the pious conversations between Matha and Valois, for example, quoted from a now lost but well-attested manuscript history of the founding of the order written by the Portuguese friar Antonio Raposo. Figueras also made some use of alternative sources, such as inscriptions and poems, but he does not seem to have adopted the trend toward incorporation of archaeological or material evidence into the writing of history.[50]

Together, these new biographical details and newly discovered sources refigured the early history of the Trinitarians, placing John of Matha at the center of current events and at the heart of the order's early history. Figueras's *Annales* revealed that far from being neglected, Matha had long been venerated both within the Trinitarian Order and within the Church universal. Upon the founder's death, for example, Pope Innocent III and the entire college of cardinals came to San Tommaso in Formis to venerate his body. The pontiff ordered that Matha would lie in state for four days to accommodate the faithful, who flocked to San Tommaso in Formis to pay their respects and to petition for miraculous cures.[51] Afterward, the pontiff and his entourage returned to bury Matha in the marble tomb. Even better, fifty years later, both Matha and Valois were honored with a formal canonization. While as recently as 1625 Benoit Gonon had flatly asserted that neither Matha nor Valois had been canonized, Figueras pointed to multiple authorities and to papal bulls with seals, "which," claimed Figueras, "we saw with our own eyes when we were in Rome," that proved that both founders had already been raised to the altars on October 4, 1263, by Pope Urban IV.[52] In testimony of this fact, Figueras quoted the liturgical office for the two saints contained in the English breviary—the same source about which, as we saw in chapter 2, witnesses had been questioned in 1630. The Trinitarians, claimed Figueras, had long remembered their founder with prayers and antiphons (sung responses) in both the morning (Lauds) and the evening (Vespers) gatherings for community prayer.[53] In fact, as early as 1218, the order's leaders had begun collecting information about the virtues and miracles of the two Trinitarian founders in order to advance their canonization by the pope. As late as the mid-fourteenth century, he said, this testimony had been kept in a box in the Trinitarian monastery in Paris, together with the original copy of the order's constitutions as written out by St. John of Matha himself.[54] Together, these startling pieces of information promised to jump-start the Trinitarians' quest to win papal recognition of Matha's immemorial cult.

But Figueras was not just an archival sleuth and solid historical scholar—he was also a skilled and inventive forger. His specialty was trawling through histories and bibliographies of the British Isles in search of obscure authors and titles that could stand as cover for his historical inventions. Of his many forged sources, the most important was a history of the Trinitarian Order supposedly written around 1346 by one George Innes, a Trinitarian friar from Aberdeen, Scotland. This history drew on "ancient manuscripts" written on parchment to craft a full history of the order from its founding.[55] Figueras seems to have found the inspiration for this obscure Scottish friar and his detailed history in a brief mention in Thomas Dempster's (1579–1625) *Historia ecclesiastica gentis Scotorum*. In this book, published in Bologna in 1625, the inventive Dempster aimed to fill the void of Scotland's ecclesiastical history by creating a list of Scottish saints, popes, cardinals, missionaries, kings, and other holy men—a task that he accomplished (as one later commentator charged) by "filching of Saints, Confessors and other Authors, from *England, Ireland*, and other Nations; and putting them all off, as the proper Manufacture of his own Countrey."[56] In entry number 723 in his list of Scotland's notable men, Dempster described George Innes as a man "of the most famous lineage and innocent manners" who had served the order as provincial for Scotland and Ireland and had died in 1414 somewhere outside of Scotland. Dempster attributed four works to Innes: two works on the Holy Land, one on the sorrows of the Virgin, and one treating the founding of the Trinitarian order.[57] Where Dempster dug up this reference, or whether he crafted it himself, remains unclear—I can find no references to Innes before the appearance of the *Historia ecclesiastica gentis Scotorum*. It seems probable that this brief entry, published in a book that Figueras encountered in the course of his studies (he cites it directly several times in the *Annales*), provided the seed material for Figueras's more elaborate inventions.[58]

Figueras's second-most-cited source was a manuscript history on the ages of the world, supposedly "published" (that is, completed and entered into circulation) in London in 1478 by John Blakeney (or Blackeney), the head of the order's monastery at Ingham. Like Innes, Figueras appears to have found Blakeney's name in a list of illustrious men of the British Isles—in this case, in a work by John Pitts, aka Pitseus (1560–1616), an English Catholic priest active in France who today is best known for his work as a continuator of John Bale, the great English bibliographer. Pitts's account of Blakeney's life and works was closely based on the one found in Bale's 1557 *Scriptorum illustrium maioris Brytanniae*, but it seems unlikely that Figueras ever saw Bale; instead, he cited Pitts directly.[59] Blakeney makes his appearance as entry number 829 in Pitts's *Relationum historicarum de rebus anglicis* (Paris, 1619; a text better known as *De Illustribus Angliæ Scriptoribus*).[60] An Englishman from the county of Norfolk, Blakeney had been a member of the Trinitarian house at Ingham around 1447, under the reign of Henry VI. According to Pitts, Blakeney was the author of several volumes on grammar, rhetoric, letter writing, and poetry, a five-part treatise on Boethius's famous *On the Consolation of Philosophy*, and a volume on the ages of the world, among others. Unlike the texts attributed to Innes, at least one of Blakeney's works on rhetoric can be found today in libraries in Britain and Ireland, and a copy of that same work seems to have circulated in the sixteenth century.[61] The others appear to have been as lost in the seventeenth century as they are today, and it was the last item on the list, *De mundi aetatibus*, that provided Figueras with the necessary fodder for his invented 1478 manuscript.

Nor were Blakeney and Innes the only spurious sources fabricated by the inventive Figueras. Other "facts" of Trinitarian history he drew from a manuscript chronicle composed around 1421 by an anonymous Carthusian monk from Dumfries, in Scotland. No such chronicle is known to have ever existed, nor does there seem to have ever been a Carthusian monastery in Dumfries.[62] Another source, a history of the establishment of monasticism in England supposedly written by the Benedictine writer "Guillerminus Spina," or William Thorne (fl. 1397), is likewise unknown.[63] Some of Figueras's archival sources, including several royal decrees, were clearly fabricated, while many others were questionable or had suspicious interpolations inserted into their texts.[64] However, many others, like those that recorded the foundation of the order's monasteries in Marseilles and Avingaña, were genuine documents still extant today or attested to by other, less problematic writers.[65]

Rather than developing from scratch both the authors and the texts with which he would rewrite his order's past, Figueras ensured greater credibility for his forgeries by attributing his invented writings to known or attested writers. Using the names, titles, and dates he had gathered from Dempster and Pitts, Figueras forged texts to match. Others, like the Dumfries chronicles, he seems to have created ex nihilo. Using these spurious sources— Innes, Blakeney, Thorne, the Dumfries chronicles, and others—Figueras rewrote both the life of the Trinitarians' founder and the history of the order as a whole. Testimony from Innes's history transformed Matha into a virtuous exemplar who, out of humility, repeatedly turned down appointments to bishoprics and archbishoprics, whose ascetic bodily discipline shocked his Muslim captors, and who, in a display of heroic patience, prayed and sat vigil at the bedside of the sick and dying.[66] Figueras also mined Innes for Matha's many miracles. In his account, Matha freed a tormented demoniac, calmed a dangerous storm, and raised a wind that brought a ship full of redeemed captives from Tunisia to Rome in a mere six hours.[67]

Even more dramatic was Figueras's reworking of the first three centuries of the Trinitarian Order's existence. Innes and Blakeney in particular provided him with names and dates for hitherto-unheard-of Trinitarian houses that he sprinkled liberally throughout Flanders, Holland, Germany, Scandinavia, Bohemia, Hungary, Poland, Lithuania, Russia, Bosnia, Serbia, Albania, Dalmatia, Dacia, Greece, Cyprus, Italy, Sicily, the Holy Land, and most especially the British Isles, a site of particular fantasy for Figueras. These spurious monasteries housed scores of previously unknown learned and pious friars of note who had occupied important positions as cardinals, patriarchs, bishops, and archbishops or led dozens of heretofore-unheard-of missions to free Christian prisoners from Muslim captors in Granada, North Africa, and other places on the Muslim-Christian frontier. It is from Innes and Blakeney, for example, that we learn of figures like Richard, a friar of the Trinitarian monastery at Knaresborough, in Yorkshire, who was executed by the Turks in 1220 while redeeming captives; or the twelve Trinitarian martyrs who accompanied the sainted French king Louis IX (1214–1270) on his ill-fated excursion into Tunis; or Robert Kett, a Scottish friar supposedly active around 1267, who, having studied theology at Oxford, served in key leadership roles in Scotland and Ireland and was rewarded by Pope Clement IV with the titles of bishop of Bethlehem and patriarch of Antioch.[68] In effect, just as Figueras's retelling of Matha's life placed the Trinitarians' founder at the heart of his era and of the order's devotional life, so too did his *Annals* rewrite the order's once-obscure medieval past around a dazzling crowd of pious and high-achieving notables spread thickly across Europe and the Middle East. Unlike other mendicant orders, the early modern Trinitarians remained firmly focused on Old World conflicts rather than New World conversions—the order did not expand into the Americas until well into the nineteenth century. Figueras's narrative reflected and fostered this emphasis by reimagining medieval Trinitarian history as one of inexorable geographic expansion that brought the whole of Europe to focus on the order's characteristically Mediterranean orientation.

In this reworked past, the Trinitarian Order enjoyed close ties to the most prominent and powerful figures in medieval society. Some of these royal and papal connections were grounded in verifiable fact, like the founding of the Trinitarian monastery in 1211 in Aberdeen by King William "the Lion" (ca. 1142–1214) or the establishment of the Trinitarians at Fontainebleau in 1259 by Louis IX. Others, however, seem to have been entirely fictitious, like the establishment of the Trinitarian monastery at Knaresborough in 1218 by Richard of Cornwall, king of the Romans.[69] Throughout Figueras's narrative, he cited bulls, letters, edicts, and other legal instruments that conferred privileges and properties on the order and testified to the esteem in which it had long been held by popes and kings. While many of these were genuine documents whose authenticity can be confirmed, others, such as two writs of privilege supposedly granted to the order by King Ferdinand IV of Castile in 1311 and 1312, were of very questionable authenticity.[70] Some, like a papal bull issued by Pope Clement V in 1305 that conceded indulgences to the order's benefactors, were very probably forgeries.[71] The cumulative effect of these vaunted royal and papal ties was to bolster the Trinitarians' long-standing eminence, especially in the face of competing claims from their perennial rivals, the Mercedarians. Figueras devoted several pages to the Order of the Blessed Virgin of Mercy, citing numerous papal grants of indulgence and royal writs of privilege in favor of the Trinitarians.[72] In his brief retelling of the origins of the Mercedarians, the friars were Johnny-come-latelies, established only in 1223, some twenty-five years after the Trinitarians, and without the same level of papal endorsement of their work as redeemers of captives.[73]

To advance this account, Figueras deployed a methodology of accumulative or agglutinative citation, layering quotations from authors both authentic and spurious to weave together invented and genuine sources into a dense and interconnected rewriting of the Trinitarians' past. That is, Figueras's preferred kind of forgery did not depend on manufacturing fake documents on parchments in antiquated scripts but on crafting plausible historical sources to be quoted within his own text. This technique drew on a strategy frequently deployed by early modern historians, who sought to offset the questionable fidelity of many historical sources not by simply rejecting them but by recuperating at least part of their content by extracting, compiling, synthesizing, and comparing historical data from a wide range of sources.[74] It was also a technique common to Renaissance forgers, who lent credibility to their inventions by highlighting their conformity with known, accepted sources and by drawing attention to their own scholarly skill.[75] For example, the *Annales*' entry for Matha's entrance into the priesthood in 1192 consisted of quotations from six authors, four of whom described a miraculous column of fire that appeared over the saint's head at the moment of consecration. One of the four was Innes, Figueras's key forged source, while the other three were González Dávila's 1630 *Compendio histórico* and two other texts that drew directly on González Dávila's work. González Dávila gave no source for the story, but he very probably received the story of the column of fire and other hagiographic details straight from Figueras himself. González Dávila certainly knew Figueras, since he mentioned both him and his chronicle, then a work in progress, twice within the text.[76] It seems likely that Figueras provided his fellow historian with transcriptions of the spurious material; in so doing, he shored up its provenance by ensuring its use by a well-known and respected author. Figueras followed up the quotations from his imaginary George Innes and from González Dávila by comparing them to passages in two other recent writers who did not mention the miraculous column. He made no commentary beyond noting the discrepancy between the sources, but Figueras's purpose was clear: such displays of evenhandedness ensured his bona fides as a historian and lent greater credibility to his invented sources.

In a like manner, Figueras provided thick layers of quotations from four sources, all nonexistent, as evidence for Matha's heretofore-unknown canonization at the hands of Pope Urban IV.[77] Elsewhere in the *Annales*, he offered additional evidence for the event by citing related honors, including a 1291 decision to celebrate the feast days of both Matha and Valois and a 1318 authorization by Pope John XXII of Matha's office and Mass to be celebrated by Trinitarian friars in England, Scotland, and Ireland (a clear reference to the English breviary text). These details, like the canonization, rested on a dense web of interdependent citations of unfindable or inaccessible documents; like the canonization, they are very likely to have been the products of Figueras's productive historical imagination. The germ or spark for this early canonization very probably came from a genuine archival document, a 1498 letter from Minister General Robert Gaguin to Andrés Sedano, provincial of Castile and head of the Trinitarian house in Burgos. The letter no longer exists; we know it only from Figueras's transcription. However, the precision and specificity of its provenance—originally held in the archive of the Valladolid monastery, the document was a gift to Figueras from Friar Martín Galindo in November 1629—suggests that it was most likely to have been genuine and not one of his many historical forgeries. In the letter, which accompanied a manuscript copy of Gaguin's chronicle of the origins of the order and of its minsters general, Gaguin lamented the order's inattention to its own history but pointed to existing sources with which the past could be reconstructed: "You will complain that among us hardly a trace of the foundation of the order is left. Our elders are not at fault. For just as their holiness of life was approved, so are their deeds yet extant in parchment codices, and those carried out by the ministers general one hundred and eighty years ago are still extant and preserved."[78] It seems likely that Figueras expanded on Gaguin's vague comment that the sanctity of the Trinitarians' elders (*maiores nostri*)—that is, founders—had been proved or approved (*probati sunt*) to invent a full papal canonization for the order's founders. It may also express an oral tradition that circulated among the Trinitarians and their supporters.[79] In any case, it is within the *Annales* that the supposed canonization first emerged as part of the written history of the Trinitarians and their founder.

These and other new details of Matha's life and of the history of the order as a whole had apparently been circulating for some time. Figueras, like most other scholars of his era, did not work in splendid isolation but instead exchanged letters, transcriptions of archival documents and inscriptions, and other materials with friends and associates. References to sources received from colleagues around Europe are scattered through the *Annales*, and while his letters no longer survive, stray comments in the works of other scholars reveal that he had been preparing the groundwork for some time by passing to colleagues and correspondents drafts of his forgeries and of the histories that promoted them.[80] As we have seen, the inventive friar was also very likely to have been the source for many of Gil González Dávila's miracles. Similarly, Martín Carrillo's (1561–1630) posthumous *Annales y memorias cronológicas* (Zaragoza, 1634), a general history of key events in Spain from antiquity through 1620, drew heavily on Figueras and his manuscript history of the order for the names and deaths of the many mythical martyrs in England and Ireland.[81] Chatter about Figueras and his forged George Innes can be found in letters sent from Lisbon by Bernardino de San Antonio, an eminent member of the Calced branch, to Juan de la Torre, a Calced Trinitarian based in Madrid. In May 1632, for example, the Portuguese friar told his correspondent that he had not yet had the opportunity to see Innes's chronicle for himself but that he hoped to, since "it is from a time closer to the [founders]"—that is, it was a more direct historical source than any other.[82]

While Figueras's favored modus operandi centered on crafting texts for quotation, there is some evidence that he may also have dabbled in other forms of forgery. A March 1640 letter sent from Lisbon by Friar Antonio de la Trinidad y Torre to Alonso Yañez mentioned that "Father Figueras brought to this monastery [in Lisbon] a book the size of the [Trinitarian] constitutions of Castile, printed, that said George Innes, *General Chronicle* of our holy religion."[83] The reference is not wholly clear, but Antonio de la Trinidad y Torre's aside hints that Figueras may have gone beyond quotes and fabricated a complete codex of Innes to show to eager scholars. Other evidence suggests that in the course of his research, Figueras may have taken advantage of his official position as chronicler to seed the order's archives with fabricated documents that would support the case for Matha's immemorial cult. In June 1665, investigators gathering testimony to be submitted to the Congregation of Sacred Rites examined a book held in the archives of the Calced Trinitarian house in Burgos. On the twentieth folio of the "large, ancient" volume—a *libro becerro*, or ledger in which the monastery's privileges, properties, benefices, and other important records were transcribed for posterity—they found the following words: "Also, another bull of Pope John XXII, sent from Avignon, in France, in the year 1318 on August 6 [of] the second year of his pontificate, in which he concedes the office of the saintly founders St. John of Matha and St. Felix of Valois, founders of our order, to the provinces of England, Ireland, and Scotland, at the request of the provincial of the province of England, called friar Robert Hundeslow, [during the rule of the] general of the aforementioned religion, Etienne du Mesnil-Fouchard."[84] Unfortunately, the witnesses did not describe the hand or the ink that inscribed the register, but given that the Burgos archive is one that Figueras relied on and from which he was known to have removed key documents, it seems possible that the insertion of this fabricated bull is the inventive friar's own handiwork.[85]

While it remains unclear who knew about these impostures, Figueras's selection as the Calced Trinitarians' general chronicler was not uncontroversial. In a letter dated July 31, 1632, Bernardino de San Antonio gossiped about Figueras, saying, "He has the drive to work, but I would be happy if this job of chronicler were undertaken by a person of greater authority and good talent." The Portuguese friar acknowledged that Figueras "doesn't lack [talent], and he's seen a lot [of documents?], which is important for a chronicler," but he implicitly suggested that Figueras lacked other qualities, like "being truthful and certain about the times, and astute, and choosing good [evidence] with truth and with inquiry into it. In these days [this practice] is lacking is some [writers], who, in order to say a lot, tell everything, good and bad, false and true, without verifying the truth, which is the soul of history."[86] Perhaps Friar Bernardino had aspired to an official chronicler's position himself, since he noted that his correspondent had erroneously called him "chronicler": "I am not that; this [title] is for another person."[87] Figueras was by no means the only Trinitarian actively researching his order's history. By 1630, for example, the Portuguese friar Antonio de la Trinidad y Torre had already completed a manuscript history of the order and its saints, but it seems to have remained unpublished.[88] Other Trinitarians are known to have been working on or completed similar studies around the same time, including Alonso Yañez and Hortensio Paravicino, the latter of whom was one of the Calced Trinitarians' most illustrious leaders.[89] Their works have not survived, however, and one might speculate that perhaps Figueras's imaginative approach to filling the gaps in the order's past made him an appealing choice. Bernardino de San Antonio's skepticism about Figueras's suitability may also suggest that the Portuguese provincial was not privy to the decision-making process through which Figueras had been selected. Neither, it seems, was the Trinitarians' central leadership in France, since in May 1635, Figueras was censured by the general chapter in Cerfroid and prohibited from publishing, on suspicion of having propagated fictions and impostures.[90] At the same meeting, the general chapter also suppressed Friar François Aloès's 1634 French translation of González Dávila's history of the order. The Spanish, remarked Minister General Louis Petit, were a nation "much given to exaggeration."[91]

While the censure of the Trinitarians' central authorities in France may have prevented Figueras's *Annales* from reaching print, it did not prevent the spread of Figueras's invented history into an ever-increasing number of works both by Trinitarian writers and by authors outside the order. Some received Figueras's revised Trinitarian history through the published work of Gil González Dávila's *Compendio histórico*. In the Calced Trinitarian Pablo Aznar's (d. 1624) posthumous 1630 *Exercicios espirituales*, for example, he drew on Figueras via González Dávila for his account of Matha's life and for the text of the English breviary.[92] Similarly, Ippolito Marracci (1604–1675; not a Trinitarian but a member of the Clerics Regular of the Mother of God), cited Figueras, Innes, and Blakeney alongside González Dávila in his 1643 treatise on religious orders and devotion to the Immaculate Conception.[93] Few of the Marian miracles that Marracci attributed to Figueras and his forged sources appear in the *Annales*, however, which suggests that Marracci received the accounts directly from the inventive Trinitarian.[94] Others also received information straight from Figueras. Bernardino de San Antonio, for example, reported receiving exciting (and false) historical details from Figueras in a letter written from Rome in 1637.[95] Similarly, a 1640 letter from the Portuguese friar Antonio de la Trinidad y Torre to his Castilian colleague Alonso Yañez alluded to transcriptions received from Figueras.[96] Other direct recipients probably included Friar Pasquale Guasque, author of a 1639 treatise on the order's origins and indulgences, and Pedro López de Altuna, a Calced Trinitarian who in 1637 published a general chronicle of the Trinitarian order with the full authorization of the Spanish province's leadership.[97] Altuna tacitly drew on Figueras for many details of Matha's life and the history of the order, so much so that one twentieth-century critic theorized that Figueras ghost-wrote the text.[98] The continued dissemination of Figueras's forgeries is testimony to the continuing importance of manuscript text culture in an age of print.

Thus, censure does not seem to have prevented the inventive chronicler from spreading his forgeries by circulating passages and transcriptions to his friends and correspondents. Nor did the Cerfroid general chapter's condemnation stop him from publishing forever. In 1642, Figueras published a short biography of St. Pedro Pascual (d. 1299/1300), aka Pedro de Valencia, a bishop of Jaén who died a martyr in Granada. Figueras used the evidence provided by his invented George Innes and other imaginary sources to transform into a Trinitarian this murky figure, whom the Mercedarians were themselves busily appropriating for the greater glory of their own order, and rechristened him Pedro Figueras Carpi, bestowing on the famous martyr his own family names.[99] Like the *Annales*, this book fostered controversy. According to one Trinitarian apologist, Figueras held an "indiscreet fervor" of hatred for the Order of the Blessed Virgin of Mercy, and his treatise on the saint struck yet another blow in the endless struggles between the two rival orders.[100] His revision of St. Pedro Pascual's institutional loyalties (and name!) came to feature as just one element in a larger attempt to beef up the Trinitarian Order's thinly populated roster of saints by appropriating an increasingly famous and underdocumented candidate from the order's Mercedarian antagonists. The effort, which seems to have continued into the 1670s, was unsuccessful, and by September 3, 1661, Figueras's biography of the saint was condemned by the Congregation of Sacred Rites, together with all representations of St. Pedro Pascual that depicted him in Trinitarian, rather than Mercedarian, garb.[101]

A few years later, Figueras published again.[102] In 1645, while resident in Naples, Figueras put out his *Chronicum Ordinis Sanctissimae Trinitatis de redemptione*, a trimmed-down epitome of his *Annales* that omitted the long quotes from invented authors but that conveyed the same vision of Matha's life and of the order's medieval past. The *Chronicum* bore a license to publish signed by Louis Petit, the minister general, but given the odd choice to have the work printed in Verona rather than Naples, Figueras's inability to attend to the printing personally and the subsequent confused and error-ridden quality of the text, and the rumor that Petit's imprimatur was actually false, it seems possible that the circumstances that surrounded the publication were complicated, perhaps even clandestine.[103] Whatever the case may be, despite the *Chronicum*'s exceptionally poor editing and jumbled style, it quickly became one of Figueras's most successful and influential works.

About half of the volume comprised a history of the Order of the Most Holy Trinity and of the Captives from its origins through 1642, organized chronologically and structured around the succession of the Trinitarians' ministers general. Just as in the *Annales*, Figueras combined truth and fiction, the real and the imaginary, into a knot nearly impossible to disentangle. He stripped out much of the detail found in the *Annales*, limiting himself to a bare-bones recounting of key events and figures within the history of the order, especially the foundation of monasteries, the receipt of privileges, the deaths of martyrs, and the names and works of saintly and scholarly friars, many of whom were imaginary or appropriated from other religious orders (and at least one of whom, the celebrated Scholastic philosopher Henry of Ghent [ca. 1217–1293] was not a monastic at all, let alone a Trinitarian). Figueras also used the *Chronicum* to correct minor inconsistencies in his forgeries. Its brief recounting of the life and works of his supposed chronicler George Innes hewed much more closely to Dempster's version, which listed Innes's death as occurring in 1414, rather than the details scattered through the *Annales*, which had described Innes as actively writing in 1346. Figueras dropped the *Annales*' regular recounting of excursions into Islamic lands for the redemption of captives and much of its considerable apparatus of transcribed documents and quotes from authors both authentic and invented; instead, most sources appeared as brief citations within the text or in the margins. This extended narrative of the Trinitarians' past was followed by papal bulls, royal decrees, donations, and other archival sources organized around themes that related to controversies ongoing both within the order and with its adversaries: the Trinitarian rule and its modifications over the centuries; a list of all known Trinitarian houses, many of which existed only in Figueras's imagination; redemptions carried out by the Castilian and Portuguese provinces; internal governance and term limits; liturgical celebrations for the feast of St. Agnes; the struggle with the chapter of St. Peter over the possession of San Tommaso in Formis; royal and papal support for the establishment of the order in the kingdom of Aragon and its mission of redemptions; the history of the founding of the Order of Merced; the intersections between the Trinitarian rule and that of St. Benedict. As in the *Annales*, from which it was drawn, the *Chronicum*'s apparatus of primary sources combined genuine materials with invented ones.

Despite the *Chronicum*'s many flaws, it nevertheless became a vector point from which Figueras's reworking of the order's past was disseminated into Trinitarian historical scholarship. In coming decades, his dense web of interrelated inventions would spread into an ever-greater number of hagiographies of Matha and Valois and histories of the order, acquiring in the process both greater distance from its originator and greater authority and credibility from the sheer number of authors, each one citing his predecessors. Well into the nineteenth century, it served as a key reference for nearly all Trinitarian scholars writing on Matha and on the history of the order.[104] For example, the *Chronicum* was an important source for Francisco de Macedo's hagiographic *Vitae SS. Ioannis de Mattha, et Felicis de Valois, fundatorum Ordinis SS. Trinitatis* (Rome, 1660).[105] The author, a Portuguese Franciscan working under the sponsorship of the Spanish Discalced Trinitarian leadership, relied heavily on Figueras and his many spurious medieval sources.[106] Similarly, the *Chronicum* furnished key facts for Ignace Dilloud's *Les vies des Saints Jean de Matha et Félix de Valois, patriarches de l'Ordre de la Sainte Trinité, & Redemption des Captifs* (Paris, 1695). Dilloud, a member of the Reformed branch of the French Trinitarians, bolstered Figueras's credibility by noting that he was cited "par d'habiles Auteurs," including the celebrated Jesuit essayist Dominique Bouhours.[107]

Dilloud's invocation of Bouhours points to the ways in which the imagined past contained in the *Chronicum* also found its way beyond the limits of Trinitarian history. A single anecdote offers us an example of Figueras's wide readership. Citing materials said to be housed at the Portuguese royal archive and at the Trinitarian monastery in Lisbon, Figueras retold the story of Friar Pedro da Covilhã, a Portuguese Trinitarian who accompanied Vasco da Gama on his historic voyage to India and who supposedly predicted the coming of the Jesuits to India and the evangelizing work of St. Francis Xavier.[108] Covilhã was no figment of Figueras's imagination—he also appears in other, earlier Trinitarian sources, including Bernardino de Santo Antonio and López de Altuna—but the detail of his foretelling of the Jesuit mission in Asia appears to be Figueras's invention.[109] This hagiographical tidbit, coupled with the reference back to the *Chronicum*, soon found its way into the mainstream of biographies of Xavier, such as those by Bouhours (1683) and Francisco da Sousa (1710).[110] Sometimes, as in Francisco García's 1672 life of Xavier, the anecdote appeared without a direct citation of the *Chronicum* but with Figueras's exact wording.[111]

While Figueras's *Chronicum* was quite successful in propagating the Trinitarian Order's revised and expanded history, it was less useful in advancing the case for Matha's immemorial cult, partly because it omitted the full document citations that filled the pages of the *Annales* and partly because it left out the English breviary.[112] By the late 1640s, this document and, to a lesser degree, the supposed 1263 canonization had already come to occupy a central place in the campaign to win papal recognition of the immemorial cult of Sts. John of Matha and Felix of Valois. For example, the prayers and antiphons in honor of Matha and Valois figured prominently in both

González Dávila and Aznar in 1630—the same year in which, as we saw earlier, the leadership of the Calced Trinitarians of Castile attempted to win extension of that same office to the whole order. None of the witnesses who gave evidence in support of that effort had actually seen the breviary, but all confirmed that it was well known that Pope John XXII had granted the office and that the manuscript volume that preserved it was located in London. Somewhat different testimony came from witnesses questioned in late 1629 in connection with the Calced Trinitarians' case for Matha's immemorial cult. In interviews conducted in November and December of that year, twenty prominent worthies from Toledo, both clerics and laymen, gave evidence in favor of the antiquity of Matha's veneration. Intriguingly, several mentioned that images of the two founders, printed with the prayers and chants in honor of the saints drawn from the English breviary, were currently circulating in the area.[113] The inclusion of the English breviary in the questions asked of witnesses and the circulation of the saints' office, together with devotional images, reveals the growing importance of this document in the Trinitarians' efforts to ensure their founder's cult. Indeed, so central was the breviary to the campaign for Matha's immemorial cult and equivalent canonization that Jerónimo Vélez Matute—the same friar who, as we saw, came under heavy criticism from the commissioners for the Congregation of Sacred Rites in 1630 during their visit to the church of San Tommaso in Formis—on that very occasion (or, as we will see in chapter 4, perhaps another) had taken the opportunity to insert into Matha's tomb the slip of parchment with the prayer and chant from the mysterious English text: a transparent attempt to provide properly "medieval" evidence of veneration.[114]

Vélez Matute's extraordinary actions and his use of the English breviary strongly suggest that the campaign to manipulate evidence for Matha's immemorial veneration originated among the top leadership of the Spanish Calced Trinitarians. I have no smoking gun, but it seems highly probable that the English breviary, with its prayers and sung responses in praise of the Trinitarians' founders, was another of Figueras's useful historical inventions. There is no evidence of its existence prior to 1629—that is, one short year after Figueras's nomination to the position of general chronicler. Its original location was always described vaguely or as inaccessible (somewhere in Protestant London) or given no physical location at all. The breviary's earliest appearances are in texts by authors known to be in direct contact with Figueras, whose invented chronicler George Innes provided key support for its authenticity. In sum, the English breviary was a suspiciously convenient piece of evidence for Matha's immemorial cult—and, after the theft in 1655, for the identification of his stolen bones. Moreover, these facts also hint that Friar Figueras was no lone-wolf forger; rather, he worked in cooperation with or abetted by the Spanish Calced leadership.

The breviary texts appeared again in 1634 in François Aloès's ill-fated translation of González Dávila and again in 1637 in López de Altuna's chronicle. By the late 1640s, the Discalced wing of the Spanish Trinitarians seems to have begun to involve itself in the case for Matha's immemorial cult, and in 1649, the Discalced leadership arranged to have the English breviary prayers specially printed in Rome at the press of the Apostolic Camera with the required imprimatur of the master of the Apostolic Palace. In so doing, they assured the prayers' status as authentic and authoritative documents from the order's medieval past. In the 1649 printing, the apocryphal texts, which had appeared undated both in Figueras's *Annales* and in González Dávila, Aznar, and Aloès, acquired a specific date: "Commemorations for Saints John and Felix, taken from the breviary of the English province of the Order of the Most Holy Trinity Redemption of Captives, printed 1432." (A marginal note resolved the apparent anachronism of a printed book that predated Gutenberg by noting, "that is, written by hand on a leaf of parchment.")[115] The establishment of a date helped shore up the "medievalness" of the texts, a quality already signaled by Figueras's grammatical choices, such as a reliance on many connecting words (*ad, de*) and a preference for *et* as a conjunction between phrases, rather than the more classical *-que*. The 1649 edition also fixed the text, which had differed slightly from author to author. González Dávila and his translator Aloès had cited only the collect, or group prayer, to be said at Vespers in honor of the two founders, while Aznar's version mirrored that found in Figueras's *Annales* by including a second collect to be said at Lauds, as well as the antiphons and versicles that followed both. The inclusion of these details in the 1649 edition gave the prayers a proper liturgical framing within well-known, appropriate musical and textual references and, in so doing, made them that much more convincing as genuine medieval texts (figs. 2 and 3).

The 1649 printing of the invented English breviary was a brilliant success—it quickly came to figure as an essential reference for anyone, Trinitarian or otherwise, who wrote about the life of Matha or the history of the Trinitarian Order. The Discalced Trinitarians in particular made it a key proof in the developing case for Matha's immemorial cult and featured it prominently in a growing body of publications aimed at advancing the order's arguments in the court of public opinion and at deepening devotion to the founder. For example, both it and the other elements of Figueras's rendition

Fig. 2. Printed prayers and antiphons from the English breviary, 1649. Image drawn from the holdings of the National Library of Spain.

of the lives and works of the Trinitarians' founder featured prominently in *Fasciculus trium florum* (Rome, 1651), a hagiographic pamphlet published at the press of the Apostolic Camera by Juan de San Buenaventura, the Discalced branch's representative before the papal court.[116] Together, this slim publication and the 1649 English breviary edition soon found their way into a 1652 volume on the indulgences and privileges available to members of the lay confraternity associated with the order and into a 1655 sermon on the lives of Matha and Valois.[117]

Brief, ephemeral publications like these laid the groundwork for more extensive works that promoted the order's case for Matha's long-standing veneration. In the 1650s, the Discalced leadership found an ally in Juan Tamayo de Salazar (d. 1662), secretary to Inquisitor General Diego de Arce y Reinoso Ávila (1585–1665).[118] In 1659, Tamayo, a prolific and somewhat uncritical specialist in sacred history, included the breviary texts in the sixth

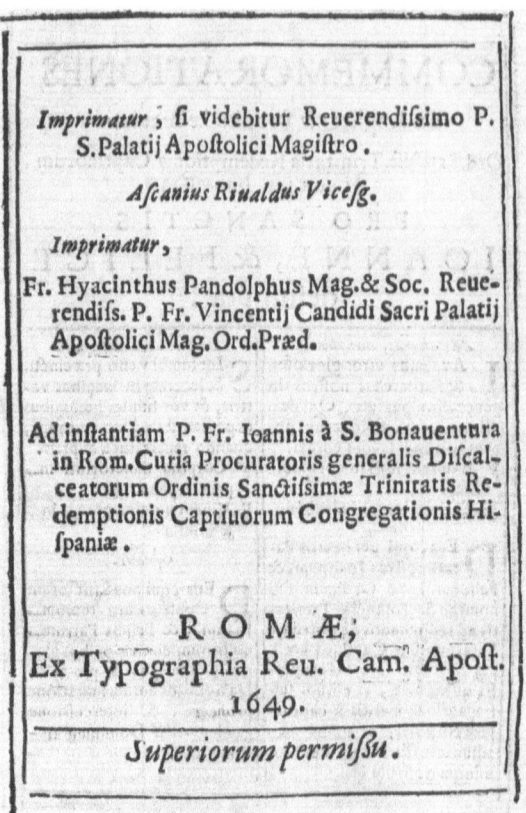

Fig. 3. Printed prayers and antiphons from the English breviary, 1649. Image drawn from the holdings of the National Library of Spain.

volume of his sprawling *Anamnesis sive Commemorationis sanctorum*, aka the *Martyrologium hispanum*. An exemplar of a growing genre of "national" hagiographies, this highly influential work aimed to catalogue the lives of "Spanish" saints, a broadly conceived category that included not merely saints from any of the kingdoms of Iberia but also the founders of any religious order with houses in the Iberian Peninsula.[119] Drawing heavily on Juan de San Buenaventura's *Fasciculus trium florum*, Tamayo supported the authenticity of the supposed canonization of Matha by Pope Urban IV in 1263 with the prayers and antiphons from the apocryphal English breviary alongside other commemorations celebrated during the first centuries of the order's existence (another of Figueras's inventions, a resolution in 1291 by the Trinitarian leadership at Cerfroid to celebrate both founders' feast days) and certain indulgences conceded by Pope Innocent X in the 1640s.[120] Similarly, the prayers and antiphons from the apocryphal English breviary featured prominently in the aforementioned *Vitae SS. Ioannis de Mattha, et Felicis de Valois, fundatorum Ordinis SS. Trinitatis* (1660) by Francisco de Macedo. This book advocated for Matha's immemorial cult by juxtaposing a full retelling of the lives of Matha and his companion as reworked by Figueras with two "corollaries," one on the Trinitarians' monastic rule, redemptions of captives, and martyrs for the faith and one on the arguments and evidence for the founders' sainthood.

The prayers and responses from the English breviary stood alongside images, altars, invocations, and other honors as powerful proofs of Matha's uninterrupted veneration over the centuries. As we saw in chapter 2, in first half of the 1650s, the Spanish Inquisition was troubled by reports of elaborate liturgical celebrations in Matha's honor held by both Discalced and Calced Trinitarians in Madrid, Andalusia, and elsewhere. These events seem to have first taken off in 1647, when the Discalced friars of Alcalá de Henares put on an elaborate and very public feast-day celebration in honor of Matha, complete with a sermon defending his long-standing veneration and an elegant new portrait of the saint above the main altar.[121] Similar celebrations were held in France, at the Discalced house in Aix-en-Provence.[122] Despite persistent controversy about the licitness of Matha's veneration, the Discalced leadership deemed the event to have been such a success that in 1650, the cult of the founders was made mandatory throughout the whole of the Discalced Trinitarian branch.[123] Celebrations in honor of Matha and his colleague continued and even increased in prominence in the second half of the decade and into the early years of the 1660s. Like the hagiographies and histories that cited the English breviary, these events were part of a larger campaign to increase the Trinitarian founders' visibility to and veneration by the wider public. They were often ostentatious affairs, advertised days in advance with public proclamations and printed handbills, lanterns, and fireworks, in order to attract the greatest number of attendees to the elaborate Mass and eloquent sermon.[124] They also often offered the incentive of plenary indulgences, secured by papal bulls.[125] Those held in Madrid sometimes attracted powerful figures at the royal court—feast-day celebrations for Matha and Valois held in the late 1640s, for example, were attended by the papal nuncio, Cardinal Giulio Rospigliosi (the future Pope Clement IX), while another in 1653 or 1654 hosted Nuncio Francesco Gaetano.[126] The sermons preached on these grand occasions extolled the order's founders and retold key moments in their legends; when funds allowed, the texts were printed to better advertise their lives and merits. The Calced Trinitarians of Madrid and Valencia, in particular, seem to have invested in publishing their sermons in honor of Matha and Valois, with at least four published in Valencia between 1655 and 1661 and two in Madrid in 1658 and 1659.[127]

Public liturgical celebrations and historical treatises advertised Matha's sainthood; so too did the dissemination of hagiographic images of Matha and his cofounder.[128] Movements to spread Matha's likeness were probably already under way by the late 1620s—the aforementioned witness testimony gathered in Toledo in 1629 included several mentions of hagiographic prints of Matha and Valois circulating in the city. Many religious orders deployed such images, often engraved or even woodcut, as affordable and portable means of promoting the fame and prestige of their particular saints, and it seems likely that the campaign to shore up Matha's cult through inventive history writing would have been accompanied by efforts to spread his image both among the order's own members and among the laity.[129] The Trinitarian leadership in Paris undertook an early initiative to spread the order's iconography when, in 1606, Louis Petit, then secretary to his uncle, Minister General François Petit, commissioned an engraving titled *Institutio ordinis SSmae Trinitatis redemptionis*, which featured the cross-armed angel, the kneeling and shackled Christian and Muslim captives, and the three persons of the Holy Trinity.[130] In 1612, Louis Petit succeeded to his uncle's office, and in the early 1630s, he revived his early efforts and developed an elaborate campaign to advance Matha's veneration through art. In 1633, he sponsored the publication of a series of elegant print engravings designed by Theodor van Thulden (1606–1669), a talented Dutch painter and engraver. These images, which reproduced a collection of twenty-four paintings created by Thulden for the Parisian Trinitarians' choir stalls, advertised the founders' holy lives and works as well as the Trinitarians' work redeeming captives in North Africa.[131] The engravings reiterated key moments of Matha's developing legend (though some elements they depicted, such as the infant John of Matha's inclination toward the baptismal font, did not appear in Figueras or his sources and may represent more local, French traditions). Petit further reinforced the hagiographic imagery of the paintings and engravings with a new main altar for the Paris church in 1647. The remodeled altar featured at its center a painting of the Trinity, flanked by statues of Matha and Valois and topped by a statue of the Trinitarians' iconic angel holding the chains of a Christian and a Muslim captive.[132]

Spanish Trinitarians were not far behind their French colleagues in creating images to advertise Matha's holy life and deeds. In 1634, the Discalced friars of Madrid undertook a similar project when they contracted with the celebrated Florentine artist Vicente Carducho (1576–1638) for a cycle of twelve paintings depicting key moments in the life of the saint. Some images, like the miraculous wind that returned a ship of freed captives from Tunisia to Rome or the vision of St. Peter that convinced the erudite but humble Matha to accept a doctoral degree, reflected the new, enhanced *vita* developed by Figueras. Others, like Matha's mystic experience at the moment of his first Mass and Innocent III's reiteration of the vision and his confirmation of the new Trinitarian order, depicted episodes that were part of the oldest strands of Matha's legend. Such images, which were commonly displayed in those sections of monastic houses not subject to cloister, instructed both the friars and their lay visitors in Matha's miracles and virtues and helped foster veneration toward him.[133] Despite the public festivities, sermons, and stories, there is little evidence for Matha's and Valois's popularity among the laity—in 1649, a widow in Rome reported that she had been healed of terrible pain through direct application of an "image of the most blessed Trinity of Redemption."[134] Among members of the order, however, a handful of prophecies fulfilled and portentous events were testimony to rising devotion to the founders.[135]

In sum, by the end of the 1650s, Trinitarians of all varieties were busily engaged in projects to advance Matha's veneration and to uncover or create proofs to support the case for his immemorial cult. Figueras's historical inventions, including the English breviary and the 1263 canonization, had found their way into a host of histories, sermons, artworks, and other discursive media that, coupled with the very public celebrations staged by Trinitarian monasteries, spread the story of Matha's life, works, and miracles. The cumulative effect of this dissemination was to put some daylight between the new hagiographical facts and their creator, transforming them into the *pública voz y fama*, common knowledge held to be true by all. It is unclear how much Figueras's fabrications and the forged sources that supported them owed to oral lore and traditions already in circulation among the friars before the 1630s—whether, for example, the miraculous wind that blew the ship from Tunisia to Rome or Matha's service as a papal legate to Dalmatia were tales that came to be told over the course of the centuries before they found their way into Figueras's *Annales* and *Chronicum*. By the 1660s, however, such stories were well on their way to being indispensable features of Matha's saintly *vita* and canonical elements of the Trinitarian Order's origin story, stories well known and accepted both by members of the order and by their lay friends and supporters. Their transformation into broadly accepted common knowledge would make them important proofs for Matha's immemorial cult, as the *pública voz y fama* of the founders was one of the categories of evidence about which witnesses would be asked to give testimony.

Whether Figueras drew on existing oral traditions or whether he fabricated them from the conventions and commonplaces of the legends of the saints (or, as is likely, did both), his inventions were not merely fabrications or falsehoods—they were also statements about what many Trinitarians must have believed their history to have been. Figueras's forgeries proved what the friars already knew to be true about their saintly founder and about their order's distinguished past. For medieval writers, forgery could be "a mode of historical writing."[136] So too for early modern historians, some of whom turned to forgery in order to validate cherished visions of the past on which were founded devotions, local patriotisms, or, in the case of the Trinitarians, institutional and corporate identity.[137] Those who adopted Figueras's inventions were not simply gullible or credulous. As Katrina Olds has demonstrated in another context, "careful consideration of one's sources, and what looks, in retrospect, like 'credulity,' were not seen as mutually incompatible by the scholars who wrote sacred history in the late sixteenth and seventeenth centuries."[138] Many writers of sacred history felt that the history of the Church should be shaped more by moral purpose than by historical accuracy—that what mattered was not just truth but Truth. This interpretive mode, grounded in the traditional notion that history should serve higher ends, required practitioners to approach the saints and their sources in a spirit of "pious affection," a generous posture that did not preclude critical inquiry but gave latitude for the imperfections of historical evidence.[139] Calls for rigorous evaluation of the sources for knowledge of the past were a commonplace among early modern historians—we have already seen such comments in the form of criticisms leveled against Figueras by Bernardino de San Antonio—but even the Portuguese friar's rhetoric of truth as "the soul of history" was not incompatible with a concern for the higher truths of doctrine.

By the same logic, neither Figueras nor the Castilian Calced Trinitarian leaders who sponsored him can be easily dismissed as unscrupulous purveyors of lies. There was more to the forgeries than the calculated manipulation of the past. The interpretive approach of pious affection, usually deployed in the critique of historical sources, perhaps can help us understand the fabrication of those same sources. While nobody openly endorsed forgery, it seems likely that a generous approach toward the sources for history may have extended to the crafting of those same sources—that is, in cases in which the needs of devotion, so closely linked to community identity, applied, the ends might conceivably have justified the means. On the other hand, it is also true that without the forgeries, the Trinitarians' case for Matha's immemorial veneration was very weak, especially given the Congregation of Sacred Rites' growing preference for documentary evidence. Figueras's censure by the general chapter in Cerfroid in 1635 makes it clear that if there was a scheme to falsify the order's history, it was not based in the central leadership in France but among the top administrators of the Castilian Calced province. The order stood to gain a great deal by Figueras's historical innovations, and it is likely that some in the Castilian leadership collaborated with the inventive friar to facilitate their dissemination and acceptance.

Indeed, it seems probable that the 1655 theft of St. John of Matha's bones from San Tommaso in Formis was a key element of this effort and of the larger project to prove Matha's immemorial cult and shore up his sainthood. While both the witnesses' testimony and later Trinitarian commentators presented the break-in and robbery as the rash act of two low-ranking lay brothers, Medina and Vidal's crime makes considerably more sense if interpreted as a ploy developed and orchestrated by their superiors to bring the relics under the order's control and transport them to Spain, where they could become the focus of veneration. "The Trinitarians needed the relics of John of Matha as an essential proof in the case for recognition of his immemorial cult," María Cruz de Carlos Varona has argued, since "the relics of John of Matha lay in a half-ruined church, without any cult or attendance by the faithful and, what was worse, forgotten for centuries. No one would believe the Trinitarians if they presented some relics saying that they belonged to their founder, even if they were authentic. They needed the [legal] proceedings about the theft to call attention to them and the [legal] proceedings about their identity to make clear their authenticity once the remains reached Madrid."[140] Decaying, abandoned, and under the control of the canons of the Vatican chapter, the little church of San Tommaso in Formis presented a serious problem for Matha's advocates. By removing his bones from the premises, the theft resolved the issue by demonstrating not the lack of cult but a devotion so ardent that the saint's devotees would willingly risk all to ensure his veneration. It also diverted attention away from San Tommaso in Formis, where material evidence of cult was utterly lacking, to sites (mainly in Castile and Aragon) where statues, paintings, and other demonstrations of veneration could be found. Indeed, aside from the inscription atop the tomb, San Tommaso in Formis scarcely figures at all among the proofs eventually submitted in 1665 to the Congregation of Sacred Rites as evidence of Matha's immemorial cult.[141]

De Carlos Varona has suggested that the masterminds behind the theft were Pedro Arias Portocarrero, the *procurador general* for the Castilian

Calced branch, and his colleague Francisco de Arcos, the minister provincial for Castile and the same figure who had brought the case of Matha's relics to King Philip IV. Arias seems to have had the reputation among his confrères of being Arcos's right-hand man. Calced Trinitarian friars who testified in the course of a 1656 investigation into Arcos's tenure as minister provincial complained that Arcos had not punished Arias for his role in the theft but instead had relied on his aid to "dishonor the religion and [further] his ambitions" and had sent Arias to Rome without consulting the senior members of the Madrid monastery.[142] To this duo of probable plotters, we might add Jerónimo Vélez Matute, the friar who had overseen the first attempts before the Congregation of Sacred Rites in 1630 and who had inserted the passages from the English breviary into Matha's tomb. The trio knew each other well, since all three were closely involved in the Calced branch's affairs both in Castile and in Rome, and it was these three men who came together in November 1655 to hand over the stolen remains to the papal nuncio. On the other hand, their duties sometimes put them in conflict; indeed, it was Vélez who, acting as an apostolic inspector for the Congregation of Bishops and Regulars, investigated Arcos in 1656 and eventually deposed him from his office.[143] Given the gap of twenty-five to thirty years between them, it seems less likely that the persons who planned the theft were also involved in facilitating the historical impostures of Juan Figueras Carpi. Instead, the two separate efforts suggest the importance of Matha's cult to the Castilian Calced wing as a site of institutional identity and memory.

In the long run, however, the pious plot backfired. In opening up the question of the identity of the relics, the theft of Matha's remains seems to have created more problems than it solved, and it may also have won the Castilian Calced Trinitarians some powerful enemies in Rome. Perhaps as a consequence, in the years that followed the theft, the Calced wing seems to have stepped back from a leadership role in the effort to win recognition of Matha's immemorial cult. Instead, it would be the Discalced branch that would shoulder the project, first of Matha's immemorial cult and saintly status and later of the identity of his relics. As the Discalced Trinitarians took up the task in the late 1650s and early 1660s, they could count on an ever more solid foundation of historical and hagiographical "facts" that were supported by a formidable array of documentary proofs and broadcast by a growing number of publications, festivities, and images that spread devotion to Matha and Valois among the rank-and-file members of the order they founded and, to a lesser degree, among the public at large.

Antonio Lupián Zapata

But something was missing. Whether it was because the key evidence was false or insufficient or, as I suspect, because Figueras's *Annales* had failed to reach print and his *Chronicum* was inadequate to the task of proving Matha's immemorial cult, the Discalced Trinitarians commissioned a new chronicle of the order. This time, they turned not to one of their own but to a historian-for-hire, a Madrid-based royal chronicler and notary of noble background from Roussillon named Antonio Lupián Zapata. Between 1661 and 1665, Lupián churned out five thick volumes of the *Chrónica general de la sagrada orden de la Santíssima Trinidad de Redención de Cautivos Cristianos*, each bristling with details about the life and works of the founder and the order's progress through the centuries. His vision of Matha and of the Trinitarian Order's medieval past differed little from that of his predecessor, Figueras, but his deep research enriched his retelling with important new particulars, such as the titles and genres of St. John of Matha's surprisingly large literary output and the Catalan origins of Matha's family.[144] Lupián's archival digging uncovered a wide array of exciting new sources, such as an early fourteenth-century history of the hermits of France by Gravelino, a Benedictine monk from Marseilles. From Gravelino, for example, we learn that before launching the Trinitarian Order, Matha had served as a member of the cathedral clergy in Paris and that Pope Urban IV—the same pontiff who supposedly canonized Matha in 1263—had been brought up at the Trinitarian mother house at Cerfroid.[145] Gravelino was also Lupián's main source for his discussion of the pious conversations that passed between Matha and his cofounder, St. Felix of Valois, conversations also documented in never-before-cited passages from the English breviary itself.[146]

The prominent role of the English breviary in Lupián's chronicle points us toward the truth of the matter: like Friar Figueras, Lupián was not who he claimed to be, and like his predecessor, he was a forger, and a prolific one to boot. According to his own accounts, Antonio Lupián Zapata (or Antonio de Lupián Zapata or Antonio Lupián de Zapata) was born in 1604 or 1605, the scion of a noble Catalan family.[147] Educated in a Benedictine monastery, Lupián pursued his interests in historical research in archives in France and Italy and throughout the Spanish kingdoms until 1639, when he assumed control of his family's patrimony after his brother's death in royal service in Flanders. In 1640, he suffered multiple injuries while fighting against invading French troops and endured heavy financial and personal losses when the family lands were burned. Lupián fled to Castile when Cataluña erupted into revolt that same year, moving first to Briviesca, then Burgos, and finally Madrid. Plunged into penury by the loss of his family lands to France in the Treaty of the Pyrenees in 1659, by the early 1660s, Lupián was earning his living by his pen while he sought a position in the royal administration for the kingdom of Aragon. By around the same time, he was also styling himself as head chaplain of Santa María de Requesens, a rural church on the border between France and Cataluña, and petitioning the king for an ecclesiastical pension.[148] He also claimed to enjoy the titles of apostolic notary, royal chronicler, and later, either dean or provost of the cathedral of Ibiza.[149] He died in Ibiza in 1667.[150]

Lupián's critics, however, told a different story. He could not have been a well-educated nobleman, said one, since "well informed people noted from his pronunciation of Latin and Castilian that he was not [a noble] Catalan, but an uneducated Catalan from the towns where Cataluña borders on France."[151] His real name, they said, was Antonio de Nobis, and he was the son not of a nobleman from Roussillon but of a surgeon from Thuir, a small town near Perpignan. Some detractors said he had frequented Benedictine monasteries throughout Spain, France, and beyond in his capacity as a skilled maker of church organs and that these connections had allowed him access to archives from which he had stolen documents and into which he had seeded false materials.[152] Others said that Antonio de Nobis had traveled to Flanders in the service of a Catalan nobleman whose surname he had assumed upon returning to the Iberian Peninsula. "Afterward, he gave himself over to stirring up papers and acquiring information about past events. He made ill use of this information, writing many false things, making up out of his own head royal and imperial privileges and even apostolic bulls, not with the aim of causing harm but of fooling many noblemen about the brilliance of their family names."[153] Some critics claimed that Lupián was neither a royal chronicler nor an apostolic notary, given that no corroborating records of the award of these positions could be found. Others contended that his priesthood was a sham, since he had never once been known to celebrate Mass.[154] Whoever he really was, it is clear that Antonio Lupián Zapata was as much of a self-inventor as his predecessor, Friar Juan Figueras Carpi.

Lupián was a prolific forger. He seems to have worked in a wide range of genres, from chronicles to genealogies to medieval documents of all sorts. The most infamous of his historical inventions was the chronicle of Hauberto, a Benedictine monk of Seville active in the second half of the ninth century. This false chronicle, which Lupián claimed to have discovered in Paris in the Abbey of Saint-Denis, provided much fodder for would-be historians writing on ancient and early medieval Iberia, periods for which there was little documentary evidence, and its impact on seventeenth- and eighteenth-century historical scholarship was deep.[155] Other notorious forgeries included a catalogue of early Christian martyrs attributed to St. Gregory of Elvira (ca. 320–393) and a document recording the voluntary incorporation of the Basque territory of Gipuzkoa into the kingdom of Castile in 1200.[156] These were but a handful of Lupián's many impostures, however, and while perhaps not every word he wrote was false, his works should be approached with extreme caution, since genuine sources regularly rubbed elbows with false and faked documents of all sorts.[157] It was not until after Lupián's death in 1667, however, that critics began to uncover his many impostures. Until then, the leaders of the Discalced branch of the Trinitarian Order were perfectly happy to sponsor his *Chrónica general*, paying him ten silver *reales* for each quire (*pliego*) of sixteen pages of manuscript text—a decent but not hugely generous sum, given that half a *real* would have bought a two-pound loaf of bread in Madrid's markets.[158]

For the structure of the text, Lupián turned to Antonio de Yepes (ca. 1552–1618), the "Cesare Baronio of his Order of St. Benedict," and his magisterial, seven-volume *Corónica general de la Orden de San Benito*.[159] Lupián took Yepes as his model, imitating his method of organization, in which each volume covered a century of the Benedictine Order's existence, starting from the birth of its founder in 480 CE, and in which Yepes's careful and exhaustive archival work was revealed not only in numerous direct citations within the text but also in an appendix of key documents included in each volume. Following Yepes's structure and using Figueras as his foundation, he expanded the scope of Trinitarian history backward from 1198 to the early twelfth century, to the birth of St. Felix of Valois in 1128, and forward to 1597. According to Lupián, the newly established Trinitarian Order absorbed a previously existing body, a military order of Trinitarian knights said to have been operating in the Iberian Peninsula in the middle of the twelfth century.[160] Among the famous members of this shadowy military order were the martyred archbishop of Canterbury, St. Thomas à Becket (d. 1170); Duke William X of Aquitaine (1099–1137); and St. Pere Nolasc, the founder of the Mercedarian Order. In support of this unexpected revelation, the appendix to the first volume of Lupián's *Chrónica general* included a copy of a 1226 agreement between the Knights Templar and the Trinitarian Knights, signed by Nolasc and others.[161]

Unsurprisingly, this document was a forgery, one of several fabricated by Lupián to bolster the Trinitarians' position in their long-running legal struggle with the Mercedarian friars over begging rights and pious bequests and one of dozens of invented sources that riddle the text of the *Chrónica general*. Like Figueras, Lupián claimed to have uncovered these new records in the course of research conducted during the 1630s and 1640s in archives throughout Spain, France, and Italy. Some sources he found reprinted in the works of other historians; still others he received from scholarly friends and informants.[162] For the most part, his account of the lives and deeds of the Trinitarians' founders and of the order's progress through the centuries followed in the path laid down by Juan Figueras Carpi and his imitators. Where his account deviated from Figueras was not so much in the interpretive bent of his historical narrative but in the details of the lives of Matha and Valois and of the order's medieval past. For example, Lupián elaborated on Matha's bare-bones genealogy as it appeared in Figueras, Macedo, and others, transforming him from the son of Eufremio de Mata, a Provençal nobleman, into a descendant of the Mataplana clan, one of the oldest and most prestigious noble families in Cataluña.[163] This new pedigree rested on multiple invented sources, including a sworn statement (dated 1192) by Maurice de Sully, bishop of Paris, that testified to the presence of "Joannes de Mataplana" as a member of the cathedral chapter of Paris, a 1201 royal order that granted the Trinitarian Order the right to collect alms within Aragon, and two 1212 donations from Sancho, Count of Rousillon.[164] It also relied on one of Lupián's many previous forgeries, a genealogy of the noble families of Cataluña attributed to the chronicler Ramon Muntaner (1265–1336).[165]

Like Figueras, Lupián manipulated the signs of authority by mixing quotations and references to writers both genuine and imagined, building on his predecessor's forgeries by listing them as authorities and by citing them alongside his own inventions. For the supposed 1263 canonization, for example, he quoted four sources: Figueras's forged chronicle of George Innes, Figueras's *Chronicum*, a 1655 French treatise based on Figueras, and an imaginary Trinitarian chronicle from the late thirteenth century that Lupián ascribed to Friar Ferrario Grait (d. 1269?).[166] This last source is yet another of Figueras's forgeries, but one for which there survives no text.[167] Lupián took up Grait's name and the title of the missing chronicle and, by means of references and quotations, expanded it into a full-fledged invented source, complete with a date (1279).[168] In other cases, Lupián seems to have crafted new documents to fit "facts" fabricated by his predecessor. In one instance, Figueras's forged source, Innes, described a number of memoranda signed by witnesses to Matha's original vision on the occasion of his first Mass, all preserved "in some ancient manuscript parchment book" of the deeds of Maurice de Sully, bishop of Paris.[169] Lupián embroidered on this detail by crafting a letter, dated 1193 and signed by the head of the Abbey of Saint-Victor in Paris, that provided eyewitness testimony of Matha's miraculous vision of Christ and the two captives. This forgery, together with other documents both genuine and fake, he inserted into the appendix to the first volume of the *Chrónica general*. In his capacity as a notary, he certified these transcriptions as faithful copies of the originals. In so doing, he imbued them with his *fides publica*, his authority as the bearer of the public trust, and transformed them into not just historical evidence but also legal evidence with probative force.[170]

For Lupián, the truth value of a historical text was closely connected to the authoritativeness of the documents on which it rested and the archives that held those documents. Archives and their contents, he opined, are "the perfection and the quintessence of histories"; histories are rectified and corrected by archival documents, since they are "of greater credence than histories."[171] Lupián regularly employed documents to correct the accounts of other historians. In the case of Minister General Thierry de Vareland (r. 1410–13), for example, he cited Figueras's brief account from the *Chronicum* but corrected and expanded it with (invented? genuine?) materials that he claimed to have received from the Franciscan historian Luke Wadding. López de Altuna's version, he lamented, was in error: "and it grieves me to find in this author so many things that go against the truth of history."[172] Both his reliance on archival sources and his name-dropping of respected figures like Wadding were strategies to shore up his bona fides and ensure the acceptance of his forgeries; so too were his indications of the locations of particular bulls, donations, or other documents. Alongside his regular references to the archives of individual Trinitarian monasteries throughout France and the Iberian Peninsula, Lupián cited materials housed in prestigious Benedictine and Cistercian monasteries and convents; in royal and cathedral archives in cities like Lisbon, Barcelona, Burgos, Toledo, and Paris; and in the library of the Count of Gondomar and the private archives of numerous noble Catalan and Aragonese families.[173]

Unlike Figueras, who depended primarily on print books and manuscripts, Lupián supplemented his written materials with a wide range of nontextual sources. He regularly cited paintings and frescoes as testimony to the holy lives and deeds of celebrated sons and daughters of the order and ruins as evidence for monasteries and convents no longer standing. Local oral traditions, too, provided Lupián with much material, especially for more recent centuries. In general, however, both as a historian and as a forger, his methods resembled those of his predecessor, whose forgeries remained firmly anchored to his historical text and to the thick snarl of interwoven references and quotations that both constituted them and supported them.[174] Like Figueras, Lupián built up the credibility of his invented sources by seeding them into the works of unsuspecting colleagues. For example, one of his more frequently cited apocryphal (?) writers was one Pierre de Espoleto, the author of works on the saints and bishops of Paris and of Meaux, on England's King Henry VIII, and on "the bishops of England, Scotland, Ireland, Flanders, and Germany, some of which catalogs have gone to press."[175] I can find no references to this shadowy figure anywhere, except in a life of the Benedictine mystic St. Gertrude the Great (1256–ca. 1302), published in 1663 by the prolific Jesuit historian Alonso de Andrade (d. 1672). According to Andrade, Espoleto ("an erudite man, of great reputation in his nation") made a French translation of an early life of St. Gertrude the Great of Helfta; his version was later translated into Spanish by "learned people, devotees of the saint," who then passed them on to Andrade.[176] Might these "learned people" have been Antonio Lupián Zapata? It seems possible, since five years later, Andrade published a hagiographic life of St. John of Matha and St. Felix of Valois that was based closely on Lupián's manuscript *Chrónica general* and its forged sources.[177] In the prologue, Andrade noted that he had met and conversed with Lupián when the latter had been living in Madrid—that is, precisely when Lupián was busily writing his history of the Trinitarian Order.[178]

Like Figueras, Lupián also developed wholly new events and records in support of the founders' long-standing veneration and the Trinitarians' reimagined past. One example, dated August 10, 1219, documented a pact between the friars at Cerfroid and the bishop and cathedral chapter of Meaux. In this contract, the bishop and chapter pledged to come to the monastery and recite the canonical hours with the Trinitarians each year "on Trinity Sunday and [on the feast of] the confessor Felix, who rests in that very place, famous for his merits," while the Trinitarians promised to come to the cathedral for the feasts of the Assumption and the Nativity of Mary.[179] No such agreement can be found in Figueras, and while the archive of the Trinitarians at Cerfroid has long been dispersed and cannot be directly consulted, no such contract appears in a 1634 inventory of the monastery's important records. Instead, it seems clear that Lupián fabricated the whole affair, since both the event and the document that recorded it made their first appearance in November 1661 in the appendix to Lupián's *Annales*. It later resurfaced in October 1664, in Lupián's deposition before a panel of investigators seeking testimony about Matha and Valois's immemorial cult (on which, more shortly).[180]

Lupián also built on his predecessor's work by providing critical support for the English breviary. The breviary's accounts of the Trinitarians' founders, he claimed, were grounded not in false or apocryphal narratives but in archival documents, "authentic histories that are very authoritative and guarded," including one signed by Pope Innocent III himself and held in the library of Cardinal Barberini in Rome.[181] Though the original English breviary itself had unfortunately "passed into the flames" in the persecution launched by Henry VIII, transcriptions could be found in Benedictine monasteries in Flanders and Ireland.[182] Its prayers to St. John of Matha could also be found in several late thirteenth- and early fourteenth-century manuscripts held in several Benedictine monasteries in Cataluña and Castile.[183] Moreover, Lupián alleged that the English hymns and hagiographical readings on Matha could be found in medieval texts in Albi and other French dioceses and that commemorations of the Trinitarians' founders were also preserved in liturgical texts in Elna, San Millán de la Cogolla, and elsewhere. Those imaginary sources demonstrated that devotion to Matha and his cofounder had long been widespread throughout the order; they also allowed Lupián to expand on the existing breviary texts and to invent several more extracts that fleshed out his treatment of the order's founders, especially of Matha's colleague St. Felix of Valois. Felix, he claimed, could also be found in the liturgical calendars of the Spanish Benedictine monasteries of Rosas (Girona) and Santo Domingo de Silos and in the martyrology of the Benedictine monastery at Châteauponsac—proof positive of his long-standing veneration.[184]

Eventually, Lupián seems to have taken the next step and become a forger in a more material sense, one whose historical inventions mimicked not only the textual qualities of medieval documents but also their physical appearance. Over the course of several days in October 1664, Lupián gave sworn evidence in his capacity as an expert witness about the history of St. John of Matha's long-standing veneration. His declaration formed part of a larger dossier of witness statements gathered in Rome, Madrid, and in other Spanish cities that formed a key part of the Discalced Trinitarians' case before the Congregation of Sacred Rites for Matha's immemorial cult. In his testimony, Lupián listed all of the many books, both printed and manuscript, that referred to John of Matha as a saint or discussed his life and works. Among these were the many liturgical books that preserved the English breviary's prayers and responses in praise of St. John of Matha. While he left their locations vague, he described the books carefully in words calculated to convey their distance in time, their very medievalness. For example, a breviary he claimed to have seen in the French diocese of Meaux he described this way: "handwritten on parchment in very ancient letters . . . in the French hand they used before there was printing, with wooden covers, and hinges, straps, and clasps of copper, which all argues for great age, although I don't remember where in the bishopric I saw the aforementioned breviary."[185] In another case, however, Lupián went much further. From a copy of the English breviary that he claimed to have read in Flanders, although he could not "remember in what place it was," he not only read into the record the full text of the liturgical lesson for Matha's cofounder St. Felix of Valois but also presented what he claimed were pages extracted from the original manuscript itself (figs. 4, 5, and 6). He insisted that they be included with the dossier, saying,

> As a demonstration of the quality and antiquity of the aforementioned breviary, I exhibit these two pages from it, and I ask that your Eminence order that the originals be sent with this dossier. I would turn over all the other pages if I had them with me, since I have them a hundred and twenty-two leagues away from this court in the church of my priory of Santa María de Requesens. [But] since the fragments of the aforementioned breviary are in among a great apparatus of papers and it would be very difficult or impossible for anyone other than me to extract them or understand them, and [since] I cannot go myself because I am at present occupied in pressing obligations as chronicler to his Majesty at this court, I therefore do not [go], nor can I present the breviary for now. But I have already sent for them and as soon as those fragments arrive in my hands I am ready and disposed to send them to the Congregation of Sacred Rites.[186]

The check, it seems, was in the mail.

I have not yet determined whether the manuscript parchment pages that he enclosed with the dossier are authentic medieval documents lifted from some archive or library or forgeries crafted by Lupián to give verisimilitude to his inventions. Either seems plausible, since after his death, his critics accused him of stealing genuine manuscript documents from archives and

Fig. 4. Medieval breviary pages, date unknown. Archive of San Carlino alle Quattro Fontane, leg. 16c, pieza XVI/16: "Culto immemorial de nuestros Santos Patriarcas S. Juan y S. Félix (Madrid) (1663–1664)," n.p. Photo: author.

Fig. 5. Medieval breviary pages, date unknown. Archive of San Carlino alle Quattro Fontane, leg. 16c, pieza XVI/16: "Culto immemorial de nuestros Santos Patriarcas S. Juan y S. Félix (Madrid) (1663–1664)," n.p. Photo: author.

Fig. 6. Medieval breviary pages, date unknown. Archive of San Carlino alle Quattro Fontane, leg. 16c, pieza XVI/16: "Culto immemorial de nuestros Santos Patriarcas S. Juan y S. Félix (Madrid) (1663–1664)," n.p. Photo: author.

altering them for his own purposes and of baking papers in order to give them the appearance of age. Others claimed to have seen the tools of forgery—special pens and inks—in his study.[187] However, if they are fakes, they are very good ones, and given their appearance, I am inclined to think that they are genuine manuscripts from the fourteenth or fifteenth centuries.

In either case, these pages offer us a window into early modern engagements and encounters with the Middle Ages. The breviary pages reveal seventeenth-century ideas about medieval manuscripts—what they should look like and sound like, what made them convincing as medieval manuscripts—and the power of one written object to stand in for another, absent one. These parchment folios had nothing to do with John of Matha—the prayers and lessons they contained honored St. Clare of Assisi, St. Bernard of Clairvaux, St. Euphemia, and St. Martha of Bethany. Instead, they evoked other, imaginary pages in honor of the Trinitarians' founder and a larger imaginary text that testified to the order's long-standing devotion to its saints and to its many centuries of history. The material dissimilarity between the colorful parchment leaves, with their medieval Latin script, and the paper pages of witness testimony inscribed in a tidy seventeenth-century hand with black ink (now browning) hammered home their distance in time and evoked not just the missing English breviary but the whole of the Trinitarian Order's long past.[188] Their presence within the dossier revealed not just Lupián's awareness of the Middle Ages as distant in time but also his willingness to deploy that distance and visible difference to convey graphically his larger argument for Matha's continuous veneration. It was a medievalism that did not mourn or fetishize the past but deployed it for practical purposes, an "old wine [that] was definitely being bottled for immediate consumption and 'appreciation,' not for storage or aging."[189]

The breviary pages also highlight Lupián's reliance on the truth claims embedded in his insistence on his role as an eyewitness and as a notary. The *Chrónica general* teems with assertions of having personally seen and consulted rare, inaccessible, or lost original documents, images, and other evidence, such as paintings he saw as a student in Lérida or the foundation charter for a new church built in Burgos in 1366: "which [papers] I have held in my unworthy hands."[190] In other cases, Lupián's evidence was grounded in other kinds of personal experience, for example, an incorrupt corpse of a Trinitarian lay sister encountered in 1644, a miracle witnessed in 1646, relics of St. Thomas à Becket and St. Hilarion inspected in Burgos, or festivities for a St. Farriolo.[191] The medieval breviary pages included in the witness dossier rely on similar claims of eyewitness experience but also on Lupián's trustworthiness as a historian and as a notary. For both Lupián and his predecessor, such trustworthiness was critical to their success as forgers. Their credibility was rooted in large part in their fidelity in reproducing the sources on which they drew—as one follower of Figueras commented, "And I believe Master Figueras, for any authors I sought in him I found faithfully cited."[192] That same fidelity to the known sources rendered their invented and falsified sources that much more believable.

The invented sources' credibility may also have been linked to their personal connections to the institution whose history they chronicled and to the purposes and contexts in which they wrote. Figueras's status as a son of the Trinitarian Order may have made him that much more believable, at least for his fellow friars and nuns, readers who shared that affiliation. His impostures were created not for lucre but for the greater glory of the religious order to which he belonged. Lupián, by contrast, was a hired pen, paid for his labors by the Discalced Trinitarians—a fact seized on by critics who noted that "[Lupián's] authority still is of less estimation than that of Figueras, since the latter spoke for passion, and the former for pay."[193] While it is difficult to measure how much Lupián's outsider status affected his credibility and the long-term success of his historical inventions, his forgeries seem to have attracted much more vehement critical opposition, due in no small measure to their prominent role in the never-ending struggles between the Trinitarian and Mercedarian Orders. Figueras's forged documents touched on the history and origins of the Order of the Blessed Virgin of Mercy, but his interventions were fewer and less heavy-handed than those of Lupián, who seems to have manufactured a wide array of royal privileges and other historical sources for his Trinitarian patrons.[194] These forged materials, deployed as ammunition in the legal struggles between the two rival orders over the right to seek alms and donations within the kingdom of Aragon, were far more visible than those of Figueras, and Lupián's reputation suffered as a result. By the end of the seventeenth century, his name had become synonymous with fraud and scholarly bad faith. Lupián makes an appearance, for example, alongside famous rebels and con artists in a 1680 book of political and moral guidance.[195] By contrast, Figueras's standing as a sound and citable scholar remained largely intact well into the eighteenth century.[196] While some invested readers might take a posture of pious affection toward sacred history and the imperfect evidence on which it rested, others, operating in different contexts with different assumptions, might be less inclined to overlook impostures and falsifications. Forgery, it seems, offended more in some situations than in others.

The apocryphal English breviary, together with the other invented and genuine historical sources listed in Lupián's expert testimony, became a crucial piece of evidence in the Trinitarians' case for the long-standing veneration of John of Matha and Felix of Valois. Members of the order had been collecting these proofs for some time. Before they set aside the project in the wake of the 1655 relic theft, the Calced Trinitarians had already gathered depositions in 1649 and 1650 about images of the saints venerated in monasteries in Rome and in Úbeda, Spain.[197] They had also received the backing of the French monarch, King Louis XIV, who in 1650 wrote to the pope in support of the effort.[198] By 1661, however, the Calced Trinitarians seem to have stepped back from their efforts to win papal recognition of the founders' immemorial cult; instead, they continued their campaign to have the English breviary's liturgical commemoration of Matha and Valois extended to the whole of the order.[199]

The campaign for Matha's immemorial cult was taken up by the Discalced branch, which, in 1663 and 1664, began collecting testimony in

Burgos, Rome, Cuenca, Madrid, Córdoba, Granada, Valencia, and elsewhere about Matha and Valois's ancient veneration and their ongoing fame for sanctity. The witnesses' depositions highlighted proofs like paintings and images of the saints, processions and liturgical celebrations in their honor, and their venerable reputation as saints. Many of these witnesses were Discalced or Calced members of the order; others were expert painters and sculptors who testified to the appearance, craft, and antiquity of the many representations of Matha and Valois that could be found in Trinitarian monasteries and convents throughout Spain, Portugal, and France.[200] Lupián's testimony was a critical part of this evidence. As we have seen, liturgical texts like the English breviary figured heavily in his long catalogue of manuscript and printed materials, but they were not the only kinds of sources. The list ranged widely, from discussions by contemporary historians, including Figueras and many of his followers, to mentions in medieval chronicles. Papal letters and other official documents were cited to prove that Matha and Valois had always been honored with the title of saint. Many other proofs—some genuine, some forged—were letters, privileges, and other documents issued during Matha's lifetime that attested to his life, work, and virtues. Such sources stood alongside the testimony of the other witnesses, providing crucial chronological depth and evidentiary authority that compensated for the lack of eyewitnesses from the saint's own era.[201] There was not, however, any mention of the theft in 1655 or of the lack of cult in San Tommaso in Formis that had so angered the Congregation of Sacred Rites' commissioners in 1630; indeed, the little church merited mention only as the site of the inscription that marked Matha's tomb. While Medina and Vidal's daring robbery of their founder's remains created a new host of problems that would take decades to resolve, it had thrown up a very effective smokescreen that obscured an otherwise intractably embarrassing situation.

The testimony and texts gathered by the Discalced Trinitarians soon bore fruit. On July 31, 1665, Cardinal Ginetti, the judge delegated to the case by the Congregation of Sacred Rites, ruled that "with respect to the title or name of saints, the erection of altars, the public exposition of images, the keeping of lighted lamps, the celebration of Masses, the recitation of antiphons and prayers particular to the same [saints], it is established [as constituting] cult from time immemorial, and beyond the memory of men"—that is, he confirmed that the veneration of the Trinitarians' founders had existed since time out of mind.[202] With this act of recognition, which was approved by the Congregation of Sacred Rites on August 14, 1666, and confirmed by Pope Alexander VII on October 21 of that same year, Matha and Valois's cult—and by extension, their position as acknowledged saints—was assured.[203] As word of Ginetti's ruling became known in Rome, Trinitarians of every branch and nationality rejoiced at the news. The Discalced Trinitarians' solicitor general recalled, "I ordered that they ring the bells, and the Calced fathers of Italy did the same, [as did] the Discalceds of France, and our convent of Spaniards in Rome, which are [all] on the same street, the Via Felice. That night, we displayed lanterns and fireworks, the bugles and trumpets of the pope and of the French embassy played, and great festivities were put on, with solemn octaves."[204] Trinitarian houses elsewhere celebrated with similar festivities. The Discalced Trinitarians of Valencia, for example, went all out with five days of processions, solemn Masses and sermons, elegant altars decorated with elaborate hieroglyphs, a poetry competition, and bullfights.[205]

These celebrations suggest that for many members of the Trinitarian Order, Ginetti's ruling was much more than a mere confirmation that Matha and Valois had enjoyed veneration for hundreds of years. The cardinal's judgment and the subsequent ratifications by the Congregation of Sacred Rites and the pope himself were taken as clear statements on the sainthood of the Trinitarians' founders—a canonization in all but the name. For example, for Alonso de Andrade, a Jesuit historian writing on behalf of the Discalced Trinitarians shortly after the decision, the ruling amounted to a redeclaration of Matha's "canonization" by Innocent III—that is, the pope's veneration of the newly dead saint and participation in his burial and funeral honors. If the prayers and other texts from the English breviary, together with the images, festivities, processions, and other indicators of Matha's long-standing veneration, were important even when Innocent III's authorizing act was not well known, he said, "how much more must one do these rogations and novenas now that, after such a long and rigorous examination, the Apostolic See has declared his ancient canonization against those who impugned it, and not only [declared] his cult to be permitted, just like other solemnly canonized saints, but also proposed [Matha and Valois] to the Church universal, so that they be venerated as such."[206] The Calced Trinitarian preacher Manuel Guerra y Ribera voiced a similar interpretation in his celebratory sermon: "The [papal] bull is not an explicit canonization because it does not observe the precise ceremonial details ordered by Innocent III. It is, thus, a declaration of sainthood so ancient that it exceeds our memory: *Cultu excedente memoriam hominem*."[207] Other publications contended that the 1666 ruling was proof that Matha and Valois had been canonized by Urban IV in

1263.[208] In effect, the declaration of immemorial cult confirmed for the friars what they already knew: that their founders were truly saints.

With Matha's and Valois's sainthood secured, over the next three decades, the different branches of the order built on the affirmation of their immemorial cult by petitioning and receiving permission to celebrate the two saints with ever-more-solemn honors and in an ever-wider geographical area. Three years later, in 1669, Pope Clement IX granted the Trinitarian Order the privilege of a Mass and generic office (that is, a "common" office in the category of saintly confessors) in honor of its founding fathers, and by 1671, the two had been inserted into the Roman Martyrology, the Church's official calendar of saints and blesseds.[209] In 1682, Matha and Valois received their own, individualized liturgical commemorations (a "proper" Mass and office), and in 1694, observation of the feasts of the two saints was finally extended to the whole of the Catholic world.[210]

The histories compiled and the documents fabricated by Juan Figueras Carpi and Antonio Lupián Zapata mobilized the past to achieve results in the present—they exalted the Trinitarian Order against its rivals, and they elevated its claims to antiquity, erudition, piety, and service to Crown and Church as well as the sanctity of its founders. The hagiographic facts they manufactured became cornerstones of Trinitarian history and, by extension, load-bearing supports in the case for the identity of Matha's remains. The English breviary in particular would soon become an essential piece of evidence in proving that the bones once held in the little church in Rome were the same as those handed over to the nuncio in Madrid. With Matha's status as a saint successfully resolved, the Trinitarian Order could finally turn to the question of his stolen bones. By 1668, the friars were ready to take up the task.

4

UNCERTAIN SAINT

The Case Before the Congregation of Sacred Rites

By July 1668, the Discalced Trinitarians of Castile had launched the case for the identity of the stolen bones of St. John of Matha. Perhaps still reveling in their recent success in cementing their founders' sainthood, the Discalced leaders seem to have decided that the time was right and the evidence strong enough to present the question before the Congregation of Sacred Rites. The political situation was not terribly encouraging—while Alexander VII had favored Spanish interests, his successor, Clement IX (r. 1667–69), a member of the faction of independent-minded cardinals known as the *squadrone volante*, the "flying squadron," tended toward positions that advantaged France and its powerful monarch, Louis XIV. Clement himself knew Spain well, having served as papal nuncio to Madrid between 1644 and 1653, but his affiliation with the reforming and rigorist *squadrone* and his opposition to Spanish influence pushed him closer to France. Worse, the death of King Philip IV in September 1665 had left Spain and its far-flung empire arguably weaker, with its government in the hands of Queen Mariana of Austria, who ruled as regent for her young son Charles II. The Marquis of Astorga, the current Spanish ambassador to the Holy See, was probably of little use as an intercessor, given his reputation as a somewhat ham-handed diplomat.[1] But the Trinitarians were an international order with roots in both France and Spain, and St. John of Matha himself was French, so perhaps the Discalced authorities gambled that their arguments might find support among the cardinals who would decide the case. Moreover, the prefect, or head, of the

Congregation of Sacred Rites was none other than Cardinal Marzio Ginetti di Velletri, the order's official patron or protector at the papal court.[2] Given these factors, the Discalced Trinitarians seem to have judged the stars sufficiently aligned to test their luck. They had already been collecting the necessary documents. In November 1667, witnesses to the 1655 handover at the nunciature in Madrid and to the 1657 depositions of Medina, Vidal, and Arias Portocarrero before the nuncio's judge confirmed their testimony, and other witnesses at the French and Spanish Discalced monasteries in Rome spoke on the record about what they knew about the theft.[3]

It was customary for religious orders, bishoprics, and other large religious institutions to maintain representatives in Rome to lobby on behalf of their interests and to supervise unresolved petitions and proceedings before the Holy See. It seems likely that responsibility for overseeing the case for the identity of Matha's stolen bones fell to the Discalced Trinitarians' *procurador general*, or solicitor general, in Rome, Felipe de Jesús (1602–1687). Confessor to the powerful Cardinal Francesco Barberini and adviser to several convents in Rome and in surrounding towns, this Portuguese Trinitarian was well connected to Rome's noble ecclesiastical elite.[4] Friar Felipe would need these friendships and ties in his work as the Discalced representative at the papal court. The work of the *procurador general* was demanding; it required the soft skills of tact, patience, and modesty and an ability to maneuver within Rome's complex networks of patronage and influence. As one later solicitor general commented, it was no job for an overscrupulous friar more concerned with spending his days "saying Mass, praying, and commending himself to God" than attending to the order's affairs.[5] Nor was it an asset to have too fastidious a conscience, since negotiating often required "gifts" and promises that might trouble the overly scrupulous, "and so they attain nothing." In addition to dancing attendance on cardinals and their staff, solicitors general had to be ready to hand out tips to the secretaries and to the "lackeys, valets, and gentlemen of the lord cardinals, since in this way not only will they facilitate access to their bosses, but often one can achieve through these [servants] some business that without them, even with much resolve, one could not achieve before."[6]

Gifts and promises might help a religious order achieve its aims in Rome, but they could not entirely substitute for careful arguments and sound evidence. Procurador General Felipe de Jesús would have to make his case with care. In centuries past, the act of theft did not necessarily imperil the authenticity of relics. For medieval Catholics, acquisition by ruse or by violence (rather than by gift, sale, or discovery) guaranteed that a relic was indeed exactly what—or who—it was said to be.⁷ By the early modern period, however, the heyday of *furta sacra* was long past, and relic theft seems to have raised more questions than it solved. The depositions at the papal nuncio's residence in Madrid in 1655 and 1657 were the first steps in creating the necessary documentation, but the problem of the identity of the relics remained. How could the authorities in Rome, perhaps still aggrieved at the thieves' audacious act, be sure that the bones in Madrid were truly those of St. John of Matha? How, indeed, could one be sure of the identity of any of the relics and remains held up to the faithful as those of saints?

The Council of Trent had sought to address these concerns by specifying that bishops confronted with new miracle claims or new relics (i.e., newly discovered bodies of established saints, rather than remains of wholly unknown saints or candidates for canonization) were to consult with "theologians and other devout men and decide as truth and devotion suggest."[8] In the century that followed the close of the council, officials slowly codified and clarified the procedures and evidentiary requirements by which true holy relics might be recognized and known. Two leading reformers, Cardinal Carlo Borromeo (1538–1584), archbishop of Milan, and Cardinal Gabriele Paleotti (1522–1597), archbishop of Bologna, elaborated on Trent's bare-bones directions, drawing on medieval precedents to establish modern procedural examples that shaped the responses of later prelates tasked with the investigation and verification of supposed relics.[9] Among the rules for proper treatment and veneration of relics elaborated by Borromeo's Fourth Council of Milan (1574) was a set of guidelines for the investigation of relics.[10] Presiding bishops were to examine first the "writings, records, documents, reliable annual accounts, or memorials of any sort" found in and around churches or attached to reliquaries, followed closely by witness testimony of "ancient and constant tradition."[11] The results of their investigations and transcriptions of the evidence were to be carefully recorded and placed in the episcopal archive for posterity. Four years later, similar criteria were brought to bear by Cardinal Paleotti on the remains of Sts. Agricola and Vitalis. Before conducting a solemn translation, or transfer, of the two early Christian martyrs, the cardinal himself examined books, authenticating writings, liturgical texts, and other written materials that documented the previous locations and translations of their remains, and subjected the relics to a careful physical inspection. Records of these investigations, "made for the memory of future generations," were later placed in the episcopal archive.[12]

Precedents like the acts of Cardinals Borromeo and Paleotti helped foster a growing consensus that privileged legal instruments and written records as indispensable proofs of a relic's identity and authenticity—proofs that, thanks to the illegal actions of Medina and Vidal, the body of St. John of Matha sorely lacked. As Cécile Vincent-Cassy has noted, "after the Council of Trent, in the face of Protestant critics, the search for veracity led the Catholic Church to demonstrate the relics' historicity."[13] While miracles, sensory experiences, tests, and other forms of creating knowledge about holy bodies were not wholly set aside, relic investigations like those conducted by Borromeo and Paleotti were exercises firmly grounded in historical sources, methods, and modes of thought. This trend paralleled ongoing developments in canonization. Since the twelfth century, the process of saint-making had become increasingly centralized and standardized. These tendencies gained momentum after Rome's resumption of canonizations in 1588 after a sixty-five-year "failure of papal nerve."[14] Early modern canonizations, especially those of long-venerated but never authorized holy figures like Matha and Valois, relied heavily on historical sources—documents, inscriptions, accounts by ancient and modern writers, carefully recorded witness testimony—and on the critical assessment of those sources that was increasingly expected of historians. Miracles remained key to the saint-making process but were increasingly subject to similar critical review.

It is within the context of this "shrinking of the saintly possible" that the case of the stolen bones of St. John of Matha came before the Congregation of Sacred Rites.[15] It was urgent that the case be resolved—without clearly establishing that the human remains stored in the nuncio's chapel in Madrid were those of their founder, neither the Calced nor the Discalced Trinitarians would be able to make a plausible claim to the body, nor would they be able to put it forward to the faithful for veneration. Without a body to venerate, any effort to promote the cult of the newly canonized Matha would be seriously hampered. This was a grave matter that could affect the whole order's public standing and potentially hinder its ability to collect the monetary donations on which its redemption efforts in North Africa and elsewhere depended. Worse, without veneration, Matha's bones were in grave danger of losing their special status as sacred remains. To the naked eye, there was little that distinguished a holy person's bodily remains from those of a common sinner. The difference between the two lay not in their physical appearance but in their place in the hearts and memories of the faithful: "Relics might become precious objects, capable of confirming prestige on their possessors and donors, but like any currency, their value was never fixed: even an authenticated relic, without a cult, becomes just a bone."[16] The Discalced Trinitarians collected a letter from the Countess de la Fuente petitioning the pope that Matha's body be transferred to their monastery in Madrid, where she was building a chapel, but even with the support of the wealthy and well connected, nothing could be done until the identity issue was put to rest.[17]

Given these high stakes, how were the Discalced Trinitarians to establish that the bones they claimed belonged to their founder were indeed his? What kinds of proofs could they present that would convince the Congregation of Sacred Rites that the bones in Madrid were the same as those that had been in Rome? This chapter explores the evidence and arguments put forward by the Discalced Trinitarian leaders and their legal advisers in hearings before the congregation in 1668 and 1669. While theoretical discussions of how relics might be identified pointed to a wide array of possible proofs, from divine revelations and miracles to pilgrimages and processions, in practice, investigating Church authorities regularly preferred physical evidence and documents as tools for evaluating both relic identity and the closely related issue of relic authenticity. In the coming pages, I examine how Procurador General Felipe de Jesús and the Discalced Trinitarian legal team linked the question of the identity of Matha's relics—that is, their sameness through time—to their unchanging material qualities, especially their size and color, and to the documentary support provided by the extracts from the English breviary, a text that developed out of the invented history in support of Matha's immemorial cult. That they derived this information from the fallible testimony of humans opened them to doubts about the credibility and certainty of their evidence, doubts that they sought to accommodate by arguing that while some things could be known absolutely with metaphysical or mathematical certainty, relics called for a lesser form of certainty known as "moral certainty." Together, these two arguments reflected the inherent ambivalence of relics and defined them as acceptably contingent and probable.

As we saw in chapter 3, the main focus of the Congregation of Sacred Rites' complex administrative apparatus was the beatification and canonization of holy men and women. Saint-making was an increasingly complex process, and the cardinals and administrative staff that ran the congregation's regular operations sought to know and to recognize the saints through a wide array of evidentiary forms and modes of inquiry. In effect, the making of saints was also an exercise in the making of knowledge, a process in which the congregation's administration played a critical role. The rising number of publications dedicated to unpacking the processes and problems associated with the examination of would-be saints is testimony to ways in which the making of holy people and holy knowledge was bureaucratized and routinized over the course of the seventeenth century.[18] These publications, and the Congregation of Sacred Rites as a whole, are also indicative of the degree to which the early modern papacy sought—not always successfully—to submit the diverse, vibrant cult of the saints to the homogenizing, centralizing control of Rome.

Relics could also come under the congregation's purview if they were of candidates for beatification or canonization or, in the case of the physical remains of established saints, if they were so doubtful or their circumstances so confused as to be beyond the jurisdiction of the bishop in whose diocese they were discovered. Full-blown relic identity cases like that of St. John of Matha seem to have been infrequent, even rare. I have uncovered only a scant handful of cases that reached the level of the Congregation of Sacred Rites, though there may be others hidden within the largely inaccessible archive of the Congregation for the Causes of Saints, the present-day successor to the early modern institution. It is very likely that the paucity of identity cases is due to the fact that, as we will see, other Roman institutions frequently weighed in on questions of relic identity and authenticity. Moreover, rather than taking up the labor-intensive (and potentially controversial) task of a complete investigation of a relic's identity and authenticity, the congregation often preferred to respond to requests for permission to render special liturgical honors to the remains of some saint with the cautious words, "[Permission is granted] as a boon, but without approval of the relic."[19] Petitioners were probably not eager to undergo the intense scrutiny of the congregation's judges; instead, most newly discovered, poorly documented, or otherwise uncertain bodies of the saints were not investigated in Rome but instead were handled locally by bishops and their agents.

Whether at the episcopal level or at that of the congregation, officials seeking to investigate and authenticate relics needed guidance. Like the saints themselves, relics became the subject of a specialized knowledge, known through an ever more precisely identified body of accepted forms of evidence and modes of inquiry. And just as a wave of specialized publications explained the processes of beatification and canonization, so too did a small boom in treatises on relics begin to appear over the course of the 1600s. The texts, which seem to have made their first appearance in the first decade of the seventeenth century, gathered together the discussions scattered through legal works, apologetic treatises, summae of moral theology, confessors' manuals, the decrees of ecumenical and provincial councils, hagiographies, and histories to examine the divine and historical origins of the cult of relics and to explore the legal, moral, and liturgical issues they might present.[20] What was a relic and what was not? Where did the veneration of the bodies of the saints come from? How were relics to be contained, displayed, and handled, and by whom? How was one to deal with an uncertain or questionable relic? These questions were theoretical but also practical, born from the confusion and doubts of investigating ecclesiastical authorities and also from the very materiality of the holy objects themselves. They responded both to the criticism of Protestants and to the devotional excesses of the faithful, as well as to the tension between the transcendent and the material that was inherent to relics. The Council of Trent had sought both to reaffirm the validity of the cult of the saints and their relics and to underscore the boundaries between sacred and profane people, places, and things. In the decades that followed the close of the council in 1563, theologians and confessors investigated the roots of the cult and systematized the disparate array of beliefs and practices that surrounded the bodies of the saints. However, their attempts to impose order had to take into account the ontological blendedness of relics, in which were combined distinct or even opposed categories or qualities (e.g., the celestial and the earthly, the fragment and the whole, the absent and the present, the dead and the living).

The emergence of this literature reflects ongoing changes within Catholic veneration of relics and of the saints more generally. Prior to the reforms put in place by the Council of Trent, relics belonged not to dogma but to popular devotion; their veneration was grounded not in the pronouncements of theologians but in the practices of the faithful. "Until Trent," notes the medievalist Julia M. H. Smith, "relics were *habitus*, not creed."[21] In the century and a half that followed the closing of the council in 1563, Church authorities sought to bring rationalizing order to the cult of relics by establishing clear guidelines and procedures. One approach was to limit what could be considered to be a proper relic. Whereas in earlier centuries a relic might be dust gathered from a martyr's shrine, a piece of string used by a pilgrim in Jerusalem to measure the Holy Sepulcher, a hair of the Virgin or Mary Magdalen, a shred torn from the shroud of a holy man or woman, or any other, similar material object, by the early decades of the eighteenth century, only the bodies of the saints could be considered to be true, "distinguished" relics.[22] Similarly, ecclesiastical officials sought to enforce long-standing rules about how relics could be stored and who could touch them. Just as the post-Trent Church sought to better distinguish between holy and profane people, places, and things by requiring members of the clergy to dress and behave differently from their lay neighbors, so too did it seek to ensure that holy remains could not be confused with the bones of the common dead. The minigenre of relic treatises that emerged during the seventeenth century offered Church officials clear guidelines on how to transform these concerns into practical action.

The Counter-Reformation Church's drive for control over the cult of relics logically extended to a concern for the authenticity and identity of the remains of the saints. Relic treatises gathered and codified the rules of evidence by which authorities could ensure that alleged relics were genuine holy remains, not fakes or frauds, and that they were properly attributed to the correct saint or saints. The most detailed of these manuals, the 1647 *Disquisitio Reliquiaria: sive De suspicienda, et suspecta earumdem numero reliquiarum, quae in diversis ecclesiis servantur, multitudine* of Jean Ferrand, a Jesuit rhetorician and theologian, explained the reasons for the repetition and multiplication of individual relics so mocked by Protestant critics and outlined the forms of evidence by which one might recognize the real relics of the saints.[23] Ferrand identified three types of evidence for discerning the true relics from the false: human, divine, and mixed human-divine. Among the varieties of human evidence, he included the physical appearance of the remains, multiple forms of textual documentation, witness testimony, and local tradition. Divine evidence, by contrast, consisted of things like the miraculous qualities of the holy body (its incorruptibility, its emission of light, its capacity for movement, its subtlety), divine revelations, marvelous effluvia, and other miracles, while the mixed category included trial by fire; submersion of relics and other methods for achieving cures; and sermons, offerings, miracle books, pilgrimages, processions, and liturgical commemorations. For each form of evidence, Ferrand offered multiple examples and a careful analysis of its potential limitations.[24]

The Council of Trent left the examination of newly discovered relics of established saints to bishops but noted that particularly difficult cases must be handed over to provincial councils and that the pope himself must be consulted. In practice, this meant that in instances in which the evidence was problematic or contradictory or that had aroused a great deal of conflict, local authorities must place the problem in the hands of a third party for adjudication. In 1576, for example, the bishop of Córdoba announced that the recently discovered remains of three early Christian martyrs were indeed authentic holy relics. However, the finds had provoked a great deal of controversy among competing ecclesiastical establishments in the city, and the bishop chose not to declare whether the relics might be venerated. When one of the participants in the quarrel petitioned Pope Gregory XIII to confirm the bishop's decree and to grant permission to venerate the remains, the pontiff remanded the issue to a provincial council in Toledo. The council opted to split the difference by issuing a decree in January 1583 that declared the remains to be authentic relics that must be given proper veneration but that left room for the claims of the opposing party.[25]

The establishment of the Congregation of Sacred Rites in 1588 brought the bodies of the saints under its jurisdiction, and the committee regularly handled questions related to their veneration and treatment. In practice, however, questions about relics might be addressed to several different bodies at the papal court. Some inquiries were handled by the Congregation of the Council, a standing committee established in 1564 to oversee the implementation of the Council of Trent and to respond to any questions that might arise out of its decrees. In 1581, 1648, and 1668, for example, the Congregation of the Council handled inquiries from bishops in Zaragoza, Albi, and Albano about whether ancient relics that had long been venerated but lacked names or documentation could be displayed to the faithful for veneration.[26] At the same time, issues relating to relics, especially questionable ones, might also be taken over by the Congregation of the Holy Office of the Inquisition. This powerful institution, which was charged with policing orthodoxy, was first established in 1542 in response to dangers posed by Protestantism.[27] By the end of the sixteenth century, the Inquisition had expanded its competence into an ever broader area, including many issues that fell under the jurisdiction of the Congregation of Sacred Rites.[28] In 1638 and 1641, for example, the Holy Office intervened to suppress the display and veneration of dubious relics in Assisi and Matelica.[29] In both of these cases, the complaint was made directly to the Holy Office; in other incidents, such as the remains of supposed martyrs discovered in 1638 in Taormina, Sicily, cases originally presented to the Congregation of Sacred Rites were redirected to the Holy Office, presumably because they dealt with relics of uncanonized individuals or of questionable provenance or relics that were the subject of superstitious beliefs and practices.[30] The dividing line between the two institutions was not always apparent, however, and it is often not perfectly clear why a given case was taken over by the Congregation of Sacred Rites, rather than the Inquisition, or the other way around. After 1669, relics might also come under the jurisdiction of a new body, the Congregation of Indulgences and Relics. Little is known about this committee, especially for its earliest years, but it seems to have dedicated more of its attention to regulating indulgences than relics.[31]

The problem of the identity of the relics of St. John of Matha, however, seems to have been understood as one that was plainly under the jurisdiction of the Congregation of Sacred Rites. Unlike some of the other divisions of the papal administration, like the Congregation of Bishops and Regulars, which met on Friday mornings, or the Congregation of the Inquisition, which met on Thursdays, the Congregation of Sacred Rites did not have a fixed day for meeting. Instead, upcoming meetings were advertised by means of notices posted at the residence of the congregation's secretary.[32] This powerful official was no mere clerk but was instead the second in command within the congregation's extensive hierarchy. At the head of the congregation's administrative structure sat the prefect, who was often but not always the most senior of the twenty or more cardinals assigned by the pope to the congregation.[33] The cardinals' deliberations were aided by numerous advisers and experts, the most prominent of whom was the *promotor fidei*, or promoter of the faith. Popularly known today as the "devil's advocate," this legal expert was introduced into the saint-making process in the 1630s and was tasked with raising questions about and objections to the petitions brought before the congregation. In beatification and canonization cases, for example, the promoter of the faith pointed out weaknesses in candidates' records of heroic virtue and inconsistencies in witness testimony and offered natural explanations for alleged miracles. Other participants in the congregation's proceedings included three judges from the Rota (the highest court of appeals within the Church's legal system), legal and theological consultants, attorneys, archivists, notaries, and others. For the examination of alleged miracles performed by candidates for sainthood, doctors, surgeons, and even mathematicians might be called to give their learned opinions.[34]

The case of St. John of Matha, however, was a bit different. With the saint in question freshly canonized and his remains safely locked away in the nuncio's residence in Madrid and thus protected from unauthorized veneration, the issue was whether the bones said to be those of the Trinitarians' saintly founder were indeed his. The arguments developed around St. John of Matha's bones can be found scattered through a wide range of documents, some printed, some manuscript. Advocates for the petitioning party presented their arguments in a printed *positio*, a position statement crafted by the promoter of the cause, or *promotor causae*, assigned to the case, and supported those arguments with carefully organized evidence, printed in a summary, or *summarium*. While both of these documents survive at the National Library of Spain, in Madrid, no trace can be found of the customary printed *animadversiones*, or counterarguments, raised by the *promotor fidei* and refuted by the *promotor causae* in a printed *responsio*.[35] However, at least some of the promoter of the faith's objections and the Trinitarians' rebuttals can be gleaned from the manuscript legal briefs created for the case. These short texts, typically only one or two folios in length, can be found scattered in archives and libraries around the city of Rome.[36] While there was no clear division between the two, these briefs fit broadly into two types: *informationes in facto*, statements that sought to establish the facts relevant to the case, and *informationes in jure*, statements that laid out the pertinent legal issues. While it is impossible to re-create the exact course and trajectory of the congregation's deliberations, which were guarded in secrecy, it is clear that some were written in direct response to objections and concerns raised in the meetings. Contrary to what modern observers might assume, printed texts carried no greater force or probatory value than those in manuscript; for this reason, we must consider both, together.[37]

While it is difficult to determine the precise authorship of many of these documents, there are some clues hidden among them. Certainly, the Discalced Trinitarians' solicitor general Felipe de Jesús must have had a key role in framing the order's arguments, and while he was not directly named in any of the materials, one of the manuscript briefs specified that it made its pleas on behalf of the Discalced Trinitarians' *procurador general*.[38] Other documents had names attached. The printed *positio* and several of the manuscript briefs, for example, bore the name of Claude Bouillaud, a legal expert who served the Congregation of Sacred Rites as *promotor causae* in a number of prominent beatification and canonization cases in the 1660s and 1670s and who seems to have had an important role in the development of the Discalced Trinitarians' case, since one of the manuscript briefs mentions "my lord Claudius."[39] Another brief was signed by Angelonus de Angelonis, a lawyer. It is likely that other participants supplemented the work of these three figures—additional consultants, perhaps, and scribes—but because nearly all the materials are anonymous, it is impossible to know who these figures may have been.

We can, however, make some educated guesses at the likely audience for the arguments. Both cardinals and consultants were supposed to read carefully the written materials generated by the case as well as listen to the oral arguments presented in the congregation's meetings.[40] Several of the manuscript briefs are directed to Cardinal Ginetti, the Trinitarians' protector, or to Cardinal Angelo Celsi (1600–1671), who substituted for an absent or indisposed Ginetti during some of the proceedings. Others can be found among the papers of Cardinal Sigismondo Chigi (1649–1678), a junior member of the committee, while another is addressed to Monsignor Francisco Maria Febei (1616–1680), a well-positioned cleric who had once been secretary of the Congregation of Sacred Rites and, by 1669, was serving its administration as a consultant.[41] It is likely that the printed materials were also distributed to the cardinals and consultants involved in the case. While prior to 1661, *positiones, summaria*, and other texts generated in beatifications and canonizations were printed only after a case's conclusion, a papal edict in July of that year streamlined the congregation's processes and lowered costs by authorizing their printing while the processes were still ongoing. It seems probable that similar latitude would have extended to relic identity cases like that of St. John of Matha.[42]

The documents, both printed and manuscript, described the question before the congregation as one of the "identity" (*identitas*) of the body of St. John of Matha. While today we tend to speak of "identity" as referring to a sense of self, of individuality, or to social identity as defined by membership, attributes, or behaviors, the word as it was used in the sixteenth and seventeenth centuries derived from law and philosophy and signified sameness, including the sameness of things that might not appear identical. For example, the 1729–38 edition of the *Vocabolario degli Accademici della Crusca* defined it as *medesimità*, sameness, while the Spanish equivalent, the 1734 *Diccionario de Autoridades*, explains the word as "the reason by virtue of which two things that seem different are in reality the same thing."[43] Beyond this specialized meaning, however, "identity" as it was applied to relics often included questions of the real and the false, the genuine and the fake. This usage seems to have been in place at least by the early seventeenth century. A 1604 hagiography of St. Maurice and the martyrs of the Theban Legion, for example, described certain relics of these saints as bearing documentation that "testified to [their] realness and identity."[44] The act of examining and establishing a relic's identity—and, by extension, its genuineness—was often referred to as one of "recognition" or "qualification." This was the term used by the Council of Trent and by Cardinal Charles Borromeo's Fourth Council of Milan (1574), which cemented many of the norms and procedures for the examination of relics, especially the growing preference for written legal documentation.

The proofs and the paperwork generated in formal acts of recognition were necessary for making relics "authentic." Here too is another word that twenty-first-century readers need to approach with caution. We tend to think of authentic things and authentic people, whether individuals or collectivities, as real, original, pure, genuine, undisguised, and without dissembling, of a known and proven provenance or bearing the necessary characteristics that mark their membership in a category or collectivity.[45] For early modern Europeans, by contrast, authenticity was not some moral act or inner virtue or state of being; rather, it was a status of veracity conferred or confirmed by legal procedures and documentation. This is the meaning we find in early modern dictionaries, like Sebastian de Covarrubias's 1611 *Tesoro de la lengua castellana*: "Authentic, that which is authorized and approved as true and legal," and "Authenticate is the same as authorize public documents." Further, an authenticated document in one that a "scribe or notary public authorizes . . . by signing and autographing it, making witness of its legality."[46] Similarly, the first edition of the *Vocabolario degli Accademici della Crusca* (1612) defined "authenticate" as "to clarify as valid and authoritative, and with public testimony, worthy of belief, and, for the most part, [it] is said of writings."[47] Authentic relics were thus those that boasted full documentation, often produced though formal acts of recognition. By extension, they stood in opposition to those that were sham, false, or doubtful.

Identity, recognition, authentication, truth, falseness—these were nested and interrelated ideas, not easily disentangled. To address one was to invoke them all. Thus, the question of whether the bones in the nuncio's residence in Madrid were the same as those that had previously lain in the tomb in the little church in Rome was tacitly a question of whether the crime of relic fraud had accompanied that of relic theft. To be sure, not everyone agreed that the question of whether a relic really was what people said it was was particularly important. Even King Philip II of Spain (1527–1598), the proud possessor of one of the sixteenth century's largest relic collections, acknowledged that while a good many of the supposedly holy bodies that were sent to him were probably fakes, it was of little consequence: "They won't fool us; we don't lose our merit before God by revering his saints in bones, even if they are not theirs."[48] Many commentators argued that for ancient relics, long venerated, it was better not to inquire into their identity at all. Domenico Anfossi, for example, argued that this was the case "especially in the matter of relics, in which it is unnecessary to prove identity, which is presumed in such pious affairs."[49] Nevertheless, in a case like that of the bones of John of Matha, the question of identity (and authenticity) was so obvious and the stakes so high for the Trinitarian Order that it had to be resolved before the relics could be put forward for veneration.

Identity, Evidence, and Change

Faced with the task of proving that the bones in Madrid were those that had previously been in Rome, the Discalced Trinitarians focused in on identity in its limited, specialized meaning of sameness. More specifically, they framed the issue as one of diachronic identity, sameness over time—and, in this case, through space. Conceptually, the question of identity was closely connected with the problem of individuation—that is, what accounts for and what structures the individuality of a given person or thing. The question of individuation and of the principles, or causes, of individuation was a common topic within medieval Scholastic philosophy, and well into the seventeenth century, inquiries into identity were often categorized as inquiries into individuation. By the middle of the century, however, the two were beginning to be separated out as discrete issues, and discussion of individuation began to decline as the question of identity through time began to take center stage.[50]

Felipe de Jesús and his legal advisers drew on commonplace Scholastic ideas about individuation and identity as the foundation for their arguments in favor of Matha's bones. "Sameness is one in itself, and different from everything else. Identity is unity, which a thing has in itself, with diversity from everything else," began one of the manuscript briefs, while another expanded on the point: "Identity is unity . . . which a thing has in itself with diversity, distinction, and difference from everything else."[51] This definition drew directly on St. Thomas Aquinas's commentary on the fifth book of Aristotle's *Metaphysics*, in which the philosopher examined the terms or concepts that structured his investigation of being. It did not, however, reiterate the complexities of Aquinas's explanation of Aristotle's treatment of sameness and difference but instead gestured broadly toward them and the questions of unity, oneness, and being with which they were intimately connected. It also tacitly invoked Aquinas's emphasis on the key role of matter as the principle of individuation, the thing that accounts for the specificity or uniqueness of a given individual, including but also beyond that individual's numerical distinctness. According to Aquinas (following Aristotle), all things within nature created by God had both matter and form. It was "undesignated matter" (*materia communis*) that tied the individual to another of its kind and made both people equally part of the group we call "human beings." It was a different sort of matter, "designated matter" (*materia signata*), that individuated and made two people distinct, unique individuals within the larger category of human beings.[52] The specific designated matter of each individual was fundamental to its identity, its sameness. Said Aquinas, "In order for something to be numerically the same, its essential principles have to be identical. Hence, whenever an individual's essential principles vary, its identity necessarily varies as well. Now, the parts of an individual's nature constitute its essential principles. Matter and form, for instance, are essential principles of things. So, if an individual's accidents vary and change, while its essential principles remain, the individual itself will remain the same."[53] That is, as the scholar Christopher Hughes has explained, "A material thing cannot go from having this matter to having that matter, because a thing cannot go from having this individual essence to having that individual essence, and the individual essence of a material thing just is a bit of signate matter together with a (matter-individuated) substantial form. So things, and *a fortiori* things of the same species—existing at the same time, or at different times—are identical only if they have the very same matter."[54]

But as the manuscript brief signed by the lawyer Angelonus de Angelonis noted, the case of St. John of Matha's bones "concerns proving only identity, since [their] existence is indubitable."[55] The question at hand was not one of ontology, of categories, but of epistemology, of knowing. The issue was not what individuated and distinguished one person or thing from another but instead how one individual was to be recognized and known as different from another. It was matter that individuated, and it was through matter that human beings understood the world around them. "For with respect to us, who derive our knowledge from material things," commented the Jesuit philosopher Francisco Suárez, "the distinction among individuals is often taken from matter or from the accidents which follow matter, such as quantity and other properties."[56] Following this logic, the Discalced Trinitarians argued that discernment of sameness was to be found in external markers and characteristics apprehended and interpreted by human intelligence. Thus, "the intrinsic identity of any one thing cannot become known to us except by exterior signs, especially speaking in the present case of the bodies of the saints, either through tradition or through revelation."[57] In effect, the Trinitarians sought to make the case that the facts surrounding the theft and the characteristics of the bones themselves—their exterior signs—demonstrated that the matter of St. John of Matha's relics remained unchanged, and so too did their identity. The only real change was a change of location; the bones themselves remained constant even as they moved through space and time.

Matha's advocates again drew on traditional concepts to frame their discussion of the relics' movement through space and time. In this case, the reference was to Aristotle's ideas about change and persistence. In his treatise on physics, the philosopher indicated that "every change is *from* something and *to* something." These two points, the *terminus a quo*, or end from which, and the *terminus ad quem*, or end to which, are known collectively as the *termini* of change. In the case of Matha's stolen bones, the two *termini* were the church of San Tommaso in Formis and the nuncio's residence, the physical sites at either end of the journey from Rome to Madrid. The *termini* and, to a lesser degree, the *medium*, the intervening space of transition between them, were established by laying out the facts of the case and the evidence for the presence of the relics at each stage, while the stable sameness of the bones was established through the unchanging exterior signs that marked them at each point along their journey.[58]

This organizing logic underlay almost all of the materials created around the case of Matha's relics to be heard by the Congregation of Sacred Rites in 1668 and 1669. To take just one example, the printed *positio* signed by Bouillaud organized its numbered arguments roughly according to the relics' movement from Rome to Madrid. Arguments 1 through 3 sought to establish the presence of Matha's body in the church of San Tommaso in Formis from his death in 1213 until 1655 and the physical indicators that marked his holy body, while arguments 4 through 10, plus two other unnumbered paragraphs, marshaled evidence for the transition of the relics from Rome to Naples and from Naples to Madrid, together with witness testimony of physical markers seen while in transit. Finally, arguments 8 through 11 established Matha's arrival in Madrid and the handover to Nuncio Massimo and the exterior signs seen on the relics there. Bouillaud concluded by summing up and restating each of the *termini* and the key proofs adduced for each one, together with the most important of the external markers by which the identity of Matha's bones was known. The *summarium*, which contained the witness testimony that supported the arguments laid out in the *positio*, was organized in the same way.

Procurador General Felipe de Jesús and his legal team sought to bring the evidence both for the *termini* and for the exterior signs in line with a developing consensus about how the identity of these holy objects might be recognized, a consensus most clearly articulated in the relic manuals genre. While classification schemes differed, most writers agreed that the required forms of evidence fell into certain basic types. We have already seen Jean Ferrand's three categories of evidence (human, divine, and mixed human-divine). While the Discalced Trinitarians did not deploy Ferrand's vocabulary—though they definitely were familiar with his book—the evidence they presented to establish the *termini* of change and the exterior signs that identified Matha's relics fit squarely into Ferrand's tripartite schema.[59]

Of Ferrand's three categories, it was divine evidence that carried the least weight for the Discalced Trinitarians. Miracles had held probative force since the earliest origins of the cult of the saints, and they remained obligatory proofs of sanctity for seventeenth-century candidates for beatification and canonization. They were not, however, unquestioningly accepted. As Church authorities tightened the juridical structure of beatification and canonization to better discern God's true saints, miracles too came under greater scrutiny.[60] While the first saints elevated to the altars after 1588 tended to have many miracles attributed to them but only few witnesses for each, as the seventeenth century wore on, candidates for canonization were increasingly put forward with fewer miracles but more and better testimony, the better to weather the careful scrutiny of the *promotor fidei*.[61] In the case of the remains of the saints, commentators pointed to miracles as important corroborative or even decisive evidence for determining the identity and authenticity of holy remains, but in practice, they could not stand alone.[62] The congregation itself had pointed to the limited value of miracles as proofs for relics in 1643, when it considered the case of a newly rediscovered relic of St. Bruno (1049–1143), bishop of Segni. Asked to confirm the identification of a skull fragment alleged to be that of the saint but attested to only by a miraculous light, the assembled cardinals could not come to a consensus and handed the question back to the town's bishop for judgment.[63] Similarly, in the case of the stolen bones of St. John of Matha, miracles seem to have taken second billing to the congregation's preference for legal documentation. The testimony of the two thieves, Medina and Vidal, one of the Discalced Trinitarians' key sources for evidence, contained one miracle—a rather lackluster incident in which "[while] passing by the monastery of the Spanish Discalced [friars] of their order at two o'clock at night, an hour when no bell should ring, they heard one sound in the aforementioned Discalced monastery, and they held it to be a miracle because they carried with them the said holy relics."[64] Though this supposed miracle was pointed out in several of the manuscript briefs, it may have been judged too weak to stand up to scrutiny, since Bouillaud made no mention of it in the printed *positio*.[65]

Instead, the Discalced Trinitarians pointed to evidence that fell within Ferrand's categories of "humana praesidia," or human evidence or aids to knowledge of relics, and "praesidia ex humanis, & diuinis mixta," or mixed human and divine evidence. As one manuscript brief noted, Matha's relics were "rerum naturae," things within the realm of the natural, material world; thus, it was evidence that reflected this reality that carried the most probative force.[66] In Ferrand's definition, human evidence was a broad category that included the physical characteristics of holy remains—their size, shape, color, and smell—but also documentary evidence, witness testimony, Church tradition, images, and the pilgrimages and celebrations of devotees. The Discalced Trinitarian legal team deployed multiple forms of human evidence to establish the *termini* and the physical characteristics of the remains. To fix the *terminus a quo* in Rome, for example, they pointed to the long-standing tradition that St. John of Matha had died and been buried there, as documented by the inscription on his tomb, testimony gathered from Trinitarian friars in 1630 (in connection with the case for his immemorial cult) and in 1655, a 1571 papal bull, and eleven non-Trinitarian historians (presumably more impartial and thus more trustworthy than members of the order). The bones' transition from Rome to Madrid was established through letters and through testimony from the two thieves, Medina and Vidal; their superior, Arias; and others; their arrival at the *terminus ad quem* in the nuncio's residence was documented by the testimony of Arias and the two thieves as well as the declaration by Nuncio Massimo.

At each stage in the journey, witness testimony attested to the relics' unchanging characteristics, especially their size and color. As the brief signed by lawyer Angelonus de Angelonis remarked, "Another [proof] is surely taken from [the fact that] at the time of the removal from the tomb, the bones of the body were white and large, and such are those that today are found at the residence of the lord nuncio, . . . which qualities, indeed, since they are not natural in other bodies, work well for resolving [their] identity."[67] The unusual color and size of the bones was testified to by a host of witnesses at each stage of the relics' journey and stood as a key indicator that marked the bones as those of Matha and differentiated them from those of the other two bodies that had accompanied him in the tomb. For example, one Discalced Trinitarian friar testified that he had visited the fugitive Pedro Arias Portocarrero in his hideout in the hospital of San Giacomo degli Spagnoli. Arias, he said, had shown him Matha's bones, which were "large and very white," and, in another box, the bones of Matha's two successors and tomb-mates, "which were of a very distinct yellow color."[68]

The bones' unusual size and color tied the question of Matha's relics to long-standing hagiographical tradition and ecclesiastical practice. In the fourth century, St. Ambrose had recognized the newly discovered remains of Sts. Gervasius and Protasius in part by their size and color. To do so again now was no innovation but was instead an explicit invocation of a powerfully authoritative precedent.[69] It also aligned St. John of Matha with the rest of the saints in a traditional interpretive mode called "typology," in which writers and readers overlaid images or figures from one tradition on another as a means of articulating their meaning. Most commonly applied to the Bible, in which the characters and events of the Old Testament were regularly read as prefigurations of Christ as described in the New Testament, typology allowed readers to expand the field of meanings around a person or happening through parallels and ideal types. Using typology, the Discalced Trinitarians made sense of the unique characteristics of Matha's bones by aligning them with other saints whose relics were uncontroversial and uncontested.

By emphasizing the relics' uncommon physical characteristics, the Discalced Trinitarian legal team also underscored their dual nature as both sacred objects and historical artifacts. Relics could be both "powerful natural matter" and material evidence of the past.[70] The Discalced Trinitarians also linked the identity case directly to the invented history developed by Figueras and Lupián in support of the canonization effort. In their arguments, the Discalced Trinitarians connected the size of the bones to stories circulating among the friars, noting that "the bones of the founder are large, since he was of tall stature, as an enduring tradition of his order holds, but the remaining ones [are] of middling size."[71] The first written mention of this "enduring tradition" appeared in Figueras's *Annales*. Quoting his invented source, Innes, Figueras described Matha as a conventionally handsome but tall man, some nine palms high, with "straight shoulders, long arms, large but delicate hands, [and] long, rounded fingers."[72] While there may have been a preexisting tradition with the order about Matha's unusual height, given the collaboration that may have existed between Figueras and members of the Spanish Calced Trinitarian leadership, it seems possible that his oddly specific portrayal of Matha's uncommon height might be informed by (authorized? unauthorized?) openings of the tomb and viewings of the remains, especially that of Jerónimo Vélez Matute in 1630, who, as we saw in chapter 3, took advantage of the Congregation of Sacred Rites' inspection of the tomb to open it and insert the slip of parchment with passages from the English breviary.

Those liturgical passages and the breviary from which they supposedly came, which fell within Ferrand's third, blended category, were the linchpin of the Discalced Trinitarians' arguments, as critical to the case for the relics' identity as they had been to the canonization effort. As one member of the legal team pointed out, some of the experts who advised the cardinals of the Congregation of Sacred Rites had sought more information about the prayer and antiphon inscribed on the slip of parchment on Matha's head, "for they judge that it most strongly points in favor of [the relics'] identity."[73] Just as an ornate reliquary could signal the special holiness of the human remains contained within, so too was paperwork a key marker that established a relic's bona fides. Labels and tickets affixed to a bone, provenance paperwork, and other kinds of documentation were all known as *authentica*; without them, it was difficult, even impossible, to tell the remains of a common mortal from those of a saint. The parchment slip that marked Matha's skull and differentiated it from those of average men served as the foundation of the Discalced Trinitarians' case—together with the physical characteristics of the bones, it appeared in almost every brief as the crucial *authenticum* that proved their identity and authenticity. Its frequency in the case file is indicative of the weight carried by documentary evidence in relic identity cases. For seventeenth-century Catholic authorities, holiness in all its aspects was a profoundly historical project, and just as written evidence was increasingly preferred for beatification and canonization cases, so too does it seem to have held pride of place as proof of the historicity, and thus authenticity, of the bodies of the saints.

By contrast, the two explanatory notes—one left in the tomb on the two thieves' return visit to San Tommaso in Formis, its twin accompanying Matha's bones in Madrid—seem to have held less importance. Composed, penned, and signed by Arias, the two texts were retroactive attempts to manufacture the kind of documentation usually created in legal relic translations. The two notes, identical in their wording and inscribed by the same hand, were meant to circumvent the lack of a notary's record, and the Discalced Trinitarian legal team put them forward in the *positio* and *summarium*, together with expert testimony from two handwriting specialists who affirmed that both had been written by Arias, as secondary evidence that demonstrated the connection between the *terminus a quo* in Rome and the *terminus ad quem* in Madrid.[74] The notes do not seem to have been considered particularly decisive proofs, however, since there is scarcely a single mention of them in the manuscript briefs. As *authentica*, they seem to have been less important or convincing than were the unchanging physical characteristics and the accompanying documentation from the English breviary that marked and identified the bones as those of the Trinitarians' founder.

Interpreting Evidence: Moral Certainty

The second of the Discalced Trinitarians' two-pronged strategy was to shape the way that the evidence for the identity of the relics, those unchanging markers, was interpreted. The printed *positio* signed by Claude Bouillaud noted that numerous legal scholars and the relic theorist Jean Ferrand all had argued that to prove the identity of a thing, it was sufficient to have "presumptive proofs" and "moral certainty."[75] The former, presumptive proofs, were a type of proof within a larger grouping of presumptions, conjectures, indications, probable arguments, and other indirect evidence that sat at the lowest rank of the legal hierarchy of evidence. Less determinative than the demi-proofs, half proofs, full proofs, or confession, the so-called *regina probatitionum*, or "queen of proofs," this lesser form of evidence was insufficient for beatifications and canonizations.[76] However, it seems to have been acceptable in cases related to proving the identity of relics, especially old ones for which, barring a miracle, there was only ancient, unbroken tradition and reputation.[77] The second category, moral certainty, was the proper interpretive lens through which the Discalced Trinitarians' presumptive proofs were to be presented. As a lesser form of certainty that accommodated doubt and the potential for error in human testimony and human understanding, moral certainty was critical to their case.

While moral certainty was repeatedly invoked throughout all of the paperwork generated around the stolen bones of St. John of Matha, the Discalced Trinitarians' most coherent statement on its applicability to the case was in one of the manuscript briefs found among the papers of Cardinal Sigismondo Chigi.[78] Barely twenty years old and only recently raised to the cardinalate, Cardinal Chigi would not have been a particularly important participant in the Congregation of Sacred Rites' deliberations, but his papers offer an interesting view into the committee's inner workings in the late 1660s. The brief in question is directed to the congregation's prefect, Cardinal Ginetti. Its author is anonymous, but internal references within other manuscript briefs demonstrate that it was one of several written by a central figure within the Discalced Trinitarian legal team, perhaps even Procurador General Felipe de Jesús himself.

The Chigi brief opened by laying out five propositions that were then proved in the rest of the text. The first three framed the question of saintly relics in the terms and concepts of Aristotelian logic and, in so doing, established the terms and parameters of the debate over the relics of St. John of Matha. Citing St. Augustine together with some of the leading lights of sixteenth- and seventeenth-century moral theology, the author first contrasted metaphysical certainty with moral certainty.[79] He argued,

> While metaphysical certainty is found only in situations or acts of supernatural faith, because they rely on divine authority, with which falsity or the telling of falsehood is incompatible, . . . moral and human certainty pertains to those things that for the most part are so, yet can sometimes fail; such that such a certainty is altogether infallible, nor is it incompatible with [the possibility] that a matter or someone's assent to something that at present is judged to be sure

> is in fact false. . . . On the contrary, [moral] certainty can be greater than the other [kind of certainty] because it is grounded on better and more efficacious foundations.[80]

Moral, not metaphysical, certainty, asserted the author in the second proposition, was the standard by which the bodies of the saints were judged, "but it is not impossible that the bodies that are venerated as holy are not of those saints."[81] Three examples illustrated the potential for error. In the catacombs underneath Rome, inscriptions and grave goods marked the tombs of martyrs, but because the graves of the saints lay right next to those of common Christians, confusion between the two might easily occur. Similarly, though historians disagreed about the fates of the bodies of St. Peter and St. Paul and the locations of the remains of St. Benedict and St. Scholastica, "these things notwithstanding, when other principles are considered, it is judged that the identity of such bodies is morally certain, and they are exposed for public veneration."[82]

The third proposition argued that moral certainty was not undermined by the possibility of contradiction, opposition, or the danger of falseness. The fact that moral certainty coexisted with the possibility of falseness did not abrogate it, since "as the axiom says, *ab actu ad potentiam bene valet consequentia*, but not from potential to actual."[83] The author of the brief illustrated with a commonplace example this traditional principle of Scholastic logic, that while what really exists must also be judged to be possible, there is no valid inference from what is possible to what is actual. It was, he noted, certainly possible that he himself might have some defection of intention in his baptism and ordination and thus might not truly be a priest and that therefore the Host might not be consecrated. Refusal to adore the consecrated Host on that mere possibility, however, was neither pious nor prudent.[84]

The category here invoked, that of moral certainty, *certitudo moralis*, was no innovation. First articulated by Jean Gerson (1363–1429) in response to the theological confusion fostered by the Great Western Schism (1378–1417), moral certainty signified "a certainty that suffices for action," in which "moral risk avoidance becomes unnecessary and an agent is entitled to trust his beliefs without fear of error" because he has attained a level of certainty that is adequate to avoid sin.[85] Gerson grounded this principle from his reading of a well-known passage in Aristotle's *Nichomachean Ethics*, in which the philosopher noted that "it is the mark of an educated man to look for precision in each class of things just so far as the nature of the subject admits: it is evidently equally foolish to accept probable reasoning from a mathematician and to demand from a rhetorician demonstrative proofs."[86] Both moral certainty and other varieties of uncertain certainty, such as probable certainty, which was an "opinion, an assent to one proposition, coupled with the acknowledgement that its opposite might be true," found new life in the wake of the Protestant Reformation, as competing claims to theological truth forced partisans on both side of the confessional divide to articulate definitive positions.[87] In the face of Protestant arguments for the assurance of salvation granted to those to whom God had given the gift of faith, for example, the Council of Trent reiterated St. Thomas Aquinas's rejection of absolute certainty, asserting that "no one can know, by that assurance of faith which excludes all falsehood, that he has obtained the grace of God."[88] Later Catholic apologists elaborated on this idea. Cardinal Robert Bellarmino, for example, contended that while one may have a "probable opinion" of one's own justification, absolute certainty is beyond human beings.[89]

By the latter decades of the sixteenth century, Gerson's concept of moral certainty became particularly important in casuistry, the early modern science of the conscience. Predominantly (though not exclusively) a Jesuit specialty, casuistry anatomized moral decision-making, especially in cases of uncertainty. Its enormous popularity in the early modern period suggests that casuists' moral systems hit a nerve in their response to the uncertainties of the age. Casuistry "sought to bolster confidence about certain values and principles; although . . . it was the assurance of moral probability rather than certitude."[90] Probabilism, the dominant strain of casuistic reasoning until 1656, was pioneered in 1577 by the Dominican theologian Bartolomé de Medina (1527–1581). Medina's medieval predecessors had argued for a moral doctrine that demands that "in doubtful matters, the safer path is to be chosen."[91] That safer path, the option that will not lead to sin, was known at least in part by its probability—a concept understood by Thomas Aquinas as "an opinion warranted by authority, and such probabilities vary in probative force according to the probity of the authority."[92] Medina elaborated on these older understandings by conflating doubt and opinion and suggesting instead that "if an opinion is probable it is licit to follow it, though the opposite be more probable."[93] This approach proved enormously successful among moral theologians and casuists alike, since it offered an acceptance of doubt and an acknowledgment of the limits—but not the impossibility—of human knowledge. Probabilist theologians elaborated a hierarchy of certainty that took these constraints into account. Juan Caramuel Lobkowitz (1606–1682), for example, described three types of certainty: metaphysical, physical, and moral. Metaphysical certainty was that "which necessarily is true, because from the absolute power of God it is not able to be otherwise."[94] Physical certitude was a step down. It was known by the regular physical behavior of things and the usual connections between cause and effect but did not exclude the possibility of a miracle operating outside the natural order. By contrast, moral certainty, the weakest type, described things that could possibly be other than what they usually are not only because of divine intervention but also because of the actions of human beings.[95] Moral certainty "represented a certainty which was beyond reasonable doubt, but which did not entail logical necessity."[96]

Moral certainty's important role in casuistry was paralleled by its rise to prominence in other, related fields. By the second half of the seventeenth century, natural philosophers, both Protestant and Catholic, increasingly deployed the concept of moral certainty as a means of discussing scientific "facts" grounded in experiment and in human testimony.[97] In law, moral certainty came to occupy an important place in categories of proof and in criteria for judicial decision-making.[98] Canon lawyers, for example, expanded the role of moral certainty in the process of beatification, a status of sanctity that, over the course of the seventeenth century, came to be understood as a precursor to full canonization.[99] While theologians and jurists increasingly argued for the full certainty of papal inerrancy in canonization, most agreed that rulings on beatification should be understood as merely morally certain and potentially subject to error. The language of beatification and canonization decrees reflected the difference between the two, in that beatifications merely permitted veneration within a region or a particular religious order but canonizations decreed and defined a holy person as a saint to be venerated by all of the faithful. In Pope Gregory XV's 1622 bull beatifying Peter of Alcántara (1499–1562), for example, he "concede[d] and permit[ted]" the holy man's veneration by members of the Franciscan Order, while in 1669, Pope Clement IX's bull of canonization "decreed and defined Blessed Peter of Alcántara to be a saint and inscribed him in the catalogue of the saints."[100]

The extension of the category of moral certainty to relics appears to have emerged in the last decades of the sixteenth century. Leading moral theologians like Francisco Suárez (1548–1617) argued that relics could not be equal in their level of certainty (older relics, for example, were more uncertain) and that those publicly venerated by the universal Church were subject to more stringent evidentiary demands than those given private cult. There was no risk of formal theological error, "since in human affairs no greater certainty [than moral certainty] is required."[101] By the second half of the seventeenth century, the application of moral certainty to relics was commonplace among moral theologians, casuists, and other writers who dealt with relics. The treatment of Francesco Bordoni (1594–1671) was typical.[102] In the course of his consideration of a contested relic, said to be a thorn from Christ's crown, Bordoni noted that human knowledge was divided into three types—"scientific" (i.e., complete, perfect, true) knowledge, "opinion," and human testimony. The first two categories corresponded to two kinds of certainty. Scientific knowledge corresponded to a certainty that "touches on the truth of the principles of knowledge, in which nothing false can be concealed—this one pertains to natural wisdom and to divine faith, which is most reliable, in which it is impossible for anything false to be concealed," while opinion corresponded to moral certainty, to which the thinking intellect arrived when it judged a thing to be true, or close to true, on the basis of strong arguments. Unlike the first sort of certainty, moral certainty had to admit the possibility of doubt, error, or falseness, since it was grounded on opinion.[103] The third sort of knowledge, the knowledge of human testimony (*fides humana*), was grounded in the words or authority of others; "therefore, in this mode, we believe rather than know." This belief was particularly useful—even necessary—for the study of history, especially the ancient past.[104] Bordoni did not explain what kind of certainty could be ascribed to human testimony, but it seems likely that the corresponding category was also moral certainty, since both opinion and trust were necessary for the understanding of moral matters and thus for relics. Thus, "applying the adduced learning to our case, scientific knowledge is not necessary for proving the truth of the fact, but knowledge based on opinion suffices, and moral certainty, by which one thus reasonably and not rashly believes himself to regard the matter."[105]

While the validity and importance of the veneration of the remains of the saints was treated as a theological certainty, known through divine faith and through the tradition and consensus of the universal Church, the teachings of the early Church fathers, miracles and signs, and the decrees of popes and councils, individual or particular relics were understood to require a lesser degree of certainty.[106] Indeed, at least one author maintained that subjecting relics to more stringent standards of proof and a higher level of certainty would create grave problems. Carlo Felice de Matta (1622–1701) argued in his 1678 book on canonization and beatification that "it is very difficult, or rather impossible, to judge the identity of relics, because in order to have physical identity, two witnesses must depose that, for example, such and such a bone was removed from the body of such and such servant of God, known to them and that they themselves were present and watched it being stored in such a place from which, as they themselves knew, it was never removed, nor could it ever at any time or moment be taken away, without their having become aware of it themselves, giving compelling reasons."[107] Given these limitations, de Matta urged that decrees approving relics for veneration be carefully phrased, using words like "held [to be authentic] or similar, by which will be excluded approbation of physical identity."[108] Were uncertain holy bones subjected to more demanding standards of proof, warned Prospero Lambertini (Pope Benedict XIV; 1675–1758), "all holy relics would be exposed to the danger of uncertainty."[109] In effect, just as probabilist casuists sought certainty by accommodating doubt and uncertainty in moral decision-making, writers on relics upheld the authenticity of holy remains while finding a place for ambiguity and the characteristic blendedness and ambivalence of the bodies of the saints. Relics were inherently a bit uncertain, but tolerably so.

But to apply the category of moral certainty to relics was not simply to tolerate or to permit their intrinsic uncertainty but to recognize them for what they were. For early modern natural philosophers and others writing in the first half of the seventeenth century, an object of knowledge, often described as an "objective concept"—that is, not an idea of a thing or the thing itself but an interstitial concept of the thing insofar as it was known—had an "objective certainty," a type of certainty inherent to the nature of the object known.[110] In a discussion of the distinctions between moral, physical, and metaphysical certainty, for example, the Jesuit scholar Rodrigo de Arriaga (1592–1662) gave as an illustration his moral certainty that the city of Naples existed, a confidence grounded in the statements of "prudent and truthful men" but one that admitted the physical possibility that all were lying.[111] As Peter Dear has noted, "It would be simple, and correct, to analyze 'moral certainty,' with its reliance on properly accredited testimony, as the social grounding of belief. It is guaranteed by 'prudent and truthful men' rather than by the possibility of independent confirmation or some similar universal epistemic procedure. But it is crucial to note that Arriaga and the rest (including Descartes) do not themselves analyze it in that way. The assumption is always that moral certainty can be identified by its appeal to testimony, but that it is not in itself constituted by such testimony."[112] Testimony did not create moral certainty but instead served as a marker or indicator that it was the proper form of certainty to be applied.

For the investigator and authenticator of relics, then, the task was one of discernment, of properly reading the evidence from testimony that pointed to the moral certainty of the remains. In the case of the stolen bones of St. John of Matha, it was also that same evidence drawn from testimony that pointed to their identity. The Chigi brief's two remaining propositions shifted in traditional form from universals to particulars, from general principles to the specifics of the case at hand. As we saw earlier, individuation was understood to be rooted in matter, and it was through matter that identity might also be recognized. Thus, the anonymous author argued that "the intrinsic identity of any given thing cannot be known to us except through external signs (particularly speaking of the present case of holy bodies) or through tradition or through revelations."[113] Just as moral certainty was signaled by testimony, so too was an object's identity identified by similar means. In the case of Matha's relics, the historical evidence of the epitaph on the saint's tomb and the physical proofs provided by the two confessed thieves, including the bones' location, disposition, size and color, and the identifying documentation from the English breviary, established the moral certainty of the remains. As a comparison, the brief's author pointed to the thousands of martyrs thought to lie buried within the Roman catacombs. Like the bones of St. John of Matha, the moral certainty of the identification of their remains depended on extrinsic indicators like inscribed epitaphs, insignia, and the so-called vial of blood that pointed to the presence of the holy. The brief's author also offered a handful of parallels of stolen or mysteriously moved holy objects drawn from Catholic hagiographic tradition, such as the Holy House of Mary at Loreto, the hand of St. Gregory the Great at Cesena, and the bodies of St. Peter and St. Paul. Since in such cases one proceeded "from the definition to the thing defined, and the converse works as well," what was important was not the means by which the body was moved or where it ended up but rather that the indicators of identity and sanctity that were found in Rome were the same as those found in Madrid.[114] The brief's author concluded by waving away potential objections, such as the possibility that the two friars mixed up the bodies in the tomb and the impropriety of accepting evidence proffered by criminals, as both unlikely and irrelevant. The thieves had been interrogated, had confessed, and had been punished. If their testimony could serve as the source for knowledge of the very crime itself, surely it could also serve as the source for the unchanging markers that indicated the body of the saint, "and therefore identity [is proven] with sufficient moral and human certainty that it may be venerated, as the aforementioned examples and exact analogies quite effectively recommend."[115]

The Discalced Trinitarians' inventive arguments cut no ice with the hardnosed members of the Congregation of Sacred Rites. After multiple discussions since July 1668, the assembled cardinals, prelates, and legal experts ruled on January 12, 1669, that "the identity of the body of St. John of Matha is not established, since [the relics] have not been proven in proper form or according to law. Let different proofs be brought forth and handed over to the congregation."[116] It appears that the cardinals and consultants of the congregation did not contest the application of moral certainty; instead, they rejected the evidence adduced as proof. Without more information, such as the counterarguments put forward by the promoter of the faith, it is difficult to know precisely which of the Discalced Trinitarians' proofs were declined, but the arguments presented in the *positio* and the manuscript briefs suggest several problems.

One issue that seems to have been raised was the lack of evidence about the status of the relics during their move from Rome to Madrid—that is, whether they were carried by Pedro Arias Portocarrero alone or whether the two thieves were also in possession of the remains while in transit. The question had no bearing on the case, argued one of the manuscript briefs. Just as the genuineness of locally created canonization case files did not depend on the person or persons who carried the papers to Rome but on the seals and signatures that guaranteed them, and as catacomb relics sent from Rome to churches around the Catholic world were judged not by their bearers but by the documents that authenticated them, so too was the identity of a thing unaffected by either the quantity or the quality of the agents involved in its transfer.[117]

The issue of who carried the relics was far less important, however, than the larger problem to which it pointed: the use of testimony from convicted criminals. The depositions gathered from the two thieving friars and their superior were the Discalced Trinitarians' primary source of information for both the facts of their theft and transfer from Rome to Madrid and for the unchanging physical characteristics of the relics, their location within the tomb, and the parchment that marked them as objects of veneration. The fact that the witnesses' delinquency was raised repeatedly throughout the paperwork generated by the case suggests that the issue was a pressing one. The Discalced Trinitarian legal team countered by pointing to the opinions of several prominent canon and civil lawyers, who argued that the testimony of criminals could be admitted in cases in which there were no other possible witnesses and in which the offending witnesses did not stand to gain from providing their statements to the court. Given the committee's request for "exempla . . . dissimilia," however, it seems probable that it was not convinced. Likewise, if one recognized a morally certain thing by the testimony that signaled it, then the questionable credibility of the two thieves probably accounted for the congregation's distinction between the bones' "formal" and "moral" identification.

The question of the credibility—the *fides*—of criminals cut to the heart of the Discalced Trinitarians' case. It was a commonplace of Roman law that the credibility of testimony depended in no small part on the social standing of the witnesses. Men were to be preferred to women, for example, and persons of higher social status had more credibility than those lower in the social hierarchy. Mere quantity could not make up for "quality," or social condition; as the jurist Baldus de Ubaldis (1327–1400) put it, "A small number of noble witnesses are to be preferred to a multitude of rustics and peasants."[118] Such was the case both in civil and in criminal law; it was also the norm in beatification and canonization cases. In the tighter juridical structure of canonization and growing concerns about discerning true miracles from diabolical illusions, true holy people from imposters, the credibility of miracles was tied ever more firmly to the trustworthiness and social standing of the witnesses who testified to them.[119] Relic identity cases, too, could be won or lost on the quality of witnesses. In 1709, for example, the Congregation of Sacred Rites declined to permit the veneration of two relics, a miter and a garment said to have belonged to Blessed Pius V and Blessed Felice of Cantalice (both of whom were later raised to sainthood in 1712), since the evidence for their identity rested exclusively on the recollections of a single elderly nun.[120] Certain categories of witnesses—heretics, people in "dishonorable professions," for example, or people whose relationship to the case might affect their testimony—were also (usually) disqualified from giving evidence. But *facti*—facts but also events—were established through testimony and through the *series facti*, the historical sequence of events crafted from witness testimony. The narrative arc that tracked the relics from the *terminus a quo* to the *terminus ad quem* represented the Discalced Trinitarians' attempt to create and constrain the facts of the case, especially the physical characteristics of the bones and the presence of the parchment bearing the extracts from the English breviary—key proofs that depended primarily on the compromised *fides* of the two thieves and their superior.

Qualms about witness *fides* intersected with another concern: the lack of proper documentation. Though the congregation did not explain its opposition to the examples offered in the briefs, the comments of an anonymous official associated with the papal nunciature in Madrid around 1671 make it clear that at least part of the reason for the committee's negative response was the inadequate paper trail: "The Trinitarian Order, both Calced and Discalced, claimed that the holy body should be turned over to them, and to this end introduced their petition in the Congregation of [Sacred] Rites. But because it was removed from Rome without [proper] proceedings or any documentation, they could not prove the identity of the relic, [and] so not only could they not obtain its handover, but neither could it be exposed for public veneration."[121] The anonymous commentator's emphasis on the lack of proper legal proceedings (*diligenza*) and formal documentation (*autentica*) suggests that the cardinals and consultants of the Congregation of Sacred Rites required better documentary evidence for the identity of the bones, such as a notarized attestation of the opening of the tomb and the transfer of the remains.

While the committee's objections on this point may be in part an attempt to punish the Trinitarian Order for the theft, they are also indicative of the degree to which the evidentiary norms for would-be relics had come to privilege legal instruments and written records.[122] Just as the process of saint-making had come over the course of the sixteenth and seventeenth centuries to rely ever more heavily on written evidence, so too did the methods for investigating and authenticating the remains of long-dead holy women and men. And as we saw, the tightened procedures and growing preference for reliable documentation were at least in part a response to both Protestant and Catholic reformers, whose devastating criticisms laid bare the questionable beliefs and practices at work in the traditional veneration of the saints and their bodies. Their mockery was not, however, the sole driver behind the increased attentiveness to evidence in the cult of the saints. The Congregation of Sacred Rites' preference for documentation was also fostered by the new attitudes and methods being adopted by writers of hagiography, ecclesiastical history, and other, related forms of sacred history. The Jesuit hagiographers known as the Bollandists, for example, aimed to found their studies of the lives of the saints firmly on the oldest, most reliable, most vetted of documentary materials, to submit them to careful analysis, and, in so doing, to purge the cult of the saints of falsehoods and fables.

The same critical approach to the sources of hagiography encouraged the members of the Congregation of Sacred Rites to ask questions about the documents offered as proofs by Matha's defenders. The same judges who saw the prayer and antiphon as key evidence in favor of the identity of the remains asked for more information about when the parchment with the two extracts had been placed on Matha's skull.[123] While I can find no evidence that the cardinals and consultants expressed any reservations about the contents of the document or the appropriateness of its insertion into the tomb, there is some evidence that their question had the potential to undermine the parchment's status as an authorized, official piece of documentation. The Discalced Trinitarian legal team appears to have argued that the English breviary extracts were inserted in 1630 by Friar Jerónimo Vélez Matute, when the grave was opened as part of a formal inspection of Matha's tomb in San Tommaso in Formis, a visit that, as we saw in chapter 3, was part of the Calced Trinitarians' bid to have the English breviary extended to the whole of the order.[124] This version of events was, in fact, at least partly a convenient fiction, since Vélez's testimony does not actually mention an unsealing of the grave during the inspection. It also appears that the Discalced Trinitarians created other convenient fictions by manipulating the evidence to eliminate any mention of previous openings of the tomb. A note inscribed on the back of one of the manuscript briefs notes that in Arias's 1657 statement before the nuncio in Madrid, he mentioned that "through the work of a father *procurador general* who was called Friar Agostino de Cardoso, a Spaniard, the aforementioned body of the aforementioned Venerable John of Matha was removed from a more common sepulcher and placed in the tomb from which it was extracted [in 1655]."[125] These words are missing from Arias's testimony in the printed *summarium*, but they do appear, carefully crossed out but still legible, in a 1714 draft version of the same evidence. The Discalced Trinitarian legal team quietly suppressed them from the witness statement, most probably because they demonstrated not only that the tomb had been opened extrajudicially and without authorization (probably in 1605) but, worse, that the tomb and its inscription were not the original one in which Matha's bones had lain since his death in 1213.[126] Had this testimony come to the attention of the Congregation of Sacred Rites, the order would surely have lost its case.

But the maneuver was successful, and it seems that the congregation's critical approach to the presented evidence did not extend to the English breviary documentation or the tomb and its inscription. For some contemporaries, historical criticism intersected with and was amplified by the expanding influence of ancient and modern skepticism and Cartesian doubt to create a crisis of historical credibility, of *fides historica*.[127] While it is difficult to parse the congregation's laconic response, the wording of its ruling and its reported preference for documentation suggest that in this case, at least, the problem was less a philosophical one than one of judicial procedure. Just as commentators on canonization procedure increasingly grounded their arguments for papal inerrancy in saint-making not in theology but in practical questions of legal procedure and proof, the cardinals cut the larger question of the identity of Matha's remains down to size by focusing on the evidence presented and its problematic source.[128] When the congregation ruled on the question of sainthood itself, "true *scientia* [was] only that which is juridically (even more than theologically) founded."[129] The same seems to be true of the bones of the saints. The congregation's declaration that the bones of St. John of Matha "have not been proven in proper form or according to law" and its request for different proofs suggest that the problem lay in the evidence adduced by the briefs' authors—the issue was not so much *fides historica* in general but the faulty *fides* of the two confessed criminals and the lack of notarized legal proceedings.

Part of the problem, too, may have been the historical parallels brought to bear on the case, especially the briefs' frequent references to relics uncovered in the Roman catacombs. In the wake of the accidental discovery of a previously unknown tomb complex in 1578, the catacombs, major pilgrimage sites and sources of relics since the early Middle Ages, became the focus of renewed devotional enthusiasm.[130] Over the course of the succeeding centuries, Rome's underground tombs were ransacked for remains of martyrs that were then sent to churches and chapels around the Catholic globe.[131] Though most Catholics assumed that most, if not all, of the bodies in the catacombs were those of ancient martyrs for Christ, Protestant derision and Catholic skepticism had called into question the criteria used in distinguishing the remains of the martyrs from those of the common dead.[132] A special committee convoked in the early 1630s to consider which inscriptions, grave goods, and other markers were to be considered sure indicators of sanctity failed to resolve the problem. By 1668, just as the the case of St. John of Matha came before the Congregation of Sacred Rites, questions surrounding the identification and treatment of catacomb relics had become so urgent that Pope Clement IX created a new oversight body, the Congregation of Indulgences and Relics, which quickly issued rulings about which inscriptions and objects could be considered reliable indicators of the presence of martyrs' remains and which could not. At least one person who probably helped craft that legislation was also a member of the committee that examined the case for Matha's relics. The papal sacristan Ambrosio Landucci (d. 1669) served as consultant to both the Congregation of Sacred Rites and the Congregation of Indulgences and Relics and was intimately familiar with the catacombs and the problems surrounding the recognition of martyrs' remains.[133] In the light of this contemporaneous debate and at a time when the evidence for and moral certainty of catacomb relics were themselves the subject of considerable anxiety, comparisons between the identification of ancient martyrs' bones and the identification of the bones of St. John of Matha may have been less than convincing.[134]

Though the members of the Congregation of Sacred Rites rebuffed the evidence and the precedents offered in the briefs, they do not seem to have rejected the Discalced Trinitarians' fundamental premise that a saintly body could be recognized by external signs derived from its physical matter and that this matter could remain constant between a *terminus a quo* and a *terminus ad quem*. Indeed, to do so would have been to destabilize some of the logic that underpinned the cult of relics as a whole. St. Thomas Aquinas had argued that the remains of the saints should be venerated "not on their own account as dead objects, but for the sake of the souls to which they were united and for the sake of the God whose ministers the saints were." While it was the soul that made the saint's body, living or dead, worthy of veneration, Aquinas also understood that there was a "concrete and real material continuity between a saint's living body and their relics."[135] This principle of "material continuity," or *identitas materiae*, was intimately linked to a host of hotly debated questions that concerned the relationship between holiness and matter—questions surrounding personal continuity and the Resurrection of the body; questions of transubstantiation, consubstantiation, and Christ's real presence in the Eucharist; questions of the incarnation and of salvation itself. These issues were far from academic; rather, they marked the fault lines that separated the Catholic Church and the many Protestant confessions from each other. The very human materiality of relics recalled the promise of resurrection. To push back against the possibility of their constancy through time and space would have been to call into question far more than the stolen bones of a single saint.

The assembled cardinals also seem to have accepted that moral certainty was the appropriate form of certainty to apply to the identity of the remains of St. John of Matha and to relics in general. Here, too, the congregation's approach to relics paralleled that of many hagiographers and other writers of sacred history. Some, like Jean Bolland himself, accommodated uncertainty and doubt about events within the lives of the saints by handing back to the reader the task of discernment.[136] Others adopted a different, complementary interpretive mode, one that dealt with the saints and their sources critically but gently, in a spirit of "pious affection." As we saw in chapter 3, this hermeneutic asked scholars to temper their criticism and their evidentiary demands and to approach the history of the saints and their remains with at least one eye on its moral purpose.[137] A marriage of careful criticism with an acknowledgment of the limits and imperfections of historical evidence and testimony, pious affection intersected neatly with moral certainty. As the noted Spanish humanist Ambrosio de Morales put it, questions of pagan antiquity did not require conclusive evidence or arguments but instead "a good moral probability deduced from good principles and foundations, from which one forms reasons." If this was the case for the pagan past, it was even more so with matters of sacred history, which must be understood "morally" and with "pious affection" but also with critical judgment and attention to detail.[138] Indeed, even Daniel van Papenbroek (1628–1714), one of the most prominent of the Bollandists, acknowledged that when dealing with the relics of the saints, one must often proceed out of "a feeling of pious credulity" rather than "certain knowledge." Written or ocular evidence demonstrated relics' trustworthiness, but the evidence was often thin or imperfect and could often be deceptive.[139] Lesser certainty required lesser proofs, so moral certainty required only moral evidence—that is, as the Jesuit canonist Antonio de Quintanadueñas put it, it was sufficient that moral certainty be "deduced from probable arguments; moreover, it does not have to be necessary, clear, and unerringly conclusive."[140] In effect, the application of pious affection and moral certainty to relics—and to sacred history more generally—allowed scholars to rescue religious truth from the more destabilizing aspects of critical historical scholarship and to find a middle path between naïve credulity and the extremes of skepticism.[141]

More broadly, the Congregation of Sacred Rites' willingness to admit the application of moral certainty is indicative of the concept's broad acceptance as a common feature on the scientific and philosophical landscape of the seventeenth century. The Catholic cult of the saints did not stand alone and isolated from the cultural and intellectual movements at work in other areas of inquiry. Seventeenth-century canonization cases (and inquisitorial investigations) were, as Jacalyn Duffin has observed, "centered on a forensic, even skeptical, approach to assertion, argument, and interpretation. They were predicated on doubt and demonstration."[142] Officials investigating miracles and candidates for sainthood, for example, increasingly employed techniques of observation and experimentation usually associated with early modern natural philosophy.[143] By the same token, the priests and prelates who engaged the thorny problems of relic identification and authentication participated with natural philosophers, historians, lawyers, and others in a wider culture of proof that incorporated doubt and uncertainty into the epistemological foundations of their respective fields.[144]

This accommodation of doubt was a response to the broad and thoroughgoing crisis of certainty in early modern European culture. As explorers expanded the limits of the known world and scholars engaged the classical past in new ways, long-established truths were increasingly cast into question. The encounter with the peoples of the Americas, for example, forced Europeans to reconsider traditional modes of explaining and engaging with alien cultures, while rampant inflation and an expanding credit economy produced churning anxieties as budding economists struggled to comprehend the rapid fluctuations and devaluations of gold, a substance traditionally understood to be stable and unchanging in value.[145] Most disorienting of all were the religious transformations of the sixteenth and seventeenth centuries, as Protestant and Catholic Reformations compelled Europeans to confront conflicting claims to theological truth and competing claims to the certainty of those truths. For early Protestants, for example, certainty of salvation and of scriptural interpretation was to be sought in the human experience of the Holy Spirit, while Catholic controversialists contended that certainty could only be found in the Church, the true location of the Holy Spirit.[146] But could true knowledge of God be found in human experience? And how was one to know the true church from the false, the divine from the demonic, reality from appearance, being from seeming? And while both sides came to embrace human knowledge as a means to faith, its limits and potential for error remained a site of much anxiety. So too was its potential to undermine the very theological truths that apologists sought to uphold—on both sides of the confessional divide, for example, the deep scholarship brought to bear in defense of religion threatened to undermine the foundational texts of Christianity.[147] Cases like that of the stolen bones of St. John of Matha connect to a central question that, as Stefania Tutino has noted, addresses "the very nature of Catholic theology and its relationship to a central feature of modernity. How can the absolute truth of theology relate to, and engage with, the probable certainty of human affairs? How could the supernatural maintain centrality in a world that was increasingly dominated by the human?"[148]

Both for relics in general and for the particular case of Matha's purloined remains, moral certainty offered one solution to the problem of uncertainty by accommodating doubt and imperfect knowledge. In doing so, it also reaffirmed the ambivalent character of the remains of the saints, in which were combined the mundane and the sacred, the fragment and the whole, the animate and the inanimate. "Matter and body were problematic," noted Helen Hills, "in spite of and because of being redeemed. The privileging and denying of change fuelled the ecclesiastical authorities' and theorists' attempt to authenticate relics, and to deny that divine presence might inhere in matter."[149] The application of moral certainty to saintly relics may also be seen as a development within a larger, cross-confessional reaction to what Caroline Bynum has called the late medieval "crisis of confidence in

Christian materiality," a crisis precipitated by the radically paradoxical nature of late medieval Catholicism.[150] Bynum posited that Protestant rejections and Tridentine reforms of the cult of the saints were engendered at least in part by fourteenth- and fifteenth-century Catholicism's simultaneous emphasis on inner focus and exterior action, mysticism and materiality. The moral certainty of holy remains, I suggest, expanded on Trent's reforming clarifications by responding both to the uncertainties raised by critics and to the ambiguities inherent in relics themselves.

Procurador General Felipe de Jesús and his legal advisers, their arguments rejected, were surely bitterly disappointed. The bones of St. John of Matha would remain locked away in the nuncio's residence, deprived of the veneration that a newly authorized saint would normally enjoy. But all was not lost. By specifying that different proofs were required, the Congregation of Sacred Rites had left the door open for another attempt.

5

"A VERY DIFFICULT BUSINESS"
Proving the Bones of St. John of Matha in 1715 and 1721

Disappointed though the Discalced Trinitarians must have been, they wasted no time in setting the wheels in motion to gather new evidence and present the case anew. In May 1671, the Congregation of Sacred Rites authorized another formal viewing of the bones of St. John of Matha in the nuncio's Madrid residence.[1] In the presence of the assembled Spanish leadership of both the Discalced and the Calced wings of the Order of the Most Holy Trinity and of the Captives, together with notaries, witnesses, and the two surviving members of the thieving trio from 1655, Nuncio Galeazzo Marescotti (1627–1726) broke the seals and untied the cords that bound the boxes that held the relics. Opening them, he found inside a bundle, wrapped in white taffeta. Beneath the taffeta, he discovered some white cotton batting and several documents, including the original extract from the English breviary that had marked Matha's skull. With his own hands, the nuncio removed the cotton and laid bare the skull and some bones, "which were very white, extremely bright, without having suffered any stain." He elevated the skull and offered it to the onlookers to kiss and raised up another large bone, but "out of respect, he neither moved nor recounted the other bones."[2] After taking more testimony from the attending witnesses, Marescotti replaced the contents, inserted a notarized record of the solemn procedure and of his findings, and resealed the boxes. Afterward, a second notarized copy of the record was sent to the Congregation of Sacred Rites.[3]

Much like Nuncio Massimo's viewing of the relics in 1655, the gathering at the nuncio's residence in 1671 was a formal act of seeing, a procedure known as a relic "recognition." These ceremonies were essential elements within the larger body of processes for identifying and authenticating the remains of the holy dead, especially newly discovered saintly bodies and relics that lacked proper documentation. As legal acts performed in front of a notary, relic recognitions generated the paperwork—legal instruments and written records—that authorities increasingly preferred as proofs. In some cases in which other written sources were unavailable or inadequate, a formal recognition might even provide the historical evidence needed to fix anonymous bones with a name and a life story. In 1625, for example, since documentation could not be found, the abbot of the Cistercian monastery of Nuestra Señora de Sandoval undertook a formal examination of a much-venerated but ill-identified skull in the monastery's relic collection. In front of the assembled members of his monastery, the abbot meticulously removed the many layers of multicolored silk gauzes and taffetas that enveloped the relic. Eventually, he uncovered the skull and a tiny parchment tag, inscribed in Greek, that identified the remains as those of St. Hieroteo, the legendary first bishop of Segovia.[4]

Unfortunately for the eager Trinitarians, Marescotti's act of recognition did not uncover any previously unknown tags or labels that might cement the identity of the relics of St. John of Matha, which would remain uncertain for some time to come. This chapter follows the case of Matha's stolen bones from 1669 into the first decades of the eighteenth century. Though the Discalced Trinitarians made repeated efforts on Matha's behalf, it was not until 1714 that they were able to win another hearing before the Congregation of Sacred Rites. The testimony generated in 1671, together with a renewed emphasis on the Trinitarians' invented past and on the forged documents on which it relied, formed the foundation of the order's second attempt in 1714. However, the new, enhanced dossier was not enough to convince the members of the congregation, and the petition was denied. By 1721, the friars were ready to try again, this time with the support of some powerful friends. As we will see, the intervention of *promotor fidei* Prospero Lambertini, who later became Pope Benedict XIV, proved critical to the Discalced Trinitarians' final effort. Using an eyewitness account written by a Trinitarian close to the case, I examine how under Lambertini's guidance, the Trinitarians reframed the evidence to meet the changing standards of early Enlightenment historical criticism as developed by scholars like Jean Mabillon and Ludovico Antonio Muratori. In the end, I find, it was as much canny political maneuvering as it was arguments and evidence that finally pushed the cardinals of the congregation to confirm the identity of Matha's stolen remains.

Recognitions and Rivalries, 1669–1720

If the arguments made before the Congregation of Sacred Rites in 1668 and 1669 had centered on the category of moral certainty and on the bones' material qualities, the documentary apparatus that accompanied them, and their place with Trinitarian history and tradition, Marescotti's recognition of Matha's remains invoked another traditional form of relic knowledge, one grounded in sight. Practices of unwrapping, of visual inspection, and of physical examination were some of the most ancient forms of relic authentication; to engage in them was to evoke the same typological web of precedents and parallels that we saw at work in chapter 4.[5] But these were not casual visual encounters; these were formal acts of witnessing that fixed the remains into known and knowable objects, with established shapes, sizes, and characteristics. The knowledge created in relic recognitions rested not only on the nuncio's inspection but also on the participation of sworn eyewitnesses and the documenting of the event by a notary. It was not merely an act of seeing but an act of seeing *together*. Moreover, the participants in the collective witnessing were nearly all high to midranking clerics or noblemen or were scribes and secretaries attending in their professional capacities. As we saw in chapter 4, not all witnesses bore the same degree of credibility and competency; therefore, relic viewings like the one undertaken by Nuncio Marescotti required not just any onlookers but witnesses appropriate to the occasion. In cases in which long-lost relics were discovered by humble laymen like construction workers or masons (as not infrequently happened in the course of renovations or repairs), investigating clerics regularly recorded their testimony but also took care to enact staged viewings by high-ranking and erudite members of the local ecclesiastical leadership. In the case of the discovery of the bones of St. Cecilia in Rome in 1599, for example, Cardinal Paolo Emilio Sfondrati held off on opening the tomb until the arrival of "idonei fidei testes," that is, appropriate, faithful witnesses, all eminent, scholarly ecclesiastics or members of the cardinal's entourage.[6]

Relic recognitions and the knowledge they produced thus bear some resemblance to the experimental culture and the scientific truths agreed to by the English gentlemen scientists described by Steven Shapin; that is, the knowable "facts" of saintly remains—in this case, the bones' size, color, and markers—were socially constructed, agreed on by an in-group of ecclesiastical elites bonded together by a shared clerical culture.⁷ As knowledge-making events, these viewings also operated within a likewise traditional culture of information gathering that relied on the five human senses. Smell, for example, could be an important evaluation tool, since the famous odor of sanctity was a traditional marker of holiness. While no one seems to have claimed that Matha's bones possessed any special fragrance, ineffable scents and the emotional responses they provoked were very commonly noted in records that documented relic discoveries and recognitions.⁸ Relic recognitions relied primarily on sight, of course, a faculty that was customarily closely aligned with knowledge. The records generated by the 1671 viewing reveal none of the uncertainties that increasingly surrounded vision for so many early modern European thinkers; rather, Cardinal Marescotti's act of recognition reflects older, more traditional currents of thought.⁹

Knowledge production in relic recognitions could also be highly empirical. Where the physical substance of a would-be relic was ambiguous, investigating ecclesiastical authorities might call on artisan experts to perform tests or might even undertake tests themselves. For example, in 1614, confronted with a newly discovered vial filled with dirt mixed with what was presumed to be clumps of coagulated blood of martyrs, clerics in Sassari, Sardinia, conducted a test aimed at distinguishing between the two. After moistening a small portion, "one could see clearly that it was so, that that one was earth and this one was blood, because when squeezed between the fingers, the earth fell apart and the blood crumbled into little bits, showing more of its red color."¹⁰ Such quasi-scientific tests are indicative of a relic culture that could include a pragmatic and empirical approach to the holy—another reminder that the Catholic cult of the saints, and the ecclesiastics who administered it, did not stand alone and isolated from the cultural and intellectual movements at work within the broader culture. However, that the nuncio's inspection of Matha's body did not extend to moving or recounting the bulk of the bones may suggest that the categories of knowledge created through the formal viewing of a relic recognition were specific and constrained. While Cardinal Marescotti refrained from reducing the remains to known objects by describing, counting, or measuring them, other, less formal kinds of relic viewings and handlings often produced such comprehensive information. The paperwork that accompanied relics extracted from Rome's ancient catacombs, for example, often included detailed measurements and descriptions.¹¹ Mathematical precision, it seems, may have been a different kind of knowledge, generated through different kinds of seeing.

The goal of the 1671 recognition ceremony seems to have been to produce new, more credible testimony to be put forward in a new presentation of the case of Matha's bones before the Congregation of Sacred Rites. A speedy resolution was not to be, however, and the years stretched into decades. As it had been in 1669, the campaign to secure the identity of Matha's stolen bones was a project undertaken exclusively by the Discalced wing of the order, perhaps in part because of continuing hostility in Rome toward the Calced Trinitarians, the authors of the original crime. The Discalced Trinitarians seem to have benefited from their confrères' ill repute. In 1686, Nuncio Marcello Durazzo (1633–1710) entrusted the remains of St. John of Matha to the Discalced Trinitarians of Madrid, who placed them below the altar in a small chapel in the cell once occupied by Tomás de la Virgen (1587–1647), a Discalced friar famed for his sanctity. Though the body remained unidentified and the friars were still not allowed to present the body for veneration by the faithful, the transfer of possession was a potent indicator of Rome's positive attitude toward the Discalced branch. In the intervening decades, the friars made at least one attempt in the 1690s to bring the matter of Matha's stolen remains to the attention of the pope, but their efforts went nowhere.[12]

Hidden away in the chapel, Matha's relics ran the risk of diminishment.[13] Moreover, without a body to venerate, Matha's potential for popularity was limited. A religious order's prominence and reputation depended in no small part on its saints, and while relics were not absolutely necessary for fostering popular devotion and the social, political, and economic clout that came with it, their quality of making the holy present could be important aids in establishing a cult. Miracle-working images could be potent alternatives—in the case of the Trinitarians, the Discalced friars worked hard to promote veneration of Jesus of Medinaceli, an image of Christ ransomed from captivity in Morocco in 1682, while their Calced colleagues sought to expand the cult of Our Lady of Remedy.[14] Their emphasis on these devotions reflected the Order of the Most Holy Trinity and of the Captives' core mission of redeeming captives in the Mediterranean slave trade, its perennial rivalry with the Mercedarians, and the rising number of redemptions carried out by all branches of the order during the seventeenth and eighteenth centuries.[15] Though the Trinitarians could not put Matha's relics forward for veneration by the laity, they continued to promote their founder and the invented history on which his recent canonization had relied. For example, the Calced Trinitarian Salvador de Mallea's hagiographical *Epítome de las vidas de los gloriosos S. Jvan de Mata, y S. Félix de Valoys* (Rome, [1665 or 1673?]) relied heavily on both Figueras and Lupián Zapata, as did Alonso de Andrade's

Vidas de los gloriosíssimos Patriarcas San Iuan de Mata, y S. Félix de Valois, fundadores de la ínclita religión de la Santíssima Trinidad Redención de Cautiuos (Madrid, 1668).[16] Later publications continued the tradition. Some were written by members of the order's French branches, such as Bonaventura Baro's *Annales Ordinis SS.mae Trinitatis Redemptionis Captivorum . . . tomus primus* (Rome, 1684) and Ignace Dilloud's *Les vies des Saints Jean de Matha et Félix de Valois, patriarches de l'Ordre de la Sainte Trinité et Redemption des Captifs* (Paris, 1695).[17] Others, like the hagiographic life of Matha and Valois published in Prague in 1726 and the life of Matha that appeared in Turin in 1698, were connected with the Spanish Discalced branch's expansion into Italy, Poland, and the territories of the Austrian Habsburg monarchy.[18]

Until the question of identity was resolved, the Trinitarian Order could not present Matha's relics to the faithful for veneration and thus could not point to any miracles worked directly by his stolen bones. Instead, Trinitarian writers promoted their patron by recounting the marvelous healings and wonderous rescues effected through images and objects associated with the saint. For example, Melchor del Espíritu Santo's 1707 life of Matha listed dozens of cures worked by means of prints, medals, paintings, and statues of the saint, hagiographic pamphlets, cross-emblazoned stones, and little bread rolls marked with Matha's name, as well as a storm calmed through the use of a relic of Matha sent by Cardinal Ginetti to Minister General Pierre Mercier in 1656.[19] Another text, Diego de Jesús's 1687 hagiography of Matha and Valois, even included a miracle worked by the English breviary, the same forged text that, as we saw in chapter 3, was printed in 1649 in order to further the canonization effort and that served as a key piece of evidence in the case for the identity of Matha's stolen remains.[20] Few of these works mentioned the 1655 theft; those that did treated it as a heroic act of piety on the part of the Calced wing.[21]

These efforts were not enough, however. With the identity and thus the authenticity of the relics of the Trinitarians' founder in question and with the Calced wing of the order locked in a schism between the French and the Spanish leaderships that lasted from 1688 to 1704, all Trinitarians were tarred with the brush of scandal.[22] We know little about how the order weathered the War of the Spanish Succession (1701–14), but the fighting and chaos in both the Iberian Peninsula and in the Papal States surely hampered the ability of the Discalced Trinitarians to pursue the case for Matha's relics in Rome. It was not until 1714 that the friars were ready to try their luck again. As we will see, the new case file incorporated some ingenious new arguments and documents, including the new records generated by the 1671 recognition and the 1686 transfer of possession. But, as one Calced Trinitarian critic acidly commented, "[The Discalced friars] made a pretty dossier with more bulk, but not with better or stronger instruments," and their efforts were to no avail.[23] On July 2, 1715, the Congregation of Sacred Rites again issued its damning decision: *non constare de identitate*. It is unclear what moved the members of the committee to vote down the petition, but the new arguments put forward may well have raised some eyebrows, and the old ones very probably elicited many of the same critiques that they fostered in 1669.

Defeated once more, the Discalced Trinitarians turned to different maneuvers. By late 1716, they had collected letters of support from Philip V, founder of the new Bourbon dynasty in Spain, and from the queen, Maria Luisa Gabriella di Savoia, as well as letters from the archbishop of Toledo and from the municipal and ecclesiastical councils of Madrid. In January 1717, Cardinal Francesco Acquaviva d'Aragona, Spain's ambassador to the Holy See, presented Pope Clement XI with the letters and a petition from the Discalced Trinitarians that requested a third hearing before a special committee of the Congregation of Sacred Rites. In the meantime, however, a new obstacle arose. A stray remark in a hagiographic life of St. John of Matha, published in 1707 by the Discalced Trinitarian friar Melchor del Espíritu Santo, let the cat out of the bag that the saint's remains were no longer in the nuncio's residence but were instead in the Discalced Trinitarian monastery in Madrid.[24] Shocked and furious, the Calced Trinitarians protested mightily—or they would have, if only they could. In 1709, tensions between Clement XI and Philip V over the pope's endorsement of Charles III, the rival claimant to the Spanish throne, prompted the closing of the nunciature in Madrid and with it the nuncio's tribunal, a key component in Spain's complicated system of ecclesiastical legal courts. As a result, "there was no one to go to to undo the injustice."[25] Nor could they complain to Rome, since the king had prohibited any communication with the Holy See or appeals to its tribunals.[26]

Only with the reestablishment of diplomatic ties in 1717 under the guidance of Nuncio Pompeo Aldrovandi were the Calced friars able to pursue their grievance by demanding an inquiry into the matter. A search of the nunciature's archives found no records of the handover in 1686 to the Discalced Trinitarians, and when questioned by Aldrovandi's investigator whether it was true that Matha's body had been deposited with them, the Discalced Trinitarians of Madrid allegedly hedged that "they had heard it [said] so."[27] When a copy of the printed *positio* from the second failed attempt before the Congregation of Sacred Rites finally arrived from Rome, the jig was up, since among the few new pieces of evidence it put forward was the notary's account of the 1686 transfer of custody. The reluctant Discalced

Trinitarians of Madrid were forced to admit that they did indeed have possession of Matha's remains, and in response, on the evening of January 11, 1718, Aldrovandi sent a judge from the nunciature's tribunal to their monastery to take back the bones of St. John of Matha and to return them to the nuncio's palace. The friars refused to hand over the relics and appealed both to Rome and to the Council of Castile, the central governing body of the Spanish Crown and a competing appellate jurisdiction to the court of the nuncio. In so doing, they transformed the squabbling over Matha's stolen bones into a minor diplomatic kerfuffle over ecclesiastical versus civil jurisdiction. Such contests were fairly common, especially in cases of internal disputes within religious orders—not for nothing did the outgoing nuncio to Madrid warn his successor in 1675 that "the entanglements and effort that the nuncio encounters because of friars and nuns are incredible, and if he could refrain from dealing with them and seeing them, he would be rid of [those entanglements] completely."[28] In 1718, however, with diplomatic relations between Madrid and Rome still only freshly reestablished, even such a marginal dispute merited the personal intervention of Pope Clement XI himself.[29]

The aggrieved Calced Trinitarian friars also pursued the matter in Rome, where they circulated damaging rumors that their rivals had broken the seals that protected the relics and had dressed the bones in a Discalced habit "so as to inform the world that the saint wore the habit of Discalceds and not of Calceds."[30] Their representative, José de Castañeda, lobbied the pope, the Congregation of Sacred Rites, and Cardinal Acquaviva, the Trinitarians' designated protector at the papal curia.[31] In December 1716, he succeeded in having the Calced wing's claim recognized and a *nihil transeat* imposed on the case of the identity of Matha's remains, which meant that no judgment or concession could be executed without first informing all the interested parties, both Calced and Discalced alike, and without Friar Castañeda first having had a chance to have his say.[32] For the Discalceds, these Calced strategies meant that any new effort to win the Congregation of Sacred Rites' confirmation of the identity of Matha's remains would be even riskier and more troublesome. Even the smallest development meant another skirmish.[33] More significant was the fact that the Vatican chapter—the victim of the original theft—stood in the way of the identity case and would not allow its resolution until the warring Trinitarian branches could come to an accord over the possession of the relics.[34] The disagreement seems to have dragged on until late 1719–early 1720, when the rival Trinitarian branches hammered out an agreement to place Matha's remains in the care of the Jesuits of Madrid and began to discuss the possibility of collaborating in the effort to win recognition of the relics' identity.[35]

New Arguments for Old Bones

In July 1720, Pope Clement XI authorized the Discalced Trinitarians to bring the endless case of the bones of St. John of Matha yet again before a special committee of the Congregation of Sacred Rites, but the gears of the Roman bureaucracy ground slowly, and in early 1721, the question was still pending. The pope's death in March 1721 opened a new opportunity, however, and the Discalced Trinitarians' *procurador general*, Miguel de San José (1682–1757), scrambled to take advantage of the conclave of cardinals to elect a new pontiff and the reshuffling of offices that would accompany a new administration.[36] While a Calced critic would later allege that the Discalced Trinitarians sought to exploit a temporary lapse in the Calced wing's representation in Rome, an eyewitness account of the affair by a Discalced friar revealed that Friar Miguel "resolved to take up the business of the identity [of the relics] because there were at that time in this curia many new cardinals and because many of the old ones who had been against it had died."[37] Miguel de San José also sought to turn to his advantage the assistance of a new ally, Prospero Lambertini, the promoter of the faith. The erudite Lambertini, who would later become Pope Benedict XIV, developed a close friendship with Friar Miguel, and the two consulted closely on many of the Discalced Trinitarians' dealings in Rome.[38] Indeed, so much involved was Lambertini in the Discalced Trinitarians' business before the Congregation of Sacred Rites that he pursued the order's petitions "with such tenacity, as if they were his own."[39] Lambertini not only helped guide the process through the committee but was a key contributor to the Discalced Trinitarians' reframing of their arguments. According to Lambertini's own discussion of the case—included in his landmark manual on the beatification and canonization process, *De servorum Dei beatificatione et beatorum canonisatione*, first published in Bologna between 1734 and 1738—for the case of Matha's stolen bones, he occupied two apparently contradictory positions, serving both as promoter of the faith and as a consultant to the congregation. Moreover, as a member of the Vatican chapter, Lambertini was well positioned to help overcome any objections that might come from that powerful institution.

Once Friar Miguel had gotten the matter of Matha onto the congregation's agenda, he turned to Lambertini for advice on how to structure the case file. Together, Lambertini and Miguel de San José quickly put together the *positio*, or position statement (which they put forward under the name of Giovanni Franchellucci, a lawyer attached to the Congregation of Sacred Rites) and the summary of evidence, "removing from the old one some superfluous things."

They had them printed together with Lambertini's old *animadversiones*, or counterarguments, from 1715, "since His Grace had declared that he had no new objections to add."[40] The *positio*, Lambertini opined, "was the most difficult thing, not knowing whom to trust, since it was a very difficult business, given that [though] the statement could not be a new thing since there were no new documents, it had to appear so to lynx-eyed [readers] like those that take part in a congregation."[41] The problem was that there was no new evidence to present—the only thing that had changed since 1715 was the composition of the committee. The solution, it seems, was to rework the arguments and the evidence to make them more compatible with contemporary notions about historical criticism and the interpretation of sources.

At the end of the seventeenth century, the drive to defend and to shore up the foundations of the Catholic Church by submitting its history to careful critique continued unabated. The reassessment of sacred history by figures like Baronio and Bolland, undertaken in great part to refute the assertions of Protestant foes, continued on in less overtly controversialist tones as Catholic scholars engaged contemporary intellectual trends, turning new approaches and methods to the old stories and sources on which the faith was founded. Their work, like that of others who laid the groundwork for the Catholic Enlightenment, sought "to use the newest achievements of philosophy and science to defend the essential dogmas of Catholic Christianity by explaining them in a new language, and . . . to reconcile Catholicism with modern culture."[42] For some, the popularity of philosophical skepticism sharpened ongoing debates about historical practice by calling into question the reliability of historical evidence and even the possibility of historical knowledge. Responses to historical skepticism at their most extreme could lead to critical readings like those of the Jesuit librarian Jean Hardouin (1646–1729), who became notorious for his contention that almost the entire body of classical literature, including Cicero, Virgil, and most of the patristic texts, were forgeries perpetrated by a conspiracy of medieval monks. While Hardouin's views found few adherents, his methods and goals were very much in the mainstream of contemporary scholarship.[43] Historical criticism, an intellectual approach and a method of inquiry that relied in great part on the experienced scholar's discerning interrogation of the authenticity and trustworthiness of sources, was very much ascendant.

Among those who put the texts and traditions of Catholic Christianity under the loupe were the historians known as the Bollandists and the Maurists. The former, a school of Jesuit scholars based in Antwerp, took up the project of hagiography. In their great work, the encyclopedic *Acta sanctorum*, the Bollandists brought the methods of historical criticism to the lives of the saints, sometimes ruffling pious feathers in the process. In the 1680s and 1690s, for example, the Bollandists and their leading scholar, Daniel van Papenbroek, found themselves locked in a bitter controversy with the Carmelite Order, which objected to the doubt cast by Papenbroek on their legendary foundation by the prophet Elijah. In 1695, the Carmelites succeeded in having the offending volumes of the *Acta sanctorum* condemned by the Spanish Inquisition, a decree that was not lifted until 1715. The Maurists were a collection of erudite Benedictine monks who devoted their attentions to a wide range of scholarly studies in sacred history broadly understood—the history of monasticism, the lives of ancient and medieval saints, editions of medieval monastic writers, and much more. The most prominent of the Maurists was Jean Mabillon (1632–1707), a scholar's scholar most famous for his landmark *De re diplomatica* (1681), which established the field of diplomatics, a historical science devoted to the critical analysis of documents. Like Papenbroek, Mabillon sometimes came under attack for his willingness to question cherished saints and stories, including those of his own order.[44] For his own part, Mabillon insisted that the critical scholar's gimlet eye should not be turned on theological truths: "We must always remember that the Christian religion is not an art or a human science, where everyone is allowed to seek, invent, subtract, and add. It is only a matter [for the scholar] of collecting and faithfully preserving the deposit of tradition, recorded for us in ancient ecclesiastical monuments. The Church alone pronounces and decides; our duty is to listen to her and not to set ourselves up as censors of her decisions."[45]

The "deposit of tradition" was not, however, to be accepted wholly uncritically, and if the lives of the saints were not exempted from examination, neither were their remains. Partaking in both traditional and modern modes of thinking about and interpreting saints and sanctity, practitioners of the new historical methods did not hesitate to apply their tools of criticism to even the most venerated of relics. During Mabillon's tour of Italy in 1685 and 1686, for example, he visited the catacombs of Rome and came away unconvinced that all of the ancient bodies buried under the Eternal City could confidently be identified as those of ancient martyrs for Christ. By 1691, he was circulating a treatise that denounced the criteria by which supposed catacombs were known and the practices that surrounded the distribution of supposed catacomb relics into the wider Catholic world. Five years later, he sent the text to his friend Cardinal Leandro Colloredo (1639–1709), a member of both the Congregation of the Index and of the Congregation of Sacred Rites, who advised him not to publish it. Too many copies were already in circulation, however, and in 1698, threatened with an unauthorized edition, Mabillon published his treatise anonymously as *Eusebii Romani ad Theophilum Gallum Epistola de cultu sanctorum ignotorum*. It made a splash, quickly appearing in multiple editions in Paris, in reprintings in Utrecht, Brussels, Tours, and Grenoble, and in French and German translations.[46]

The mind-set and methods advanced by the Bollandists and Maurists in Flanders and France found a ready reception among like-minded historians in Italy, of whom Ludovico Antonio Muratori (1672–1750) was the most prominent representative.[47] A multifaceted scholar best known for his studies in medieval Italian history, Muratori was familiar with Mabillon's work and may have read the *Epistola* when it circulated in manuscript.[48] Muratori published his own highly critical discussion of catacomb relics in 1698, and while his 1719 takedown of the so-called Iron Crown of Lombardy, a medieval crown preserved in Monza said to contain one of the nails from the True Cross, irritated the pious and patriotic Monzesi, neither text incurred censorship or proscription. By contrast, Mabillon's opponents in Rome pushed hard to have the *Epistola* censored or prohibited, and it was only through the protection of Cardinal Colloredo and Cardinal Nephew Pietro Ottoboni (1667–1740) that the Maurist avoided the Index of Prohibited Books. However, some of Muratori's later works that more directly advocated reforms or critiqued contemporary devotional practices did come in for censure.[49] The opposition faced by Mabillon's study on catacomb relics and the accusations of errors, of pandering to Protestants, even of heresy, that were leveled against Muratori later in his career remind us that scholarship exists in close dialogue with contemporary political, theological, cultural, and even economic trends. To apply historical criticism to the saints and to their bodies might suggest particular political positions, like the Gallican bent of Mabillon and his fellow Maurists, or theological orientations, like the Jansenist or Jansenish leanings of figures like Muratori. While the case for the identity of St. John of Matha's stolen remains did not directly raise these kinds of theological or political questions, Miguel de San José and Lambertini would have to keep in mind the cluster of associations and alignments that their reworking of the historical evidence could evoke.

The *promotor fidei* and future pope Prospero Lambertini traveled in the same reforming scholarly circles as Muratori and Mabillon and thus was well placed to reshape the case for the identity of Matha's remains in ways that reflected the developing new historical norms. In the first decades of the eighteenth century, still at the beginning of his celebrated scholarly career, Lambertini was "one of the most devoted and zealous members" of the

Accademia dei Concilii, an erudite gathering dedicated to critical approaches to Church history founded by Giovanni Giustino Ciampini (1633–1698), a versatile scholar who also founded Rome's premier scientific society, the Accademia Fisico-matematica. During this period, Lambertini also may have intersected with other like-minded figures on Rome's cultural scene, like the historian Francesco Bianchini (1662–1729) and the antiquarian Scipione Maffei (1675–1755).[50] Later, as Pope Benedict XIV and a key figure of the Catholic Enlightenment, he would reestablish the defunct Accademia dei Concilii and create three other new historical academies, "a response to academic Europe—the response of sacred erudition—and a sign of renewed harmony between Rome and the critical method."[51] Such policies were characteristic of Benedict XIV's central place within the "third party" of moderate reformers, a diverse group of erudite churchmen who, like Muratori, sought to renew Catholicism through reforms in theology, education, liturgy, and more.[52]

But this lay far in the future. For now, Lambertini and Procurador General Miguel de San José reworked the evidence and arguments to better fit the new critical approaches to the past. Their starting point, the *positio* and *summarium* from the 1714–15 attempt, had taken a very different approach.[53] In that version, the Discalced Trinitarian legal team had largely jettisoned the language of *terminus a quo*, *medium*, and *terminus ad quem* and downplayed the discussion of moral certainty. Instead, the new position statement focused on four key questions: (1) whether the remains of the saint were physically distinct from the bones of the two successors with whom he had shared the tomb, (2) whether the body handed over to the nuncio in 1655 was the same as the one that had lain in Rome, (3) whether the remains entrusted to the Madrid Discalced Trinitarians in 1686 were the same as those that had been held by the nuncio, and (4) whether the testimony of the three key witnesses—the two thieves and their superior—could be accepted despite the fact that they were convicted criminals. Shoehorned into this schema were the same pieces of evidence as presented in 1669 and some new ones, including testimony from Nuncio Marescotti's 1671 recognition, records from the 1686 handover to the Discalced Trinitarians of Madrid, and a handful of materials originally produced for the case for Matha's immemorial cult in 1666. These latter sources created a new overarching structure for the case, one that contextualized the theft and its outcomes within a broader sweep of historical time.

In effect, the 1714 *positio* and *summarium* positioned the question of the identity of the stolen bones within the new history of Matha and the Trinitarian Order crafted for the canonization effort, stressing the unbroken veneration of the saint from the thirteenth century (or before) to the present and downgrading the crime into one of misguided devotion. The position statement, for example, opened with paragraphs that highlighted the founder's reputation for sanctity during his life and the honors received from Innocent III, who not only had been Matha's student in Paris but who "canonized" his teacher in his confirmation of the Trinitarian rule.[54] The summary of the evidence made the case even more plainly. Of the fourteen items put forward as proofs, the first three pointed to Matha's holiness and his veneration by Innocent III both before and after Matha's death, while the last four documented the 1666 recognition of immemorial cult, the supposed prior canonization by Urban IV, privileges and indulgences in honor of Matha and Felix de Valois granted by popes since 1643, and the extension of the two founders' feast days to the whole of the Church in 1694. Prominent among the evidence were sources either appropriated or fabricated by Juan Figueras Carpi and Antonio Lupián Zapata, such as the invented account from the abbot of Saint-Victor describing Matha's first vision of the angel and the two captives, letters of Innocent III that documented the saint's alleged diplomatic mission in Dalmatia, and forged texts extracted from Figueras, Lupián, and their followers that testified to the 1263 canonization. None of these materials had any direct bearing on the case; rather, their purpose seems to have been to reframe the original crime to stress the culprits' pious aims and lack of motive to deceive.

The 1714 *positio* also brought in a category of evidence largely left out in the materials developed for the 1668–69 hearings before the Congregation of Sacred Rites: miracles. As evidence proving the identity of the stolen bones, the Discalced Trinitarians pointed to four "prodigies" that occurred in the course of the theft: the three chilling howls issued by the "Infernal Enemy" to scare off the thieves, the ease with which the two opened the tomb, their success in closing it again, and the bell heard from the Discalced Trinitarian monastery at San Carlo alle Quattro Fontane as they made their way back to their own Calced monastery several streets away. In performing these miracles, argued Matha's defenders, God honored the holy relics and identified them as such. The miracles also implied that the thieves' unsanctioned actions bore the stamp of divine approval.[55]

Without further evidence, it is impossible to know exactly why the Congregation of Sacred Rites rejected the Discalced Trinitarians' second attempt to secure the identity of Matha's stolen bones. However, the fact that, in drafting the case file for the 1721 attempt, Lambertini and Friar Miguel stripped out all of these elements suggests that if they were not actually objectionable, they were at least considered unconvincing and ineffective. For example, while miracles were a traditional means for recognizing authentic remains of saints, the "prodigies" put forward in the 1714 case file were quite weak and failed to conform to the healings, rescues, or other conventional miracle types usually associated with relics. It may also be that the Congregation of Sacred Rites' "lynx-eyed" readers may have objected to some of the new documentation contained in the 1714 *summarium*, such as the historically implausible mission to Dalmatia or the letter from the abbot of Saint-Victor. By 1721, Antonio Lupián Zapata's reputation as a forger was well known, especially among the Trinitarians' perennial foes, the friars of the Mercedarian Order, who stressed his ill repute in legal briefs as a means of calling into question the documents he produced.[56] While the two rival religious orders regularly fought their legal battles in Madrid before the Council of Castile and the Council of Aragon, their endless struggle may well have found its way to Rome and into the hands of Cardinal Pietro Ottoboni, a member of the Congregation of Sacred Rites and protector of the Mercedarian Order since 1690. We have already seen that Ottoboni was familiar with Mabillon's critical methodology. He also intersected with figures like Ciampini, whose scientific academy he sponsored, and Bianchini, who served him as librarian. While I do not know whether Ottoboni served on the subcommittee that examined the case for Matha's bones in 1714–15, he certainly would have been well placed to point out the many problems with the new evidence.

By removing the dubious documents and questionable miracles, Lambertini and Miguel de San José brought the evidence into closer relationship with the demands of historical criticism.[57] The 1721 *positio* also simplified and streamlined the argumentation, minimizing digressions while covering the same ground. The position statement opened by first tracing the history of the case from the death of Matha in 1213 and his burial in San Tommaso in Formis to the theft in 1655 and then through the various legal moves through the seventeenth century, culminating in the two failed attempts before the Congregation of Sacred Rites in 1669 and 1715. It then laid out the case for the moral certainty of relics and disposed of new concerns raised by legal experts on the case that relics authenticated by the Congregation of Sacred Rites required stronger proofs than those examined by bishops or other, lower-level authorities.[58] The *positio* walked through the evidence demonstrating that the bones in Madrid were the same as those in Rome, offering many of the old arguments (including the bones' distinct size and color) and adding a handful of new arguments (mostly related to reputation and motive).[59] It then refuted the *promotor fidei*'s objections, which had been recycled from the 1714–15 hearings. In particular, the position statement argued that the compromised *fides* of the culprits was no obstacle since the Church had a long history of accepting the testimony of relic thieves—an argument it substantiated with a long list of parallel cases drawn from the lives of saints from the fourth through the sixteenth centuries. Almost none of these examples mentioned miracles, nor were miracles necessary in relic identity cases, "setting aside the prodigious whiteness of the sacred bones of St. John and some other things to which the witnesses in our case testify." The *positio* concluded by noting that unlike the remains of some saints, there was no other contender vying to be recognized as the body of St. John of Matha. "Everyone agrees that either the body is that which is preserved in the Madrid monastery, or that the body of St. John of Matha does not exist in the material world"—that is, does not exist at all.[60]

Once printed, the hastily composed materials were handed over to Cardinal Francesco Acquaviva d'Aragona (1655–1725), protector of Spain and the Spanish Crown's ambassador to the Holy See, who ensured that they were distributed to all of the cardinals of the congregation—not, as was customary, in the name of the Trinitarian Order but in the name of the king and queen of Spain, who had requested the special committee.[61] Meanwhile, Félix Cornejo y Alemán (1675–1735), a key Spanish envoy, "attended to the case with much finesse, making personal visits to those cardinals with whom he could deal without inconvenience."[62] The participation of these high-ranking diplomats and the intervention of the monarchs point to the fact that by 1721, the case for the identity of Matha's stolen bones was as much about politics as it was about the culture of relics and discerning the true bodies of the saints from the false. The divisions of the War of Spanish Succession were still fresh, it seems. According to the anonymous account written by a Discalced Trinitarian close to the case, though Cardinal Michael Friedrich von Althann (1682–1734) and Cardinal Francesco del Giudice (1647–1725) were members of the Congregation of Sacred Rites, they were not given copies of the printed materials since they were outspoken adherents of the Imperial party and opposed to Franco-Spanish pretensions.[63] The Discalced Trinitarians need not have worried about any potential resistance from the two cardinals, however, since though they both received letters from Holy Roman Emperor Charles VI's minister of foreign affairs, Philipp Ludwig Wenzel von Sinzendorf (1671–1742), instructing them to attend the meeting, neither did so.[64]

Instead, opposition came from a different source: the *zelanti* faction, a group of traditionalist cardinals dedicated to upholding papal power and prestige and to defending the traditional exemptions and privileges of the clergy. The chief adversary against the Discalced Trinitarians' bid for Matha's bones was Cardinal Pier Marcellino Corradini (1658–1743), an influential member of the cardinalate and a leading member of the *zelanti* faction who had adamantly opposed the case in 1715. In May 1721, however, Corradini was selected by the newly elected Pope Innocent XIII to serve as the head of the Apostolic Datary, a key office within the curia that was charged with, among other things, handling marriage dispensations, benefices, and other papal favors. Corradini remained a member of the Congregation of Sacred Rites, but his new post seems to have prevented him from appearing at its deliberations; together with the conclave, the opportunity presented by this new appointment had been the impetus to Procurador General Miguel de San José's sudden push to try one more time.[65] Because Corradini could no longer attend the congregation's meetings, the Discalced Trinitarians made sure that he did not receive a copy of the *positio, summarium*, or other materials, but their opponent persisted in actively speaking out against the case and "did no little damage in the meetings he had with some of the cardinals on the occasion of some chapel functions."[66] Joining Corradini in opposition was Cardinal Francesco Barberini *iuniore* (1662–1738), another member of the *zelanti* who, said the anonymous Discalced Trinitarian commentator, "had declared himself so contrary to our cause [that it was] as if it were a mania for his own rights or interests."[67] Coupled with the roadblocks thrown up by the Vatican chapter, the opposition of the two *zelanti* cardinals suggests that the case of the stolen bones of St. John of Matha was about more than faithful witnesses or trustworthy evidence; it was also about the defense of papal property and jurisdiction.

Together, Corradini and Barberini lobbied their colleagues against Matha's bones and were successful in turning a good number of cardinals to their side. Cardinal Fabio degli Abati Olivieri (1658–1738), for example, rarely attended the meetings of the Congregation of Sacred Rites, due to his competing obligations as secretary of briefs. Lobbied by both Princess Teresa Virginia Albani (1699–1792) and Félix Cornejo, Olivieri agreed to come to the meeting and support the cause, but "he later begged off and implied that he was of the contrary opinion than what he was believed to be, because he had conferred with Barberini and Corradini."[68] Others, like Cardinals Nuno da Cunha e Ataíde (1664–1750) and Henri-Pons de Thiard de Bissy (1657–1737), likewise made positive noises but failed to show up for the meeting, perhaps because they too had had conversations with Corradini and Barberini. Though the elderly Cardinal Marescotti was not a member of the Congregation of Sacred Rites, petitions were made to him, since as nuncio, he had personally examined Matha's relics and venerated them. He too declined to intervene in support of the case, "although at first he showed signs of wanting to do so."[69] Another member of the committee, Cardinal Ottoboni, was pressured by an agent of the Duke of Medinaceli to come to the meeting and vote in favor but demurred because he "had some difficulty with the cause because of modern [historical] criticism and other human respects [of the case]."[70] Ottoboni is best known as a lavishly generous patron of the arts, but as we saw, he also was well informed about the new historical methods. While his terse reply did not explain which parts of the Discalced Trinitarians' case he found wanting, it did suggest that not everyone found it convincing. Indeed, at one point, Procurador General Miguel de San José sought to delay the case in order to prepare an entirely new investigation and case file, citing the "inevitable prejudice" that would arise when the case came before the membership of the congregation.[71]

In the end, though, prejudgments and doubts about the case were only a few of the factors at play. The involvement of Spain's new Bourbon monarchs and the alignment of the case with broader cultural and political movements suggest that perhaps these factors mattered as much as or even more than arguments and evidence. On the morning of September 6, 1721, the special committee of the Congregation of Sacred Rites gathered at the Quirinal Palace to consider the question of Matha's stolen bones. While the task of presenting the case had originally been assigned by Innocent XIII to his nephew Cardinal Annibale Albani (1682–1751), that chore was handled instead by Cardinal Fabrizio Paolucci (1651–1726), prefect of the congregation. Of the twelve cardinals in attendance, the majority were allied to a greater or lesser degree with the Franco-Spanish faction, and only two—Barberini and Carlo Agostino Fabroni (1651–1727), the head of the *zelanti* faction in the recently concluded conclave—voted in opposition.[72] Thus, more than sixty-five years after the theft of the bones and more than fifty years since the Discalced Trinitarians first made the case for the relics' identity before the Congregation of Sacred Rites, they had finally won a ruling in their favor—sort of. Not long before the meeting, the Discalced Trinitarians shifted tactics and changed their petition, abandoning their quest to have the identity of Matha's relics formally affirmed and instead seeking only permission to expose the remains for public veneration.[73] Thus, the cardinals' verdict did not actually weigh in on the identity of the body but rather declared that "it is ascertained from sufficient proofs to the effect that the body of St. John of Matha may be exposed to public veneration."[74] This was a compromise judgment, one that sidestepped the vexed question of authenticity but preserved the power of the ecclesiastical hierarchy to determine religious belief and practice.[75]

These distinctions mattered little to the jubilant Discalced Trinitarian friars of San Carlo alle Quattro Fontane, who greeted the news sent from the Quirinal Palace by Cardinal Antonio Felice Zondadari (1665–1737), the erstwhile nuncio to Spain, with "universal rejoicing" and a Te Deum, the traditional hymn of celebration and thanksgiving. Despite some last-ditch efforts on the part of their Calced rivals to stall or scuttle the process, the pope confirmed the decree ten days later, and on September 29, the Spanish Discalced Trinitarians of Rome celebrated their triumph with pyrotechnics, music, and a pontifical Mass.[76] When the news reached Madrid on November 17, Nuncio Aldrovandi and Alejandro de la Concepción (1672–1739), general of the Discalced Trinitarians, staged a ceremony in which the nuncio, accompanied by numerous powerful grandees, venerated the relics and performed a formal inspection of the coffers and their seals (though not of the bones themselves). Three days later, on the feast day of Matha's legendary collaborator St. Felix of Valois, the capital erupted at noon as the bells of all the parish churches, hospitals, monasteries, and convents rang out, the clocks were made to strike, and Matha was saluted with gun salvos, bugles, and drums. Five days of liturgical festivities followed, "as everyone, both clergy and laity alike, congratulated one another, exaggerating that it was a true stroke of luck for Spain to be the possessor of so great a treasure."[77] In the months that followed, Calced and Discalced Trinitarian monasteries around Spain celebrated the restoration of Matha's cult—and, by extension, the confirmation of the relics' identity—with fireworks, festivities, and sermons in praise of the saint.[78]

It is difficult to know what the deciding factor was that convinced the attending cardinals finally to vote in favor of the relics. Was it Miguel de San José and Lambertini's evidence and arguments? Was it the pressure of political alignments? Or was it the last-minute strategy change of dropping the case for identity and taking the less contentious route of seeking only authorization to present the remains for veneration? Lambertini's remarks on the case suggest that in the long run, it may well have been the tactical shift away from identity to the lesser goal of permission that made the difference. In the first edition of his magnum opus, *De servorum Dei beatificatione et beatorum canonizatione* (Bologna, 1738), he reprinted the 1721 *positio*, lightly edited, and the congregation's decree, together with some brief comments. He noted that, given the difficulty of proving relic identity and authenticity, such cases were rare and that most postulators before the congregation preferred to avoid the question by seeking only approval to honor the saint in question with an office and a Mass. This observation and the example he offered (the Holy Lance) made up almost the entirety of his comments on the case, which suggests that his point may have been that the strategy was a winning one.[79] Further comments appended in later editions hinted that all along the stumbling block may have been the question of accepting the tainted testimony of thieves.[80]

In allowing the cult of Matha's relics to go forward, the Congregation of Sacred Rites seems to have opted for a moderate position that tacitly endorsed tradition as a key factor in the discernment of relics. Reputation, local lore, stories passed down from parents to children—these were time-honored criteria for evaluating the authenticity of relics, especially newly discovered saintly remains. An increasing preference for documentary evidence, however, coupled with the methods of modern historical criticism and a priestly mistrust of popular devotion could mean that tradition could be narrowly defined. For example, Jean-Baptiste Thiers (1636–1703), who provoked a celebrated public debate with Mabillon with his uncompromising refutation of a much venerated but very questionable relic known as the Holy Tear of Vendôme, argued that there were only three kinds of acceptable, genuine tradition: divine tradition, "which is a dogma that Jesus Christ taught to his disciples, and which the Catholic Church has always believed"; apostolic tradition, "which was established by the apostles, and which is not found in their writings"; and ecclesiastical tradition—that is, one that was introduced by a council or a pope or a bishop and that passed into force of law slowly, over time, by the tacit consent of the whole community. Vendôme's supposed tear shed by Christ was none of these, claimed Thiers: "It is only a popular tradition, which has no foundation, and which is stripped of all truth."[81] By contrast, Lambertini and Miguel de San José's arguments for the relics of St. John of Matha demonstrated not only that it was publicly known both in Madrid and in Rome that the bones were those of the Trinitarians' founder but that this "not slight but solid, not interrupted but continuous" common opinion was documented by the official recognitions in 1655 and 1671 and by the 1686 transfer. Such public knowledge, they noted, "alone is not sufficient, but greatly contributes to the proving of the identity of relics."[82]

While we cannot know for sure which arguments proved persuasive to the committee, the cardinals' decision could be read as a gesture in support of reputation and long-standing tradition as a means of discerning true saintly remains. In sustaining tradition, the 1721 *positio* and the Congregation of Sacred Rites' decision tempered the more radical potential of modern criticism, which, in the hands of figures like Thiers, threatened to sweep away cherished devotions and beliefs. They also simultaneously reaffirmed the importance of the new historical methods and perspectives within the epistemological culture that surrounded the bodies of the saints in the seventeenth and early eighteenth centuries. Relic authentication, and saint-making more generally, were profoundly historical projects, and for some people, the challenges posed by the new historical criticism to traditional authority and traditional forms of knowledge threatened to undermine even the oldest devotions by pulling them out of time immemorial and inserting them into historical time.[83] Others—including, it seems, Lambertini and the Congregation of Sacred Rites—were able to take an accommodationist stance that could embrace both a rigorous critique of sources and a generous posture toward what the Discalced Carmelite historian Honoré de Sainte-Marie (1651–1729) identified as "pious traditions," another category of tradition that "holds the middle ground between apostolic and ecclesiastical traditions, on the one hand, and the traditions that the critics call 'popular' on the other."[84] It was a moderate position not dissimilar to the position that, over the course of the seventeenth century, the Congregation of Sacred Rites came to adopt toward miracles, which remained indispensable for would-be candidates for sainthood but which were also increasingly subject to the critical scrutiny of doctors and surgeons, as well as theologians and judges. Just as the process of saint-making developed and changed over time, so too did relic culture and the ways in which relics were known. The congregation's decision preserved the evidentiary status of reputation and tradition but refined it according to its growing "intensely legalistic rather than theological cast" and "thirst for written evidence."[85] Even the most time-honored categories of relic evidence were adjusted to meet the new historicizing norms and rendered intelligible to the expectations of the examining authorities.

Lambertini's more general discussion in *De servorum Dei beatificatione et beatorum canonizatione* on proving the identity of relics underscored the intimate connection between long-standing tradition and moral certainty, that category of certainty that, as we saw in chapter 4, had by the late seventeenth century come to be broadly accepted as the form most correctly applied to the remains of the saints. In ancient times, he noted, trial by fire had been a customary means of proving the identity of relics, "but, since all this is now ceased and [trials by fire] are avoided . . . today, whether one pursues [a case of] identity of bodies and relics in the court of the ordinary or in the court of the Congregation of Sacred Rites, one must establish the identity of bodies and relics through solid proofs, and, if not metaphysical or physical evidence, at least certain proofs through moral evidence." While miracles could cement a case, much of the moral evidence could come "from tradition and from ancient and constant reputation." He supported this with examples drawn from late antiquity of relics proven by or disproven by the lack of the testimony of senior clerics and other older people and stories told by parents to children. While identity cases adjudicated at the apostolic rather than the ordinary (episcopal) level required weightier evidence, the operative principle of moral certainty remained the same. Were uncertain saints' bones subjected to more demanding standards of proof, "it would destroy the identity of holy relics."[86]

While politics remained largely outside of Lambertini's discussion, the final resolution of the long-running case of Matha's relics highlights the ways in which the veneration of the saints and their relics could be intimately connected to politics. As a religious order of French origin but with deep roots in the Spanish kingdoms, the Order of the Most Holy Trinity and of the Captives was arguably well placed to make connections with the new Bourbon monarchs of Spain. Though it is difficult to gauge the impact of the interventions of Philip V and his queen and the lobbying performed by diplomats representing the Spanish Crown, they remind us that while early modern princely power cannot be said to have derived from sacred objects, royal manipulation remained one of the many ways in which saints and their bodies were sites on which different groups worked out their agendas.[87] Relics performed what Jane Tomkins has called "cultural work"; that is, like the nineteenth-century novels she examined, they "provide[d] society with a means for thinking about itself, defining certain aspects of a social reality which the authors and their readers shared, dramatizing its conflicts, and recommending solutions."[88] While the French kings seem not to have taken any particular interest in the case, for the new Spanish monarch, Matha's remains may have offered a chance to connect with a cult that, according to the Discalced Trinitarians, had come under royal protection since the relics first arrived at the court in 1655. For the cardinals associated with the Franco-Spanish faction of the recent wars, a vote in favor of the relics offered an opportunity to articulate and to affirm their allegiance, while for those affiliated with the *zelanti*, their opposition expressed their political program of defending papal authority in the face of pressures exerted by secular powers.

In truth, the question of the stolen bones of St. John of Matha was a fairly minor matter, both for the new Bourbon dynasty, which seems to have taken less of an interest in the politics of canonization than its Habsburg predecessors did, and for the cardinals of the Congregation of Sacred Rites themselves.[89] For the Trinitarian friars, however, whether they were Calced, French Reformed, or especially Discalced, Matha's relics were a cause worth pursuing for decades because of their deep importance to their founder's burgeoning cult and, by extension, to the order's internal shared sense of institutional history and mission and to the projection of that history and mission to the world. For them, the cultural work of the body of their founder was to bring the past into the present, making concrete and material their "family" bond and reinforcing their commitment to its unique calling. In the words of one Discalced Trinitarian preacher who celebrated the congregation's decree, "May you be congratulated, my glorious father and patriarch; now may your cult live for eternities, so that so great a triumph may be acclaimed around the whole orb. . . . And may your Trinitarian religion of mine live for eternities, so that [the friars] may be your echoes, triumphs, announcements, and memories of such sovereign virtues."[90] The relics were also important to the Trinitarians' endless lawsuits with the Mercedarians, which persisted until the early 1770s.[91] The remains of a founding saint were potent guarantees of an order's prestige, its charism, and its institutional culture, and as the two rival redemptive orders jockeyed for position, they regularly called into question each other's claims to antiquity and, thus, prominence. There was even an attempt in the 1680s to transform St. John of Matha and St. Felix of Valois into the true founders of the Order of the Blessed Virgin of Mercy, rather than St. Pere Nolasc.[92] For the Trinitarians, Matha's remains were a potent symbol of their order's preeminence, one that could not be allowed to molder away unvenerated.

Though the Congregation of Sacred Rites' decision dodged the difficult question of the identity of Matha's remains, the Trinitarian Order greeted the decree as an affirmative judgment that the stolen bones were indeed those of its spiritual father, and over the course of the eighteenth, nineteenth, and twentieth centuries, that interpretation became firmly lodged in the order's historiography. Much like the invented past crafted by Juan Figueras Carpi and Antonio Lupián Zapata, the decree told the friars what they already knew in their hearts: that the body in Madrid was truly that of their founder and that the remains were one and the same as those that had lain undisturbed for centuries in Rome. Relics and the specialized knowledge that surrounded them thus did not stand alone but were embedded in the larger body of stories, legends, and beliefs that underpinned a community's sense of itself. While the knowledge created around the relics and the evidence presented to the congregation reflected the shifting standards and norms of the larger evidentiary environment, they also responded to the needs and expectations of the Trinitarian Order and its members. In this sense, evidence was situational and depended on its context and its relation to the community to which it spoke. If holy bodies were "good to think with" and their peculiar materiality was a flexible interpretive tool with which to contend with the ambiguities and uncertainties of early modern Catholic culture, for the members of the Trinitarian Order, the knowledge that was produced around them rested on and reinforced the certainties of their own community, its history and mission, its unique charism and way of being in the world. For the nuns and friars of the Order of the Most Holy Trinity and of the Captives, then, the Congregation of Sacred Rites' 1721 decree was far more than simply a confirmation of the identity of the stolen bones of St. John of Matha; it was a confirmation of their identity as the spiritual daughters and sons of their founder and of their order itself.

EPILOGUE

While Trinitarians of all stripes heralded the 1721 ruling by the Congregation of Sacred Rites and the restoration of St. John of Matha to full veneration, the shared heritage he represented and the shared devotion he now enjoyed did not prevent the Calced and Discalced wings of the order he founded from continuing to war with each other over his remains. In 1722, the Vatican chapter formally donated Matha's relics to the Discalced Trinitarians of Madrid, who spent heavily to install the remains in a lavish shrine and silver reliquary and commemorated the event with a jasper inscription mounted on the wall of the monastery church.[1] The Calced Trinitarians of Castile, dismayed to find themselves with no relic at all, petitioned Giovanni Battista Tolomei (1653–1726), the order's new cardinal protector, for either the skull or half of the body. They prepared a lawsuit to support their claim, but in the long run, they were forced to make do with two lesser bones, an arm bone and a rib, and to promise to drop permanently any demands for more. They made the best of a bad situation, however, by putting on a grand procession and a cycle of sermons in 1723 that, according to the outraged Discalced *procurador general* Miguel de San José, misled the public into thinking that they had half, if not more, of Matha's body.[2] Further conflict erupted in 1724, when there surfaced in Toledo an unauthorized relic of the saint, extracted and donated to the Calced friars of that city by Francisco de Arcos, the same celebrated Trinitarian preacher who had first brought the case to the attention of Philip IV in 1655 and who probably had been one of the masterminds behind the theft.[3]

On the matter of possession of the body of the Trinitarians' founder, however, by the middle of the 1720s, the Discalced and Calced branches seem to have come to some kind of detente. The 1749 gift of Matha's original sarcophagus from San Tommaso in Formis to the Discalced Trinitarians of Madrid by Pope Benedict XIV—that is, Prospero Lambertini himself—made scarcely a ripple.[4] The lack of conflict over Matha's relics did not, however, portend unity between the various wings of the Trinitarian Order. In 1769, a royal commission forcibly reduced the French Calced, Discalced, and Reformed branches into a single institution named the Canons Regular of the Most Holy Trinity, and in 1771, the French Discalced and Reformed were formally suppressed by Pope Clement XIV.[5] Divisions between Calced and Discalced Trinitarians remained in place in Iberia, however, where the Spanish Discalced Trinitarians continued their development, founding new monasteries in Portugal and expanding into Italy and eastern Europe.[6] By the end of the eighteenth century, however, the political, social, and cultural turmoil of the French Revolution completely extinguished what remained of the order in France, and new state policies dramatically reduced its presence in Poland, Lithuania, and Austria. In Spain, both Calced and Discalced Trinitarians persisted until the 1820s and 1830s, when the Spanish state expropriated Church properties and suppressed religious orders. Similar government actions in Italy in the 1860s and 1870s further reduced the Trinitarians almost out of existence. While the changing political climate in Spain after 1875 saw a resurrection of the Discalced branch, by the end of the nineteenth century, the Calced Trinitarians had dwindled down to a handful of friars, all living in the general curial house at Santissima Trinità degli Spagnoli, on Rome's Via Condotti.[7] Antonio Martín Bienes (1806–1894), the last leader of the Calced Trinitarians, died there in 1894 and with him the whole of that ancient, original branch of the order. A zealous defender of the Calced Trinitarian tradition, Martín Bienes preferred to hand over the Via Condotti complex to the Dominicans for use as a training institute for missionaries headed to the Philippines rather than allowing the property to fall into the hands of his Discalced rivals.[8] The extinction of the Calced Trinitarians was finalized in 1900, when the surviving wing dropped the Discalced name, becoming simply the Order of the Most Holy Trinity and of the Captives.[9]

Throughout these upheavals, the majority of Matha's bones remained in Madrid in their place of honor on the main altar of the monastery of the Discalced Trinitarians, until, faced with exclaustration and suppression in the 1830s, the friars found it advisable to transfer the relics to Madrid's convent of Discalced Trinitarian nuns. A century later, alarmed by the declaration of the Second Spanish Republic in 1931, the sisters entrusted Matha's body to the prominent Navarro Reverter family for safekeeping, but the reliquary holding the bones was stolen during the chaos of the Spanish Civil War (1936-39), only to turn up again safe and sound in the basement of the church of San Isidro, Madrid's temporary cathedral.[10]

After the war, the relics were returned to the custody of the Discalced Trinitarian nuns until 1966, when they were transferred yet again to the order's church in Salamanca. There they remain today, housed not, as is traditional, in the main altar but in a special vitrine installed in a palm-shaped column in the center of the sanctuary. Matha's place at the heart of the Salamanca church is testimony to the success of the efforts on the part of the Trinitarians during the seventeenth century to ensure their founder's sainthood and to prove the identity of his relics, as well as to the centrality of the founder's charism in the order today. It is also emblematic of the ways in which the meanings invested in the saints and their bodies shift and change with the times. The Trinitarians' newly constructed church in Salamanca, which was completed in 2000, reflects a very contemporary view of sainthood that emphasizes the saint's accessibility and connection to the faithful. "The idea is a saint in the midst of the people," explained the superior of the Salamanca Trinitarians in a 2014 interview. That accessible holiness conveyed by the relics' central location takes on a larger meaning in relation to the symbolism of the palm tree column. "It comes from a part of the Bible that says the righteous—that is, the saint—will grow like a palm; holiness produces fruits, and the Holy of Holies is Jesus Christ."[11] Were St. John of Matha alive today, commented the Salamanca superior in another interview, he would work "for the respect of human rights, concretely for the right of religious expression."[12] For today's Trinitarians, Matha's mortal remains are a reminder of the founder's charism in the order today and the fundamental theological truths of Christianity. For their seventeenth-century predecessors, too, the relics of St. John of Matha pointed to key concepts and values. For example, one preacher who celebrated the 1721 ruling noted that just as "the identity of this holy body that the Church declares today is not the identity of one part alone, like the head, hand, or arm, but also the identity of all of that whole body," so too was the whole of the body of Christ present in the Eucharist and present in the hearts of believers: "the same identity that we adore in the Sacrament, we receive in our hearts."[13]

But in the climate of uncertainty fostered by the deep cultural shifts of the early modern period, the doubts raised by Gonzalo de Medina and José de Vidal's daring robbery took on a larger significance. The questions that surrounded the case of St. John of Matha's stolen bones—questions of materiality, of truth and falsity, of certainty and uncertainty, of evidence and ways of knowing—assumed a special salience. The crime lay bare the tensions embedded in relics as powerful material objects. The theft removed Matha's remains from their identifying, individualizing context within the sepulcher in San Tommaso in Formis; in doing so, it potentially endangered them by rendering them nameless and generic, mere bones rather than relics. With the relics stuffed into an improvised sack, stripped of the identifying inscription on the tomb's lid (but, crucially, not the key passage from the English breviary that proved so important in the identity case), their ability to *be* the saint and make visible his invisible presence was dangerously imperiled. The ensuing legal wrangling demonstrates some of the ways in which early modern Catholic relic culture confronted this "complicated dynamic of seen and unseen" that lay at the heart of the materiality of saintly remains.[14]

As we have seen, to question the identity of Matha's relics was also to question their authenticity. Questions of truth and falsity surrounded St. John of Matha—both in the case of his stolen remains and also in the evidence produced in the campaign to prove his immemorial cult and affirm his status as a recognized saint. Unlike Giovanni Calà, the "fake saint" examined by Stefania Tutino, no one doubted that the founder of the Order of the Most Holy Trinity and of the Captives was a true historical figure.[15] But much like Calà or St. Pere Nolasc or many other holy figures of ancient or medieval Christianity, some of the key sources on which Matha's life story rested were invented, fabrications or forgeries crafted by the saint's partisans. Even in an age of increasingly exacting expectations for historians and growing rigor and legalism in saint-making, forgeries like those crafted by Juan Figueras Carpi and Antonio Lupián Zapata remained viable resources for some of those who sought to promote the saints and their veneration. Modern readers should not presume, however, that early modern readers were simply credulous or that the promoters of the fictions that surrounded St. John of Matha were merely unprincipled liars. For some, devout ends may have justified deceptive means. Critical, even skeptical approaches to the past and its sources existed alongside or in conjunction with interpretive modes like pious affection that put the truth of doctrine before the truth of history. Further, selective retellings of the past played a key role in supporting the cherished beliefs that knit together community solidarities. The invented history that came to adhere around St. John of Matha was also an articulation of just who the members of the Trinitarian Order—Calced, Discalced, or Reformed alike—thought themselves to be.

Such uses of history will probably be familiar to many twenty-first-century readers. Today, Americans are locked in an increasingly bitter struggle over how to teach about the place of systemic racism in their nation's history. For some, the issue is one of speaking difficult truths about the past and, in so doing, fostering a new, more inclusive national civic community; for others, such truths cannot be truths, in part because they call into question the shared beliefs that undergird the status quo and the sense of national belonging as they understand it. Now as then, history is vital to creating communities; now as then, history is sometimes shaped around imagined pasts or even "alternative facts."

Problems of truth and falsity were also problems of doubt and certainty. Hermeneutic strategies like pious affection and the extension of moral certainty to Matha's bones mirrored sixteenth- and seventeenth-century European culture's struggle with questions of certainty and uncertainty and remind us of the ways in which early modern relic culture and the cult of the saints more generally reflected the larger society in which they were immersed. Contrary to the impression one might receive from popular books on the subject, the veneration of the saints and their bodies did not peter out with the Protestant Reformation but continued on into the modern era, shifting and changing with the times.[16] Evidentiary expectations, new ways of knowing and thinking about the world, and new values all shaped the cult of relics as it moved through the seventeenth century and into the early decades of the Enlightenment. The case of St. John of Matha's stolen bones demonstrates how the veneration of the saints and their bodies was not a timeless holdover of a bygone era but was instead intimately connected to some of the most vital questions of the day. The saints were indeed "good to think with."[17]

At some point after the mysterious reappearance of Matha's remains in the church's basement, they were subjected to yet another examination, this time conducted by Manuel Pérez de Petinto (1892–1981), a celebrated specialist in forensic medicine. Pérez de Petinto seems to have had something of a sideline specialty in identifying holy relics—in 1942, he deployed ultraviolet light to distinguish the remains of St. Francis Borgia, which had been destroyed by arson in 1931.[18] According to one Trinitarian history, in his examination of the relics of St. John of Matha, the doctor found that they were intact and undisturbed, but an unsigned, undated document housed in the archive of the Trinitarian monastery in Rome suggests that either in this examination or in another one, new uncertainties arose.[19] Typed on the monastery's letterhead and tucked in with the centuries-older documents related to the case of Matha's stolen bones, the document sought solutions to new concerns surrounding the relics. It seems that the urn holding the relics contained one femur too many. Even more distressing, there was some possibility that one of the femurs was smaller and perhaps was that of a woman.[20] The outcome of these deliberations is unknown, but the questions they raised demonstrate the ways in which, deep into the twentieth century and indeed today, relics remain objects of a specialized culture of knowledge that shifts to reflect and reinforce new ways of knowing and proving the holy.[21]

Notes

Abbreviations

AASG	Archivo de la Abadía del Sacromonte, Granada
AAV	Archivio Apostolico Vaticano, Vatican City
ACDF	Archivio della Congregazione per la Dottrina della Fede, Vatican City
AHN	Archivo Histórico Nacional, Madrid
ASC	Archivo de San Carlino alle Quattro Fontane, Rome
ASDS	Archivio Storico Diocesano di Sassari, Sassari
ASVR	Archivio Storico del Vicariato di Roma, Rome
BA	Biblioteca Angelica, Rome
BAV	Biblioteca Apostolica Vaticana, Vatican City
BNE	Biblioteca Nacional de España, Madrid
BPPM	Biblioteca Pública del Estado de Palma de Mallorca
PL	*Patrologia Latina*, edited by Jacques-Paul Migne, 217 vols. (Paris, 1841–55)
Positio 1666	*Congregatione Sacrorum Rituum siue Eminentissimo, ac Reurendissimo D. Card. Ginetto. Romana Canonizationis Seruorum Dei Ioannis de Matha, & Felicis de Valois Fundatorum Ordinis Sanctissimae Trinitatis Redemptionis Captiuorum. Positio super dubio an sententia Eminentissimi Cardinalis Vicarii super casu excepto fit confirmanda, vel infirmanda, in casu &c.* Rome, 1666.
Positio 1669	*Congregatione Sacrorum Rituum siue Eminentissimo, ac Reurendissimo D. Card. Ginetto Hispaniarum identitatis corporis Sancti Ioannis de Matha Fundatoris Ordinis Sanctiss. Trinitatis Redemptionis Captiuorum. Positio super identitate corporis Sancti Ioannis de Matha.* Rome, 1669.
Positio 1714	*Sacrorum Rituum Congregatione. Emo, & Rmo. D. Cardinali Casino ponente Hispaniarum identitatis corporis S. Ioannis de Matha fundatoris Ordinis Sanctissimae Trinitatis Redemptionis Captiuorum. Positio super identitate dicti corporis.* Rome, 1714.
Positio 1721	*Sacra Rituum Congregatione. Eminentissimo, & Reverendissimo D. Card. Paulutio pro Eminentissimo, & Reverentissimo D. Card. Annibale Albano*

	ponente Hispaniarum identitatis corporis S. Ioannis de Matha Fundatoris Ordinis Sanctissimae Trinitatis Redemptionis Captivorum. Positio. Rome, 1721.
RAH	Real Academia de la Historia, Madrid
Summarium 1669	*Hispaniarum identitatis corporis Sancti Ioannis de Matha alterius ex Fundatoribus Ordinis Sanctissimae Trinitatis Redemptionis Captiuorum: Summarium.* Rome, 1669.
Summarium 1714	*Hispaniarum identitatis corporis S. Joannis de Matha. Summarium.* Rome, 1714.
UG-BHR	Universidad de Granada, Biblioteca del Hospital Real

Prologue

1. Lucás de la Purificación, *Historia del sagrado cuerpo*, 10–14.
2. On the Calced Trinitarian monastery of St. Francesca Romana in the Via Sistina, see Armellini, *Chiese di Roma*, 370, 374.
3. Vega y Toraya, *Crónica*, 250, 271–77. For the lengthy lawsuit over possession of the church, see BAV, Archivio del Capitolo di S. Pietro in Vaticano, Miscellanea I, XV. On the history of S. Tommaso in Formis, see Svizzeretto, "Chiesa e l'ospedale"; Svizzeretto, "Passaggio"; Antonino dell'Assunta and Romano di S. Teresa, *S. Tommaso in Formis sul Celio*.
4. Morbidelli, "*Ecclesie sint plani operis*."
5. According to Vega y Toraya (*Crónica*, 278), Medina was a Castilian whose home monastery was the Calced house in Madrid, while Vidal was Aragonese and based in Mallorca.
6. Svizzeretto, "Passaggio," 407.
7. Fita, "Sarcófago marmóreo."
8. Antonino dell'Assunta, *Ministrorum Generalium*, 9–10, 14–18.
9. For the note, see Lucás de la Purificación, *Historia del sagrado cuerpo*, 16–17.
10. On the shoe, see *Summarium 1669*, 7.
11. *Summarium 1669*, 4–9; *Summarium 1714*, 9–22; Arcos, *Memorial*, 17r.
12. *Summarium 1669*, 38.
13. For Arias's disguise, see ASC, leg. 16a, pieza XVI/3, "Hispaniarum. Identitatis corporis Sancti Joannis de Matha alterius ex fundatoribus Ordinis Sanctissimae Trinitatis Redemptionis Captivorum" (manuscript draft of *Summarium 1669*, testimony of Friar Juan de San Francisco [witness 11]), n.p. Throughout, my ASC citations refer to the shelf mark of a single bundle (*legajo*) of documents, which is internally divided into numbered sections (*piezas*) but unpaginated, so references will also include the incipit, the first lines of the substantive text (after the honorific addresses to the recipients or the indication of the subject matter).

Chapter 1

1. Lucás de la Purificación, *Historia del sagrado cuerpo*, 11.
2. This date is disputed. See Wisniewski, *Beginnings of the Cult of Relics*, 159–79.
3. Bartlett, *Why Can the Dead Do Such Great Things?*, 17.
4. Augustine, *De opere monachorum*, in *PL*, vol. 40, col. 575.
5. K. Schreiner, "Discrimen veri ac falsi"; Malo, "Pardoner's Relics."
6. Brown, *Cult of the Saints*, 69–85.
7. Russell, *Luther's Theological Testament*, 126.
8. Calvin, *Treatise on Relics*, 56. See Fabre and Wilmart, "*Traité des reliques* de Jean Calvin."
9. Walsham, "Skeletons in the Cupboard," 123.
10. Julia, "Église post-tridentine et les reliques."
11. Council of Trent, session 25, December 3–4, 1563, "On invocation, veneration and relics of the saints, and on sacred images," in Tanner, *Decrees of the Ecumenical Councils*, 775–76.

12. Julia, "Église post-tridentine et les reliques," 72.
13. For an introduction to the saints and their place in medieval life, see Bartlett, *Why Can the Dead Do Such Great Things?*; Vauchez, *Sainthood*. On the saints in early modern domestic devotions, see Brundin, Howard, and Laven, *Sacred Home*.
14. Bartlett, *Why Can the Dead Do Such Great Things?*, 239–332. On relics in diplomacy, see Bozóky, *Politique des reliques*; Rollason, *Saints and Relics*; Osborne, "Politics, Diplomacy and the Cult of Relics"; Buettner, "Past Presents."
15. Geary, *Furta Sacra*; Harris, "Gift, Sale, and Theft."
16. G. Clark, "Victricius of Rouen," 392.
17. Thomas Aquinas, *Summa Theologiae*, 205 (III, q. 25, a. 6, ad 2); Foyer, "Quand le corps fait signe," 35.
18. Bartlett, *Why Can the Dead Do Such Great Things?*, 27–84.
19. Ibid., 317.
20. Smith, "Relics," 47.
21. Dozio, *De signis Ecclesiae Dei*, 117–24.
22. Ferrand, *Disquisitio Reliquiaria*.
23. Bouley, *Pious Postmortems*, 2–3.
24. Fernando Vidal, "Miracles, Science, and Testimony"; Bouley, *Pious Postmortems*. Other examples include Daston, "Marvelous Facts and Miraculous Evidence"; Duffin, *Medical Miracles*; Gentilcore, *Healers and Healing*; Park, "Criminal and the Saintly Body"; Pomata, "Malpighi and the Holy Body"; Siraisi, "Signs and Evidence"; Ziegler, *Medicine and Religion*.
25. Ditchfield, "Thinking with Saints," 553.
26. Hazard, *Crisis of the European Mind*; S. Schreiner, *Are You Alone Wise?*; Robbins, *Arts of Perception*; Tutino, *Shadows of Doubt*; Fuchs, García-Arenal, and Cañete, *Quest for Certainty*.
27. S. Clark, *Thinking with Demons*; Sluhovsky, *Believe Not Every Spirit*; Zagorin, *Ways of Lying*; Eliav-Feldon, "Religious Dissimulation"; García-Arenal, *After Conversion*.
28. Zarri, *Finizione e santità*; Schutte, *Aspiring Saints*; Keitt, *Inventing the Sacred*; Sluhovsky, *Believe Not Every Spirit*.
29. For early modern forgery, see Grafton, *Forgers and Critics*. On sacred history, see Ditchfield, *Liturgy, Sanctity and History*; Olds, *Forging the Past*; Van Liere, Ditchfield, and Louthan, *Sacred History*. On historical truth and doctrinal truth, see Tutino, *Shadows of Doubt*; Tutino, *Fake Saint*.
30. Olds, "Ambiguities of the Holy"; Tausiet, *Dedo robado*; Sosa Mayor, "Experimenting with Relics."
31. On materiality in late medieval and early modern religion, see Bynum, *Christian Materiality*. On material religion among Protestants, see Heal, "Visual and Material Culture." See also Ivanič, Laven, and Morrall, *Religious Materiality*; Ivanič, "Early Modern Religious Objects."
32. Sosa Mayor, "Experimenting with Relics," 239. On lay Catholic understandings of material religion, see especially Ivanič, *Cosmos and Materiality*.
33. Brodman, *Charity and Religion*, 150–62; Brodman, "Trinitarian and Mercedarian Orders"; Cipollone, *Studi intorno a Cerfroid*; Cipollone, *Mosaico*; Cipollone, *Cristianità—Islam*.
34. Pujana, *Reforma de los Trinitarios*; Porres Alonso, *Libertad a los cautivos*.
35. Hershenzon, *Captive Sea*. See also G. Weiss, *Captives and Corsairs*.
36. Carlos Varona, "Imagen y santidad"; Beaven, "Robbing the Grave."

Chapter 2

1. Hunt, *Vacant See*.
2. Geary, *Furta Sacra*. For early modern examples, see Tausiet, *Dedo robado*; Joseph de Santa Teresa, *Resunta de la vida*, 123–25.
3. Herrmann-Mascard, *Reliques des saints*, 386–402.
4. Fagundes, *Tractatus*, 19–20.
5. AHN, Inq., leg. 1079, fol. 469v.
6. Dandelet, *Spanish Rome*.

7. On zones of diplomatic immunity in Rome, see Anselmi, *Palazzo*, 169–93; Napolitano, "Prospects of Statecraft"; Pastor, *History of the Popes*, 342–61.
8. Dandelet, *Spanish Rome*, 121–59.
9. On the Trinitarian rule, see Gross, *Trinitarians' Rule of Life*; Pagano, "Testo della Regola dei Trinitari."
10. González Fernández, "Contexto histórico," 157; Romano di Santa Teresa, *Ordine trinitario in Italia*.
11. For Trinitarian holdings in the Levant, see Aurrecoechea and Moldón, *Fuentes históricas*, 120–25, 178–81. On the Trinitarians in England, see Gray, *Trinitarian Order in England*, 10–15. On the early expansion of the order more generally, see Brodman, "Trinitarian and Mercedarian Orders," 211–43.
12. Moreau-Rendu, *Captifs libérés*, 50–51. For the gradual modification of this requirement, see Aurrecoechea and Moldón, *Fuentes históricas*, 23, 288–89. On the Trinitarian house in Paris, see Deslandres, "Couvent et l'église."
13. Cipollone, "Indole non-militare."
14. Aurrecoechea and Moldón, *Fuentes históricas*, 33–34.
15. Pujana, *Reforma de los Trinitarios*, 31–33.
16. Aliaga Asensio, "Claves políticas," 250; Deslandres, *Ordre des Trinitaires*, 1:35. On the 1568 split between the Andalusian and Castillian provinces, see Pujana, *Reforma de los Trinitarios*, 125–38. For the Trinitarians in Great Britain, see López, *Noticias históricas*, but on this text, see McRoberts, "Three Bogus Trinitarian Pictures."
17. Aurrecoechea and Moldón, *Fuentes históricas*, 38–40.
18. Deslandres, *Ordre des Trinitaires*, 1:190, 221.
19. Le Fur, "Renaissance d'un apostolat."
20. Pujana, *Reforma de los Trinitarios*, 44–47.
21. On the French Reformed Trinitarians, see Pujana, *Reforma de los Trinitarios*, 255–60; Diefendorf, *Planting the Cross*, 110–29.
22. Pujana, *Reforma de los Trinitarios*; García Oro and Portela Silva, "Felipe II y la reforma."
23. Ginarte González, *Orden Trinitaria*, 144–45. For the papal decrees authorizing the independence of the Spanish Discalced branch, see *Exemptio fratrum discalceatorum*, which is included in BNE, ms. 18174, fols. 58r–61v.
24. Deslandres, *Ordre des Trinitaires*, 1:160.
25. Diego de la Madre de Dios, *Chorónica*, 50–52; Ginarte González, *Orden Trinitaria*, 100–102.
26. Deslandres, *Ordre des Trinitaires*, 1:247–48. On Petit's portrait, see Liez, "Portrait comme affirmation d'autorité." For Petit's opinions on the French Reformed branch, see his letters in BNE ms. 18238, fols. 164r, 168r.
27. Porres Alonso, *Libertad a los cautivos*, 484–85.
28. Porres Alonso, "Dos primeros pleitos," 880. Used as a base for the turbans worn throughout the Mediterranean Islamic world, Spanish-made red caps (*bonetes*) were an important commodity in the redemption trade. See Martínez Torres, "Plata y lana para el 'infiel.'"
29. *Summarium* 1669, 10.
30. Reported by Bernardino de San Antonio, *Epitome*, fol. 71r–v.
31. Hershenzon, "[P]ara que me saque cabesa por cabesa," 11–12.
32. Hershenzon, "Towards a Connected History of Bondage," 1.
33. Hershenzon, *Captive Sea*, 2. There is much scholarly disagreement over just how many people were caught up in the Mediterranean slave trade. Cf. Davis, *Christian Slaves, Muslim Masters*, and Matar, *British Captives*, 9–11.
34. For a survey of captivity in the early modern Mediterranean, see Hershenzon, "Towards a Connected History of Bondage."
35. Cipollone, *Cristianità—Islam*, 506; Maillard, *Papes et le Maghreb*, 53–54, 430.
36. Hernando, "Tertia pars."
37. Porres Alonso, *Libertad a los cautivos*.
38. Hershenzon, *Captive Sea*, 47–48.

39. On French redemptions during the sixteenth century, see Porres Alonso, *Libertad a los cautivos*, 197–98.
40. Skilliter, "Hispano-Ottoman Armistice of 1581."
41. For Iceland, see Egilsson, *Travels*.
42. Porres Alonso, *Libertad a los cautivos*, 316–19.
43. Lecerf, "Missions de rédemption."
44. Martínez Torres, *Prisioneros de los infieles*, 82.
45. Ibid., 77–99.
46. Porres Alonso, *Libertad a los cautivos*, 23; Martínez Torres, "Corso turco-berberisco."
47. G. Weiss, *Captives and Corsairs*, 212–20.
48. Kaiser, "Économie de la rançon."
49. Porres Alonso, "Hospitales trinitarios"; Porres Alonso, *Libertad a los cautivos*, 175–84; Friedman, *Spanish Captives*, 91–102.
50. Porres Alonso, *Libertad a los cautivos*, 161–73. On Jesuits, see Andújar Castillo, "Rescates de cautivos"; Fabre, "Affaire Jean de la Goutte." On Lazarists, see G. Weiss, *Captives and Corsairs*, 46. On other religious orders, see Barrio Gozalo, "Tolerancia y vida religiosa."
51. Prologue of the 1272 Constitutions of the Mercedarian Order, in Brodman, *Ransoming Captives*, 127. On the Mercedarians' foundation date, see ibid., 15–16.
52. Ibid., 66, 135.
53. Porres Alonso, *Libertad a los cautivos*, 173. See also Hershenzon, *Captive Sea*, 47–48; Le Fur, "Renaissance d'un apostolat."
54. Farge, *Orthodoxy and Reform*, 38.
55. Perdrizet, *Calendrier parisien*, 256.
56. Berty, *Topographie historique du vieux Paris*, 332–34.
57. Denifle, *Chartularium Universitatis Parisiensis*, 525–26, 544–46; Collard, "Entre fardeau et honneur."
58. Deslandres, *Ordre des Trinitaires*, 1:204, 206.
59. Arbois de Juvainville, *Histoire des ducs*, 531; Deslandres, *Ordre des Trinitaires*, 2:62.
60. Thornton, *Prophecy*, 159–60. See Aurrecoechea and Moldón, *Fuentes históricas*, 35–36.
61. Cueto, "Some Observations"; Soria Ortega, *Maestro Fray Manuel de Guerra y Ribera*, 55–59.
62. Culliere, "Bernard Dominici."
63. Aliaga Asensio, *San Simón de Rojas*; Hoffman, *Raised to Rule*, 63–64.
64. Quintana, "Tomás de la Virgen."
65. On Paravicino, see Real Academia de la Historia, "Hortensio Paravicino y Arteaga." For other prominent Trinitarians at court, see Negredo del Cerro, *Predicadores de Felipe IV*. On Almoguera, see Ortiz Juárez, *Biografía de Fray Juan de Almoguera*.
66. Pedro Aranda de la Puente (ca. 1466–1545), auxiliary bishop in Mallorca; Antonio del Puerto (d. 1532), auxiliary bishop of Jaén; Philippe Musnier, auxiliary bishop of Châlons-sur-Marne. On claims that the Mallorcan cardinal Antoni Cerdà i Lloscos (ca. 1390–1459) was a Trinitarian, see Cassanyes Roig, "Antoni Cerdà," 109–35.
67. Cal Pardo, *Episcopologio mindoniense*, 447–70.
68. Aliaga Asensio, *San Simón de Rojas*, 226.
69. López de Altuna, *Primera parte*, 616–37.
70. Lucás de la Purificación, *Historia del sagrado cuerpo*, 11.
71. Gotor, *Beati del papa*, 285–319.
72. Vauchez, *Sainthood*, 22–32.
73. The process for establishment of *casus exceptus* status and immemorial cult was complex, and my description is simplified. The most comprehensive discussion is Benedict XIV, *Beatificazione*, but see also Veraja, *Beatificazione*, 113–90; Parise, "Casus exceptus"; De Matta, *Novissimus de sanctorum canonizatione tractatus*, 412–13; Brosch, *Der Heiligsprechungsprozess*.
74. Castro, "Iter canónico," 673.
75. *Positio* 1666, 59.
76. Taylor, *Structures of Reform*, 6.
77. Benedict XIV, *Beatificazione*, vol. I/2, 25–38. For the documents, see Colombo,

Vida del glorioso patriarca San Pedro Nolasco, 441–64.
78. Castro, "Iter canónico."
79. Taylor, *Structures of Reform*, 399–411.
80. This early version of Matha's *vita* does not mention St. Felix.
81. "Hoc fuit initium," Bibliotèque Nationale de France, ms. lat. 9753, fol. 10v, published in Deslandres, *Ordre des Trinitaires*, 2:141–43, and Marchionni, *Note*, 321–23. See Romano di Santa Teresa, *S. Giovanni di Matha*, 347–93; Marchionni, *Note*, 73–81. For a Spanish translation, see Porres Alonso, *Libertad a los cautivos*, 104; Aurrecoechea and Moldón, *Fuentes históricas*, 224–27.
82. Thomas of Eccleston, *De adventu*, 103.
83. Svizzeretto, "Chiesa e l'ospedale," 397–402; Cipollone, *Mosaico*; Liez, "Sceaux de l'ordre des Trinitaires."
84. Liez, "Sceaux de l'ordre des Trinitaires."
85. "Dictus ordo fuit institutus a Domino." Urban IV, "Ad hoc ordo vester," May 15, 1263, in Antonin de l'Assomption, *Origines*, 122–23. It remains unclear why the figure of an angel came to supplant that of Christ, but by the 1500s, it was so much the norm that commentators on the mosaic sought explanations for its imagery. E.g., Panciroli, *Tesori nascosti*, 121.
86. On Innocent III's Trinitarian ties, see Cipollone, *Cristianità—Islam*, 393–447; Keyvanian, *Hospitals and Urbanism*, 173–80.
87. "Deus creator omnium," Bibliotèque Nationale de France, ms. lat. 9753, fol. 12v, published in Deslandres, *Ordre des Trinitaires*, 2:143–47; Antonin de l'Assomption, *Origines*, 133–37. See Marchionni, *Note*, 93–115, 325–29; Aurrecoechea and Moldón, *Fuentes históricas*, 228–37. Medieval Trinitarians also bought Muslim captives to exchange for Christians. E.g., Archivo de la Corona de Aragón, Canc., reg. 1894, 159v, published in Aurrecoechea and Moldón, *Fuentes históricas*, 170–73.
88. Antonin de l'Assomption, *Origines*, 138–43; Collard, *Robert Gaguin*, 67–68.
89. British Library, ms. Egerton 3143, fols. 60v–63v, "De initio creacionis ordinis Sancte Trinitatis," published in Bazire, *Metrical Life*, 72–76.
90. In this text, Felix remained in Rome, while John returned to Cerfroid. Antonin de l'Assomption, *Origines*, 144–45; Aurrecoechea and Moldón, *Fuentes históricas*, 648–51.
91. Antonin de l'Assomption, *Origines*, 138–39, 145–45.
92. Jacques Bourgeois, "Institutio seu inventio O.SS.T.," in *Regula et statuta fratrum Ordinis Sanctissimae Trinitatis* (Douai, 1586), 1–5, reprinted in Antonin de l'Assomption, *Origines*, 148–50; Aurrecoechea and Moldón, *Fuentes históricas*, 650–57. See Deslandres, *Ordre des Trinitaires*, 1:xvi–xvii.
93. Romano di Santa Teresa, *S. Giovanni di Matha*, 16.
94. *La institución o fundación*, fol. 30v.
95. *Regula et constitutiones*, n.p.; *Institutio siue fundatio*, fol. 12v.
96. On Trinitarian liturgy, see Molin, "Introduction."
97. Pujana, *Orden de la Santísima Trinidad*, 38; Lebigue, "Modèle liturgique." There is substantial evidence that many Trinitarian houses in France, Portugal, and the British Isles followed the Augustinian rule and that this may account for the veneration given to St. Augustine rather than to the Trinitarians' founder. See Aliaga Asensio, "Orden de la Santa Trinidad."
98. Liez, *Art des Trinitaires*, 165.
99. *Breviarium ad usum Fratrum*; *Ceremonial y processionario*, 448.
100. Cf. Deslandres, *Ordre des Trinitaires*, 2:224.
101. Deslandres, *Ordre des Trinitaires*, 1:136; Calixte de la Providence, *Vie de Saint Jean de Matha*, 284–89.
102. Humbert of Romans, *De eruditione praedicorum*, in De La Bigne, *Maxima bibliotheca*, 469; Antonin de l'Assomption, *Origines*, 62.
103. Deslandres, *Ordre des Trinitaires*, 2:146; Antonin de l'Assomption, *Origines*, 135–36. Cf. Bazire, *Metrical Life*, 74.

104. Antonin de l'Assomption, *Origines*, 144–45.
105. *Institutio, regula, priuilegia*, fol. 6v.
106. Pampalone, "Restauro."
107. Antonino dell'Assunta and Romano di Santa Teresa, *S. Tommaso in Formis sul Celio*, 81–83.
108. Panciroli, *Tesori nascosti*, 121.
109. Román y Zamora, *Repúblicas del Mundo*, 292–97.
110. Morigia, *Historia*, fol. 178r–v. See Gagliardi, *Historia dell'origine di tutte le religioni*.
111. Ávila, "Antiguo convento," 741; Collar de Cáceres, "Convento de la Trinidad." For Bourgeois's poem, see Deslandres, *Ordre des Trinitaires*, 2:185–89.
112. Bouchet, *Ad sanctissimum d.n.d. Gregorium papam decimum tertium*. See Figueras Carpi, *Chronicum*, 502. Bouchet's address celebrated a brief restoration of San Tommaso in Formis to the order. *Institutio, regula, priuilegia*, fol. 3r.
113. *La institución o fundación*, fol. 25r; *Institution et fondation*, 10.
114. Antonino dell'Assunta and Romano di S. Teresa, *S. Tommaso in Formis sul Celio*, 65–66; Svizzeretto, "Passaggio," 405.
115. Antonino dell'Assunta and Romano di S. Teresa, *S. Tommaso in Formis sul Celio*, 230.
116. In 1920, the Vatican chapter conceded the church to the Trinitarians. See ibid., 239–41.
117. Juan Bautista de la Concepción, "Memoria de los orígenes de la descalcez trinitaria," in *Obras completas*, 149. See also the miraculous tales of the order's origins that convinced a youthful Pablo Aznar (d. 1624) to take the habit. Antonino de la Asunción, *Diccionario*, 1:82.
118. Pujana, "Juan de Mata y Félix de Valois."
119. Quoted in Pujana, *San Juan Bautista de la Concepción*, 618.
120. Juan Bautista de la Concepción, "Memoria de los orígenes de la descalcez trinitaria," 149.
121. Ibid., 149–50.
122. ASC, leg. 16c, pieza XVI/16, "Copia authentica processus Romae in 1630 fabricatus," fols. 22v, 25v, 31r, 34r, 37r–v.
123. "Felice anachoreta Valesiensi." Robert Gaguin, *Chronicon de majoribus ministris ordinis sacrosanctissimae Trinitatis*, in *Gallia christiana*, col. 1732.
124. Gonon, *Vitae et sententiae*, 373.
125. Ibid.
126. On the legend of St. Felix of Valois, see Antonin de l'Assomption, *Origines*, 144; Romano di Santa Teresa, *S. Giovanni di Matha* 15; Willibrord de Paris, "Félix de Valois"; Delooz, "Toward a Sociological Study," 200, 213–14; *Bibliotheca Sanctorum*, cols. 566–73. In 1969, St. Felix of Valois was removed from the General Roman Calendar. *Calendario Romanum*, 146.
127. González Dávila, *Compendio histórico*.
128. On Gónzalez Dávila (d. 1658), see Millares Carlo, *Tres Estudios*.
129. Cf. Bernardino de San Antonio, *Epitome*, fol. 16r.
130. Cf. Deslandres, *Ordre des Trinitaires*, 1:2–3. On Gónzalez Dávila's links to Figueras Carpi, see Antonino de la Asunción, "Autoridad."
131. Cf. Vega y Toraya, *Crónica*, 441–65 (Calced), and Lucás de la Purificación, *Quarta parte*, 103–30 (Discalced). See also Alejandro de la Madre de Dios, *Chrónica . . . : Tercera parte*, 148.
132. ASC, leg. 16c, pieza XVI/16, "Copia authentica processus Romae in 1630 fabricatus," manuscript dated 1650. For a 1646 copy, see AAV, Congr. Riti, Processus 912. Vélez was also charged with advancing the case for the canonization of Simón de Rojas and of Juan del Águila (1563–1613), Juan de Palacios (1560–1616), and Bernardo de Monroy (1559–1622), three Calced Trinitarian friars who died as prisoners in Algiers. On Vélez, see Porres Alonso, *Trinitarios en Burgos*, 201.
133. This strategy may have stemmed from a 1642 addition to the reforms enacted in 1625 and 1634. This text specified that *casus exceptus* status could be grounded

not just in the required hundred years of cult but also in a papal concession of liturgical honors or permission from the Congregation of Sacred Rites. In a case like Matha's, in which evidence for long-standing veneration was scarce, the extension of the prayers from the English breviary to the whole of the Trinitarian Order might have offered an alternative route to *casus exceptus* standing. See Gotor, *Beati del papa*, 324–26; Veraja, *Beatificazione*, 72–73; Papa, *Cause*, 354–55. For the text of the 1642 amendment, see Urban VIII, *Decreta*, 20.

134. *Memoriale. Pro Concessione*, n.p., included in ASC, leg. 16c; Vega y Toraya, *Crónica*, 455–57; Carlos Varona, "Imagen y santidad," 145–51.
135. Vega y Toraya, *Crónica*, 456. On the 1628 decree, see Veraja, *Beatificazione*, 117.
136. AHN, Inq., leg. 1079, fols. 469v–470v.
137. BNE, ms. 18238, fol. 201r.
138. Ibid., fols. 202v–203r.
139. Arcos, *Memorial*, fol. 26r–v. See AAV, Congr. Riti, Processus 912.
140. Vega y Toraya, *Crónica*, 459–60.
141. Lucás de la Purificación, *Historia del sagrado cuerpo*, 11.
142. Deslandres, *Ordre des Trinitaires*, 1:263–65.

Chapter 3

1. *Summarium* 1714, 24, 35.
2. Ponz, *Viage de España*, 69–74.
3. Lucás de la Purificación, *Historia del sagrado cuerpo*, 18; *Summarium* 1669, 37.
4. On the estimate of three weeks, see *Summarium* 1714, 24.
5. On Arcos, see Antonino de la Asunción, *Diccionario*, 1:47–49.
6. For a printed version of Massimo's account of the handover, see *Summarium* 1714, 35–36. For a draft version of the same text, see BA, ms. 1659, fol. 278r. According to Vega y Toraya (*Crónica*, 283–84), Arcos consulted the leadership of the Madrid Calced monastery before handing over the bones. See also Alejandro de la Madre de Dios, *Chrónica . . . : Tercera parte*, 133.
7. *Summarium* 1714, 35.
8. Vega y Toraya, *Crónica*, 284.
9. *Summarium* 1714, 24, 35–36.
10. Vega y Toraya, *Crónica*, 285.
11. Alejandro de la Madre de Dios, *Chrónica . . . : Tercera parte*, 133–34. On the palace of the nuncio, see Vázquez Barrado, "Palacio de la nunciatura."
12. Wintroub, "Translations," 1194–97.
13. AAV, Arch. Nunz. Madrid, 22.
14. Vega y Toraya, *Crónica*, 285.
15. This division was first laid out by the Fourth Lateran Council (1215) and later reproduced in Gregory IX's decretals of 1234. Boiron, "Définition et statut juridique"; Dooley, *Church Law on Sacred Relics*.
16. Council of Trent, session 25, December 3–4, 1563, "On invocation, veneration and relics of the saints, and on sacred images," in Tanner, *Decrees of the Ecumenical Councils*, 776.
17. Ditchfield, *Liturgy, Sanctity and History*, 219. Cf. Daston, *Classical Probability*, 320–22.
18. Ditchfield, *Liturgy, Sanctity and History*, 212–69.
19. Quoted in Pujana, *Reforma*, 9.
20. García Torralbo, "Real monasterio," 77. However, it seems certain that Trinitarian houses that also served as the order's educational centers also boasted working libraries. For one example (a library established in 1428 in Valladolid), see Porres Alonso, *Trinitarios en Burgos*, 129.
21. E.g., the modest holdings of the mother house at Cerfroid, inventoried in 1790. Calixte de la Providence, *Vie de S. Félix de Valois*, 334.
22. Collard, *Robert Gaguin*, 99–100; Rodríguez de Castro, *Biblioteca española*, 364–70.
23. Robert Gaguin, *Chronicon de majoribus ministris ordinis sacrosanctissimae Trinitatis*, in *Gallia christiana*, cols. 1732–35.

24. Deslandres, *Ordre des Trinitaires*, 1:610.
25. Jotischky, *Carmelites and Antiquity*; Dunphy, "Franciscan Chronicle Tradition."
26. Huijbers, "'Obervance' as Paradigm," 113–18.
27. Atienza López, "Crónicas."
28. Taylor, *Structures of Reform*, 417–18.
29. Antonino de la Asunción, *Diccionario*, 2:141, 262–63, 333. The first two of these texts are now lost but existed well into the eighteenth century. The third is known only from Figueras Carpi's *Chronicum*. The Portuguese Trinitarians underwent their own, Crown-led reform earlier in the sixteenth century. That these early histories are documented as held in the Lisbon house lends added weight to the correlation between monastic reform and historiographical production.
30. Grafton, *Forgers and Critics*.
31. Orlandi, Caldelli, and Gregori, "Forgeries and Fakes."
32. On Annius, see Stephens, "When Pope Noah Ruled the Etruscans." On Inghirami, see Rowland, *Scarith of Scornello*.
33. Bizzocchi, *Genealogie incredibili*.
34. Collins, *Reforming Saints*; Frazier, *Possible Lives*; Webb, "Sanctity and History."
35. Guazzelli, "Cesare Baronio." For Baronio's source criticism, see Ditchfield, *Liturgy, Sanctity, and History*, 283–84; Tutino, *Shadows of Doubt*, 84–87.
36. Knowles, *Great Historical Enterprises*, 1–32; Van Ommeslaeghe, "Acta Sanctorum"; Godding et al., *Bollandistes*.
37. Harris, "Immense Structure of Errors."
38. Olds, *Forging the Past*; Rowe, *Saint and Nation*, 43–44.
39. Rowe, *Saint and Nation*, 40–44.
40. Atienza López, "Crónicas," 43.
41. Rano Grundin, "Maestro agustino," 13–16.
42. These biographical details were reported in a now lost 1751 manuscript by José Moreno Curiel (d. 1755) and quoted in Calvo, *Resumen*, xxiv–xxvii. Two copies of Figueras's *Annales sacri Ordinis Ssmae. Trinitatis de Redemptione Captivorum* exist today: one at the Trinitarian house in Rome (ms. 244, covers 1153–306) and one at the Biblioteca Pública de Palma de Mallorca (mss. 55, 56, 57, covers 1153–333). I have used the Mallorcan copy, which was transcribed from the original manuscript during the eighteenth century. Figueras claimed to have completed four more volumes, but their location today is unknown. Figueras Carpi, *Chronicum*, "Ad fratres exhoratoria epistola," n.p., 322.
43. *Probabilis Assertio Iuridica Pro . . . Fr. Ioanne de Figueras, alias de Sancto Roberto . . . Contra Maiorem Domus Sanctae Trinitatis Geruifrigid capitalis Ministrum, necnon totius Ordinis Generalem, & praecipue aduersus eius Scolum Procuratorem de Vrbe Fratrem Alfonsum Domenech . . . surtin um Siculum vulgo nuncupatum Carne de Penna* (Naples?, 1644?), as discussed in Porres Alonso, "Dos manuscritos autógrafos."
44. For the allegation that the Trinitarians' minister general ordered Figueras's arrest, see Esteve, *Demonstración legal*, 24–25; Pedro de la Asunción, *Nihil nouum*, 61–62. Cf. the latter's rebuttal with Figueras's complaints about the minister general and his agent in Rome in the aforementioned pamphlet, *Probabilis Assertio Iuridica*, and in BNE, ms. 3584, fol. 67v. See Porres Alonso, "Dos manuscritos autógrafos."
45. BPPM, ms. 55, fol. 65r. On Cathars and Waldensians, see ibid., fols. 42v–50r, 63v–65r, 73v, 191v–196v.
46. Ibid., fols. 166v–169r.
47. Bzovius, *Annalium Ecclesiasticorum*, 40–43; Binius, *Concilia generalia, et provincialia*, 665; *Innocentii Romani pontificis regestorum siue epistolarum*, doc. 525, in *PL*, vol. 214, cols. 727A–29B.
48. BPPM, ms. 55, fols. 176r–178r.
49. Ibid., fols. 69v–72v.
50. On historical scholarship and antiquarian engagement with the material remains of the past, see

Momigliano, "Ancient History and the Antiquarian"; R. Weiss, *Renaissance Discovery*; Woolf, *Social Circulation of the Past*, 141–82; Stenhouse, *Reading Inscriptions*.
51. BPPM, ms. 55, fol. 238v.
52. Gonon, *Vitae et sententiae*, 373; BPPM, ms. 56, fol. 430r.
53. BPPM, ms. 55, fol. 242r.
54. BPPM, ms. 56, fol. 282r–v.
55. BPPM, ms. 55, fols. 89r, 119v.
56. Nicolson, *Scottish Historical Library*, 208 (emphasis in the original).
57. Dempster, *Historia ecclesiastica gentis Scotorum*, 285.
58. E.g., BBPM, ms. 55, fol. 223r; ms. 56, fol. 276v. On Dempster, see Morét, "Early Scottish National Biography"; Durkan, "Thomas Dempster."
59. Figueras Carpi, *Chronicum*, 183. See Bale, *Scriptorum illustrium maioris Brytanniae*, 588; Pitts, *Relationum historicarum*, 639.
60. Pitts, *Relationum historicarum*, 639. See also Harpsfield, *Historia anglicana ecclesiastica*, 640.
61. Sharpe, *Handlist*, 217, lists copies of Blakeney's *Modum rhetoricandi* at the British Library and at Trinity College, Dublin. See also Bale, *Index*, 183.
62. Figueras gave no location for this supposed source, and most of the details that he attributed to it can be found in other, verifiable sources, including Boece, *Scotorum historiae*; and Buchanan, *Rerum Scoticarum historia*.
63. Pitts, *Relationum historicarum*, 529.
64. Porres Alonso, "Dos manuscritos autógrafos"; Antonino de la Asunción, "Autoridad del P. Juan Figueras."
65. Antonin de l'Assomption, *Origines*, 90–92.
66. BPPM, ms. 55, fols. 215v, 216v, 230r.
67. Ibid., fols. 216r–217r, 228v.
68. BPPM, ms. 56, fols. 278r, 452r; BPPM, ms. 57, fol. 469r.
69. BPPM, ms. 56, fols. 250r, 267v, 397r.
70. BPPM, ms. 57, fols. 625r–626v, 629v–630r; Porres Alonso, "Dos manuscritos autógrafos," 272.
71. E.g., BPPM, ms. 57, fol. 609r–v. Figueras's sole source for this bull was Innes.
72. BPPM, ms. 57, fols. 560r–563r, 595v–600r.
73. BPPM, ms. 56, fol. 287r–v. On this assertion, which Figueras based on Innes, see Cavero, *Informe*, 259–60.
74. Popper, "Ocean of Lies."
75. See Findlen, "Inventing the Middle Ages."
76. González Dávila, *Compendio histórico*, fols. 15r, 51r.
77. Figueras cited Innes, Blakeney, Thorne, and a manuscript Trinitarian martyrology for which he gave no date or location.
78. BPPM, ms. 55, fols. 81v–82r.
79. One witness interviewed in 1630 testified that it was public knowledge in France that Matha and Valois had been beatified by the Apostolic See and opined that the bull of beatification must have been lost. ASC, leg. 16c, pieza XVI/16, "Copia authentica processus Romae in 1630 fabricatus," fols. 16v–17r.
80. E.g., BPPM, ms. 55, fols. 81v, 115v, 175v, 179r, 181v; BPPM, ms. 56, fol. 284r.
81. Carrillo, *Annales y memorias cronológicas*, 343.
82. BNE, ms. 18238, fols. 187r–188v.
83. AHN, Códices 154, fol. 205r.
84. ASC, ms. 251: "Processos de n[uest]r[o]s Santos, uno echo en Burgos, otro en Roma. 1663 y 1664," fol. 111r.
85. Figueras sprinkled references to materials housed in the Calced monastery in Burgos liberally throughout the *Annales* and had several independently printed. Antonino de la Asunción, "Autoridad del P. Juan Figueras," 18–19; Porres Alonso, "Dos manuscritos autógrafos," 260. On materials removed from the Burgos archive, see José Rodríguez, *Copia fidelíssima*, n.p. The entry contains a historical error: Robert of Hounslow and Etienne Mesnil-Fouchard were active in the order around 1414, not 1318.
86. BNE, ms. 18238, fol. 189r.
87. Ibid., fol. 189v.

88. Antonino de la Asunción, *Diccionario*, 2:438–39.
89. Ibid., 2:473–74; Carrillo, *Annales y memorias cronológicas*, 343; Diego de la Madre de Dios, *Chorónica*, prologo al lector (n.p.). For some of Paravicino's papers collected for this project, see BNE, ms. 18238.
90. Porres Alonso, "Dos manuscritos autógrafos," 255; Deslandres, *Ordre des Trinitaires*, 1:5.
91. Deslandres, *Ordre des Trinitaires*, 1:5; González Dávila, *Abrégé historique*.
92. Aznar, *Exercicios espirituales*, fols. 229v–243r.
93. Marracci, *Fundatores Mariani*, 94–96.
94. Porres Alonso, "Advocación y culto."
95. Reported in Jerónimo de San José, *Historia chronologica*, 61, which cited Bernardino de San Antonio's four-volume manuscript *Chronica da Ordem da SS. Trindade de Portugal*.
96. AHN, Códices 154, fol. 205v.
97. Guasque, *Celeste institutione*. Two of the licenses and permissions for this text were issued in Genoa in 1634—during Figueras's tenure in that city. One of the licenses, issued by a certain "Giovanni Fernández," cited both Innes and the *Annales*. Given these clues, it seems likely that "Giovanni Fernández" was Juan Figueras Carpi himself.
98. López de Altuna, *Primera parte*. See, for example, page 142, which closely followed Gónzalez Dávila on the English breviary but also mentions its supposed authorization by the Avignon pope John XXII—a detail found in Figueras's *Annales* and in the rumors that circulated among the friars in the early 1630s. BPPM, ms. 56, fol. 430r; ASC, leg. 16c, pieza XVI/16, "Copia authentica processus Romae in 1630 fabricatus." For the suggestion that Figueras ghost-wrote López de Altuna's text, see Antonino de la Asunción, "Autoridad," 23.
99. Figueras Carpi, *Compendio histórico*. On Figueras's invented sources for this text, see Antonio, *Biblioteca Hispana Antigua*, 98–99. The martyred bishop first appears as a Trinitarian in the *Annales* but as "Pedro de Valencia," rather than "Pedro Figueras Carpi." BPPM, ms. 57, fols. 601r–604r.
100. Pedro de la Asunción, *Nihil nouum*, 63.
101. *Decretum sac. Rit. Congregationis*; BPPM, ms. 54: Lorenzo Reynes, *Bullarium Ordinis Sanctissimae Trinitatis Redemptionis Captivorum*, 3:103–5. On St. Pedro Pascual as a Mercedarian, see Pedro Pascual, *Sobre la secta mahometana*, 63–70; Taylor, *Structures of Reform*, 406–10; Riera y Sans, "Doble falsificació." On the Trinitarian effort to appropriate this saint, see Antonino de la Asunción, *Diccionario*, 1:181–82; Antonino de la Asunción, *Diccionario*, 2:309–10; Carlos Varona, "Imagen y santidad," 90–99.
102. Numerous authors cite another publication, a *Compendio histórico de la Orden de la Santíssima Trinidad* (Venice, 1642), but I have not been able to locate this text.
103. See Figueras Carpi, *Chronicum*, "Ad benevolum lectorem," n.p. For the rumor of a false *imprimatur*, see Esteve, *Demonstración legal*, 24–25.
104. For two nineteenth-century examples, see Prat, *Histoire*; Calixte de la Providence, *Vie de Saint Jean de Matha*.
105. On Macedo, see Sousa Ribeiro, *Fr. Francisco de Santo Agostino de Macedo*.
106. Internal evidence suggests that the real author of this text was Juan de la Concepción, head of the Discalced house in Rome and the Discalced wing's Roman representative from 1659 to 1668. Antonino de la Asunción, *Diccionario*, 1:179–82.
107. Dilloud, "Avertissement," in *Les vies des Saints Jean de Matha et Félix de Valois*, n.p.
108. Figueras Carpi, *Chronicum*, 205.
109. Bernardino de San Antonio, *Epitome*, fols. 61v–62r; López de Altuna, *Primera parte*, 304–6.
110. Bouhours, *Vie de saint François Xavier*, 109–10; Sousa, *Oriente conquistado*, 477.

On Covilhã, see Gonçalves Guimarães, "Entre a hagiografia e crónica," 105.
111. García, *Vida y milagros de San Francisco Xavier*, 4.
112. While the *Chronicum* did not mention the breviary, it did cite the supposed canonization in 1263 by Urban IV, citing Innes "et alia" as the source. Figueras Carpi, *Chronicum*, 87–88.
113. Carlos Varona, "Imagen y santidad," 147–50.
114. *Summarium* 1669, 36. Vélez Matute's act was mentioned as an aside in the records of Nuncio Massimo's November 1655 examination of Matha's stolen remains.
115. *Commemorationes ex Anglicanae Prouinciae Breuiario*, n.p.
116. Juan de San Buenaventura, *Fasciculus trium florum*. Cf. ASC, 77a: Juan de San Buenaventura, "Relatione del convento di S. Carlo alle Quattro Fontane di Roma," 1–16. See Montijano García, "Libro della fabbrica."
117. Alós y Orraca, *Sermón panegírico*. The breviary did not appear in the 1649 edition of Jennyn, *Vera confraternitatis*, but according to Tamayo Salazar, *Anamnesis*, 550, and Alós y Orraca, *Sermón panegírico*, 38, it was cited in the second edition (Rome, 1652), and both it and Buenaventura appear in the third edition (Brussels, 1666). See also Francesco di S. Lorenzo, *Compendio Memorabile*; and Francesco di S. Lorenzo, *Compendio della vita*. Many of these titles were placed on the "Index of Prohibited Books" in 1666. *Index librorum prohibitorum*, 300.
118. Alejandro de la Madre de Dios, *Chrónica . . . : Segunda parte*, 127.
119. Tamayo Salazar, *Anamnesis*, 536–50. See Henriet, "Collection hagiographique et forgeries."
120. BPPM, ms. 56, fol. 430r–v.
121. Alejandro de la Madre de Dios, *Chrónica . . . : Segunda parte*, 122–25.
122. Antonino de la Asunción, *Diccionario*, 1:541.
123. Alejandro de la Madre de Dios, *Chrónica . . . : Segunda parte*, 127.
124. Arcos, *Memorial*, fol. 20r–v.
125. Ibid., fol. 17r–v. E.g., Alós y Orraca, *Sermón panegírico*. For plenary indulgences, see José de Jesús María, *Bullarium*, 535–37, and BPPM, ms. 54.
126. Arcos, *Memorial*, fol. 20v. Arcos does not specify the date, but it must have been between 1644 and 1647, since the sermon was delivered by the royal preacher Bernardo Suchet (d. 1647) and since Rospigliosi's term as nuncio in Madrid began in 1644.
127. Valencia: Alós y Orraca, *Sermón panegírico*; Miralles, *Sermón panegyrico*; Sisternes de Oblites, *Sermón panegyrico*; José Rodríguez, *Ostentación magnífica*. Madrid: Rojas, *Declamación evangélica*; Rojas, *Laudatoria eungélica* [sic]. See also Carruesco y Sessé, *Sermón panegírico*.
128. Carlos Varona, "Imagen y santidad."
129. Rodríguez G. de Ceballos, "Ciclos pintados," 5–6.
130. Du Breul, *Théâtre des antiquités*, 488.
131. Le Fur, "Renaissance d'un apostolat."
132. Cousinié, *Saint des saints*.
133. Rodríguez G. de Ceballos, "Ciclos pintados," 4–5.
134. ASC, leg. 16a, pieza XVI/1, n.p. The reference is unclear, but this was probably an inexpensive print that included depictions of Matha and Valois, since the recipient mentioned "la gratia que riceve da questi benedetti santi."
135. Alejandro de la Madre de Dios, *Crónica . . . : Segunda parte*, 124–27.
136. Hiatt, *Making of Medieval Forgeries*, 9.
137. Atienza López, "Crónicas."
138. Olds, *Forging the Past*, 16.
139. Ibid., esp. 193–95.
140. Carlos Varona, "Imagen y santidad," 136.
141. *Positio* 1666.
142. BAV, Ott. lat. 1123, fols. 31v, 64r.
143. Ibid., fols. 109v–110r; Deslandres, *Ordre des Trinitaires*, 1:67–68.
144. BNE, ms. 6161, fols. 279v–281r, 74r–v. Cf. Antonio de la Trinidad y Torre's contention that Matha was of Portuguese descent. AHN, Códices 154, 204v.
145. BNE, ms. 6161, fol. 91v; BNE, ms. 6162, fol. 165v.

146. BNE, ms. 6161, fol. 96r–v.
147. Gayangos, *Catalogue*, 394, lists a 1659 memorandum in which Lupián calls himself "Don Antonio de Lupián Zapata y Aragón" (citing British Library, Add. 13,997, no. 45, fol. 406). Lupián's own accounting varied. In BNE, ms. 6164, fol. 3r, which is dated August 1662, he claimed to be sixty-three years old, thus born in 1599.
148. Pellicer de Ossau y Tovar, *Tropheo*, fols. 38v–39v.
149. E.g., his *aprobación*, or censor's approval, printed in Núñez de Castro, *Coronica*, n.p. Cf. the list of titles laid out in Pellicer de Ossau y Tovar, *Tropheo*, fol. 8r.
150. For Lupián's final testament, see RAH, Salazar y Castro, M-75, fols. 170–172.
151. Josep Rodríguez, *Biblioteca Valentina*, 529–30.
152. Pellicer de Ossau y Tovar, *Tropheo*, fol. 47v, citing testimony gathered in 1675.
153. Roig y Jalpi, *Resumen historial*, n.p. (emphasis in original).
154. Roig y Jalpi, *Dulze desengaño histórico*, 87–88; Pellicer de Ossau y Tovar, *Tropheo*, fols. 45r–48r.
155. Godoy Alcántara, *Historia crítica*, 265–305.
156. Orella Unzué, "Geografías guipuzcoanas." For more complete lists of Lupián's forgeries, see Antonio, *Censura*, 683; Pellicer de Ossau y Tovar, *Tropheo*.
157. Cf. Salvador Martínez, *Berenguela la Grande y su época*, 26–28.
158. Andrés Ucendo, "Abasto de pan." BNE, ms. 4354: Esteve, *Symbolo de la Concepción de María*, fol. 18v, alleged that Lupián's wage was only two *reales* per *pliego*.
159. BNE, ms. 6161, fol. 7r.
160. The Trinitarian Knights made their first appearance in López de Altuna, *Primera parte*.
161. BNE, ms. 6161, fol. 386v.
162. Lupián's informants on the first century of the Trinitarian Order's existence included Diego Morante de Ayala, an antiquarian scholar of Burgos active in 1627; Pedro Magarola Fontanet, bishop of Elna from 1622 to 1627; Juan Reart, nephew of Bishop Onofre Reart of Girona; the celebrated Franciscan scholar Luke Wadding; the Benedictine historian Antonio de Cantabrana (1597–1662); and Jerónimo Pardo (1576–1643), a prominent member of the cathedral chapter of Burgos. BNE, ms. 6161, fols. 168v, 176r, 246v, 345r, 370r, 371v, 399r.
163. BPPM, ms. 55, fol. 171r–v; Figueras Carpi, *Chronicum*, 2.
164. BNE, ms. 6161, fols. 372v, 392v–393v, 408v–410r.
165. Godoy Alcántara, *Historia crítica*, 266.
166. BNE, ms. 6162, fols. 136r–137r. The French treatise, which I have not yet succeeded in locating, is Jacobus a S. Marco, *Triumphus Ordinis SS. Trinitatis Redemptionis Captivorum* (Aix-en-Provence, 1655).
167. Ferrario Grait was a leading member of the order, active in Aragon and Valencia after 1250. For Grait's biography (based on BPPM, ms. 56, fols. 456r–457v), see Latassa, *Bibliotecas antigua y nueva*, 507–8. Grait's supposed writings first appear in Ippolito Marracci's *Fundatores Mariani*, 96. Marracci probably received his information directly from Figueras, since he cites him but also mentions a miracle that does not appear in the existing *Annales* manuscript.
168. ASC, leg. 16c, pieza XVI/16: "Culto immemorial de n[uest]r[o]s Santos Patriarcas," fol. 25r. After Lupián, events derived from Grait wormed their way into Trinitarian historiography. See Sales, *Memorias históricas*, 59.
169. BPPM, ms. 55, fol. 73r.
170. Tutino, *Fake Saint*, 42, 108–13.
171. BNE, ms. 6161, fols. 284v, 361r. See also ibid., fol. 154v.
172. Figueras Carpi, *Chronicum*, 171–72; BNE, ms. 6163, fol. 235r.
173. Benedictine and Cistercan houses: Santo Domingo de Silos (BNE, ms. 6161, fol. 298v), San Millán de la

Cogolla (BNE, ms. 6162, fol. 35v; BNE, ms. 6163, fol. 12r), Santa María la Real de las Huelgas (Burgos; BNE, ms. 6163, fol. 15v); royal archive of Aragon: BNE, ms. 6164, fols. 141v, 362r; Count of Gondomar: BNE, ms. 6163, fols. 66v, 74v; noble Catalan and Aragonese families: BNE, ms. 6162, fol. 270r (Cruilles); BNE, ms. 6162, fol. 276r (Lupián); BNE, ms. 6163, fol. 105r (Corbera); BNE, ms. 6163, fol. 230r (Cerbellón); BNE, ms. 6162, fol. 258r (barons of Anglesola); BNE, ms. 6163, fol. 204v (Marquina); BNE, ms. 6164, fol. 51v (Malla); BNE, ms. 6164, fol. 137r (Carroz and Gotór); BNE, ms. 6164, fol. 247v (Moncada, marquises of Aytona).

174. E.g., BNE, ms. 6162, fol. 247v; BNE, ms. 6163, fols. 183v, 192v (images); BNE, ms. 6163, fols. 109v, 168v, 200r (ruins); BNE, ms. 6164, fols. 135v, 367v (traditions).
175. BNE, ms. 6164, fol. 350v.
176. Andrade, *Vida de la gloriosa señora Santa Gertrudis la Magna*, prologue by the Carmelite friar José Haro de San Clemente, n.p.
177. A second piece of evidence is a curiously Cataluña-specific geographic reference contained within Andrade's life of St. Gertrude and attributed to the mysterious Pierre de Espoleto. Nearly all of Lupián's personal asides and local references were to sites in northern Cataluña and southern France, often in regions that border on the Pyrenees. In this case, the reference is to an area bordering on Puigcerdá. Andrade, *Vida de la gloriosa señora Santa Gertrudis la Magna*, 198.
178. Andrade, *Vidas de los gloriosíssimos Patriarcas*, fol. 6r.
179. BNE, ms. 6161, fol. 414r–v.
180. This invented document was published in full in Baro, *Annales*, 120. It later found its way into the antiquarian Pierre Janvier's (1618–1689) manuscript history of the diocese of Meaux and from there into Duplessis, *Histoire*, 110. As late as 1978, this forgery was still being cited as evidence for Matha's cofounder. See Cipollone, *Studi intorno a Cerfroid*, 45–49; Pujana, *Orden de la Santísima Trinidad*, 36.
181. BNE, ms. 6161, fols. 301v–302r.
182. Ibid., fol. 302r.
183. Ibid., fols. 299r–300r.
184. Ibid., fols. 296v–303r.
185. ASC, leg. 16c, pieza XVI/16: "Culto immemorial de nuestros Santos Patriarcas S. Juan y S. Félix (Madrid) (1663–1664)," fol. 20r.
186. Ibid., fol. 20v.
187. BNE, ms. 4354: Esteve, *Symbolo de la Concepción de María*, fols. 17v–18r.
188. Gumbrecht, "Identifying Fragments," esp. 15.
189. Eisenbichler, introduction to *Renaissance Medievalisms*, 24.
190. BNE, ms. 6163, fols. 121r, 149r.
191. Ibid., fol. 128r–v (corpse); BNE, ms. 6164, fol. 52r (miracle); BNE, ms. 6164, fol. 11v (relics); NBE, ms. 6163, fol. 253v (St. Farriolo).
192. Macedo, *Vitae SS. Ioannis de Mattha, et Felicis de Valois*, 190.
193. Amada y Torregrosa, *Parangón histórico y iurídico*, fol. 18r–v. Lupián obscured the monetary exchange behind his scholarly efforts by claiming a special emotional attachment to the Trinitarian Order, an affinity born of having been witness in 1625 to the murder of a Spanish Trinitarian friar at the hands of a mob of angry French Protestants. BNE, ms. 6161, fols. 4v–6r.
194. E.g., Alonso de San Antonio, *Gloriosos títulos*, a 1661 anti-Mercedarian treatise in which appear the Mataplana name, the Trinitarian Knights, and the donations and privileges granted by Count Sancho and others, together with a direct reference to Lupián's then-ongoing work.
195. Ferrer de Valdecebro, *Templo de la fama*, 136.
196. Later Trinitarian writers elevated Innes to the status of cardinal. By the 1800s, he was well enough entrenched in Scottish history to become the subject of a short

biography. See López, *Noticias históricas*; McRoberts, "Three Bogus Trinitarian Pictures"; Geddes, "Memoirs of the Life."
197. ASC, leg. 16a, pieza XVI/1: Rome, 1649; ASC, leg. 16a, pieza XVI/2: Úbeda, 1650, and Rome, 1649. See García Torralbo, "Patrimonio artístico."
198. See Calixte de la Providence, *Vie de S. Félix de Valois*, 248, which provides neither source nor location for the document.
199. A brief entry included in a June 1659 list of beatification and canonization cases currently in process before the Congregation of Sacred Rites suggests that by this date, the Trinitarians' campaign for their founders' immemorial cult was at a standstill. BAV, Chig. B.II.16, fol. 39v.
200. ASC, ms. 251: "Processos de n[uest]r[o]s Santos, uno echo en Burgos, otro en Roma. 1663 y 1664"; ASC, leg. 16b, pieza XVI/16: testimony from Córdoba, Cuenca, Rome, Granada, Valencia. See Carlos Varona, "Imagen y santidad."
201. Gutiérrez, "Prove sussidarie."
202. *Romana canonizationis Sanctorum Ioannis de Matha*.
203. ASC, leg. 16a, pieza XVI/13; José de Jesús María, *Bullarium*, 564–67.
204. Juan de la Concepción, *Canonización de los gloriosos patriarcas San Juan de Mata y San Féliz de Valois* (Madrid, 1674), 23, quoted in Llona Rementería, *Fundador y redentor*, 445.
205. José Rodríguez, *Sacro, y solemne novenario*; Mínguez Cornelles, "Declaración," 21–42.
206. Andrade, *Vidas de los gloriosíssimos Patriarcas*, fol. 203r–v.
207. Guerra y Ribera, *Sermones*, 16.
208. E.g., Lucás de la Purificación, *Quarta parte*, 130.
209. José de Jesús María, *Bullarium*, 573–77, 585–86. Matha's commemoration was added to December 17, while Valois's was scheduled on November 4. In 1679, their feasts were moved to February 8 and November 20, respectively. Ibid., 616–18.
210. Llona Rementería, *Fundador y redentor*, 446–47; José de Jesús María, *Bullarium*, 624–26; BPPM, ms. 54, 98–99, 123–24, 126, 150–51. For the new office, see Baro, *Annales*, 307–13.

Chapter 4

1. Signorotto, "*Squadrone Volante*"; Rodén, *Church Politics*.
2. On Ginetti, see Tabacchi, "Ginetti, Marzio." On cardinal protectors, see Witte, "Cardinal Protectors."
3. *Summarium* 1669, 25–39.
4. Felipe de Jesús served as visitor general for convents associated with the powerful Farnese and Barberini families. Antonino de la Asunción, *Diccionario*, 1:397.
5. ASC, ms. 282, "Noticia chronológica de los negocios de nuestra sagrada religión de Trinitarios Descalzos Redentores de Cautivos Xpianos," 7–8.
6. Ibid., 9.
7. Herrmann-Mascard, *Reliques des saints*, 364–65.
8. Council of Trent, session 25, December 3–4, 1563, "On invocation, veneration and relics of the saints, and on sacred images," in Tanner, *Decrees of the Ecumenical Councils*, 776.
9. On medieval procedures, see Herrmann-Mascard, *Reliques des saints*, 106–42.
10. Pius XI, *Acta ecclesiae mediolanensis*, cols. 300–302.
11. Ibid., col. 300.
12. Paleotti, *Archiepiscopale bononiense*, 279.
13. Vincent-Cassy, "Search for Evidence," 143.
14. The expression is from Burke, "How to Become a Counter-Reformation Saint," 49.
15. Kleinberg, "Proving Sanctity," 205.
16. Hills, "Nuns and Relics," 18. See also Geary, "Sacred Commodities."
17. For the letter, dated October 19, 1668, see ASC, leg. 16a, pieza XVI/3.
18. E.g., Rocca, *De canonizatione sanctorum*; Contelori, *Tractatus et praxis*; Scacchi, *De cultu*; De Matta, *Novissimus*.
19. Benedict XIV, *De servorum Dei beatificatione et beatorum canonizatione*,

3rd ed., 829 (part 2, chap. 25, no. 54). For a 1614 example, see *Analecta juris pontificii*, 7th ser., col. 132.

20. Segni, *Reliquiarium*; Anfossi, *De sacrarum reliquiarum cultu*; Dávila y Toledo, *De la veneración que se deve*; Ferrand, *Disquisitio Reliquiaria*. See also Ricciulli, *Lucubrationum*.

21. Smith, "Relics," 50.

22. Ibid. On measurement relics, see Bynum, *Dissimilar Similitudes*. For an example, see Osuna Cerdá, "Descripción y catalogación," 63.

23. On Ferrand, see Sommervogel, *Bibliothèque de la Compagnie de Jésus*, cols. 660–63.

24. Julia, "Église post-tridentine."

25. *Sentencia y decreto*. On the Córdoba discoveries, see Morales, *Cinco libros postreros*, fols. 268r–289r.

26. AAV, Congr. Concilio, Libri Decret. 3, fols. 16r, 18A, fol. 456v; 25, fol. 551r–v; Pallottini, *Collectio omnium conclusionum*, 643.

27. Mayer, *Roman Inquisition*.

28. Gotor, *Beati del papa*.

29. ACDF, S.O., St. St., B4 e, fasc. 13; ACDF, S.O., St. St., B4 e, fasc. 16. On the Assisi case, see Gotor, *Beati del papa*, 338–40.

30. ACDF, S.O., St. St., B4 e, fasc. 12. Notations on the back of the letter show that notification about the events in Taormina was first sent to the Congregation of Sacred Rites but was then diverted to the Inquisition. On Taormina, see Gotor, *Beati del papa*, 338.

31. Moroni, *Dizionario di erudizione*, 16:216–20. My impression is based on the decrees published in Prinzivalli, *Resolutiones*.

32. ASC, ms. 282, 11.

33. Weber, *Die ältesten päpstlichen Staatshandbücher*, demonstrates that membership numbers in the Congregation of Sacred Rites varied over the decades. In 1668, the congregation had twenty-one cardinals.

34. On the congregation's personnel, see Papa, *Cause*, 64–98; Benedict XIV, *Beatificazione*, vol. I/1, 357–442.

35. BNE, 4/42284(8): *Positio* 1669; BNE, 4/42284(9): *Summarium* 1669.

36. Three manuscript briefs can be found at the Vatican Library among the papers of Cardinal Sigismondo Chigi (1649–1678), one of the members of the Congregation of Sacred Rites in 1669. See BAV, Chig. E.II.47, fols. 244r–247v, 248r–249v, 282r–282v. Another is held at the Biblioteca Angelica, part of a collection of printed and manuscript materials originally owned by the powerful Massimo clan. See BA, ms. 1659, fols. 272r–273r. Many more—ten, in total, including drafts—are preserved at San Carlino alle Quattro Fontane. Citations include the shelf mark, section, and incipit. Where multiple briefs have the same incipit—for example, multiple iterations or drafts of the same document—I have cited them by the shelf mark, section, and incipit and a number relating to where they appear in relation to the beginning of the *legajo*. For example, ASC, leg. 16a, pieza XVI/3, Commissa fuit relatio-1; ASC, leg. 16a, pieza XVI/3, Commissa fuit relatio-2.

37. Benedict XIV, *Beatificazione*, vol. I/1, 437. There is a great deal of crossover between the manuscript and the printed materials, but the manuscript briefs were not mere drafts of the printed versions. Rather, they need to be read in tandem.

38. ASC, leg. 16a, pieza XVI/3, "In sede vacante." Cf. BA, ms. 1659, fols. 272r–273r.

39. ASC, leg. 16a, pieza XVI/3, "Relinquendo omni arbitrio." Bouillaud appeared as *promotor cause* in multiple cases during the 1660s and 1670s. In 1668, he published a short pamphlet on the festivities held in Rome for the beatification of Rose of Lima. In July 1677, Bouillaud seems to have fallen afoul of the reforming regime of Innocent XI (r. 1676–89), since he was imprisoned by the Congregation of Sacred Rites, probably for graft. For the pamphlet, see Bouillaud, *Breve*

Relatione. For Bouillaud's legal troubles, see *Analecta juris pontificii*, 8th ser., cols. 1207–8.
40. Benedict XIV, *Beatificazione*, vol. I/1, 370–71.
41. On Febei, see Mayer, *Roman Inquisition*, 136–39. According to Moroni, *Dizionario*, 40:179, in January 1663, Bernardino Casali became secretary of the Congregation of Sacred Rites, while Febei became a consultant to the congregation.
42. Benedict XIV, *Beatificazione*, vol. I/1, 433–35.
43. Accademia della Crusca, *Vocabolario*, 4th ed., 709; Real Academia Española, *Diccionario de la lengua castellana*, 203.
44. Baldesano, *Sacra historia*, 363.
45. Lindholm, "Rise of Expressive Authenticity."
46. Covarrubias Orozco, *Tesoro*, fol. 105v.
47. Accademia della Crusca, *Vocabolario*, 1st ed., 99.
48. Lazure, "Possessing the Sacred," 60.
49. Anfossi, *De sacrarum reliquiarum cultu*, 158.
50. Thiel, *Early Modern Subject*, 18–26.
51. ASC, leg. 16a, pieza XVI/3, "Supplicatur adverti sequentia"; BAV, Chig. E.II.47, fol. 245v.
52. Thiel, *Early Modern Subject*, 20.
53. Aquinas, *Thomas Aquinas's Quodlibetal Questions*, 169 (Quodlibetum XI, q. 6).
54. Hughes, "Matter and Individuation in Aquinas," 6.
55. ASC, leg. 16a, pieza XVI/3, "Corpus Sancti Joannis de Matha."
56. As quoted in Thiel, "Individuation," 218.
57. BAV, Chig. E.II.47, fol. 245v.
58. On the greater importance of the *termini* than the *medium*, see ASC, leg. 16a, pieza XVI/3, "Supplicatur adverti sequentia."
59. Citations of Ferrand include *Positio* 1669, 6, and BAV, Chig. E.II.47, fols. 248r–249r.
60. E.g., Vidal, "Miracles, Science, and Testimony"; Ditchfield, "Thinking with the Saints," 567; Laverda, "Revising the Supernatural."
61. Duffin, *Medical Miracles*, 20.
62. Benedict XIV, *De servorum Dei beatificatione et beatorum canonizatione*, 3rd ed., 801–6 (part 2, chap. 24, nos. 10–16); Ricciulli, *Lucubrationum*, 71.
63. *Analecta juris pontificii*, 7th ser., col. 295; Benedict XIV, *De servorum Dei beatificatione et beatorum canonizatione*, 3rd ed., 801 (part 2, chap. 24, no. 9). On the head of St. Bruno of Segni, see Navarra, *Filippo Michele Ellis*, 136–39.
64. *Summarium* 1669, 30.
65. ASC, leg. 16a, pieza XVI/3, "Supplicatur adverti sequentia."
66. BAV, Chig. E.II.47, fol. 282r. Cf. ASC, leg. 16a, pieza XVI/3, "Hic notantur aliquas scitu digna."
67. ASC, leg. 16a, pieza XVI/3, "Corpus Sancti Joannis de Matha."
68. *Summarium* 1669, 38.
69. *Positio* 1669, 7.
70. Ivanič, "Early Modern Religious Objects," 325.
71. BAV, Chig. E.II.47, fol. 282r.
72. BPPM, ms. 55, fol. 241r.
73. ASC, leg. 16a, pieza XVI/3, "Relinquendo omni arbitrio."
74. On handwriting experts as witnesses, see Antonucci, "Scrittura giudicata"; Antonucci, "Tecniche dello scrivere."
75. *Positio* 1669, 6.
76. On the hierarchy of proofs, see Palazzolo, *Prova legale e pena*; Marchetti, *Testis contra se*, 87–128.
77. Royo Mejía, "Algunas cuestiones"; Benedict XIV, *De servorum Dei beatificatione et beatorum canonizatione*, 3rd ed., 800–801 (part 2, chap. 24, no. 9).
78. BAV, Chig. E.II.47, fols. 244r–247v.
79. The brief cites Francisco Suárez, S.J. (1548–1617), Gabriel Vázquez, S.J. (1549?–1604), and Pedro de Lorca (1561–1612).
80. BAV, Chig. E.II.47, fol. 244r.
81. Ibid., fol. 244r–v.
82. Ibid., fol. 245r.
83. Ibid., fol. 244v.
84. Ibid., fol. 245v. The example recalls the ancient Donatist heresy.
85. Schüssler, "Jean Gerson," 453.

86. Aristotle, *Nichomachean Ethics* 1.2.1094b, in *Complete Works of Aristotle*, 1730.
87. Jonsen and Toulmin, *Abuse of Casuistry*, 165–66.
88. Council of Trent, session 6, January 13, 1547, "Decree on justification Chap. 9. Against the vain confidence of the heretics," in Tanner, *Decrees of the Ecumenical Councils*, 674.
89. Strehle, *Catholic Roots*, 7.
90. Jonsen and Toulmin, *Abuse of Casuistry*, 148. See also Franklin, *Science of Conjecture*.
91. Deman, "Probabilisme," col. 464; Kantola, *Probability and Moral Uncertainty*; Schüssler, "On the Anatomy of Probabilism."
92. Daston, "Probability and Evidence," 1112.
93. Franklin, *Science of Conjecture*, 75.
94. Fleming, *Defending Probabilism*, 123.
95. Ibid., 123–24.
96. Schüssler, "On the Anatomy of Probabilism," 107.
97. Serjeantson, "Proof and Persuasion," 157–62; Daston, "Probability and Evidence," 1116–22.
98. On the shift in Roman and canon law from a fixed hierarchy of "full" and "partial" proofs to degrees of certainty and probability, see Padoa-Schioppa, *Italia ed Europa*, 280–87; Rosoni, *Quae singula non prosunt collecta iuvant*. On moral certainty in English law, see Shapiro, *Beyond Reasonable Doubt*.
99. Papa, *Cause*, 170–214; Veraja, *Beatificazione*.
100. Alcalá, *Chrónica*, 497–511. On moral certainty in canonization, see Gutiérrez, "Certezza morale"; Royo Mejía, "Algunas cuestiones." On papal infallibility in canonization, see Giovannucci, *Canonizzazioni*; Prudlo, *Certain Sainthood*.
101. Suárez, *Commentariorum*, 614–15 (Disp. 55, sec. 1 and 2, on Aquinas, *ST* 3, q. 25, art. 6). Cf. T. Sánchez, *Opus morale*, 600 (bk. 2, chap. 43, nos. 13–14).
102. On Bordoni, see Zanot, *Francesco Bordoni*.
103. Bordoni, *Operum*, 165 (resol. 117, nos. 42–44).
104. Ibid.
105. Ibid.
106. E.g., Suárez, *Commentariorum*, 612–13 (Disp. 55, sec. 1, on Aquinas, *ST* 3, q. 25, art. 6, ra 3).
107. De Matta, *Novissimus*, 437.
108. Ibid.
109. Benedict XIV, *De servorum Dei beatificatione et beatorum canonizatione*, 3rd ed., 816 (part 2, chap. 25, no. 20). This passage is quoted from *Positio* 1721, 4.
110. Dear, "From Truth to Disinterestedness."
111. Arriaga, *Cursus philosophicus*, 224–26.
112. Dear, "From Truth to Disinterestedness," 623.
113. BAV, Chig. E.II.47, fol. 245v.
114. Ibid., fol. 246v.
115. Ibid., fol. 247v.
116. Ibid., fol. 266r. According to notes jotted down on this same folio, the attending cardinals were Carlo Gualterio, Flavio Chigi, *seniore*, Scipione Pannocchieschi d'Elci, Angelo Celsi, Sigismondo Chigi, Federico Sforza, Cesare Faccinetti, and Paolo Savelli. The attending prelates were Bernardino Casali, the congregation's secretary; Pietro Paolo Bona and Fulvio Servanzio, papal masters of ceremonies; Pietro Francesco de Rossi, *promotor fidei*; Aloysius de Aquino, apostolic protonotary; and Ambrosio Landucci, papal sacristan. Notes contained in ASC, leg. 16a, pieza XVI/3, n.p., give the date on which the committee came to its decision as February 16, 1669, but other sources, including notes scrawled on BAV, Chig. E.II.47, fol. 266r, indicate that the judgment was made on January 12. For other decisions made that day, see *Decreta authentica*, 421–22.
117. ASC, leg. 16a, pieza XVI/3, "Supplicatur adverti sequentia." Cf. ASC, leg. 16a, pieza XVI/3, "Relinquendo omni arbitrio."
118. Quoted in Ullmann, "Medieval Principles of Evidence," 83.

119. Vidal, "Miracles, Science, and Testimony."
120. Benedict XIV, *De servorum Dei beatificatione et beatorum canonizatione*, 3rd ed., 807–8 (part 2, chap. 25, nos. 1–2).
121. AAV, Arch. Nunz. Madrid, 22.
122. E.g., Bordoni, *Operum*, 161 (resol. 117, nos. 14–18).
123. ASC, leg. 16a, pieza XVI/3, "Relinquendo omni arbitrio."
124. Ibid.
125. ASC, leg. 16a, pieza XVI/3, "Supplicatur adverti sequentia." The handwriting dates from 1714, when the case came before the Congregation of Sacred Rites for a second time.
126. On Agustín Cardoso, see Vega y Toraya, *Crónica*, 275. The date of 1605 is given by a document created for the 1714 hearing. ASC, leg. 16a, pieza XVI/3, "E visto los papeles." For papers related to Cardoso's work in Rome, see BNE, ms. 18238.
127. Borghero, *Certezza e la storia*; Völkel, "*Pyrrhonism historicus*" und "*fides historica*."
128. Giovannucci, *Canonizzazioni*, 197–202.
129. Giovannucci, "Prospero Lambertini e la prova," 66.
130. Osborne, "Roman Catacombs"; Oryshkevich, "History of the Roman Catacombs"; Ghilardi, "Catacombe di Roma nel Medioevo."
131. Baciocchi and Duhamelle, *Reliques romaines*.
132. For one Protestant's critique, see Munday, *English Romayne lyfe*, 42. For a Catholic skeptic, see Cirot, *Mariana, historien*, 418–23.
133. On Landucci, see Moroni, *Dizionario di erudizione*, 60:189.
134. De Rossi and Ferrua, *Sulla questione del vaso di sangue*. See also Ghilardi, *Sanguine tumulus madet*; Bartolini, *Congregazione particolare dei Sagri Riti*, 23.
135. Fitzpatrick, *Thomas Aquinas on Bodily Identity*, 165–66.
136. Machielsen, "Heretical Saints and Textual Discernment."
137. Olds, *Forging the Past*, esp. 193–95. In pious affection's emphasis on combining critical scholarship with the needs of faith, it shared the *semper eadem* orientation to the past found also in ecclesiastical historians like Baronio and writers on positive theology. Quantin, *Catholicisme classique*, 103–11.
138. Morales, *Cinco libros postreros*, 272.
139. Papenbroeck, *Responsio*, 365–66. Cf. Imbruglia, "Dalle storie di santi," 56–62.
140. Quintanadueñas, *Singularia theologiae moralis*, 194. See Díaz Moreno, "Antonio de Quintanadueñas, S.J."
141. Quantin, "Reason and Reasonableness," 418–26. The hermeneutic of pious affection seems to have been extended primarily to old or ancient relics, since the bodies of the recent holy dead were subject to the increasingly stringent evidentiary requirements and procedures of canonization and were thus less likely to be called into question.
142. Duffin, *Medical Miracles*, 15.
143. E.g., Pomata, "Malpighi and the Holy Body"; Vidal, "Miracles, Science, and Testimony"; Bouley, *Pious Postmortems*.
144. Shapiro, *Probability and Certainty*; Harrison, "Miracles"; Hillman, "Putting Faith to the Test."
145. Vilches, *New World Gold*.
146. S. Schreiner, *Are You Alone Wise?*
147. See Mortimer and Robertson, "Nature, Revelation, History"; Levitin, "From Sacred History."
148. Tutino, *Fake Saint*, 126.
149. Hills, "Through a Glass Darkly," 39.
150. Bynum, *Christian Materiality*, 272–73.

Chapter 5

1. ASC, leg. 16a, pieza XVI/3, n.p.: "Reconocimiento de las Reliquias hecho ante el Sr. Nuncio en Madrid a 26/V/1671"; *Summarium* 1714, 41–44. For lists of those who were in attendance, see Lucás de la Purificación, *Historia del sagrado cuerpo*, 19, and Vega y Toraya, *Crónica*, 286. AAV, Arch. Nunz. Madrid 16 and 22 both

indicate that the order originated in the Congregation of Sacred Rites.
2. *Summarium 1714*, 44.
3. AAV, Arch. Nunz. Madrid, 22.
4. Bravo, *Invención felicíssima*.
5. Bagnoli, "Dressing the Relics."
6. Bosio, *Historia passionis B. Caeciliae virginis*, 155–56. Cf. the case of relics discovered in Granada in 1588, in Harris, *From Muslim to Christian Granada*, 2–3; Antolínez de Burgos, *Historia eclesiástica de Granada*, 489–92.
7. Shapin, *Social History of Truth*.
8. E.g., ASDS, Fondo Capitolare, Q4, fols. 27v–29v (relic finds in 1614); AASG, C49, fols. 575r–576v (relic finds in 1595); AHN, Clero, Leg. 346-1 (relic finds in Ávila, 1519).
9. S. Clark, *Vanities of the Eye*.
10. ASDS, Fondo Capitolare, Q4, fol. 58r. On blood-soaked earth as a sign of martyrdom, see Ghilardi, *Sanguine tumulus madet*. For an example of devotees adding water to vials in order to reconstitute the "blood," see Van Cutsem, "Lettre inédite."
11. ASVR, Atti della Segreteria del Tribunale del Cardinale Vicario, t. 11, includes multiple records of relics extracted from the Roman catacombs. Many of these records include measurements as part of the relic identification apparatus.
12. ASC, leg. 16a, pieza XVI/3, "Probatur identitas corporis sancti Joannis de Matha."
13. Hills, "Nuns and Relics," 18. See also Harris, "Gift, Sale, and Theft."
14. Carlos Varona, "'Imágenes rescatadas' en la Europa moderna"; Porres Alonso, "Advocación y culto."
15. Porres Alonso, *Libertad a los cautivos*.
16. The title page of Mallea's text bears a publication date of 1665, but internal references demonstrate that it could not have been completed before 1673. According to Antonio, *Bibliotheca Hispana nova*, 275, Mallea was still living in 1670. On Mallea, see Antonino de la Asunción, *Diccionario*, 2:64–68.

17. According to Deslandres, *Ordre des Trinitaires*, 1:xxi, the real author of the text by the Irish Franciscan Baro was Ignace de Saint-Antoine, minister of the French Discalced monastery in Rome. Dilloud was a prominent member of the French Reformed Trinitarian branch.
18. Florianus a S. Josephus, *Chronicorum*, vii–li. This text is a Latin translation of Diego de la Madre de Dios, *Chorónica*. Tarizzo, *Compendio*.
19. Melchor del Espíritu Santo, *Patriarca San Juan de Mata*, 277–330. Evidently, some of Matha's remains were left behind in the tomb.
20. Diego de Jesús, *Annales*.
21. The theft is mentioned by Mallea, *Epítome de las vidas*, and by Vega y Toraya, *Crónica*.
22. Deslandres, *Ordre des Trinitaires*, 1:268–83.
23. Vega y Toraya, *Crónica*, 286.
24. Melchor del Espíritu Santo, *Patriarca San Juan de Mata*, 264.
25. Vega y Toraya, *Crónica*, 289. On the court of the nuncio, see Vatican, "Nunciatura española."
26. Fernández Alonso, "Período," 20.
27. Vega y Toraya, *Crónica*, 289.
28. AAV, Arch. Nunz. Madrid, 1, fols. 262–263, quoted in Marques, *Santa Sede*, 69.
29. Antonio de la Asunción, *Diccionario*, 1:474–77; ASC, leg. 16a, pieza XVI/3, "El sagrado cuerpo del glorioso patriarca S. Juan de Matta" (1723).
30. ASC, leg. 16a, pieza XVI/3, "El sagrado cuerpo del glorioso patriarca S. Juan de Matta."
31. ASC, ms. 282, 110–12.
32. Vega y Toraya, *Crónica*, 293.
33. E.g., the uproar provoked by the July 1720 appointment of Cardinal Annibale Albani to present the case to the Congregation of Sacred Rites, as described in ASC, ms. 282, 113.
34. ASC, leg. 16a, pieza XVI/4, "Cartas del señor Lambertini (después Bened. XIV) sobre el cuerpo de N.S.P.S. Juan de Mata," copy of letter from *promotor fidei*

Lambertini to Cardinal Luigi Priuli, protector of the Trinitarian Order, dated January 18, 1720.
35. UG-BHR, Caja MS-2-070, 246.
36. On Miguel de San José, see Criado y Domínguez, *Sabio español*.
37. ASC, ms. 66, 139. This manuscript is attributed to *procurador general* Juan de San Pablo and bears the date of 1704, but the material related to the Matha case is clearly later. The account in ASC, ms. 66, is the foundation for ASC, ms. 282, which is attributed to Miguel de San Rafael, *procurador general* from 1731 to 1741. For his description of his labors in Rome, see UG-BHR, Caja MS-2-070.
38. Antonino de la Asunción, *Diccionario* 1:467, 470.
39. UG-BHR, Caja MS-2-070, 70.
40. ASC, ms. 282, 115–16.
41. Ibid., 115.
42. Lehner, *Catholic Enlightenment*, 7. See also Lehner, "Many Faces of the Catholic Enlightenment"; Rosa, "Catholic *Aufklärung* in Italy."
43. On the response to Hardouin, see Grafton, "Jean Hardouin."
44. Mabillon, *Brèves réflexions*, 11–36.
45. Mabillon, *Traité*, 293–94.
46. Aris, "Jean Mabillon," 28.
47. For an introduction to Muratori, see Vismara, "Lodovico Antonio Muratori."
48. Bertelli, *Erudizione e storia*, 39.
49. Vismara, "Muratori 'immoderato'"; Orlandi, "L. A. Muratori negli archivi."
50. Donato, *Accademie romane*, 21; Heilbron, "Francesco Bianchini, Historian"; Giuli, "Prospero Lambertini."
51. Donato, *Accademie romane*, 87–88. On Lambertini's scholarly work, see Fattori, *Storia*; Fattori, *Fatiche*; Messbarger, Johns, and Gavitt, *Benedict XIV*.
52. Appolis, *"Tiers parti" catholique*; Monaco, "Rapporti di L. A. Muratori."
53. *Positio* 1714. Both the *positio* and the *summarium* are signed by Bernardino Peregrino, *promotor causae*.
54. *Positio* 1714, 1.
55. Ibid., 11.
56. E.g., Esteve, *Demostración legal*.
57. *Positio* 1721.
58. ASC, ms. 282, 118–19, and ASC, ms. 66, 143–44. See also ASC, leg. 16a, pieza XVI/3, "Por parte PP. Discalceatorum SS. Trinitatis Redemptionis Captivorum Congregationis Hispaniorum."
59. The evidence put forward to document the physical qualities of the bones included a passage from Figueras's imaginary Scotsman, George Innes. For Lambertini's later skeptical comments on this source, see Benedict XIV, *De servorum Dei beatificatione et beatorum canonizatione*, 3rd ed., 818 (part 2, chap. 25, no. 29).
60. *Positio* 1721, 17–18.
61. ASC, ms. 282, 116.
62. ASC, ms. 66, 142.
63. ASC, ms. 282, 116–17; ASC, ms. 66, 142. However, ASC, leg. 16a, pieza XVI/3, includes a letter petitioning for Giudice's vote. Althann was the Holy Roman Empire's ambassador in Rome. Giudice, who had once served as Grand Inquisitor of Spain, fell out of favor with Philip V in 1716 and switched his allegiance to the rival Imperial party.
64. ASC, ms. 282, 117; ASC, ms. 66, 142.
65. ASC, ms. 66, 139.
66. ASC, ms. 282, 117–18.
67. ASC, ms. 66, 142. Tabacchi, "Cardinali zelanti e fazioni cardinalizie," 157.
68. ASC, ms. 282, 117–18; ASC, ms. 66, 142.
69. ASC, ms. 66, 144.
70. ASC, ms. 282, 117; ASC, ms. 66, 14.
71. The petition is included in ASC, leg. 16a, pieza XVI/3.
72. In attendance were Cardinals Francesco Barbarini, Luis Antonio Belluga y Moncada, Giovanni Battista Bussi, Álvaro Cienfuegos Villazón, Carlo Agostino Fabroni, Filippo Antonio Gualterio, Curzio Origo, Fabrizio Paolucci, Bernardino Scotti, Armand-Gaston-Maximilien de Rohan, Giovanni Battista Tolomei, and Antonio Felice Zondadari. According to the comments scrawled in

an eighteenth-century hand on the BAV copy of *Positio* 1721, Cardinal Giuseppe Renato Imperiali, a member of the *zelanti* faction, abstained from voting.
73. The petition is included with the BAV copy of *Positio* 1721.
74. ASC, leg. 16a, pieza XVI/3, printed decree: *Decretum. Hispaniarum identitatis corporis S. Ioannis de Matha Ordiis SS. Trinitatis Redemptionis Captiuorum* (Rome, 1721).
75. Cf. a similar decision (the 1717 case of the Iron Crown of Lombardy) in Morelli, "Roman Trial."
76. ASC, leg. 16a, pieza XVI/3, "El sagrado cuerpo del glorioso patriarca S. Juan de Matta, fundador del orden de la S.ma Trinidad."
77. ASC, leg. 16a, pieza XVI/3, letter from Discalced Minister General Alejandro de la Concepción to Miguel de San José, November 29, 1721.
78. For some examples, see Lucás de la Purificación, *Historia del sagrado cuerpo*; Casal y Montenegro, *Oración panegyrica*; A. Sánchez, *Oración euangélica*; Joaquín del Espíritu Santo, *Oración panegyrica*; Elizondo, *Oración panegyrica*. See also ASC, leg. 16b, pieza XVI/15. In some places, however, Calced Trinitarians refused to stage public celebrations since the congregation's ruling represented a triumph for their Discalced rivals. Paramar, *Carta que responde*, 12.
79. Benedict XIV, *De servorum Dei beatificatione et beatorum canonizatione*, 1st ed., 246–47 (part 2, chap. 24, no. 55).
80. Benedict XIV, *De servorum Dei beatificatione et beatorum canonizatione*, 2nd ed., 185 (part 2, chap. 25, no. 56). See Saccenti, "Lunga genesi," and Saccenti, "Fonti."
81. Thiers, *Dissertation*, 121–24. See Ossa-Richardson, "Cry Me a Relic"; Julia, "Église post-tridentine et les reliques," 88–97.
82. *Positio* 1721, 9. The text cited the treatises on relics by Anfossi and Ferrand.
83. Stone, *St. Augustine's Bones*, 51.

84. Honoré de Sainte-Marie, *Réflexions*, 3–4. See Julia, "Église post-tridentine et les reliques," 95–97.
85. Ditchfield, *Liturgy, Sanctity and History*, 219.
86. Benedict XIV, *De servorum Dei beatificatione et beatorum canonizatione*, 3rd ed., 816 (part 2, chap. 25, no. 19).
87. Ditchfield, "Thinking with Saints," 580–83.
88. Tompkins, *Sensational Designs*, 200.
89. Conover, *Pious Imperialism*, 106.
90. Lucás de la Purificación, *Historia del sagrado cuerpo*, 54.
91. Vázquez, "Encuentros Trinidad-Merced," 281–82.
92. Ibid., 240–41.

Epilogue

1. See Damián de la Virgen, dedication to Alexandro de la Concepción, in *Quaresmas*, n.p.; Lucás de la Purificación, *Phoenix Redivivus*; ASC, leg. 16a, pieza XVI/3, testimony of notary Francisco Carrero, February 4, 1724.
2. ASC, leg. 16a, pieza XVI/3, "El sagrado cuerpo del glorioso patriarcha," undated report by Miguel de San José.
3. ASC, ms. 108, "Autos sobre la reliquia de Toledo de San Juan de Mata (a. 1725)"; ASC, leg. 16a, pieza XVI/10.
4. ASC, leg. 16a, pieza XVI/12; Fita, "Sarcófago marmóreo de San Juan de Mata"; Criado y Dominguez, *Sabio español*, 13.
5. Deslandres, *Ordre des Trinitaires*, 1:292–300.
6. Ginarte, *Orden Trinitaria*, 152–57; D'Errico, *Trinitarians*, 191–94; Watzka-Pauli, *Triumph de Barmherzigkeit*.
7. On the Calced Trinitarian church on Via Condotti, see Anselmi, "Chiesa."
8. D'Errico, *Trinitarians*, 238–39.
9. Ibid., 233–34.
10. Ibid., 391.
11. Holguera Illera, "Tesoro."
12. Holguera Illera, "San Juan de Mata."
13. Casal y Montenegro, *Oración panegyrica*, 10–11.

14. Bynum, *Dissimilar Similitudes*, 42–43, 172–73.
15. Tutino, *Fake Saint*.
16. E.g., Freeman, *Holy Bones, Holy Dust*.
17. Ditchfield, "Thinking with Saints."
18. See Manuel del Arco Álvarez's interview with Pérez de Petinto in *La Vanguardia*, October 6, 1961, 23. See also Pérez de Petinto y Bertomeu, *Valor jurídico*. For current scientific approaches to relics, see Van Strydonck, Reyniers, and Van Cleven, *Relics @ the Lab*.
19. D'Errico, *Trinitarians*, 391.
20. ASC, leg. 16a, pieza XVI/3, undated typescript, incipit "La documentación que se conserva."
21. Sbardella, *Antropologia delle reliquie*; Sbardella, "Against the Sacred Body."

Bibliography

Manuscript Sources
Archivio Apostolico Vaticano, Vatican City
    (AAV)
  Arch. Nunz. Madrid 16, 22
  Congr. Concilio, Libri Decret. 3, 18A, 25
  Congr. Riti, Processus 912
Archivio della Congregazione per la Dottrina
    della Fede, Vatican City (ACDF)
  S.O., St. St., B4 e, fasc. 12
  S.O., St. St., B4 e, fasc. 13
  S.O., St. St., B4 e, fasc. 16
Archivio Storico del Vicariato di Roma, Rome
    (ASVR)
  Atti della Segreteria del Tribunale del
    Cardinale Vicario, t. 11
Archivio Storico Diocesano di Sassari, Sassari
    (ASDS)
  Fondo Capitolare, Q4
Archivo de la Abadía del Sacromonte,
    Granada (AASG)
  Ms. C49
Archivo de San Carlino alle Quattro Fontane,
    Rome (ASC)
  Leg. 16a: pieza XVI/1; pieza XVI/2;
    pieza XVI/3; pieza XVI/4; pieza XVI/10;
    pieza XVI/12; pieza XVI/13
  Leg. 16b: pieza XVI/15; pieza XVI/16
  Leg. 16c, pieza XVI/16
  Mss. 66, 77a, 108, 251, 282
Archivo Histórico Nacional, Madrid (AHN)
  Clero, leg. 346-1
  Códices 154
  Inq., leg. 1079
Biblioteca Angelica, Rome (BA)
  Ms. 1659
Biblioteca Apostolica Vaticana, Vatican City
    (BAV)
  Archivio del Capitolo di S. Pietro in
    Vaticano, Miscellanea I, XV
  Chig. B.II.16
  Chig. E.II.47
  Ott. lat. 1123
Biblioteca Nacional de España, Madrid
    (BNE)
  Mss. 3584, 4354, 6161, 6162, 6163, 6164,
    18174, 18238
Biblioteca Pública del Estado de Palma de
    Mallorca (BPPM)
  Mss. 54, 55, 56, 57
Real Academia de la Historia (RAH)
  Salazar y Castro, M-75
Universidad de Granada, Biblioteca del
    Hospital Real (UG-BHR)
  Caja MS-2-070

Published Primary Sources

Accademia della Crusca. *Vocabolario degli Accademici della Crusca*. 1st ed. Venice, 1612.

———. *Vocabolario degli Accademici della Crusca*. Vol. 2. 4th ed. Florence, 1731.

Alcalá, Marcos de. *Chrónica de la Santa Provincia de San Joseph*. . . . Madrid, 1736.

Alejandro de la Madre de Dios. *Chrónica de los Descalzos de la Santíssima Trinidad Redempción de Cautiuos: Segunda parte*. Alcalá de Henares, 1706.

———. *Chrónica de los Padres Descalzos de la Santíssima Trinidad Redempción de Cautivos: Tercera parte*. Madrid, 1707.

Alonso de San Antonio. *Gloriosos títulos apostólicos y reales, originarios y privativos de la Sagrada Religión Descalça y Calçada de la Santíssima Trinidad, de Redención de Cautivos*. . . . Madrid, 1661.

Alós y Orraca, Marco Antonio. *Sermón panegírico de nuestros santos patriarcas y fundadores del Orden de la Santíssima Trinidad, San Iuan de Mata y San Félix de Valois confessores*. Valencia, 1655.

Amada y Torregrosa, Joseph Félix de. *Parangón histórico y iurídico por la Sagrada real y Militar Religión de Nuestra Señora de la Merced Redempción de cautivos christianos*. Madrid, 1663.

Andrade, Alonso de. *Vida de la gloriosa señora Santa Gertrudis la Magna*. Madrid, 1663.

———. *Vidas de los gloriosíssimos Patriarcas San Iuan de Mata, y S. Félix de Valois, fundadores de la ínclita religión de la Santíssima Trinidad Redención de Cautiuos*. Madrid, 1668.

Anfossi, Domenico. *De sacrarum reliquiarum cultu, veneratione, translatione, atque identitate*. Brescia, 1610.

Antolínez de Burgos, Justino. *Historia eclesiástica de Granada*. Edited by Manuel Sotomayor. Granada: Universidad de Granada, 1996.

Antonio, Nicolás. *Biblioteca Hispana Antigua, o de los escritores españoles que brillaron desde Augusto hasta el año de Cristo de MD*. Translated by Francisco Pérez Bayer. Madrid, 1788. 2nd ed., Madrid: Fundación Universitaria Española, 1998.

———. *Bibliotheca Hispana nova sive Hispanorum scriptorum qui ab anno MD ad MDCLXXXIV floruere notitia*. Vol. 2. Madrid, 1788.

———. *Censura de historias fabulosas*. Valencia, 1742.

Arcos, Francisco de. *Memorial que el . . . padre M. Fr. Francisco de Arcos . . . del Orden de la S.S. Trinidad de Redentores, remitió al Padre Procurador General de Roma*. . . . [Madrid?], [1661?]

Aristotle. *Nichomachean Ethics*. In *The Complete Works of Aristotle: The Revised Oxford Translation*, vol. 2, edited by Jonathan Barnes, 1729–1867. Princeton: Princeton University Press, 1984.

Arriaga, Rodrigo de. *Cursus philosophicus*. Antwerp, 1632.

Aznar, Pablo. *Exercicios espirituales: Muy prouechosos para personas deseosas de su saluación*. 3rd ed. Zaragoça, 1630.

Baldesano, Guglielmo. *La sacra historia di S. Mauritio arciduca della Legione Thebea, et de' suoi valerosi campioni*. Turin, 1604.

Bale, John. *Index Britanniae Scriptorum quos ex variis bibliothecis non parvo labore collegit Ioannes Baleus, cum aliis, John Bale's Index of British and Other Writers*. Edited by Reginald Lane Poole, with Mary Bateson. Oxford, UK: Clarendon, 1902.

———. *Scriptorum illustrium maioris Brytanniae, quam nunc Angliam et Scotiam uocant: Catalogus*. . . . Basel, 1557.

Baro, Bonaventura. *Annales Ordinis SS.mae Trinitatis Redemptionis Captivorum . . . tomus primus*. Rome, 1684.

Benedict XIV. *De servorum Dei beatificatione et beatorum canonizatione*. Vol. 4. 1st ed. Bologna, 1738.

———. *De servorum Dei beatificatione et beatorum canonizatione*. Vol. 4. 2nd ed. Pavia, 1743.

———. *De servorum Dei beatificatione et beatorum canonizatione*. Vol. 4. 3rd ed. Rome, 1749.

———. *De servorum Dei beatificatione et beatorum canonizatione / Benedictus XIV = La beatificazione dei servi di Dio e la canonizzazione dei beati / Benedetto XIV*. Vatican City: Libreria Editrice Vaticana, 2010–20.

Bernardino de San Antonio. *Epitome generalium redemptionum captivorum quae a fratribus Ordinis SS. Trinitatis sunt factae*. Lisbon, 1624.

Binius, Severin. *Concilia generalia, et provincialia, Graeca et Latina quaecunque reperiri potuerunt*. . . . Vol. 3, part 2. Cologne, 1618.

Boece, Hector. *Scotorum historiae a prima gentis origine*. . . . Paris, 1527.

Bordoni, Franceso. *Operum tomus quartus*. . . . Lyon, 1665.

Borrell, Miguel. *Reformatorium Fratrum O.SS. ac individuae Trinitatis, Redemptionis captivorum, Aragoniae Provinciae*. Barcelona, 1563.

Bosio, Antonio. *Historia passionis B. Caeciliae virginis*. . . . Rome, 1600.

Bouchet, François. *Ad sanctissimum d.n.d. Gregorium papam decimum tertium, pro toto ordine sanctissimæ Trinitatis & redemptionis captiuorum oratio*. . . . Rome, 1575.

Bouhours, Dominique. *La vie de saint François Xavier de la Compagnie de Jésus apostre des Indes et du Japon*. 2nd ed. Paris, 1683.

Bouillaud, Claude. *Breve Relatione della Solennissima Festa della Beatificatione della Beata Rosa di Santa Maria . . . fatta nella Basilica di S. Pietro, adì 15. Aprile 1668*. Rome, 1668.

Bozio, Tommaso. *De signis Ecclesiae Dei libri XII*. Vol. 2. Rome, 1591.

Bravo, Thomas. *Invención felicíssima de la Cabeça del divino Hieroteo, hallada a cinco de Abril, deste año de 1625*. . . . Valladolid, 1625. Reprinted in Ildefonso Rodríguez y Fernández, *San Jeroteo, Obispo de Segovia*. Madrid: Gabriel López del Horno, 1915.

Breviarium ad usum Fratrum sacri ordinis sanctissime Trinitaris de redemptione captiuorum. Seville, 1545.

Buchanan, George. *Rerum Scoticarum historia*. Edinburgh, 1582.

Bzovius, Abraham. *Annalium Ecclesiasticorum*. . . . Vol. 13. Cologne, 1616.

Calvo, Silvestre. *Resumen de los prerrogativas del Orden de la SSma. Trinidad, Redención de Cautivos, y de los varones ilustres que han florecido en él*. Pamplona, 1791.

Carrillo, Martín. *Annales y memorias cronológicas*. . . . Zaragoza, 1634.

Carruesco y Sessé, Pedro. *Sermón panegírico de los santos padres y patriarcas San Iuan de Mata y San Félix de Valoys*. . . . Zaragoza, 1663.

Casal y Montenegro, Juan Agustín del. *Oración panegyrica que en la plausible fiesta de la identidad del cuerpo de San Juan de Mata*. . . . Granada, [1722].

Cavero, Nicolás. *Informe de la verdad, por el real, y militar orden de Nuestra Señora de la Merced, Redención de cautivos*. [Madrid?], 1731.

Ceremonial y processionario de los frayles de la orden de la sanctíssima Trinidad, y redempción de captiuos: Agora nuevamente corregido, y concertado con el Ceremonial Romano. Seville, 1593.

Colombo, Felipe. *Vida del glorioso patriarca San Pedro Nolasco*. . . . 2nd ed. Madrid, 1769.

Commemorationes ex Anglicanae Prouinciae Breuiario Ord. Santiss. Trinitatis Redemptionis Captiuorum anno 1432. . . . Rome, 1649.

Congregatione Sacrorum Rituum siue Eminentissimo, ac Reurendissimo D. Card. Ginetto Hispaniarum identitatis corporis Sancti Ioannis de Matha Fundatoris Ordinis Sanctiss. Trinitatis Redemptionis Captiuorum. Positio super identitate corporis Sancti Ioannis de Matha. Rome, 1669.

*Congregatione Sacrorum Rituum siue Eminentissimo, ac Reurendissimo D. Card. Ginetto. Romana Canonizationis Seruorum Dei Ioannis de Matha, & Felicis de Valois Fundatorum Ordinis Sanctissimae Trinitatis Redemptionis

Captiuorum. Positio super dubio an sententia Eminentissimi Cardinalis Vicarii super casu excepto fit confirmanda, vel infirmanda, in casu &c. Rome, 1666.

Contelori, Felice. Tractatus et praxis de canonizatione sanctorum. Lyon, 1634.

Covarrubias Orozco, Sebastian de. Tesoro de la lengua castellana, o español. Madrid, 1611.

Damián de la Virgen. Quaresmas de las tres ferias mayores. Vol. 1. Zaragoza, 1722.

Dávila y Toledo, Sancho. De la veneración que se deve a los cuerpos de los sanctos y a sus reliquias.... Madrid, 1611.

Decretum. Hispaniarum identitatis corporis S. Ioannis de Matha Ordiis SS. Trinitatis Redemptionis Captiuorum. Rome, 1721.

Decretum sac. Rit. Congregationis. Giennen.... Rome, 1670.

De La Bigne, Marguerin. Maxima bibliotheca veterum patrum et antiquorum scriptorum ecclesiasticorum. Lyon, 1677.

de Matta, Carlo Felice. Novissimus de sanctorum canonizatione tractatus.... Rome, 1678.

Dempster, Thomas. Historia ecclesiastica gentis Scotorum lib. 19.... Bologna, 1627.

Diego de Jesús. Annales de la religión de la santíssima Trinidad.... Madrid, 1687.

Diego de la Madre de Dios. Chorónica de los Descalços de la Santíssima Trinidad Redentores de Cautivos. Primera parte. Madrid, 1652.

Dilloud, Ignace. Les vies des Saints Jean de Matha et Félix de Valois, patriarches de l'Ordre de la Sainte Trinité et Rédemption des Captifs. Paris, 1695.

Du Breul, Jacques. Le Théâtre des antiquités de Paris.... Paris, 1612.

Duplessis, Michel Toussaint Chrétien. Histoire de l'Église de Meaux. Vol. 2. Paris, 1731.

Elizondo, Pablo Miguel de. Oración panegyrica en la solemne pompa al descubrimiento de el cuerpo de gran patriarca S. Juan de Matha. Pamplona, 1722.

Esteve, Damián. Demostración legal, y política que manifiestan el real fisco de Su Magestad.... Madrid, 1678.

———. Symbolo de la Concepción de María sellado en la caridad y religión mercenaria.... Madrid, 1728.

Exemptio fratrum discalceatorum Ordinis Sanctissimae Trinitatis Redemptionis Captiuorum . . . Sanctiss. D.N. Vrbani Divina Providentia PP. VIII Indulta. Rome, 1637.

Fagundes, Estevão. Tractatus in quinque Ecclesiae praecepta. Lyon, 1626.

Ferrand, Jean. Disquisitio Reliquiaria: sive De suspicienda, et suspecta earumdem numero reliquiarum, quae in diversis ecclesiis servantur, multitudine. Lyon, 1647.

Ferrer de Valdecebro, Andrés. El templo de la fama, con instrucciones políticas y morales. Madrid, 1680.

Figueras Carpi, Juan. Chronicum Ordinis Sanctissimae Trinitatis de redemptione.... Verona, 1645.

———. Compendio histórico de la vida y martirio de D. Pedro Figueras Carpi de Valencia.... Venice, 1642.

Florianus a S. Josephus. Chronicorum discalceati ordinis sanctissimae trinitatis de redemptione captivorum pars prima ab exordio reformationis.... Prague, 1726.

Francesco di S. Lorenzo. Compendio della vita miracolosa de' santi Gio. de Matha, e Felice Valesio, patriarchi dell'Ordine della Santiss. Trinità del Riscatto. Rome, 1658.

———. Compendio Memorabile dell'institutione, approbatione & progresso dell'Ordine della Santissima Trinità del Riscatto. Rome, 1650.

Gallia christiana, in provincias ecclesiasticas distributa.... Vol. 8. Paris, 1744.

García, Francisco. Vida y milagros de San Francisco Xavier, de la Compañia de Iesús, apostol de las Indias. Madrid, 1672.

Gonon, Benoit. Vitae et sententiae patrum occidentis, libris VII. digestae.... Lyon, 1625.

González Dávila, Gil. Abrégé historique de la vie des glorieux S. Jean de La Matte et S. Felix de Valois.... Translated by François Aloès. Avignon, 1634.

———. Compendio histórico de las vidas de los gloriosos san Iuan de Mata i S. Félix de Valois.... Madrid, 1630.

Guasque, Pasquale. La Celeste institutione del Sacro Ordine della S.ma Trinità della Redentione delli schiavi.... Naples, 1639.

2nd ed., Velletri, 1640. 3rd ed., Naples, 1642.

Guerra y Ribera, Manuel. *Sermones varios de santos.* Madrid, 1677.

Harpsfield, Nicholas. *Historia anglicana ecclesiastica.* Douai, 1622.

Hispaniarum identitatis corporis Sancti Ioannis de Matha alterius ex Fundatoribus Ordinis Sanctissimae Trinitatis Redemptionis Captiuorum: Summarium. Rome, 1669.

Hispaniarum identitatis corporis S. Joannis de Matha. Summarium. Rome, 1714.

Honoré de Sainte-Marie. *Réflexions sur les règles et sur l'usage de la critique touchant l'histoire de l'Église.* . . . Vol. 2. Paris, 1719.

Index librorum prohibitorum et expurgandorum novissimus. . . . Madrid, 1667.

La institución o fundación de indulgencias del Orden de la Santíssima trinidad de la redempción de captivos y agora nuevamente por privilegio particular de Paulo Quinto confirmadas. Pamplona, 1611.

Institution et fondation de l'Ordre de la Tressaincte et individve Trinité, et Rédemption des captifs. Douai, 1611.

Institutio, regula, priuilegia, constitutiones, c[a]erimoniale, & formularium Ordinis Sanctissimae Trinitatis Redemptionis Captiuorum. Zaragoza, 1584.

Institutio siue fundatio Ordinis Sanctissimae ac Indiuiduae Trinitatis & Redemptionis Captiuorum. Lisbon, 1591.

Jennyn, Joannes. *Vera confraternitatis Sanctissimae Trinitatis de Redemptione Captivorum idaea originem, propagationem indulgentias, privilegia et regulas ejus complectens.* . . . Bruges, 1649.

———. *Vera confraternitatis SS. Trinitatis de Redemptione Captivorum, & B. Mariae de Remedio; nec non vita SS. Patriarchum Joannis et Felicis idaea.* . . . Brussels, 1666.

Jerónimo de San José. *Historia chronologica da esclarecida ordem da SS.Trindade, redempção de cativos, da provincia de Portugal.* Vol. 1. Lisbon, 1789.

Joaquín del Espíritu Santo. *Oración panegyrica de mi gran padre S. Juan de Matha.* Valladolid, [1722].

José de Jesús María. *Bullarium ordinis Sanctissimae Trinitatis redemptionis Captiuorum.* Madrid, 1692.

Joseph de Santa Teresa. *Resunta de la vida de n. bienaventurado padre San Juan de la Cruz.* . . . Madrid, 1675.

Juan Bautista de la Concepción. *Obras completas: Edición crítica.* Vol. 2, *La reforma trinitaria.* Edited by Juan Pujana and Arsenio Llamazares. Madrid: Biblioteca de Autores Cristianos, 1997.

Juan de San Buenaventura. *Fasciculus trium florum Ordinis SS. Trinitatis de Redemptione Captivorum seu brevissimum Compendium.* . . . Rome, 1651.

López, Domingo. *Noticias históricas de las tres florentíssimas provincias del celeste Orden de la Santíssima Trinidad, redempción de cautivos, en Inglaterra, Escocia, y Hybernia.* Madrid, 1714.

López de Altuna, Pedro. *Primera parte de la Corónica General del Orden de la Santíssima Trinidad Redención de Cautivos.* Segovia, 1637.

Lucás de la Purificación. *Historia del sagrado cuerpo del glorioso patriarcha San Juan de Matha.* . . . [Madrid], [1723].

———. *Phoenix redivivus, id est: corpus Sancti Patris Nostri Joannis de Matha . . . novo cultu reviviscens.* . . . Madrid, 1737.

———. *Quarta parte de la chrónica de los religiosos descalzos del orden de la SSma. Trinidad, Redempción de Cautivos.* Granada, 1732.

Mabillon, Jean. *Brèves réflexions sur quelques règles de l'histoire.* Edited by Blandine Barret-Kriegel. Paris: P.O.L., 1990.

———. *Traité des études monastiques.* Paris, 1691.

Macedo, Francisco de. *Vitae SS. Ioannis de Mattha, et Felicis de Valois, fundatorum Ordinis SS. Trinitatis.* Rome, 1660.

Mallea, Salvador de. *Epítome de las vidas de los gloriosos S. Jvan de Mata, y S. Félix de Valoys.* Rome, [1665 or 1673?].

Marracci, Ippolito. *Fundatores Mariani.* . . . Rome, 1643.

Melchor del Espíritu Santo. *El Patriarca San Juan de Mata, embiado de las Tres*

Divinas Personas para maestro de la más acendrada caridad. . . . Madrid, 1707.

Memoriale. Pro Concessione, seu extensione Officii, & Missarum SS. Ioannis de Mattha, & Foelicis Valois Fundatorum Religionis SS. Trinitatis Redemptionis Captiuorum. Pro dicta religion. Rome, 1631.

Migne, Jacques-Paul, ed. Patrologia Latina. 217 vols. Paris, 1841–55.

Miralles, Gabriel. Sermón panegyrico de los Santos Patriarcas, y fundadores de Nuestro Sagrado Orden de la SS. Trinidad, San Iuan de Mata, y San Félix de Valois Confessores. Valencia, 1658.

Morales, Ambrosio de. Los cinco libros postreros de la Corónica general de España. Córdoba, 1586.

Morigia, Paolo. Historia dell'origine di tutte le religioni. . . . 2nd ed. Venice, 1581.

Munday, Anthony. The English Romayne lyfe. . . . London, 1582.

Nicolson, William. The Scottish Historical Library. . . . London, 1702.

Núñez de Castro, Alonso. Corónica de los señores reyes de Castilla, don Sancho el Deseado, don Alonso el Octauo y don Enrique el Primero. . . . Madrid, 1665.

Paleotti, Gabriele. Archiepiscopale bononiense sive De bononiensis ecclesiae administratione. Rome, 1594.

Panciroli, Ottavio. I tesori nascosti nell'alma Città di Roma. Rome, 1625.

Papenbroeck, Daniel van. Responsio Danielis Papebrochii ex Societate Jesu theologi ad Exhibitionem errorum per adm. r.p. Sebastianum a s. Paulo. . . . Antwerp, 1697.

Paramar, Juan de. Carta que responde un afecto al Celestial Orden de la Ssma. Trinidad de Redemtores Calçados a una que le escribió un sujeto de esta ciudad de Granada. [Granada], [1721].

Pedro de la Asunción. Nihil nouum. Señor, Fray Pedro de la Assumpción . . . dize: Que hauiendo salido en público vn papel dirigido en forma de Memorial . . . subscripto de Don Antonio Calatayud, y Toledo . . . y de Fray Damián Esteuan . . . llebando por máxima, mouer el dictamen de V.M. en buen gouierno, y política, a que sola la Religión de la Merced, ha de exercitar los actos de la Redempción de Cautiuos en la Corona de Aragón. . . . N.p., 1682.

Pedro Pascual. Sobre la secta mahometana. Edited by Fernando González Muñoz. Valencia: Universitat de Valencia, 2011.

Pellicer de Ossau y Tovar, José. Tropheo de la verdad de la historia. . . . Valencia, 1676.

Pitts, John. Relationum historicarum de rebus anglicis. Paris, 1619.

Ponz, Antonio. Viage de España: En que se da noticia de las cosas más apreciables, y dignas de saberse, que hay en ellos. Vol. 5. Madrid, 1776.

Quintanadueñas, Antonio de. Singularia theologiae moralis: Ad septem ecclesiae sacramenta. . . . Seville, 1645.

Real Academia Española. Diccionario de la lengua castellana. . . . Vol. 4. Madrid, 1734.

Regula et constitutiones fratrum ordinis Sanctissimae Trinitatis Redemptionis Captiuorum. . . . Seville, 1573.

Ricciulli, Antonio. Lucubrationum ecclesiasticarum libri sex. Naples, 1643.

Rocca, Angelo. De canonizatione sanctorum. Rome, 1601.

Rodríguez, José. Copia fidelíssima de carta, que el reuerendíssimo padre Ioseph Rodríguez . . . escriue al Rmo. P. Fr. Vicente Domingo Henrique. . . . N.p., n.d. [1674?].

———. Ostentación magnífica con que el Real Convento de Nuestra S. del Remedio de la ciudad de Valencia celebró . . . S. Iuan de Mata y San Félix de Valois . . . en 17 de deziembre del año 1660. Valencia, 1661.

———. Sacro, y solemne novenario, públicas y luzidas fiestas, que hizo el Real Convento de N. S. del Remedio de la Ciudad de Valencia, a . . . San Iuan de Mata, y San Félix de Valois. . . . Valencia, 1669.

Rodríguez, Josep. Biblioteca Valentina. Valencia, 1747.

Rodríguez de Castro, José. Biblioteca española. . . . Vol. 2. Madrid, 1786.

Roig y Jalpi, Juan Gaspar. Dulze desengaño histórico, del año cierto en que se fundó la Sagrada . . . Orden de Nuestra Señora de la Merced Redención de Cautiuos. . . . Barcelona, 1684.

———. *Resumen historial de las grandezas y antigüedades de la ciudad de Gerona y cosas memorables suyas eclesiásticas y seculares, assí de nuestros tiempos, como de los passados.* . . . Girona, 1678.

Rojas, Juan de. *Declamación evangélica en la solemnidad qve al patriarca San Félix de Valois . . . hizo en quatro de noviembre deste año de 1658 su conuento de Madrid.* . . . Madrid, 1658.

———. *Laudatoria eungélica [sic] en la solemnidad, que a nuestro glorioso patriarcha San Iuan de Matha . . . consagró su conuento desta corte de Madrid, este año de 1659 en 17 del mes de Diziembre.* . . . Madrid, 1659.

Romana canonizationis Sanctorum Ioannis de matha, & Felicis de Valois, Fundatorum Ordinis Sanctissimae Trinitatis Redemptionis Captiuorum. . . . Rome, 1666.

Román y Zamora, Jerónimo. *Repúblicas del Mundo divididas en XXVII libros.* Medina del Campo, 1575.

Sacra Rituum Congregatione. Eminentissimo, & Reverendissimo D. Card. Paulutio pro Eminentissimo, & Reverentissimo D. Card. Annibale Albano ponente Hispaniarum identitatis corporis S. Ioannis de Matha Fundatoris Ordinis Sanctissimae Trinitatis Redemptionis Captivorum. Positio. Rome, 1721.

Sacrorum rituum congregatione. Emo, & Rmo. D. Cardinali Casino ponente Hispaniarum identitatis corporis S. Ioannis de Matha fundatoris Ordinis Sanctissimae Trinitatis Redemptionis Captiuorum. Positio super identitate dicti corporis. Rome, 1714.

Sales, Agustín. *Memorias históricas del antiguo Santuario del Santo Sepulcro de Valencia.* Valencia, 1749.

Sánchez, Agustín. *Oración euangélica que en la fiesta a la declaración de la identidad del cuerpo de San Juan de Mata.* Madrid, 1722.

Sánchez, Tomás. *Opus morale de praeceptis decalogi.* Madrid, 1613.

Scacchi, Fortunato. *De cultu et veneratione servorum Dei.* Rome, 1639.

Segni, Giovanni Battista. *Reliquiarium, sive De reliquiis et venerat. sanctorum liber unus.* . . . Bologna, 1600. 2nd ed., Bologna, 1610.

Sentencia y decreto del Concilio provincial de Toledo en el negocio de las reliquias de los santos mártires de Córdoba. n.p., n.d. [1583].

Sisternes de Oblites, Gerónimo. *Sermón panegyrico de nuestros Santos Padres San Iuan de Mata, y San Félix de Valois, Patriarcas y fundadores de la Orden de la Santíssima Trinidad.* Valencia, 1660.

Sousa, Francisco da. *Oriente conquistado a Jesu Christo pelos padres da Companhia de Jesus da Provincia de Goa.* Vol. 1. Lisbon, 1710.

Suárez, Francisco. *Commentariorum, ac disputationum in tertiam partem Divi Thomae.* Vol. 1. Venice, 1598.

Tamayo y Salazar, Juan. *Anamnesis sive Commemorationis sanctorum hispanorum.* . . . Vol. 6. Lyon, 1659.

Tarizzo, Antonio Francesco. *Compendio della vita del gloriosissimo patriarca S. Giovanni di Matha.* . . . Turin, 1698. 2nd ed., Turin: G. Olivieri, 1848.

Thiers, Jean-Baptiste. *Dissertation sur la Sainte Larme de Vendôme.* Paris, 1699.

Thomas Aquinas. *Summa Theologiae: Latin Text and English Translation, Introductions, Notes, Appendices, and Glossaries.* Vol. 50. Cambridge, UK: Blackfriars, 1964.

———. *Thomas Aquinas's Quodlibetal Questions.* Translated and edited by Turner Nevitt and Brian Davies. Oxford: Oxford University Press, 2020.

Thomas of Eccleston. *De adventu fratrum minorum in Angliam.* Edited by A. G. Little. Manchester, UK: Manchester University Press, 1951.

Urban VIII. *Decreta seruanda in canonizatione, & beatificatione sanctorum.* . . . Rome, 1642.

Vega y Toraya, Francisco de. *Crónica de la provincia de Castilla, León y Navarra, del Orden de la Santíssima Trinidad,*

Redención de Cautivos. Primera parte. Madrid, 1720.

Secondary Sources

Aliaga Asensio, Pedro. "Claves políticas en la génesis de la Reforma Trinitaria." In *San Juan Bautista de la Concepción: Su figura y su obra (1561–1613): Actas del Congreso Trinitario Internacional*, edited by Isidro Hernández Delgado, 249–61. Córdoba: Publicaciones Obra Social y Cultural Cajasur, 2000.

———. "La Orden de la Santa Trinidad, bajo la Regla de san Agustín." *Trinitarium* 9 (2000): 41–67.

———. *San Simón de Rojas: Un santo en la Corte de Felipe III y Felipe IV*. Madrid: Biblioteca de Autores Cristianos, 2009.

Analecta juris pontificii. 7th ser. Rome, 1864.

Analecta juris pontificii. 8th ser. Rome, 1866.

Andrés Ucendo, José Ignacio. "El abasto de pan en el Madrid del siglo XVII." *Studia historica: Historia moderna* 34 (2012): 61–97.

Andújar Castillo, Francisco. "Los rescates de cautivos en las dos orillas del Mediterráneo y en el mar (alafías) en el siglo XVI." In *Le commerce des captifs: Les intermédiaires dans l'échange et le rachat des prisonniers en Méditerranée, XVe–XVIIIe siècle*, edited by Wolfgang Kaiser, 133–64. Rome: École Française de Rome, 2008.

Anselmi, Alessandra. "La chiesa della Santissima Trinità degli Spagnoli." In *Roma y España: Un crisol de la cultura europea en la Edad Moderna: Actas del Congreso Internacional celebrado en la Real Academia de España en Roma del 8 al 12 de mayo de 2007*, vol. 2, edited by Carlos José Hernando Sánchez, 915–30. Madrid: Sociedad estatal para la acción cultural exterior, 2007.

———. *Il Palazzo dell'Ambasciata di Spagna presso la Santa Sede*. Rome: De Luca, 2001.

Antonin de l'Assomption. *Les origines de l'ordre de la Très Sainte Trinité d'aprés les documents*. Rome: St. Cajetan, 1925.

Antonino de la Asunción. "Autoridad del P. Juan Figueras como historiador de la orden." *Acta Ordinis Sanctissimae Trinitatis* 4 (1941): 15–40.

———. *Diccionario de los escritores trinitarios de España y Portugal*. 2 vols. Rome: F. Kleinbub, 1898.

Antonino dell'Assunta. *Ministrorum Generalium Ordinis SS. Trinitatis Series*. Isola del Liri: Soc. Tip. A. Macioce and Pisani, 1936.

Antonino dell'Assunta and A. Romano di S. Teresa. *S. Tommaso in Formis sul Celio. Notizie e documenti*. Isola del Liri: Soci Tipog. A. Macioce and Pisani, 1927.

Antonucci, Laura. "La scrittura giudicata: Perizie grafiche in processi romani del primo seicento." *Scrittura e civiltà* 13 (1989): 489–534.

———. "Tecniche dello scrivere e cultura grafica di un perito romano nel '600." *Scrittura e civiltà* 16 (1992): 265–303.

Appolis, Émile. *Le "tiers parti" catholique au XVIIIe siècle: entre Jansénistes et Zelanti*. Paris: A. et J. Picard, 1960.

Arbois de Juvainville, Henri d'. *Histoire des ducs et des comtes de Champagne*. Vol. 4, part 2. Paris: Aug. Durand, 1865.

Aris, Rutherford. "Jean Mabillon (1632–1707)." In *Medieval Scholarship: Biographical Studies of the Formation of a Discipline*, vol. 1, *History*, edited by Helen Damico and Joseph B. Zavadil, 15–32. New York: Routledge, 1995.

Armellini, Mariano. *Le chiese di Roma dal secolo IV al XIX*. Vol. 1. Rome: Edizioni R.O.R.E. de Nicolà Ruffolo, 1942.

Atienza López, Ángela. "Las crónicas de las órdenes religiosas en la España Moderna: Construcciones culturales y militantes de época barroca." In *Iglesia memorable. Crónicas, historias, escritos . . . a mayor gloria. Siglos XVI–XVII*, edited by Ángela Atienza López, 25–50. Madrid: Sílex, 2012.

Aurrecoechea, José Luis, and Antonio Moldón, eds. *Fuentes históricas de la Orden Trinitaria (s. XII–XV)*. Córdoba: Secretariado Trinitario, 2003.

Ávila, Guillermo. "El antiguo convento de la Trinidad y el Santísimo Cristo de Burgos." *Boletín de la Institución Fernán González* 157 (1962): 739–44.

Baciocchi, Stéphane, and Christophe Duhamelle, eds. *Reliques romaines: Invention et circulation des corps saints des catacombes à l'époque moderne*. Rome: École Française de Rome, 2016.

Bagnoli, Martina. "Dressing the Relics: Some Thoughts on the Custom of Relic Wrapping in Medieval Christianity." In *Matter of Faith: An Interdisciplinary Study of Relics and Relic Veneration in the Medieval Period*, edited by James Robinson, Lloyd De Beer, and Anna Harnden, 100–109. London: British Museum, 2014.

Barrio Gozalo, Maximiliano. "Tolerancia y vida religiosa de los cautivos cristianos en el norte de Africa (siglos XVI–XVIII)." *Revista de la Inquisición* 12 (2006): 99–136.

Bartlett, Robert. *Why Can the Dead Do Such Great Things? Saints and Worshippers from the Martyrs to the Reformation*. Princeton: Princeton University Press, 2013.

Bartolini, Domenico. *Congregazione particolare dei Sagri Riti con segreto pontificio deputata da Sua Santità per esaminare e difinire la questione se veramente i vasi di vetro, e di terra cotta posti fuori o dentro i loculi dei sepolti nei sagri suburbani cimiterj contenghino il sangue dei martiri; e perciò se debbano ritenersi come segno indubitato di martirio*. Rome: Tipografia della Rev. Camera Apostolica, 1863.

Bazire, Joyce, ed. *The Metrical Life of St Robert of Knaresborough Together with the Other Middle English Pieces in British Museum MS. Egerton 3143*. London: Published for the Early English Text Society by G. Cumberlege, Oxford University Press, 1953.

Beaven, Lisa. "Robbing the Grave: Stealing the Remains of the Blessed John of Matha from the Church of S. Tommaso in Formis in 1655." In *Matters of Engagement: Emotions, Identity, and Cultural Contact in the Premodern World*, edited by Daniela Hacke, Claudia Jarzebowski, Hannes Ziegler, 153–71. New York: Routledge, 2021.

Bertelli, Sergio. *Erudizione e storia in Ludovico Antonio Muratori*. Naples: Nella sede dell'Istituto, 1960.

Berty, Adolphe. *Topographie historique du vieux Paris*. Vol. 6, *Région centrale de l'université*. Paris: Imprimerie impériale, 1897.

Bibliotheca Sanctorum. Vol. 5. Rome: Istituto Giovanni XXIII nella Pontificia Università Lateranense, 1964.

Bizzocchi, Roberto. *Genealogie incredibili: Scritti di storia nell'Europa moderna*. 2nd ed. Bologna: Il Mulino, 2009.

Boiron, Stéphane. "Définition et statut juridique des reliques dans le droit canonique classique." In *Reliques et sainteté dans l'espace médiéval*, edited by Jean-Luc Deuffic and André Vauchez, 19–31. Saint-Denis: Pecia, 2006.

Borghero, Carlo. *La certezza e la storia: Cartesianesimo, pirronismo e conoscenza storica*. Milan: Franco Angeli Editore, 1983.

Bouley, Bradford A. *Pious Postmortems: Anatomy, Sanctity, and the Catholic Church in Early Modern Europe*. Philadelphia: University of Pennsylvania Press, 2017.

Bozóky, Edina. *La politique des reliques de Constantin à Saint Louis: Protection collective et légitimation du pouvoir*. Paris: Beauchesne, 2006.

Brodman, James William. *Charity and Religion in Medieval Europe*. Washington, DC: Catholic University of America Press, 2009.

———. *Ransoming Captives in Crusader Spain: The Order of Merced on the Christian-Islamic Frontier*. Philadelphia: University of Pennsylvania Press, 1986.

———. "The Trinitarian and Mercedarian Orders: A Study of Religious Redemptionism in the Thirteenth

Century." PhD diss., University of Virginia, 1974.

Brosch, Joseph. *Der Heiligsprechungsprozess per viam cultus*. Rome: Pontifical Gregorian University, 1938.

Brown, Peter. *The Cult of the Saints: Its Rise and Function in Latin Christianity*. Chicago: University of Chicago Press, 1981.

Brundin, Abigail, Deborah Howard, and Mary Laven. *The Sacred Home in Renaissance Italy*. Oxford: Oxford University Press, 2018.

Buettner, Brigitte. "Past Presents: New Year's Gifts at the Valois Courts, ca. 1400." *Art Bulletin* 83, no. 4 (2001): 598–625.

Burke, Peter. "How to Become a Counter-Reformation Saint." In *The Historical Anthropology of Early Modern Italy: Essays on Perception and Communication*, 48–62. Cambridge: Cambridge University Press, 1987.

Bynum, Caroline Walker. *Christian Materiality: An Essay on Religion in Late Medieval Europe*. New York: Zone Books, 2011.

———. *Dissimilar Similitudes: Devotional Objects in Late Medieval Europe*. New York: Zone Books, 2020.

Calendario Romanum ex decreto sacrosancto Oecumenici Concilii Vaticani II instauratum auctoritate Pauli PP. VI promulgatum. Vatican City: Typis polyglottis vaticanis, 1969.

Calixte de la Providence. *Vie de Saint Jean de Matha, fondateur de l'ordre de la Très Sainte-Trinité pour la rédemption des captifs*. Paris: F. Wattelier, 1867.

———. *Vie de S. Félix de Valois, prince du sang royal de France fondateur (avec Saint Jean de Matha) de l'Ordre de la très-sainte-trinité pour la rédemption des captifs*. Paris: Ambroise Bray, 1869.

Cal Pardo, Enrique. *Episcopologio mindoniense*. Santiago de Compostela: Instituto de Estudios Gallegos "Padre Sarmiento," 2003.

Calvin, John. *Treatise on Relics*. Amherst, MA: Prometheus Books, 2008.

Carlos Varona, María Cruz de. "'Imágenes rescatadas' en la Europa moderna: El caso de Jesús de Medinaceli." *Journal of Spanish Cultural Studies* 12, no. 3 (2012): 327–54.

———. "Imagen y santidad en la España moderna: El ejemplo de los trinitarios calzados de Madrid." PhD diss., Universidad Complutense, 2005.

Cassanyes Roig, Albert. "Antoni Cerdà (c. 1390–1459): Poder polític i promoció eclesiàstica a mitjans del segle XV." PhD diss., Universitat de Lleida, 2018.

Castro, Ernesto G. "Iter canónico y estado actual del santoral mercedario." *Estudios: Revista trimestral publicada por los padres de la Orden de la Merced* 26, nos. 90–91 (1970): 661–716.

Cipollone, Giulio. *Cristianita—Islam: Cattività e liberazione in nome di Dio: Il tempo di Innocenzo III dopo "il 1187."* Rome: Ed. Pontif. Univ. Gregoriana, 1992.

———. "L'indole non-militare dell'*Ordo Trinitatis et captivorum*: Sua espansione in Catalogna (XIII–XIVs.)." In *Actes de les primeres jornades sobre els ordes religioso-militars als països catalans (segles XII–XIX) (Montblanc, 8–10 novembre de 1985)*, 530–38. Tarragona: Diputación, 1994.

———. *Il mosaico di S. Tommaso in Formis a Roma (ca. 1210). Contributo di iconografia e iconologia*. Rome: Ordinis Trinitatis Institutum Historicum, 1984.

———. *Studi intorno a Cerfroid prima casa dell'ordine trinitario (1198–1429)*. Rome: Pontificia Universitatis Gregorianae, 1978.

Cirot, George. *Mariana, historien. Études sur l'historiographie espagnole*. Bordeaux: Féret & fils, 1904.

Clark, Gillian. "Victricius of Rouen: Praising the Saints." *Journal of Early Christian Studies* 7, no. 3 (1999): 365–99.

Clark, Stuart. *Thinking with Demons: The Idea of Witchcraft in Early Modern Europe*. Oxford: Oxford University Press, 1997.

———. *Vanities of the Eye: Vision in Early Modern European Culture*. Oxford: Oxford University Press, 2007.

Collard, Franck. "Entre fardeau et honneur: Robert Gaguin, doyen de la faculté de

Décret de l'Université de Paris à la fin du Moyen Âge." In *Église, mémoire(s), éducation: Mélanges offerts à Jean-François Boulanger*, edited by Véronique Beaulande-Barraud, 277–96. Reims: Université de Reims Champagne-Ardenne, 2014.

———. *Robert Gaguin: Un historien au travail à la fin du XVe siècle*. Geneva: Droz, 1996.

Collar de Cáceres, Fernando. "El convento de la Trinidad de Cuéllar y su ciclo pictórico." *Anuario del Departamento de Historia y Teoria del Arte* 12 (2000): 39–59.

Collins, David J. *Reforming Saints: Saints' Lives and Their Authors in Germany, 1470–1530*. Oxford: Oxford University Press, 2008.

Conover, Cornelius. *Pious Imperialism: Spanish Rule and the Cult of the Saints in Mexico City*. Albuquerque: University of New Mexico Press, 2019.

Cousinié, Frédéric. *Le saint des saints: Maîtres-autels et retables parisiens du XVIIe siècle*. Aix-en-Provence: Presses Universitaires de France, 2006.

Criado y Domínguez, Juan P. *Un sabio español del siglo XVIII; Fray Miguel de San José, general de los Trinitarios Descalzos: Indicaciones bio-bibliográficas*. Madrid: Estab. Tip. Sucesores de Rivadeneyra, 1893.

Cueto, Ronald. "Some Observations on the Trinitarian Connections—Calced and Discalced—in the Court of Philip IV." *Bulletin of Spanish Studies: Hispanic Studies and Researches on Spain, Portugal and Latin America* 81, no. 3 (2004): 293–308.

Culliere, Alain. "Bernard Dominici, trinitaire messin (c. 1517–1597)." *Les Cahiers Lorrains* 1 (1998): 29–53.

Dandelet, Thomas James. *Spanish Rome, 1500–1700*. New Haven: Yale University Press, 2001.

Daston, Lorraine. *Classical Probability in the Enlightenment*. Princeton: Princeton University Press, 1988.

———. "Marvelous Facts and Miraculous Evidence in Early Modern Europe." *Critical Inquiry* 18, no. 1 (1991): 93–124.

———. "Probability and Evidence." In *The Cambridge History of Seventeenth-Century Philosophy*, vol. 2, edited by Daniel Garber and Michael Ayers, 1108–44. Cambridge: Cambridge University Press, 1998.

Davis, Robert C. *Christian Slaves, Muslim Masters: White Slavery in the Mediterranean, the Barbary Coast, and Italy, 1500–1800*. New York: Palgrave, 2003.

Dear, Peter. "From Truth to Disinterestedness in the Seventeenth Century." *Social Studies of Science* 22, no. 4 (1992): 619–31.

Decreta authentica Congregationis sacrorum rituum. Vol. 1. Edited by Aloisii Gardellini. 3rd ed. Rome: Congregatio de Propaganda Fide, 1856.

Delooz, Pierre. "Toward a Sociological Study of Canonized Sainthood in the Catholic Church." In *Saints and Their Cults: Studies in Religious Sociology, Folklore, and History*, edited by Stephen Wilson, 189–216. Cambridge: Cambridge University Press, 1983.

Deman, T. "Probabilisme." In *Dictionnaire de théologie catholique*, vol. 13, part 1, col. 417–619. Paris: Librairie Letouzey et Ané, 1936.

Denifle, Henri, ed. *Chartularium Universitatis Parisiensis*. Vol. 4. Paris: Ex typis fratrum Delalain, 1897.

De Rossi, Giovanni Battista, and Antonio Ferrua. *Sulla questione del vaso di sangue: Memoria inedita con introduzione storica e appendici di documenti*. Vatican City: Pontificio Istituto di Archeologia Cristiana, 1944.

D'Errico, Anthony O. *The Trinitarians: An Overview of Their Eight Hundred Year Service to God and Humanity*. Rome: Tip. Cardoni, 1999.

Deslandres, Paul. "Le couvent et l'église des Mathurins de Paris (1229–1792)." *Bulletin de la Société de l'histoire de Paris et de l'Île-de-France* 61 (1934): 48–56.

———. *L'ordre des Trinitaires pour le rachat des captifs*. 2 vols. Toulouse: E. Privat, 1913.

Díaz Moreno, José María. "Antonio de Quintanadueñas, S.J. (1599–1651): Apuntes para la semblanza de un canonista extremeño." *Cauriensa* 3 (2008): 319–33.

Diefendorf, Barbara. *Planting the Cross: Catholic Reform and Renewal in Sixteenth- and Seventeenth-Century France*. Oxford: Oxford University Press, 2019.

Ditchfield, Simon. *Liturgy, Sanctity and History in Tridentine Italy: Pietro Maria Campi and the Preservation of the Particular*. Cambridge: Cambridge University Press, 1995.

———. "Thinking with Saints: Sanctity and Society in the Early Modern World." *Critical Inquiry* 35, no. 3 (2009): 552–84.

Donato, Maria Pia. *Accademie romane: Una storia sociale, 1671–1824*. Rome: Edizioni Scientifiche Italiane, 2000.

Dooley, Eugene A. *Church Law on Sacred Relics*. Washington, DC: Catholic University of America, 1931.

Duffin, Jacalyn. *Medical Miracles: Doctors, Saints, and Healing in the Modern World*. New York: Oxford University Press, 2009.

Dunphy, Graeme. "Franciscan Chronicle Tradition." In *The Encyclopedia of the Medieval Chronicle*, vol. 1, edited by Graeme Dunphy and Cristian Bratu, 633–36. Leiden, Brill, 2010.

Durkan, John. "Thomas Dempster: A Scottish Baronius." *Innes Review* 54, no. 1 (2003): 69–78.

Egilsson, Ólafur. *The Travels of Reverend Ólafur Egilsson: The Story of the Barbary Corsair Raid on Iceland in 1627*. Translated and edited by Karl Smári Hreinsson and Adam Nichols. Washington, DC: Catholic University of America Press, 2016.

Eisenbichler, Konrad. Introduction to *Renaissance Medievalisms*, edited by Konrad Eisenbichler, 15–29. Toronto: Centre for Reformation and Renaissance Studies, 2009.

Eliav-Feldon, Miriam. "Religious Dissimulation." In *Renaissance Impostors and Proofs of Identity*, 16–67. New York: Palgrave Macmillan, 2012.

Fabre, Pierre-Antoine. "L'affaire Jean de la Goutte: Religieux et laïcs dans la diplomatie jésuite en Méditerranée (1553–1555)." In *Le commerce des captifs: Les intermédiaires dans l'échange et le rachat des prisonniers en Méditerranée, XVe–XVIIIe siècle*, edited by Wolfgang Kaiser, 321–31. Rome: École Française de Rome, 2008.

Fabre, Pierre-Antoine, and Mickaël Wilmart. "Le *Traité des reliques* de Jean Calvin (1543): Texte et contextes." In *Reliques modernes: Cultes et usages chrétiens des corps saints des Réformes aux révolutions*, vol. 1, edited by Philipe Boutry, Pierre Antoine Fabre, and Dominique Julia, 29–68. Paris: Éditions de l'École des hautes études en sciences sociales, 2009.

Farge, James K. *Orthodoxy and Reform in Early Reformation France: The Faculty of Theology of Paris, 1500–1543*. Leiden: Brill, 1985.

Fattori, Maria Teresa, ed. *Le fatiche di Benedetto XIV: Origine ed evoluzione dei trattati di Prospero Lambertini*. Rome: Edizioni di storia e letteratura, 2011.

———. *Storia, medicina e diritto nei trattati di Prospero Lambertini Benedetto XIV*. Rome: Edizioni di storia e letteratura, 2013.

Fernández Alonso, Justo. "Un período de las relaciones entre Felipe V y la Santa Sede (1709–1717): Sus repercusiones en la 'nación' española de Roma." *Anthologica Annua* 3 (1955): 9–88.

Findlen, Paula. "Inventing the Middle Ages: An Early Modern Forger Hiding in Plain Sight." In *For the Sake of Learning: Essays in Honor of Anthony Grafton*, vol. 2, edited by Ann Blair and Anja-Silvia Goeing, 871–96. Leiden: Brill, 2016.

Fita, F. "Sarcófago marmóreo de San Juan de Mata." *Boletín de la Real Academia de la Historia* 16 (1880): 373–76.

Fitzpatrick, Antonia. *Thomas Aquinas on Bodily Identity*. Oxford: Oxford University Press, 2017.

Fleming, Julia E. *Defending Probabilism: The Moral Theology of Juan Caramuel*. Washington, DC: Georgetown University Press, 2006.

Foyer, Dominique. "Quand le corps fait signe . . ." *Revue des sciences humaines* 278 (2005): 31–46.

Franklin, James. *The Science of Conjecture: Evidence and Probability Before Pascal*. Baltimore: Johns Hopkins University Press, 2001.

Frazier, Alison Knowles. *Possible Lives: Authors and Saints in Renaissance Italy*. New York: Columbia University Press, 2005.

Freeman, Charles. *Holy Bones, Holy Dust: How Relics Shaped the History of Medieval Europe*. New Haven: Yale University Press, 2011.

Friedman, Ellen G. *Spanish Captives in North Africa in the Early Modern Age*. Madison: University of Wisconsin Press, 1983.

Fuchs, Barbara, Mercedes García-Arenal, and Carlos Cañete, eds. *The Quest for Certainty in Early Modern Europe: From Inquisition to Inquiry*. Toronto: University of Toronto Press in association with the UCLA Center for Seventeenth- and Eighteenth-Century Studies and the William Andrews Clark Memorial Library, 2020.

Gagliardi, Isabella. "La *Historia dell'origine di tutte le religioni* di Paolo Morigia tra memoria e censura." In *Nunca alla tempora, alii mores: Storici e storia in età postridentina: Atti del Convegno internazionale Torino 24–27 settembre 2003*, edited by Massimo Firpo, 93–110. Florence: Olschki, 2005.

García-Arenal, Mercedes, ed. *After Conversion: Iberia and the Emergence of Modernity*. Leiden: Brill, 2016.

García Oro, José, and María José Portela Silva. "Felipe II y la reforma de las órdenes redentoras." *Estudios* 54, nos. 200–201 (1998): 5–155.

García Torralbo, María Cruz. "El patrimonio artístico del convento de la Santísima Trinidad de Úbeda en los siglos XVI y XVII." *Espacio, Tiempo y Forma, Serie VII, Historia del Arte*, 7 (1994): 97–111.

———. "El real monasterio de la Santísima Trinidad de Úbeda." *Boletín del Instituto de Estudios Giennenses* 155 (1995): 61–160.

Gayangos, Pascual de. *Catalogue of Manuscripts in the Spanish Language in the British Museum*. Vol. 1. London: British Museum publications for the British Library, 1875.

Geary, Patrick J. *Furta Sacra: Thefts of Relics in the Central Middle Ages*. Princeton: Princeton University Press, 1990.

———. "Sacred Commodities: The Circulation of Medieval Relics." In *The Social Life of Things: Commodities in Cultural Perspective*, edited by Arjun Appadurai, 169–91. Cambridge: Cambridge University Press, 1986.

Geddes, John. "Memoirs of the Life of Cardinal George Innes." *Archeologia Scotica* 2 (1822): 129–33.

Gentilcore, David. *Healers and Healing in Early Modern Italy*. Manchester, UK: Manchester University Press, 1998.

Ghilardi, Massimiliano. "Le catacombe di Roma nel Medioevo: Riflessioni recenti e prospettivi di ricerca." In *Subterranea civitas: Quattro studi sulle catacombe romane dal medioevo all'età moderna*, 17–41. Rome: Edizioni dell'Ateneo, 2003.

———. *Sanguine tumulus madet: Devozione al sangue dei martiri delle catacombe nella prima età moderna*. Rome: Aracne, 2008.

Ginarte González, Ventura. *La Orden Trinitaria: Compendio histórico de los Descalzos Trinitarios*. Córdoba: PP. Trinitarios, 1979.

Giovannucci, Pierluigi. *Canonizzazioni e infallibilità pontificia in età moderna*. Brescia: Morcelliana, 2008.

———. "Prospero Lambertini e la prova dei miracoli: Ulteriori riflessioni." *Ricerche di storia sociale e religiosa*, n.s., 42, no. 84 (2013): 61–85.

Giuli, Paola. "Prospero Lambertini and the Accademia degli Arcadi (1694–1708)." In *Benedict XIV and the Enlightenment: Art, Science, and Spirituality*, edited by Rebecca Messbarger, Christopher Johns, and Philip Gavitt, 315–40. Toronto: University of Toronto Press, 2016.

Godding, Robert, Bernard Joassart, Xavier Lequeux, François De Vriendt, and Joseph van der Straeten, eds. *Bollandistes: Saints et légendes; Quatre siècles de recherche*. Brussels: Société de Bollandistes, 2007.

Godoy Alcántara, José. *Historia crítca de los falsos cronicones*. Madrid: Rivadeneyra, 1868. 2nd ed., edited by Ofelia Rey Castelao, Granada: Universidad de Granada, 1999.

Gonçalves Guimarães, Jorge. "Entre a hagiografia e crónica: A *Historia da vida do Padre Francicsco Xavier* de João de Lucena." *Revista de cultura* 19 (2006): 100–112.

González Fernández, Fidel. "El contexto histórico de la 'reconquista' española y la Orden trinitaria (Ordo Sanctae Trinitatis et Captivorum)." In *La liberazione dei "captivi" tra Cristianità e Islam: Oltre la crociata e il Ǧihād; Tolleranza e servizio umanitario; Atti del Congresso interdisciplinare di studi storici, Roma, 16–19 settembre 1998, organizzato per l'VIII centenario dell'approvazione della regola dei Trinitari da parte del Papa Innocenzo III il 17 dicembre 1198–15 safar, 595 H*, edited by Giulio Cipollone, 131–59. Vatican City: Archivio Segreto Vaticano, 2000.

Gotor, Miguel. *I beati del papa: Santità, inquisizione e obbedienza in età moderna*. Florence: Olschki, 2001.

Grafton, Anthony. *Forgers and Critics, New Edition: Creativity and Duplicity in Western Scholarship*. Princeton: Princeton University Press, 2019.

———. "Jean Hardouin: The Antiquary as Pariah." *Journal of the Warburg and Courtauld Institutes* 62 (1999): 241–67.

Gray, Margaret. *The Trinitarian Order in England: Excavations at Thelsford Priory*. Edited by Lorna Watts and Philip Rahtz. Oxford, UK: Tempus Reparatum, 1993.

Gross, Joseph J. *The Trinitarians' Rule of Life: Texts of the Six Principal Editions*. Rome: Trinitarian Historical Institute, 1983.

Guazzelli, Giuseppe Antonio. "Cesare Baronio and the Roman Catholic Vision of the Early Church." In *Sacred History: Uses of the Christian Past in the Renaissance World*, edited by Katherine van Liere, Simon Ditchfield, and Howard Louthan, 52–71. Oxford: Oxford University Press, 2012.

Gumbrecht, Hans Ulrich. "Identifying Fragments." In *The Powers of Philology: Dynamics of Textual Scholarship*, 9–23. Urbana: University of Illinois Press, 2003.

Gutiérrez, José Luis. "La certezza morale nelle cause di canonizzazione, specialmente nella dichiarazione del martirio." *Ius Ecclesiae* 3 (1991): 645–70.

———. "Le prove sussidarie nelle cause di canonizzazione." *Ius Ecclesiae* 5 (1993): 545–74.

Harris, A. Katie. *From Muslim to Christian Granada: Inventing a City's Past in Early Modern Spain*. Baltimore: Johns Hopkins University Press, 2007.

———. "Gift, Sale, and Theft: Juan de Ribera and the Sacred Economy of Relics in the Early Modern Mediterranean." *Journal of Early Modern History* 18 (2014): 193–226.

———. "'An Immense Structure of Errors': Dionisio Bonfant, Lucas Holstenius, and the Writing of Sacred History in Seventeenth-Century Sardinia." In *The Early Modern Hispanic World: Transnational and Interdisciplinary Perspectives*, edited by Kimberly Lynn and Erin Rowe, 243–67. Cambridge: Cambridge University Press, 2017.

Harrison, Peter. "Miracles, Early Modern Science, and Rational Religion." *Church History* 75, no. 3 (2006): 493–510.

Hazard, Paul. *The Crisis of the European Mind, 1680–1715*. New York: New York Review Books, 2013.

Heal, Bridget. "Visual and Material Culture." In *The Oxford Handbook of the Reformation*, edited by Ulinka Rublack, 601–20. Oxford: Oxford University Press, 2017.

Heilbron, J. L. "Francesco Bianchini, Historian: In Memory of Amos

Funkenstein." In *Thinking Impossibilities: The Intellectual Legacy of Amos Funkenstein*, edited by Robert S. Westman and David Biale, 227–77. Toronto: University of Toronto Press, 2008.

Henriet, Patrick. "Collection hagiographique et forgeries: La *Commemoratio omnium sanctorum Hispanorum* de Tamayo Salazar (1651–1659) et son arrière-plan de fausse érudition." In *Europa sacra: Raccolte agiografiche e identità politiche in Europa fra Medioevo ed Età moderna*, edited by Sofia Boesch Gajano and Raimondo Michetti, 57–82. Rome: Carocci, 2002.

Hernando, Josep. "La 'tertia pars' en la regla de los Trinitarios para el rescate de cautivos: Una forma de inversión económica, de economía evangélica." In *La liberazione dei "captivi" tra Cristianità e Islam: Oltre la crociata e il Ĝihād; Tolleranza e servizio umanitario; Atti del Congresso interdisciplinare di studi storici, Roma, 16–19 settembre 1998, organizzato per l'VIII centenario dell'approvazione della regola dei Trinitari da parte del Papa Innocenzo III il 17 dicembre 1198–15 safar, 595 H*, edited by Giulio Cipollone, 263–308. Vatican City: Archivio Segreto Vaticano, 2000.

Herrmann-Mascard, Nicole. *Les reliques des saints: Formation coutumière d'un droit*. Paris: Klincksieck, 1975.

Hershenzon, Daniel. *The Captive Sea: Slavery, Communication, and Commerce in Early Modern Spain and the Mediterranean*. Philadelphia: University of Pennsylvania Press, 2018.

———. "'[P]ara que me saque cabesa por cabesa . . .': Exchanging Muslim and Christian Slaves Across the Western Mediterranean." *African Economic History* 42 (2014): 11–36.

———. "Towards a Connected History of Bondage in the Mediterranean: Recent Trends in the Field." *History Compass* 15, no. 8 (2017): 15(8): e12391.

Hiatt, Alfred. *The Making of Medieval Forgeries: False Documents in Fifteenth-Century England*. London: British Library; Toronto: University of Toronto Press, 2004.

Hillman, Jennifer. "Putting Faith to the Test: Anne de Gonzague and the Incombustible Relic." *Journal of Medieval and Early Modern Studies* 44, no. 1 (2014): 163–86.

Hills, Helen. "Nuns and Relics: Spiritual Authority in Post-Tridentine Naples." In *Female Monasticism in Early Modern Europe: An Interdisciplinary View*, edited by Cordula van Wyhe, 11–38. Burlington, VT: Ashgate, 2008.

———. "Through a Glass Darkly: Material Holiness and the Treasury Chapel of San Gennaro in Naples." In *New Approaches to Naples c. 1500–c. 1800: The Power of Place*, edited by Melissa Calaresu and Helen Hills, 31–62. Farnham, UK: Ashgate, 2013.

Hoffman, Martha K. *Raised to Rule: Educating Royalty at the Court of the Spanish Habsburgs, 1601–1634*. Baton Rouge: Louisiana State University Press, 2011.

Holguera Illera, Jorge. "San Juan de Mata trabajaría hoy por el respeto de los derechos." *El Norte de Castilla*, December 17, 2015. https://www.elnortedecastilla.es/salamanca/201512/17/juan-mata-trabajaria-respeto-20151217100746.html.

———. "Un tesoro en San Juan de Mata." *El Norte de Castilla*, December 17, 2014. https://www.elnortedecastilla.es/salamanca/201412/17/tesoro-juan-mata-20141217091859.html.

Hughes, Christopher. "Matter and Individuation in Aquinas." *History of Philosophy Quarterly* 13, no. 1 (1996): 1–16.

Huijbers, Anne. "'Obervance' as Paradigm in Mendicant and Monastic Order Chronicles." In *A Companion to Observant Reform in the Late Middle Ages and Beyond*, edited by James D. Mixson and Bert Roest, 111–43. Leiden: Brill, 2015.

Hunt, John J. *The Vacant See in Early Modern Rome*. Leiden: Brill, 2016.

Imbruglia, Girolamo. "Dalle storie di santi alla storia naturale della religione: L'idea moderna di superstizione." *Rivista storica italiana* 101, no. 1 (1989): 35–84.

Ivanič, Suzanna. *Cosmos and Materiality in Early Modern Prague*. Oxford: Oxford University Press, 2021.

———. "Early Modern Religious Objects or Objects of Belief." In *The Routledge Handbook of Material Culture in Early Modern Europe*, edited by Catherine Richardson, Tara Hamling, and David R. M. Gaimster, 322–37. New York: Routledge, 2017.

Ivanič, Suzanna, Mary Laven, and Andrew Morrall. *Religious Materiality in the Early Modern World*. Amsterdam: Amsterdam University Press, 2019.

Jonsen, Albert R., and Stephen Toulmin. *The Abuse of Casuistry: A History of Moral Reasoning*. Berkeley: University of California Press, 1988.

Jotischky, Andrew. *The Carmelites and Antiquity: Mendicants and Their Pasts in the Middle Ages*. Oxford: Oxford University Press, 2002.

Julia, Dominique. "L'Église post-tridentine et les reliques: Tradition, controverse et critique (XVIe–XVIIe siècle)." In *Reliques modernes: Cultes et usages chrétiens des corps saints des Réformes aux révolutions*, vol. 1, edited by Philipe Boutry, Pierre Antoine Fabre, and Dominique Julia, 69–120. Paris: Éditions de l'École des hautes études en sciences sociales, 2009.

Kaiser, Wolfgang. "L'économie de la rançon en Méditerranée occidentale (xvie–xviie siècle)." *Hypothèses* 1, no. 10 (2007): 359–68.

Kantola, Ilkka. *Probability and Moral Uncertainty in Late Medieval and Early Modern Times*. Helsinki: Luther-Agricola-Seura, 1994.

Keitt, Andrew W. *Inventing the Sacred: Imposture, Inquisition, and the Boundaries of the Supernatural in Golden Age Spain*. Leiden: Brill, 2005.

Keyvanian, Carla. *Hospitals and Urbanism in Rome, 1200–1500*. Leiden: Brill, 2015.

Kleinberg, Aviad M. "Proving Sanctity: Selection and Authentication of Saints in the Later Middle Ages." *Viator* 20 (1989): 183–205.

Knowles, David. *Great Historical Enterprises: Problems in Monastic History*. London: Nelson, 1963.

Latassa, Félix de. *Bibliotecas antigua y nueva de escritores aragoneses*. Vol. 1. Zaragoza: Imprenta de Calisto Ariño, 1883.

Laverda, Alessandro. "Revising the Supernatural: The Inquiry on Miracles in Early Modern Canonization Trials." PhD diss., University of Leicester, 2017.

Lazure, Guy. "Possessing the Sacred: Monarchy and Identity in Philip II's Relic Collection at the Escorial." *Renaissance Quarterly* 60, no. 1 (2007): 58–93.

Lebigue, Jean-Baptiste. "Le modèle liturgique de Saint-Victor de Paris et son adoption par l'ordre des trinitaires." In *L'École de Saint-Victore de Paris: Influence et rayonnement du Moyen Âge à l'époque moderne*, edited by Dominique Poirel, 459–74. Turnhout: Brepols, 2010.

Lecerf, Florence. "Les missions de rédemption effectuées sur ordre des ducs de Frías." In *Captifs et captivités en Mediterranée à l'epoque moderne*, edited by Maria Ghazali, Sadok Boubaker, and Leila Maziane, 201–20. Nice: Centre de la Méditerranée moderne et contemporaine, 2013.

Le Fur, Erwan. "La renaissance d'un apostolat: L'Ordre de la Trinité et la rédemption des captifs dans les années 1630." *Cahiers de la Méditerranée* 66 (2003): 201–14.

Lehner, Ulrich L. *The Catholic Enlightenment: The Forgotten History of a Global Movement*. Oxford: Oxford University Press, 2016.

———. "The Many Faces of the Catholic Enlightenment." In *A Companion to the Catholic Enlightenment in Europe*, edited by Ulrich Lehner and Michael Printy, 1–61. Leiden: Brill, 2010.

Levitin, Dmitri. "From Sacred History to the History of Religion: Paganism,

Judaism, and Christianity in European Historiography from Reformation to 'Enlightenment.'" *Historical Journal* 55, no. 4 (2012): 1117–60.

Liez, Jean-Luc. *L'art des Trinitaires en Europe (XIIIe–XVIIIe siècles)*. Saint-Étienne: Publications de l'Université de Saint-Étienne, 2011.

———. "Le portrait comme affirmation d'autorité: L'exemple du père Louis Petit (1580–1612/1652), ministre général de l'ordre des Trinitaires." In *Les personnes d'autorité en milieu régulier: Des origines de la vie régulière au XVIIIe siècle; Actes du septième colloque international de Cercor, Strasbourg, 18–20 juin 2009*, 201–8. Saint-Étienne: Publications de l'Université de Saint-Étienne, 2012.

———. "Les sceaux de l'ordre des Trinitaires: Approche iconographique et catalogue." *Revue francçaise d'héraldique et de sigillographie* 62–63 (1992–93): 67–91.

Lindholm, Charles. "The Rise of Expressive Authenticity." *Anthropological Quarterly* 86, no. 2 (Spring 2013): 361–95.

Llona Rementería, Germán. *Fundador y redentor Juan de Mata*. Salamanca: Secretariado Trinitario, 1994.

Machielsen, Jan. "Heretical Saints and Textual Discernment: The Polemical Origins of the *Acta Sanctorum* (1643–1940)." In *Angels of Light? Sanctity and the Discernment of Spirits in the Early Modern Period*, edited by Clare Capelans and Jan Machielsen, 103–41. Leiden: Brill, 2013.

Maillard, Clara. *Les papes et le Maghreb au XIIème et XIVème siècles, étude des lettres pontificales de 1199 à 1419*. Turnhout: Brepols, 2014.

Malo, Robyn. "The Pardoner's Relics (and Why They Matter the Most)." *Chaucer Review* 43, no. 1 (2008): 82–102.

Marchetti, Paolo. *Testis contra se: L'imputato come fonte di prova nel processo penale dell'età moderna*. Milan: Giuffrè, 1994.

Marchionni, Ignazio. *Note sulla storia delle origini dell'ordine della SS. Trinità*. Rome: Arte Grafiche dei Fiorentini, 1973.

Marqués, José María. *La Santa Sede y la España de Carlos II: La negociación del nuncio Millini 1675–1685*. Rome: Iglesia Nacional Española, 1981–82.

Martínez Torres, José Antonio. "Corso turco-berberisco y redenciones de cautivos en el Mediterráneo occidental (siglos XVI–XVII)." In *Le commerce des captifs: Les intermédiaires dans l'échange et le rachat des prisonniers en Méditerranée, XVe–XVIIIe siècle*, edited by Wolfgang Kaiser, 83–107. Rome: École Française de Rome, 2008.

———. "Plata y lana para el 'infiel': La 'saca' de moneda, paños y bonetes desde España hacia el Mediterráneo y el Atlántico africano (siglos XVI–XVII)." In *Circulación de personas e intercambios comerciales en el Mediterráneo y en el Atlántico (siglos XVI, XVII, XVIII)*, 215–34. Madrid: Consejo Superior de Investigaciones Científicas, 2008.

———. *Prisioneros de los infieles: Vida y rescate de los cautivos cristianos en el Mediterráneo musulmán (siglos XVI–XVII)*. Barcelona: Bellaterra, 2004.

Matar, N. I. *British Captives from the Mediterranean to the Atlantic, 1563–1760*. Leiden: Brill, 2014.

Mayer, Thomas F. *The Roman Inquisition: A Papal Bureaucracy and Its Laws in the Age of Galileo*. Philadelphia: University of Pennsylvania Press, 2013.

McRoberts, David. "Three Bogus Trinitarian Pictures." *Innes Review* 11 (1960): 52–67.

Messbarger, Rebecca, Christopher M. S. Johns, and Philip Gavitt, eds. *Benedict XIV and the Enlightenment: Art, Science, and Spirituality*. Toronto: University of Toronto Press, 2016.

Millares Carlo, Agustín. *Tres estudios biobibliográficos: I. Juan López de Palacios Rubios; II. Antonio de León Pinelo y su "Epítome"; III. El cronista Gil Gonzálz Dávila y sus obras*. Maracaibo: Universidad de Zulia, 1961.

Mínguez Cornelles, Víctor. "La declaración de la antigua santidad de San Juan de Mata y San Félix de Valois: Celebrando santos inciertos, Valencia, 1668." In *A la luz de Roma: Santos y santidad en el barroco iberamericano*, vol. 2, *España*, *espejo de santos*, edited by Fernando Quiles García, José Jaime García Bernal, Paolo Broggio, and Marcello Fagiolo, 21–41. Seville: Enredars, Rome: Roma Tre-Press, 2020.

Molin, Jean-Baptiste. "Introduction à l'étude de la liturgie des Trinitaires." In *Actes du Colloque de Meaux sur l'histoire de l'Ordre trinitaire*, 55–62. Meaux: Meaux, ville d'art et d'histoire, 1993.

Momigliano, Arnaldo. "Ancient History and the Antiquarian." *Journal of the Warburg and Courtauld Institutes* 13, nos. 3–4 (1950): 285–315.

Monaco, Michele. "Rapporti di L. A. Muratori con i 'letterati' romani del suo tempo." In *L. A. Muratori e la cultura contemporanea: Atti del Convegno Internazionale di Studi Muratoriani, Modena, 1972*, 57–100. Florence: Olschki, 1975.

Montijano García, Juan María. "El Libro della fabbrica del convento de S. Carlino alle Quattro Fontane en Roma de los PP. Trinitarios de la Congregazione de España." In *Monjes y monasterios españoles: Actas del simposium. (1/5-IX-1995)*, vol. 1, edited by Francisco Javier Campos y Fernández de Sevilla, 547–66. Madrid: Estudios Superiores del Escorial, 1995.

Morbidelli, Monica. "'*Ecclesie sint plani operis*': Il primo insediamento trinitario a Roma: Storia e architettura." In *La liberazione dei "captivi" tra Cristianità e Islam: Oltre la crociata e il Gihad: Tolleranza e servizio umanitario: Atti del Congresso interdisciplinare di studi storici, Roma, 16–19 settembre 1998, organizzato per l'VIII centenario dell'approvazione della regola dei Trinitari da parte del Papa Innocenzo III il 17 dicembre 1198–15 safar, 595 H*, edited by Giulio Cipollone, 661–82. Vatican City: Archivio Segreto Vaticano, 2000.

Moreau-Rendu, Suzanne. *Les captifs libérés: Les Trinitaires et Saint-Mathurin de Paris*. Paris: Nouvelles Editions Latines, 1974.

Morelli, Giovanni. "The Roman Trial of the Cult of the Iron Crown." In *The Iron Crown and Imperial Europe*, vol. 2, *In Search of the Original Artifact*, part 1, *Art and Cult*, edited by Graziella Buccellati, Holly Snap, Tim Parks, and Annamaria Ambrosioni, 129–33. Milan: G. Mondadori; Monza: Società di studi monzesi, 1999.

Morét, Ulrike. "An Early Scottish National Biography: Thomas Dempster's *Historia ecclesiastica gentis Scotorum* (1627)." In *A Palace in the Wild: Essays on Vernacular Culture and Humanism in Late-Medieval and Renaissance Scotland*, edited by L. A. J. R. Houwen, A. A. MacDonald, and S. L. Mapstone, 249–69. Leuven: Peeters, 2000.

Moroni, Gaetano. *Dizionario di erudizione storico-ecclesiastica da S. Pietro sino ai nostri giorni*. 103 vols. Venice: Tipografia Emiliana, 1840–61.

Mortimer, Sarah, and John Robertson. "Nature, Revelation, History: Intellectual Consequences of Religious Heterodoxy c. 1600–1750." In *The Intellectual Consequences of Religious Heterodoxy, 1600–1750*, edited by Sarah Mortimer and John Robertson, 1–46. Leiden: Brill, 2014.

Napolitano, Elena. "Prospects of Statecraft: Diplomacy, Territoriality, and the Vision of French Nationhood in Rome, 1660–1700." PhD diss., University of Toronto, 2012.

Navarra, Bruno. *Filippo Michele Ellis: Segni e la sua diocesi nei primi decenni del '700*. Rome: Centro Studi del Lazio, 1973.

Negredo del Cerro, Fernando. *Los predicadores de Felipe IV: Corte, intrigas y religión en la España del Siglo de Oro*. Madrid: Editorial ACTAS, 2006.

Olds, Katrina B. "The Ambiguities of the Holy: Authenticating Relics in Seventeenth-Century Spain." *Renaissance Quarterly* 65, no. 1 (2012): 135–84.

———. *Forging the Past: Invented Histories in Counter-Reformation Spain*. New Haven: Yale University Press, 2015.

Orella Unzué, José Luis. "Geografías guipuzcoanas de la modernidad (V): Una novedosa y extensa geografía guipuzcoana propuesta por Antonio

Lupián Zapata (+1667) y la refutación de Gabriel de Henao en 1702." *Lurralde: Investigación y espacio* 23 (2000): 21–74.

Orlandi, Giuseppe. "L. A. Muratori negli archivi del Sant'Officio Romano: La censura dei *Rerum Italicarum scriptores*." *Lateranum* 65, no. 1 (1999): 7–39.

Orlandi, Silvia, Maria Letizia Caldelli, and Gian Luca Gregori. "Forgeries and Fakes." In *The Oxford Handbook of Roman Epigraphy*, edited by Christer Bruun and Jonathan Edmondson, 42–65. New York: Oxford University Press, 2015.

Ortiz Juárez, José María. *Biografía de Fray Juan de Almoguera, el Obispo del Libro: Córdoba 1605–Lima 1676*. Córdoba: Ediciones Escudero, 1976.

Oryshkevich, Irina Taïssa. "The History of the Roman Catacombs from the Age of Constantine to the Renaissance." PhD diss., Columbia University, 2003.

Osborne, John. "Politics, Diplomacy and the Cult of Relics in Venice and the Northern Adriatic in the First Half of the Ninth Century." *Early Medieval Europe* 5, no. 3 (1999): 369–86.

———. "The Roman Catacombs in the Middle Ages." *Papers of the British School at Rome* 52 (1985): 278–328.

Ossa-Richardson, Anthony. "Cry Me a Relic: The Holy Tear of Vendôme and Early Modern Lipsanomachy." In *Knowledge and Profanation: Transgressing the Boundaries of Religion in Premodern Scholarship*, edited by Martin Muslow and Asaph Ben-Tov, 299–329. Leiden: Brill, 2019.

Osuna Cerdá, Inés Alejandra. "Descripción y catalogación de las reliquias y relicarios de la Capilla Real de Granada: Estilo, técnica y estado de conservación." PhD diss., Universidad de Granada, 2003.

Padoa-Schioppa, Antonio. *Italia ed Europa nella storia del diritto*. Bologna: Il Mulino, 2003.

Pagano, Sergio. "Il testo della Regola dei Trinitari (1198): Redazione, annotazioni diplomatiche, aggiornamenti del secolo XIII." In *La liberazione dei "captivi" tra cristianità e Islam: Oltre la Crociata e il Ĝihād; Tolleranza e servizio umanitario; Atti del Congresso interdisciplinare di studi storici (Roma, 16–19 settembre 1998); Organizzato per l'VIII centenario dell'approvazione della regola dei Trinitari da parte del Papa Innocenzo III il 17 dicembre 1198 / 15 safar, 595 H*, edited by Giulio Cipollone, 51–117. Vatican City: Archivio Segreto Vaticano, 2000.

Palazzolo, Giorgia Alessi. *Prova legale e pena: La crisi del Sistema tra evo medio e moderno*. Naples: Jovene, 1979.

Pallottini, Salvatore. *Collectio omnium conclusionum et resolutionum quae in causis propositis apud S. Congregationem cardinalium S. Conciliii Tridentini interpretum prodierunt ab eius institutione anno MDLXIV ad annum MDCCCLX*. Vol. 15. Rome: Typis S. Congregationis de Propaganda Fide, 1867–93.

Pampalone, Antonella. "Il restauro di S. Tommaso in Formis al tempo di Alessandro VII (1655–1667)." In *Caelius I: Santa Maria in Domnica, San Tommaso in Formis e il Clivus Scauri*, edited by Alia Englen, 410–38. Rome: L'Erma di Bretschneider, 2003.

Papa, Giovanni. *Le cause di canonizazzione nel primo periodo della Congregazione dei Riti (1588–1634)*. Rome: Urbaniana University Press, 2001.

Parise, Giovanni. "Il 'casus exceptus': Storia e valore canonistico della confermazione pontificia di un culto prestato 'ab immemorabili' ad un beato." *Periodica de re canonica* 105, no. 3 (2016): 457–74.

Park, Katherine. "The Criminal and the Saintly Body: Autopsy and Dissection in Renaissance Italy." *Renaissance Quarterly* 47 (1994): 1–33.

Pastor, Ludwig von. *The History of the Popes*. Vol. 31. Translated by Ernest Graf. London: Kegan Paul, Trench, Trübner, 1940.

Perdrizet, Paul. *Le calendrier parisien à la fin du moyen âge: D'après le bréviaire et les livres d'heurs*. Paris: Les belles lettres, 1933.

Pérez de Petinto y Bertomeu, Manuel. *Valor jurídico de la identificación de reliquias*. [Madrid]: [Real Academia de Jurisprudencia y Legislación], 1952.

Pius XI. *Acta ecclesiae mediolanensis ab eius initiis usque ad nostram aetatem*. Vol. 2. Milan: Pontificia Sancti Ioseph, 1890.

Pomata, Gianna. "Malpighi and the Holy Body: Medical Experts and Miraculous Knowledge in Seventeenth-Century Italy." *Renaissance Studies* 21, no. 4 (2007): 568–86.

Popper, Nicholas. "An Ocean of Lies: The Problem of Historical Evidence in the Sixteenth Century." *Huntington Library Quarterly* 74, no. 3 (2011): 375–400.

Porres Alonso, Bonifacio. "Advocación y culto de la Virgen del Remedio en España." *Hispania Sacra* 23, no. 45 (1970): 1–77.

———. "Dos manuscritos autógrafos del padre Juan Figueras Carpi conservados en la Biblioteca Nacional de Madrid." *Trinitarium* 7 (1998): 253–73.

———. "Los dos primeros pleitos sobre redención de cautivos de los trinitarios descalzos (1619–1625)." *Acta Ordinis SS Trinitatis* 7 (1970): 849–84.

———. "Los hospitales trinitarios de Argel y Túnez." *Hispania sacra* 48, no. 98 (1996): 639–717.

———. *Libertad a los cautivos: Actividad redentora de la Orden Trinitaria*. Vol. 1, *Redenciones de cautivos (1198–1785)*. Córdoba: Secretariado Trinitario, 1997.

———. *Los trinitarios en Burgos: Historia de un convento (1207–1835)*. Córdoba: Secretariado Trinitario, 2004.

Prat, Jean-Marie. *Histoire de S. Jean de Matha et de S. Félix de Valois, fondateurs de l'Ordre de la Très Sainte Trinité pour la rédemption des captifs*. Paris, 1846.

Prinzivalli, Luigi. *Resolutiones seu decreta authentica Sacrae Congregationis indulgentiis sacrisque reliquiis praepositae ab anno 1668 ad annum 1861*. Rome: Societatis Aurelianae, 1862.

Prudlo, Donald S. *Certain Sainthood: Canonization and the Origins of Papal Infallibility in the Medieval Church*. Ithaca: Cornell University Press, 2015.

Pujana, Juan. "Juan de Mata y Félix de Valois, fundadores, según el Santo Reformador." *Trinitarium* 7 (1998): 69–99.

———. *La Orden de la Santísima Trinidad (Trinitarios)*. Salamanca: Secretariado Trinitario, 1993.

———. *La reforma de los Trinitarios durante el reinado de Felipe II*. Salamanca: Secretariado Trinitario, 2006.

———. *San Juan Bautista de la Concepción: Carisma y misión*. Madrid: Biblioteca de Autores Cristianos, 1994.

Quantin, Jean-Louis. *Le catholicisme classique et les Pères de l'Église: Un retour aux sources (1669–1713)*. Paris: Institut d'Études Augustiniennes, 1999.

———. "Reason and Reasonableness in French Ecclesiastical Scholarship." *Huntington Library Quarterly* 74, no. 3 (2011): 401–36.

Quintana, Augusto. "Tomás de la Virgen, OSST." In *Diccionario de historia eclesiástica de España*, vol. 4, edited by Quintín Aldea Vaquero, Tomás Marín Martínez, and José Vives Gatell, 2575. Madrid: CSIC, 1975.

Rano Grundin, Balbino. "El maestro agustino Fray Tomás de Herrera, principal historiador de la Orden de San Agustín." *Archivo Agustiniano* 74, no. 193 (1990): 3–81.

Real Academia de la Historia. "Hortensio Paravicino y Arteaga." Accessed December 31, 2022. https://dbe.rah.es/biografias/8295/hortensio-paravicino-y-arteaga.

Riera y Sans, Jaume. "La doble falsificació de la portadella d'un incunable (Hain 12433)." *Revista de llibreria antiquaria* 10 (1985): 5–17.

Robbins, Jeremy. *Arts of Perception: The Epistemological Mentality of the Spanish Baroque, 1580–1720*. London: Routledge; Glasgow: University of Glasgow, 2014.

Rodén, Marie-Louise. *Church Politics in Seventeenth-Century Rome: Cardinal Decio Azzolino, Queen Christina of Sweden, and the Squadrone Volante*. Stockholm: Almqvist & Wiksell International, 2000.

Rodríguez G. de Ceballos, Alfonso. "Ciclos pintados de la vida de los santos fundadores: Origen, localización y uso en los conventos de España e Hispanoamérica." In *La imagen religiosa en la monarquía hispánica: Usos y espacios*, edited by María Cruz de Carlos Varona, Pierre Civil, Felipe Pereda, and Cécile Vincent-Cassy, 3–21. Madrid: Casa de Velazquez, 2008.

Rollason, David. *Saints and Relics in Anglo-Saxon England*. Oxford, UK: Blackwell, 1989.

Romano di Santa Teresa, Angelo. *L'Ordine trinitario in Italia*. Part 1, *Trinitari Calzati*. Rome: Colegio di S. Crisogono, 1941.

———. *S. Giovanni di Matha fondatore dell'Ordine della SS. Trinità*. Vicenza: Officina Tip. Vicentina, 1961.

Rosa, Mario. "The Catholic *Aufklärung* in Italy." In *A Companion to the Catholic Enlightenment in Europe*, edited by Ulrich Lehner and Michael Printy, 215–50. Leiden: Brill, 2010.

Rosoni, Isabella. *Quae singula non prosunt collecta iuvant: La teoria della prova indiziaria nell'età medievale e moderna*. Milan: Dott. A. Giuffrè, 1995.

Rowe, Erin K. *Saint and Nation: Santiago, Teresa of Ávila, and Plural Identities in Early Modern Spain*. University Park: Pennsylvania State University Press, 2011.

Rowland, Ingrid. *The Scarith of Scornello: A Tale of Renaissance Forgery*. Chicago: University of Chicago Press, 2005.

Royo Mejía, Alberto. "Algunas cuestiones sobre la heroicidad de las virtudes y la certeza moral jurídica en las causas de los santos." *Jus Canonicum* 34, no. 67 (1994): 189–226.

Russell, William R. *Luther's Theological Testament: The Schmalkald Articles*. Minneapolis: Fortress, 1995.

Saccenti, Riccardo. "La lunga genesi dell'opera sulle canonizzazioni." In *Le fatiche di Benedetto XIV: Origine ed evoluzione dei trattati di Prospero Lambertini*, edited by Maria Teresa Fattori, 3–47. Rome: Edizioni di storia e letteratura, 2011.

———. "Le fonti del *De Servorum Dei* e il loro uso nel trattato lambertiniano." In *Storia, medicina e diritto nei trattati di Prospero Lambertini*, edited by Maria Teresa Fattori, 247–75. Rome: Edizioni di storia e letteratura, 2013.

Salvador Martínez, H. *Berenguela la Grande y su época, 1180–1246*. Madrid: Ediciones Poifemo, 2012.

Sbardella, Francesca. "Against the Sacred Body: The Processing of Remains in Catholic Circles." *Human Remains and Violence* 7, no. 1 (2021): 52–71.

———. *Antropologia delle reliquie: Un caso storico*. Brescia: Morcelliana, 2007.

Schreiner, Klaus. "'Discrimen veri ac falsi': Ansätze und Formen der Kritik in der Heiligen und Reliquienverehrung des Mittelalters." *Archiv für Kulturgeschichte* 48 (1966): 1–53.

Schreiner, Susan E. *Are You Alone Wise? The Search for Certainty in the Early Modern Era*. New York: Oxford University Press, 2011.

Schüssler, Rudolph. "Jean Gerson, Moral Certainty and the Renaissance of Ancient Scepticism." *Renaissance Studies* 23, no. 4 (2009): 445–62.

———. "On the Anatomy of Probabilism." In *Moral Philosophy on the Threshold of Modernity*, edited by Jill Kraye and Risto Saarinen, 91–113. Dordrecht: Springer, 2005.

Schutte, Anne Jacobson. *Aspiring Saints: Pretense of Holiness, Inquisition and Gender in the Republic of Venice, 1618–1750*. Baltimore: Johns Hopkins University Press, 2001.

Serjeantson, R. W. "Proof and Persuasion." In *The Cambridge History of Science*, vol. 3, *Early Modern Science*, edited by Roy Porter, Katharine Park, and Lorraine Daston, 132–75. Cambridge: Cambridge University Press, 2003.

Shapin, Steven. *A Social History of Truth: Civility and Science in Seventeenth-Century England*. Chicago: University of Chicago Press, 1994.

Shapiro, Barbara J. *Beyond Reasonable Doubt and Probable Cause: Historical Perspectives* on the Anglo-American Law of Evidence. Berkeley: University of California Press, 1991.

———. Probability and Certainty in Seventeenth-Century England: A Study of the Relationships Between Natural Science, Religion, History, Law, and Literature. Princeton: Princeton University Press, 1983.

Sharpe, Richard. A Handlist of the Latin Writers of Great Britain and Ireland Before 1540. Turnhout: Brepols, 1997.

Signorotto, Gianvittorio. "The *Squadrone Volante*: 'Independent' Cardinals and European Politics in the Second Half of the Seventeenth Century." In *Court and Politics in Papal Rome, 1492–1700*, edited by Gianvittorio Signorotto and Maria Antonietta Visceglia, 177–211. Cambridge: Cambridge University Press, 2002.

Siraisi, Nancy G. "Signs and Evidence: Autopsy and Sanctity in Late Sixteenth-Century Italy." In *Medicine and the Italian Universities 1250–1600*, edited by Nancy Siraisi, 356–80. Leiden: Brill, 2001.

Skilliter, S. A. "The Hispano-Ottoman Armistice of 1581." In *Iran and Islam: In Memory of the Late Vladimir Minorsky*, edited by Clifford Edmund Bosworth, 491–515. Edinburgh: Edinburgh University Press, 1971.

Sluhovsky, Moshe. *Believe Not Every Spirit: Possession, Mysticism and Discernment in Early Modern Catholicism*. Chicago: University of Chicago Press, 2007.

Smith, Julia M. H. "Relics: An Evolving Tradition in Latin Christianity." In *Saints and Sacred Matter: The Cult of Relics in Byzantium and Beyond*, edited by Cynthia Hahn and Holger A. Klein, 41–60. Washington, DC: Dumbarton Oaks Research Library and Collection, 2015.

Sommervogel, Carlos. *Bibliothèque de la Compagnie de Jésus*. 3rd ed. Louvain: Editions de la Bibliothèque S.J., Collège philosophique et théologique, 1960.

Soria Ortega, Andrés. *El Maestro Fray Manuel de Guerra y Ribera y la oratoria sagrada de su tiempo*. Granada: Universidad de Granada, 1950.

Sosa Mayor, Igor. "Experimenting with Relics: Laypeople, Knowledge and Relics in Seventeenth-Century Spain." In *Domestic Devotions in the Early Modern World Book*, edited by Marco Faini and Alessia Meneghin, 226–43. Leiden: Brill, 2019.

Sousa Ribeiro, Illído de. *Fr. Francisco de Santo Agostino de Macedo: Um filósofo escotista português e um paladino da Restauração*. Coimbra: Universidad de Coimbra, 1951.

Stenhouse, William. *Reading Inscriptions and Writing Ancient History: Historical Scholarship in the Late Renaissance*. London: Institute of Classical Studies, University of London School of Advanced Study, 2005.

Stephens, Walter. "When Pope Noah Ruled the Etruscans: Annius of Viterbo and His Forged Antiquities." *Modern Language Notes* 119, no. 1 (2004): 201–23.

Stone, Harold Samuel. *St. Augustine's Bones: A Microhistory*. Amherst: University of Massachusetts Press, 2002.

Strehle, Stephen. *The Catholic Roots of the Protestant Gospel: Encounter Between the Middle Ages and the Reformation*. Leiden: Brill, 1995.

Svizzeretto, Floriana. "La chiesa e l'ospedale fra il XIII e il XIV secolo." In *Caelius I: Santa Maria in Domnica, San Tommaso in Formis e il Clivus Scauri*, edited by Alia Englen, 393–404. Rome: L'Erma di Bretschneider, 2003.

———. "Il passaggio al Capitolo Vaticano nel 1395 e le transformazioni conseguenti." In *Caelius I: Santa Maria in Domnica, San Tommaso in Formis e il Clivus Scauri*, edited by Alia Englen, 405–10. Rome: L'Erma di Bretschneider, 2003.

Tabacchi, Stefano. "Cardinali zelanti e fazioni cardinalizie tra fine Seicento e inizio Settecento." In *La corte di Roma tra cinque e seicento: "Teatro" della politica*, edited by Gianvittorio Signorotto and

Maria Antonietta Visceglia, 139–65. Rome: Bulzoni, 1998.

——. "Ginetti, Marzio." In *Dizionario Biografico degli Italiani*, vol. 55, 15–18. Rome: Istituto della Enciclopedia italiana, 2000.

Tanner, Norman P., ed. *Decrees of the Ecumenical Councils*. Vol. 2. Washington, DC: Georgetown University Press, 1990.

Tausiet, Maria. *El dedo robado: Reliquias imaginarias en la España moderna*. Madrid: Abada Editores, 2013.

Taylor, Bruce. *Structures of Reform: The Mercedarian Order in the Spanish Golden Age*. Leiden: Brill, 2000.

Thiel, Udo. *The Early Modern Subject: Self-Consciousness and Personal Identity from Descartes to Hume*. Oxford: Oxford University Press, 2011.

——. "Individuation." In *The Cambridge History of Seventeenth-Century Philosophy*, edited by Daniel Garber and Michael Ayers, 212–62. Cambridge: Cambridge University Press, 2000.

Thornton, Tim. *Prophecy, Politics and the People in Early Modern England*. Woodbridge, UK: Boydell, 2006.

Tompkins, Jane. *Sensational Designs: The Cultural Work of American Fiction, 1790–1870*. Oxford: Oxford University Press, 1985.

Tutino, Stefania. *A Fake Saint and the True Church: The Story of a Forgery in Seventeenth-Century Naples*. Oxford: Oxford University Press, 2021.

——. *Shadows of Doubt: Language and Truth in Post-Reformation Catholic Culture*. Oxford: Oxford University Press, 2014.

Ullmann, Walter. "Medieval Principles of Evidence." In *Law and Jurisdiction in the Middle Ages*, edited by George Garnett, 77–87. London: Variorum Reprints, 1988.

Van Cutsem, Marcel. "Un lettre inédite du P. Gazet sur la catacombe de Saint-Hermès." *Analecta Bollandiana* 52 (1934): 334–42.

Van Liere, Katherine, Simon Ditchfield, and Howard Louthan, eds. *Sacred History: Uses of the Christian Past in the Renaissance World*. Oxford: Oxford University Press, 2012.

Van Ommeslaeghe, Flor. "The 'Acta Sanctorum' and Bollandist Methodology." In *The Byzantine Saint: University of Birmingham Fourteenth Spring Symposium of Byzantine Studies*, edited by Sergei Hackel, 155–63. London: Fellowship of St. Alban and St. Sergius, 1981.

Van Strydonck, Mark, Jeroen Reyniers, and Fanny Van Cleven, eds. *Relics @ the Lab: An Analytical Approach to the Study of Relics*. Leuven: Peeters, 2018.

Vatican, Agnès. "La nunciatura española bajo el reinado de Carlos II: Savo Millini (1675–1685)." *Cuadernos de Historia Moderna* 26 (2001): 131–47.

Vauchez, André. *Sainthood in the Later Middle Ages*. Cambridge: Cambridge University Press, 1997.

Vázquez, Luis. "Encuentros Trinidad-Merced a través de los siglos." In *Las dos órdenes redentoras en la Iglesia: Actas del I Encuentro Trinitario-Mercedario; Madrid, 7–9 de septiembre de 1988*, 231–94. Madrid: Imp. Offo, 1989.

Vázquez Barrado, Ana. "El palacio de la nunciatura de Madrid: Obras de reestructuración (1650–75)." *Hispania sacra* 52, no. 106 (2000): 507–40.

Veraja, Fabijan. *La beatificazione: Storia, problemi, prospettive*. Rome: S. Congregazione per le Cause dei Santi, 1983.

Vidal, Fernando. "Miracles, Science, and Testimony in Post-Tridentine Saint-Making." *Science in Context* 20, no. 3 (2007): 481–508.

Vilches, Elvira. *New World Gold: Cultural Anxiety and Monetary Disorder in Early Modern Spain*. Chicago: University of Chicago Press, 2010.

Vincent-Cassy, Cécile. "The Search for Evidence: The Relics of Martyred Saints and Their Worship in Cordoba After the Council of Trent." In *After Conversion: Iberia and the Emergence of Modernity*, edited by Mercedes Garcia-Arenal, 126–52. Leiden: Brill, 2016.

Vismara, Paola. "Lodovico Antonio Muratori (1672–1750): Enlightenment in a Tridentine Mode." In *Enlightenment and Catholicism in Europe: A Transnational History*, edited by Jeffrey D. Burson and Ulrich L. Lehner, 249–68. Notre Dame, IN: University of Notre Dame Press, 2014.

———. "Muratori 'immoderato': Le censure romane al *De ingeniorum moderatione in religionis*." In *Il cristianesimo e le diversità: Studi per Attilio Agnoletto*, edited by Remo Cacitti, Grado Giovanni Merlo, and Paola Vismara, 207–46. Milan: Biblioteca francescana, 1999.

Völkel, Markus. *"Pyrrhonism historicus" und "fides historica": Die Entwicklung der deutschen historischen Methodologie unter dem Gesichtspunkt der historischen Skepsis*. Frankfurt: Peter Lang, 1987.

Walsham, Alexandra. "Skeletons in the Cupboard: Relics After the English Reformation." *Past and Present*, supp. 5 (2010): 121–43.

Watzka-Pauli, Elisabeth. *Triumph de Barmherzigkeit: Die Befreiung christlicher Gefangener aus muslimisch dominierten Ländern durch den österreichischen Trinitarierorden 1690–1783*. Gottingen: V&R unipress, 2016.

Webb, Diana. "Sanctity and History: Antonio degli Agli and Humanist Hagiography." In *Florence and Italy: Renaissance Studies in Honour of Nicolai Rubinstein*, edited by Peter Denley and Caroline Elam, 297–308. London: Committee for Medieval Studies, Westfield College, 1988.

Weber, Christoph. *Die ältesten päpstlichen Staatshandbücher: Enlechus Congregationum, Tribunalium et Collegiorum Urbis, 1629–1714*. Rome: Herder, 1991.

Weiss, Gillian. *Captives and Corsairs: France and Slavery in the Early Modern Mediterranean*. Stanford: Stanford University Press, 2011.

Weiss, Roberto. *The Renaissance Discovery of Classical Antiquity*. 2nd ed. Oxford, UK: Blackwell, 1988.

Willibrord de Paris. "Félix de Valois." In *Dictionnaire d'histoire et de géographie ecclésiastiques*, vol. 6, edited by R. Aubert, col. 916–27. Paris: Letouzey et Ané, 1967.

Wintroub, Michael. "Translations: Words, Things, Going Native, and Staying True." *American Historical Review* 120, no. 4 (2015): 1185–217.

Wisniewski, Robert. *The Beginnings of the Cult of Relics*. Oxford: Oxford University Press, 2019.

Witte, Arnold. "Cardinal Protectors of Religious Institutions." In *A Companion to the Early Modern Cardinal*, edited by Mary Hollingsworth, Miles Pattenden, and Arnold Witte, 124–43. Leiden: Brill, 2019.

Woolf, Daniel. *The Social Circulation of the Past: English Historical Culture 1500–1730*. Oxford: Oxford University Press, 2003.

Zagorin, Perez. *Ways of Lying: Dissimulation, Persecution, and Conformity in Early Modern Europe*. Cambridge: Harvard University Press, 1990.

Zanot, Massimiliano. *Francesco Bordoni (1594–1671): Teologo inquisitore storico*. 2nd ed. Rome: Franciscanum, 1999.

Zarri, Gabriella, ed. *Finizione e santità tra medioevo ed età moderna*. Turin: Rosenberg and Sellier, 1991.

Ziegler, Joseph. *Medicine and Religion, c. 1300: The Case of Arnau de Vilanova*. New York: Oxford University Press, 1998.

Index

Italicized page references indicate illustrations. Endnotes are referenced with "n" followed by the endnote number.

Accademia dei Concilii, 155
Accademia Fisico-matematica, 155
Acquaviva d'Aragona, Francesco (cardinal), 149, 150, 158
Acta sanctorum, 63, 152–53
Albani, Annibale (cardinal), 160
Albani, Princess Teresa Virginia, 159
Aldrovandi, Pompeo, 149–50, 161
Alejandro de la Concepción, 161
Alexander VII (pope), 23, 103, 107
Almoguera, Juan de, 35
Aloès, François, 77, 82
Althann, Michael Friedrich von (cardinal), 158
Altuna, Pedro López de, 77, 80, 82, 95
Ana Mauricia, 34
Anamnesis sive Commemorationis sanctorum (Tamayo), 84
Andrade, Alonso de, 96, 104, 147
Anfossi, Domenico, 119
Angelonis, Angelonus de, 117, 121, 124
Annales ecclesiastici (Baronio), 63
Annales sacri . . . (Figueras Carpi), 66, 67–77, 80

Annales y memorias cronológicas (Carrillo), 75
Annius of Viterbo, 63
Antonino de la Asunción, Fray, 16
Aquinas, Thomas, Saint, 9, 120–21, 129, 139
Arce y Reinosa Ávila, Diego de, 53–54, 83–84
Arcos, Francisco de, 57–58, 90, 167
Arias Portocarrero, Pedro
  in aftermath of theft, 3
  conviction and punishment, 24
  explanatory notes regarding relics, 126
  flight to Madrid, 57
  role in theft, 89–90, 134
  surrender of relics, 58
  testimony of, 58–59, 124, 137
Aristotle, 120, 121–22, 128–29
Arriaga, Rodrigo de, 132
Astiaso Zapata, Cristóbal de, 55
Augustine, Saint, 6
Augustinian Order, 65
autopsy, 14
Aznar, Pablo, 77, 81

Bale, John, 70
Barberini, Antonio (cardinal), 39

Barberini, Federico (cardinal), 68
Barberini, Francesco (cardinal) (1597–1679), 3, 51, 108
Barberini, Francesco (cardinal) (1662–1738), 159, 160
Baro, Bonaventura, 148
Baronio, Cesare (cardinal), 63, 64, 152
beatification, 37–38, 59, 111–12, 116, 122–23, 130, 151
  See also canonization process
Beaven, Lisa, 17
Becket, Thomas à (Saint), 93
Bellarmino, Robert (cardinal), 129
Benedictine Order, 93
Benedict XIV (pope), 20, 132, 144, 151, 155, 168
Bernardino de San Antonio, 75, 76–77, 80, 88
Bianchini, Francesco, 155, 157
Binius, Severin, 68
Blakeney (Blackeney), John, 70–71, 72
Boileau, Jean, 33
Bolland, Jean, 63, 139, 152
Bollandists, 63, 136, 140, 152–53
Bonelli, Carlo (cardinal), 58
Bonfant, Dionisio, 64
Bordoni, Francesco, 131
Borrell, Miguel, 44, 45
Borromeo, Carlo/Charles (cardinal), 109, 118
Bouchet, François, 47
Bouhours, Dominique, 80
Bouillaud, Claude, 117, 122, 126
Bouley, Bradford, 14
Bourgeois, Jacques, 44, 47, 67
breviaries
  Paris (1514), 44, 47
  Roman Breviary, 63
  Seville (1545), 45
  Valencia (1519), 44, 45–46
  See also English breviary
Brodman, James, 16
Bruno, St., relics of, 123
Bynum, Caroline, 141–42
Bzowski, Abraham, 68

Calà, Giovanni, 170
Calced Trinitarians
  efforts to canonize Matha, 52–56, 90, 102
  efforts to manipulate evidence, 81–82
  promotion of English breviary, 137
  rivalry with Discalced branches, 2–3, 27, 28–29, 59, 147, 150, 167–68
  sermons, published, in honor of Matha, 85–86
Calvin, Jean, 7
canonization process
  case files, 151–52
  De servorum Dei beatificatione et beatorum canonisatione (Lambertini), 151
  documentary evidence, 60, 135–36
  equivalent canonization, 37–38
  miracles contrasted with documents, 123
  papal control of, 50–51
  promotor causae role, 116, 117
  promotor fidei role, 116
  pública voz y fama, 87–88
  reframing of evidence, 144–45
  resumption of in 1588, 110
  standardization of, 110
  testimony of criminals, 134–35
  See also sainthood
Caramuel Lobkowitz, Juan, 129
Cardoso, Agostino de, 137
Carducho, Vicente, 87
Carlos, (infante of Spain), 34
Carmelite Order, 61–62, 65, 153
Carrillo, Martín, 75
Castañeda, José de, 150
casuistry, 129–30
catacombs, Roman, 138, 153
  catacomb relics, 153–54
Cathars, 68
Catholic Enlightenment, 152–53
Ceccarelli, Alfonso, 63
Cecilia, St., 145
Celsi, Angelo (cardinal), 117
Cerfroid Mother House, 26, 49, 91
  archival material from, 96–97
Cervantes, Miguel de, 31
Charles II (Spanish king), 107
Charles IX (French king), 34
Charles V (Spanish king), 30
Charles VI (Holy Roman Emperor), 158
Charles VII (French king), 33
Chigi, Sigismondo (cardinal), 117, 127–28, 133
Chrónica general . . . (Lupián Zapata), 91, 93, 101
Chronicum Ordinis Sanctissimae . . . (Figueras Carpi), 66, 78–80

Ciampini, Giovanni Giustino, 155, 157
Cipollone, Giulio, 16
Clement IV (pope), 72
Clement IX (pope), 85, 105, 107, 130, 138
Clement V (pope), 73
Clement VII (antipope), 1
Clement VIII (pope), 32
Clement XI (pope), 149, 150, 151
Clement XIV (pope), 168
Colloredo, Leandro (cardinal), 153, 154
colors and symbolism of Trinitarian habit, 45–46
Compendio histórico (González Dávila), 60, 73–74, 77
Congregation of Indulgences and Relics, 115, 138
Congregation of Sacred Rites
  Calced Trinitarians' petition for commemoration (1630), 52–55, 81
  changing positions on evidence and miracles, 163–64
  Congregation of Indulgences and Relics, 115
  Congregation of the Council, 115
  Congregation of the Holy Office of the Inquisition, 115
  documentary evidence, 89, 116–19, 136–37
  establishment and purpose, 6, 10, 36–37, 59, 115
  identity through space and time, 119–26
  and moral certainty, 126–33
  petition for identity of Matha's relics (1669), 13, 107–11, 133–42
  petition for identity of Matha's relics (1715), 148–49
  petition for identity of Matha's relics (1721), 151–66
  process and procedures, 111–13, 115–16
  and proof of identity, 111–16
  recognition of Matha's immemorial cult (1666), 103–5
  relic recognition ceremony (1671), 143–47
  witnesses in relic identity cases, 134–35
Congregation of the Council, 115
Congregation of the Holy Office of the Inquisition, 36, 115
Congregatio Sacrorum Rituum. *See* Congregation of Sacred Rites
Cop, Nicolas, 33
Córdoba y Ronquillo, Luis de, 35

Cornejo y Alemán, Félix, 158, 159
Corradini, Pier Marcellino (cardinal), 158–59
Cosmati, Cosma, 41
Cosmati, Jacopo, 41
Council of Castile, 150
Council of Trent
  on absolute certainty, 129
  background and overview, 7, 27, 59, 62
  Congregation of the Council, 115
  veneration of miracles/relics, 113–14
  veneration of saints, 36, 37
  verification of miracles/relics, 109–10
Covilhã, Pedro da, 80
criminals, testimony of, 134–35
Cunha e Ataíde, Nuno da (cardinal), 159
Cyprian of Carthage, Saint, 63

Da Gama, Vasco, 80
Dear, Peter, 132
De Carlos Varona, María Cruz, 17, 89–90
De Gaona, Bartolomé, 62
De Illustribus Angliæ Scriptoribus (Pitts), 70
Dempster, Thomas, 70
De mundi aetatibus (Blakeney), 71
De re diplomatica (Mabillon), 153
De servorum Dei beatificatione et beatorum canonisatione (Lambertini), 151, 161–62, 163
Deslandres, Paul, 16
Díaz de Cabrera, Rafael, 35
Diego de Gayangos, 35
Diego de Jesús, 148
Diez de Cabrera, Francisco Antonio, 53–54, 55
Dilloud, Ignace, 80, 148
Discalced Trinitarians
  canonization/beatification efforts for John of Matha, 51, 82–83, 85, 90, 102–3, 110–11, 123–25
  case for identity of relics, 97–98, 107–8, 147
  celebration of 1721 decision, 161
  establishment and history of, 28, 61
  rivalry with Calced branches, 2–3, 27, 28–29, 59, 147, 150, 167–68
Ditchfield, Simon, 14
Dominici, Bernard, 34, 48
Donkey Brothers, 26
Duffin, Jacalyn, 140
Durazzo, Marcello, 147

English breviary, 80–85, 83, 84
  Lupián Zapata's forgeries, 91–92, 97–100, 99, 100
  promotion of by Calced Trinitarians, 137
  as source, 2, 69, 81
Enrique IV (Castilian king), 34
Erasmus, Desiderius, 63
Espoleto, Pierre de, 96
Eucharistic Host, 10, 139, 169
Exercicios espirituales (Aznar), 77

Fabroni, Carlo Agostino (cardinal), 160
false chronicles, 64, 65
Fasciculus trium florum (Juan de San Buenaventura), 83, 84
Febei, Francisco Maria, 117
Felice of Cantalice, 135
Felipe de Jesús, 108, 117, 120, 122, 127, 142
Felix of Valois, Saint
  canonization, 59–60
  formation of Trinitarian Order, 26
  increasing devotion to, 49–50
  Lupián Zapata's evidence for, 97
  Mass and office, 105
  privileges and indulgences 1643, 156
  sermons and images in honor of, 85–86
Ferdinand II (Aragonese king), 30, 34
Ferdinand IV (Castilian king), 73
Fernando, "Cardinal-Prince" (Spain), 34
Fernando III (Castilian king), 34
Ferrand, Jean, and categories of evidence, 114, 122–24, 125–26
Figueras Carpi, Juan
  accumulative citation, 73–76, 79
  Annales sacri . . ., 67–77
  in British Isles, 66–67
  as Calced Trinitarian chronicler, 66, 76–77
  Chronicum Ordinis Sanctissimae, 78–80
  as forger, 19, 69–70, 71–78, 88
  historical sources consulted, 68–69
  historical writings, embellishment and invention, 67, 81–82
  motivations for forgeries/inventions, 88–89
  overview of life, 65, 66
  spurious sources used by, 70–71
  used as source, 52, 94, 170
forgery
  and accumulative citation, 73–76, 79
  by Figueras Carpi, 67–77, 78–80

  and hagiography, 62–66
  and historical documentation, 12, 62–63
  and interpretive approach, 88–89
  by Lupián Zapata, 19, 91–102, 99, 100, 157
  as pious act, 64, 65
Fourth Council of Milan (1574), 109, 118
Fourth Lateran Council, 36
Franchellucci, Giovanni, 151
Franciscan Order, 62, 65
Fuentes de Albornoz, Gonzalo, 52
furta sacra (holy theft), 8, 23–24, 109

Gaetano, Francesco, 85
Gaguin, Robert, 33, 43, 44, 61, 62, 67, 74–75
Galindo, Martín, 74
Gaona, Bartolomé de, 62
García, Francisco, 80
García, Jerónimo, 35
Gaucher de Châtillon, 33
Gerson, Jean, 128–29
Gertrude the Great, Saint, 96
Gil, Juan, 31
Ginetti di Velletri, Marzio (cardinal), 52, 103–4, 108, 117, 127, 148
Giudice, Francesco del (cardinal), 158
Gómez de Lamadrid, Diego, 35
Gonon, Benoit, 50, 52, 69
González Dávila, Gil, 51–52, 60, 73–74, 75, 77, 81, 82
Grait, Ferrario, 94
Gravelino (Benedictine monk), 91
Great Western Schism, 1, 27, 128
Gregory IX (pope), 36
Gregory of Elvira, Saint, 93
Gregory X (pope), 60
Gregory XIII (pope), 47, 114
Gregory XV (pope), 130
Guasque, Pasquale, 77
Guerra y Ribera, Manuel, 35, 104
Guibert of Nogent, 6
Guzmán, Gaspar de (Count-Duke of Olivares), 34, 35

hagiography, 63–65, 133
  Bollandists, 136, 152–53
  hagiographic images, 86–87
  «national» hagiographies, 84
Halboud de Troyes, Jean, 33
Hardouin, Jean, 152
Hauberto, false chronicle of, 92–93

Henry III (French king), 34
Henry I (Navarrese king), 33
Henry of Ghent, 79
Henry VIII (English king), 97
Hershenzon, Daniel, 16
Higuera, Jerónimo Román de la, 64, 65
Hills, Helen, 141
Historia ecclesiastica gentis Scotorum (Dempster), 70
historical criticism, 152–53, 157
history
  accumulative citation, methodology of, 73–76, 79–80, 94–95, 96
  approaches to, 171
  church history, 63–65
  credibility, issues of, 137–38
  historical records, changing approaches to, 170–71
  nontextual sources, 95–96
  and relic authentication, 162–63
  Renaissance ideals and church purpose, 10
  sacred history, 63
  scholarship contrasted with forgery, 62–63
  truth value of texts, 95
holy theft *(furta sacra)*, 8, 109, 124
Honoré de Sainte-Marie, 163
hospitals, Trinitarian, 32
Hughes, Christopher, 121
Humbert of Romans, 45
Hundeslow, Robert, 76
Hynde de San Martín, Juan, 67

identity
  diachronic identity, 119–20
  and individuation, 120–21
  sixteenth and seventeenth century meanings, 118
images, miracles associated with, 148
individuation, 120–21, 133
Inghirami, Curzio, 63
Innes, George, 70, 72, 74, 75, 78, 79, 81, 94
Innocent III (pope), 1, 26, 40–44, 68–69, 87, 97, 104, 156
Innocent X (pope), 23, 55, 84
Innocent XIII (pope), 159, 160
Institutio ordinis SSmae Trinitatis redemptionis (image), 86
Isabel, Queen (Aragon), 34
Isabel de Borbón, 34
Isabella (Castilian queen), 30, 34

Jansenism, 154
Jesus of Medinaceli (image), 147
Johannes Provincialis (John of Provence), 40
  See also John of Matha, Saint
John of England, 2
John of Matha, Saint
  devotional poetry memorializing, 42–44
  devotion to, sixteenth century, 47–48
  early life, 11, 26
  feast-day celebrations, 85
  formation of Trinitarian Order, 26, 40
  González Dávila's *vita*, 51–52
  images of, 86–87, 103, 148
  liturgical celebrations in honor of, 85
  Mass and office (1682), 105
  miracle stories, 41–44, 156–57
  obscurity of, in early Trinitarian artifacts, 44–47
  ordination and holy vision, 26, 39–40, 68
  vita (1630), 25
  written accounts, *Annales sacri . . .* (Figueras Carpi), 66, 67–70, 73–75
John of Matha, Saint, canonization
  canonization, spurious, by Urban IV (1263), 69, 74–75
  conversations with Valois, 68–69
  early campaign for canonization, 50–56
  immemorial cult of, 11–12, 48, 53, 55–60, 80–81, 103–5
  recognition by Congregation of Sacred Rites (1666), 103–5
  sermons published in honor of, 85–86
John of Matha, Saint, relics
  burial in San Tommaso in Formis, 43
  chain of custody of stolen bones, 58–59, 121–22, 134–36
  Congregation of Sacred Rites, petition before (1669), 107–11, 133–42
  Congregation of Sacred Rites, petition before (1715), 148–49, 155–56
  Congregation of Sacred Rites, petition before (1721), 151–66
  dispute over return of (1718), 149–50
  in Madrid nineteenth and twentieth centuries, 168–69
  motive for theft, 5, 56, 89
  parchment slip inserted in tomb, 58, 81, 90, 125–26, 136–37
  recognition ceremony and inspection (1671), 143–47

John of Matha, Saint, relics (*continued*)
  significance of theft, 56, 89–90, 169–72
  size and appearance of bones, 2, 58, 124–25, 158
  surrender of (1655), 58
  testimony of criminals, 134–35
  theft of and flight to Madrid, 1–3, 23–24, 57
  transfer of custody (1686), 147, 149–50
  tribunal (June 1657), 58–59
John of Provence (Johannes Provincialis). *See* John of Matha, Soint
John XXII (pope), 52, 53, 74, 76, 81
Juan Bautista de la Concepción, 28, 48–49, 61
Juan de la Vega, 35
Juan de San Buenaventura, 83, 84
Juan II (Castilian king), 34

Kett, Robert, 72
Knights Templar, 93
knowledge
  created around relics, 165–66
  epistemology and identity of relics, 121
  knowledge production in relic recognition, 110, 146
  types of, 131

Laínez, Miguel, 2
Lambertini, Prospero (Pope Benedict XIV), 20, 132, 144, 151–52, 154–57, 161, 163–64, 168
Landucci, Ambrosio, 138
Leonor de Avis (Portugese queen), 34
Les vies des Saints Jean de Matha et Félix de Valois (Dilloud), 80
Ligorio, Pirro, 63
López de Haro, Juan Damián, 35
Loquet, Thomas, 33, 49
Louis IX (French king), 33, 72
Louis XIV (French king), 34, 102, 107
Lupián Zapata, Antonio
  accumulative citation, 94–95, 96
  Chrónica general . . ., 91, 93, 101
  English breviary, 97–100, 99, 100
  English breviary, critical support crafted for, 97
  forgery, 19, 91–95, 96–97
  forgery, physical, 97–101
  forgery, reputation for, 157

Hauberto, false chronicle of, 92–93
  invented sources, 101–2
  nontextual sources, use of, 95–96, 103
  truth value of historical texts, 95
Luther, Martin, 6–7

Mabillon, Jean, 20, 144, 153–54
Macedo, Francisco de, 80, 85
Madrid, Calced Trinitarian monastery, 57
Maffei, Scipione, 155
Mallea, Salvador de, 147
Marescotti, Galeazzo (cardinal), 143–44, 146, 155, 159
Maria Luisa Gabriella di Savoia (Spanish queen), 149
Mariana of Austria (Spanish queen), 107
Marquis of Astorga, 107
Marracci, Ippolito, 77
Martín Bienes, Antonio, 168
Martyrologium hispanum (Tamayo), 84
Massimo, Carlo Camillo, 58, 59, 122, 124, 144
material continuity, principle of, 139
materiality, 15–16, 142, 166, 170
Mathurins, 26, 33
Matta, Carlo Felice de, 131–132
Mattei, Girolamo (Marquis of Giove), 1
Maurice de Sully, 40
Maurists, 153, 154
medieval manuscripts, 100–101
Medina, Bartolomé de, 129
Medina, Gonzalo de
  conviction and punishment, 3, 24
  motive for theft of bones, 5
  testimony at 1657 tribunal, 58–59, 123–24
  theft of bones, 1–3
Mediterranean slave trade, 29–32
Melchor del Espíritu Santo, 148, 149
Mercedarian Order, 25, 31–32, 38–39, 62, 73, 78, 94, 164
Mercier, Pierre, 148
Mesnil-Fouchard, Etienne du, 76
Metaphysics (Aristotle), 120
Miguel de Contreras, 34
Miguel de San José, 151, 154, 155–57, 159, 160, 167
miracles
  as evidence for identity of relics, 10, 110, 123, 156, 158
  attributed to Matha, 41–44, 156–57

in canonization process, 110, 123
Catholic contrasted with Protestant approaches to, 14
moral certainty, 13, 20, 111, 126–33, 139–40, 141–42, 163
Morales, Ambrosio de, 139–40
Morcillo Rubio de Auñon, Diego, 35
Morigia, Paolo, 47
Moura, Marcos de, 62
Muget, Friar, 45
Muguet, Pierre, 42, 43
Muntaner, Ramon, 94
Murat III, 30
Muratori, Ludovico Antonio, 20–21, 144, 154
Muslims, enslaved, 29–30
Musnier, Nicolas, 45

Nanni, Giovanni, 63
Navarro Reverter family, 169
Nicholas, Minister General (d. 1257), 33
Nichomachean Ethics (Aristotle), 128
Nobis, Antonio de, 92
    See also Lupián Zapata, Antonio
Nolasc, St. Pere (Pedro Nolasco), 38, 39, 93, 165
Nonat, Ramon, 39
Núñez Sagredo, Fernando, 35

Olds, Katrina, 88
Olivieri, Fabio degli Abati (cardinal), 159
On the Consolation of Philosophy (Boethius), 71
Order of the Blessed Virgin of Mercy. *See* Mercedarian Order
Order of the Most Holy Trinity and of the Captives. *See* Trinitarian Order
Ottoboni, Pietro (cardinal), 154, 157, 160
Our Lady of Remedy, 147

Paleotti, Gabriele (cardinal), 109
Pamphili, Giovanni Battista (cardinal), 55
Panciroli, Ottavio, 46
Paolucci, Fabrizio (cardinal), 160
papacy and saint-making process, 36–37
Papenbroek, Daniel van, 140, 153
Paravicino, Hortensio Félix, 35, 55, 76
pars pro toto (a part represents the whole), 8–9

Pedro Pascual (Pedro de Valencia), 78
Pere Nolasc, Saint, 38, 39, 93, 165
Pérez de Petinto, Manuel, 171
Peter of Alcántara, 130
Petit, François, 86
Petit, Louis, 27, 28, 77, 78, 86
Philip II (Spanish king), 30, 57, 119
Philip III (Spanish king), 34
Philip IV (Spanish king), 34, 35, 55, 57–58, 90, 107, 167
Philip V (Spanish king), 149, 164
Pitts, John, 70–71
Pius V (pope), 135
Porres Alonso, Bonifacio, 16
presumptive proofs, 126–27
Prevostin of Cremona, 40
probabilism, 129–30
procurador general, role of, 108–9
Pujana, Juan, 16

Quintanadueñas, Antonio de, 140

Ramírez, Fernando, 35
Raposo, Antonio, 62, 69
Raymond de Pallas, 28–29
Reformation, Protestant, 6–7
relic culture
    authenticity of relics, 109–10, 118–19, 162–63
    collective witnessing in relic recognition, 145–46
    Council of Trent and authentication, 59
    and cult of saints, 5–10
    and "cultural work," 164–65
    evidence for, human or divine, 12, 114, 122–24
    fraud as issue, 6, 9–10
    history of veneration traditions, 5–11
    identity, proof of, 11–13, 118
    influence of Council of Trent, 7, 113–14
    as material and physical objects, 15–16
    moral certainty and authentication, 126–33
    and new historical norms, late seventeenth century, 153, 154–55
    oaths, swearing of, 9
    pars pro toto principle, 8–9
    Protestant critiques of, 6–7
    relic recognition, 20, 144, 145–46

relic culture (*continued*)
  theft of relics, 57, 108–9
  treatises on, seventeenth century, 112–14
Richard of Cornwall, 33, 72
Robert, abbot of Saint-Victor, 40
Robert d'Artois, 33
Roman Breviary, 63
Roman martyrology, 38, 63, 105
Román y Zamora, Jerónimo, 47
Rospigliosi, Guilio (cardinal), 85
Rosweyde, Heribert, 63

Sachebren, Henri, 33
sainthood
  beatification and canonization, 37–38
  contrasted with canonization, 50–51
  in cultural context of early modern period, 13–16
  importance of saints in Catholic church, 7–8
  lay female saints, 9
  missionary saints, 9
  papal power and saint-making, 36–37
  relic culture, history of, 5–11
  See also canonization process; relic culture
saint-making. *See* canonization process
Saint-Mathurin, church of, Paris, 33
Salamanca, Spain, 169
Sandoval y Rojas, Francisco Gómez de (Duke of Lerma), 28
San Giacomo degli Spagnoli (Spanish national church), 24
Santiago de Compostela, Spain, 64
San Tommaso in Formis, church
  artwork and images, 2, 46
  burial of John de Matha, 43, 69
  history of building, 1
  history of in *Annales sacri* . . . (Figueras Carpi), 68
  mosaic, 40–41, 42, 46, 52
  physical deterioration of structure, 5
  theft of bones (1655), 1–3, 89
  transferred to Trinitarian Order, 26
  Trinitarian Order's loss of and efforts to regain, 47–48
  veneration of Matha's body upon death, 69
Schism, Western, 1, 27, 128
Scholastic philosophy, 120, 128

Scriptorum illustrium maioris Brytanniae (Bale), 70
Sedano, Andrés, 74
Selim II, 30
Sfondrati, Paolo Emilio (cardinal), 145
Shapin, Steven, 145
Sigonio, Carlo, 63
Simón de Camargo, 34
Simón de Rojas, 34
Sinzendorf, Philipp Ludwig Wenzen von, 158
Sixtus V (pope), 36, 48, 59
slave trade
  Mediterranean region, 29–30
  and ransom, 16
Smith, Julia M. H., 9, 113
Soeiro, Estevão, 34
Sousa, Francisco da, 80
Spain
  Catholic Church seventeenth century, 64–65
  Spanish influence in Rome, 24
Spanish Civil War (1936–1939), 21, 169
Spanish Inquisition, 53–54, 55–56, 85, 153
Spanish Succession, War of (1701–1714), 20, 148, 158
Spínola, Agustín (cardinal), 55
squadrone volante (flying squadron), 107
Suárez, Francisco, 121, 130
Suchet de Quiñones, Bernardo, 35
Suleiman the Magnificent, 30
Sully, Maurice de, 94–95

Tagliavia de Aragón y Mendoza, Diego, 3
Tamayo de Salazar, Juan, 83–84
Theobald I (Navarrese king), 33
Theobald II (Navarrese king), 33
Thiard de Bissy, Henri-Pons de (cardinal), 159
Thiers, Jean-Baptiste, 162
Thorne, William (Guillerminus Spina), 71
Thulden, Theodor van, 86
Toledo, Spain, 64
Tolomei, Giovanni Battista (cardinal), 167
Tomás de la Virgen, 34, 147
Tomkins, Jane, 164
Torre, Juan de la, 75
tradition, role in authentification of relics, 162

Treaty of the Pyrenees (1659), 92
Trinidad y Torre, Antonio de la, 75, 76, 77
Trinitarian Order
  archival material, 17–18
  branches of, 27–29, 168
  captives, ransoming of, 29–32
  Cerfroid Mother House, 26, 49, 91, 96–97
  colors and symbolism of habit, 45–46
  Discalced branch, 2–3, 48–49
  Discalced contrasted with Calced branches, 2–3, 27, 28–29, 59, 147, 150, 167–68
  efforts to canonize founders, 49, 59–60, 65–66
  in eighteenth and nineteenth centuries, 168
  forged histories and spurious houses, 69–72
  foundational stories, 39–44, 48–49
  friars' habits, 45–46
  growth and spread in Europe, 26–27
  hagiographic imagery, 86–87
  history, documentary evidence for, 60–61, 62, 65–66
  history and overview of, 1, 11–12, 16–18, 25–35, 93
  history of in Figueras Carpi's *Chronicum Ordinis Sanctissimae*, 78–80
  Holy Trinity, dedication to, 45–46
  hospitals and needs of captive Christians, 32
  importance of founders' canonization for, 110–11
  Innocent III's role, 41–43
  libraries, 61
  liturgy, 44–45
  medieval accounts of origins, 43–44
  and Mercedarian Order, 32, 102, 157
  and miracle stories, 41–43
  motto, 44
  nuns, 26
  political connections, 34, 164

Reformed branch (1570s), 27
  and reform movements, 34–35
  scholarly pursuits, 33
  in Spain, 34–35, 57–58
Tutino, Stefania, 141, 170
typology, 124–125

Ubaldis, Baldus de, 135
Urban IV (pope), 69, 74, 84, 91, 104–5, 156
Urban VIII (pope), 28, 36, 39, 51, 55, 59, 65

Vareland, Thierry de, 95
Vélez Matute, Jerónimo, 52, 55, 58, 81, 90, 125, 137
Victricius of Rouen, 9
Vidal, Fernando, 14
Vidal, José
  conviction and punishment, 24
  testimony at 1657 tribunal, 58–59
  theft of relics, 1–3
Vincent-Cassy, Cécile, 110
Virgen, Tomás de la, 147
Vitae et sententiae patrum occidentis (Gonon), 50, 52
Vitae SS. Ioannis de Mattha (Macedo), 80, 85

Wadding, Luke, 52, 95
Waldensians, 68
War of Spanish Succession (1701–1714), 20, 148, 1
Western Schism, 1, 27, 128
William the Lion (Scottish king), 72
William X of Aquitaine (Duke), 93
witnesses, social standing of, 134–35

Xavier, St. Francis, 80

Yañez, Alonso, 75, 76, 77
Yepes, Antonio de, 93

zelanti faction, 158–159, 160, 164
Zondadari, Antonio Felice (cardinal), 161